THE HISTORY OF GARDENS

9.50

J

Overleaf   The sublime
landscape at West Wycombe,
engraved by William Woollett in
the 1770s. Today it remains one
of the most beautiful of all
landscape gardens

THE HISTORY

Christopher Thacker

OF GARDENS

UNIVERSITY OF CALIFORNIA PRESS

Berkeley and Los Angeles, California

To

PETER, MAVIS, GEOFFREY & THOMASINA

who said

GET ON WITH IT.

'Delight comes from plants and springs
and gardens and gentle winds and
flowers and the song of birds.'

—Libanios, 314–*c*.393 AD

Published in 1979 in the United States of
America by the University of California Press,
Berkeley and Los Angeles, California

This book was designed and produced in Great Britain
by London Editions Ltd, 30 Uxbridge Road, London W12 8ND

First Paperback Printing 1985
ISBN 0-520-05629-9 paper
     0-520-03736-7 cloth
Library of Congress Catalog Card Number 78-59446

Designed by John Leath

Printed in Italy by *Arti Grafiche* Vincenzo Bona - Torino

CONTENTS

INTRODUCTION

The history of gardens is like the study of icebergs: while a bit shows above the surface, much more lurks underneath. Most of an iceberg is below the water; with gardens, the majority of them have gone altogether, vanished – even the most beautiful – soon after they were made. Compared with icebergs, they are I suppose pretty long-lived; but their lifespan, like that of sandcastles and mayflies, is still inevitably short.

So a history of gardens cannot be a guide, unless you wish to be guided through gardens which no longer exist. A guide to present gardens cannot be a history, unless you want to ignore most of the past. Were this history a guide, I should be dragged – and drag my readers – through many a gruesome scene, merely because it exists and flourishes. There is no end to bad gardens, but we need not mention them. My task is far happier, since I may choose the best, among vanished and almost-vanished and existing gardens, to discuss their lovely and most fragile history.

Yet this has its melancholy side. Sometimes, I have thought this was a book of might-have-beens, repeating an Ozymandian 'nothing remains'; but the gardens I love best are – some of them – still alive: Caprarola, Lante, Ninfa, Sandemar, Edzell, Bowood, Powis, Courances, Wildenborch, and Weikersheim.

How many I regret; and most of all, Suleiman's kiosk in the sea, built in the Bosphorus four hundred years ago. Someone wrote on the wall, 'it has no equal in the world', but we can no longer judge. I regret the Leasowes, made by William Shenstone, and Fonthill, made by William Beckford, one a little, one a sumptuous paradise. Today, the Leasowes is a golf course, Fonthill is a farm.

Coming to the modern era, the problem is reversed: if so many of the wonderful gardens of the past have vanished without a trace, the choice of present-day gardens worthy of mention could with ease fill twice the length of this entire book. But being finite, my text is limited in its size and in the number of its illustrations, and by the equally finite nature of my knowledge and experience. So this book has patches, gaps and silences which anyone may remark and which concern several topics related to garden history – the vegetable garden, flower painting, the cottage garden and the smaller modern garden, especially the 'semi-detachment'. In terms of countries, I have obviously not been able to cover all the magnificent gardens which can be seen in South Africa, Ceylon, New Zealand, much of the United States and Latin America. It is sad that more space could not be devoted to the hundreds of superb gardens in North and South America, but I take some heart from the fact that so many of them are historically the offspring of the gardens of the past, which I have been able to describe more fully elsewhere in the book. I have had to choose, and have done so deliberately.

Though gardens are old, the writing of their history is still new and adventurous. This book includes many fresh pieces to fill out their puzzling picture, so that I may say, echoing La Fontaine, 'Les jardins parlent peu, si ce n'est dans mon livre.'

Yet gardens are greater than their historians, as poems and paintings tower over those who try to explain them. The Elizabethan poet Nicholas Grimald puts it best:

Seed, leaf, flowr, frute,
herbe, bee and tree
are more than I may sing.

1   A view of the Canopus at
Hadrian's villa near Tivoli,
looking from the half-domed
triclinium

1

The Beginnings

FLORA'S GARDEN

No doubt about it. The first gardens were not made, but discovered. A natural spot – a clearing in the forest, a valley opening up in a barren mountain-side, an island in a remote lake – made pleasant by a belt of trees, flowering, fragrant, and bearing fruit. The hum of bees mingles with the tinkling fall of water, for a stream winds across the tranquil scene. In the centre there is a grassy space, and the grass is rich with flowers.

No one tends this garden: it grows of its own accord. A shepherd passes from time to time; wood nymphs flit in and out of the shadows; no one may have come here for years; or, if we are in the Middle Ages, the whole place may be under a spell, like the garden walled with air in Chrétien de Troyes' *Erec et Enide*.

In the oldest accounts, such spots are the gardens of the gods, or of those favoured by the gods, so that they need do no work to keep the place in order. For refinement, they may have a rustic hut, a seat, an arbour, for here the cares that go with houses and palaces are not known. Fruit comes all the year round, as do the flowers.

Begin, then, with Homer and the Elysian fields (*Odyssey*, book IV). Menelaus, husband of Helen, is told of his destiny. At the end of his life, the immortals will send him 'to the Elysian plain at the world's end . . . in the land where living is made easiest for mankind, where no snow falls, no strong winds blow and there is never any rain, but day after day the West Wind's tuneful breeze comes in from Ocean to refresh its folk.'

Gardens, too, have many names: grove and paradise, park, landscape, wilderness and orchard. Another such *untended* garden is the orchard at the world's end, the garden of the Hesperides, where the daughters of Atlas guard 'the rich, golden apples' given by Hera to Zeus at their wedding. The dragon Ladon is coiled round the apple tree to protect the fruit. In the land of the sunset, and Hesperus, the evening star, this garden is linked with Aphrodite, a goddess concerned with gardens and in particular with apples. The site of such a garden is disputed, so that Beechey in the 1820s may imagine certain sunken fertile valleys near Benghazi to have been the Hesperides: hidden valleys which the traveller discovers, suddenly finding 'a beautiful orchard or garden, blooming in secret, and in great luxuriance, at a considerable depth beneath his feet and defended on all sides by walls of solid rock.'

Think now of another apple-garden, free of care: Avalon, where Arthur, our greatest king, went to heal him of his wounds. And of rose-gardens, growing without care: 'the place called the garden of Midas . . . wherein roses grow of themselves, each bearing sixty blossoms and of surpassing fragrance; in which garden . . . Silenus was taken captive.'

Once more to the gods, and then, alas!, to earth. 'Come, Mother of Flowers', says Ovid, and sings of the 'happy fields' over which Flora, goddess of flowers, is queen. No gardener tends this garden; here is perpetual spring. 'Ever the tree is clothed with leaves, the ground with pasture.' Her husband said 'Goddess, be queen of flowers!'

Turn now to the world we know, or would like to know: the real, natural and untended vale of Tempe in Thessaly later to be named as a fictional part of the estate of the Emperor Hadrian, in the second century AD. The vale of Tempe is the quintessential *locus amoenus,* the 'pleasant place', the unspoiled, untended meadow or glade of classical and medieval times. The pastoral pictures of Virgil's *Eclogues* or of Ovid's *Metamorphoses* give different details, but the idea is the same. Theocritus sums up this spot in his twenty-second *Idyll*. He talks of the divine twins, Castor and Pollux, who

> wandered away
> from their comrades to explore the woods together
> where trees of all sorts grew wild on the hillside.
> Beneath a smooth rock they found a brimming spring
> with water that was always clear. At the bottom
> pebbles shone like crystal or silver. Tall pines grew
> beside it, and poplars, plane trees, and cypresses,
> and all the sweet-smelling flowers that fill meadows
> in the late spring, loved and harvested by hairy bees.

Such a region is indeed destroyed if humans lay hands on it; or even if they go there often. This is the nature of the *locus amoenus*, a garden of delight, but not of usefulness, most often seen in medieval literature as the garden-in-the-forest, unexpectedly discovered by the knight errant. Commonly, the medieval garden of pleasure, whether knightly or spiritual, will centre round a 'flowery mede', a space of meadow-grass sprinkled with innumerable flowers, where Adam and Eve, Virgin and Child, knights and ladies will gather for moments of recreation and delight. Other types of garden frequently contain a gardener, with tools or clothing that indicate work, but these 'flowery medes' do not.

Much later, when Keats, in *The Fall of Hyperion* (1819), describes such a scene, he writes consciously of a garden which can no longer exist. 'Methought I stood', he writes – it is in the past and the opening of the poem is redolent of death, the poet's own oblivion. The garden which he describes is therefore imaginary, a vision:

> Methought I stood where trees of every clime,
> Palm, myrtle, oak, and sycamore, and beech,
> With plantane and spice-blossoms, made a screen,
> In neighbourhood of fountains (by the noise
> Soft-showering in mine ears), and (by the touch
> Of scent) not far from roses. Twining round
> I saw an arbour with a drooping roof
> Of trellis vines, and bells, and larger blooms,
> Like floral censers, swinging light in air;
> Before its wreathed doorway, on a mound
> Of moss, was spread a feast of summer fruits.

Keats sums up this theme – a delightful garden-grove, idyllic and almost heavenly. The reality will be a farm garden, a sacred grove, or a princely paradise.

THE SACRED GROVE

We might define the 'sacred grove' as a place apart, consecrated to a spirit or divinity, or to the memory of a hero; with trees, rocks and water, surrounding a shrine or an altar, in a temple or within a grotto or a cave. This religious or spiritual quality separates – though not always very sharply – the 'sacred grove' from the garden of Flora.

When man first felt that there was a difference between the 'atmosphere' surrounding one place and another; that some spot possessed a mysterious quality; that some mysterious or tragic event had left an emotional effect on the nearby rocks and trees and streams; that a remote locality might possess a 'spirit' of its own, a *genius loci*: at this moment, man was close to creating a 'sacred grove'.

Antiquity has many references to such places. In the Old Testament, we hear of the groves dedicated to Baal, destroyed by the Israelites; when the Romans came to Britain, they remarked on the groves used by the druids; just outside the walls of

2 The temple of the Sibyl, Tivoli. This ruined temple, perched on a cliff over the falls of the river Anio, came to fascinate both painters and gardeners, and in the eighteenth-century landscape garden it was the most frequently imitated monument of antiquity, being built – either complete or in a ruined form – in scores of gardens throughout Europe

Jerusalem there is the garden of Gethsemane, with the grotto where Christ prayed, and outside the walls of Athens were the groves of the Academy, an enclosure scattered with tombs and shrines. A similar garden, with both a religious and pleasurable intention, existed around 490 BC near Hipponium, on the southwestern tip of Italy: a 'grove exceedingly beautiful and well supplied with flowing streams, in which also there is a place called the Horn of Amaltheia, which Gelon constructed' (Athenaeus, *Deipnosophists*, book XII). Amaltheia was a goat-nymph, and goddess of fertility, and her 'Horn' (the origin of the cornucopia, the horn of plenty) would have been a shrine in her honour.

Turning to Greek and Roman imaginative literature, there are examples almost without number. In the *Odyssey*, book V, Odysseus is imprisoned on the island of the goddess Calypso. Her cave is surrounded by a grove:

> Trailing round the very mouth of the cavern, a garden vine ran riot, with great bunches of ripe grapes; while from four separate but neighbouring springs four crystal rivulets were trained to run this way and that; and in soft meadows on either side the iris and the parsley flourished. It was indeed a spot where even an immortal visitor must pause to gaze in wonder and delight.

It is the setting for the home of a goddess, and Nature has responded spontaneously in her service. This natural, untended quality of the sacred grove reappears throughout the centuries, marking the sacred grove as part of the private, romantic, natural side, rather than the public, classic and formal side of garden art. Centuries later, in a letter by the Emperor Julian, written in AD 363, there is a passage telling of a regular and tended, but clearly sacred grove where the emperor himself worshipped, at Batnae, near Antioch:

The Imperial lodging was by no means sumptuous, for it was made only of clay and logs and had no decorations; but its garden, though inferior to that of Alcinous, was comparable to that of Laertes. In it was a small grove full of cypresses and along the wall many trees of this sort have been planted in a row one after the other. Then in the middle were beds, and in these, vegetables and trees bearing fruits of all sorts. What did I do there, you ask? I sacrificed in the evening and again at early dawn, as I am in the habit of doing practically every day.

Julian's references both to religious sacrifice and to the garden of Alcinous show that the garden combined features of the 'pleasurable farm' and of the sacred grove.

At Tivoli, to the east of Rome, there remains the circular temple of the Albunean Sibyl, built in the first century BC, which overlooks the precipitous slope where the falls of the river Anio poured down from the mountains into the plain. This temple, with its oracle, is in a dramatic setting of trees, cliffs and tumbling water: it is a 'sacred landscape', and it was to influence painters and landscape gardeners in the eighteenth century more than any other single scene, so fully did it respond to their inclination to find a spiritual quality in landscape which they could reproduce.

Another remarkable survival of the sacred grove is to be seen in Cyprus, near the port of Larnaca, in the grounds surrounding the Tekké or mosque of Umm Haram. This spot, sacred to Muslims, is where the aunt of the prophet Mohammed is buried. This lady died here in AD 649. The mosque contains her tomb, which is shrouded from view beneath hangings of green cloth, but it is clear that the vast stones over and to each side of the tomb are primitive megaliths, going back to a remote period of Cypriot history. This spot has therefore been sacred for many centuries, well before Muslim, and indeed before Christian times, and the surrounding grove – of cypresses, palms, vines, carobs, and oranges – has probably been here practically as long.

Apart from such rare exceptions, what survives of the sacred grove? Where is the grove of Calypso now?

The original groves, established thousands of years ago, have been altered, destroyed, obliterated. But their spirit survives in secluded shady spots, cut off from disturbance by an angle of wall, by rocks and irregular stones. A statue, an urn, a single column of stone invite our contemplation; ferns grow in the shady soil, and water drips from ledge to ledge. Often we may not see what it is that draws our attention – the 'sacred grove' is far away – but it is this primitive element which lies behind such pensive scenes.

THE GODS OF THE GARDEN

Curiously, the sacred grove is not often connected with an actual god or goddess of gardening. In Greek mythology, there are deities responsible for agricultural prosperity and for general fertility – for example Demeter, corn-goddess, mother of Persephone, and Dionysus, god of the vine. But only the little-known god Priapus seems to have had definite responsibility for gardens. The principal centre for his worship was at Lampsacus, on the Hellespont. The son of Aphrodite, the goddess of love, whose flower is the rose and whose fruit is the apple, and Dionysus, Priapus is a god both of fertility and of the garden. Images of him show him to be ugly, small in stature, but with enormous genitals, and carrying a sickle or a pruning-knife.

By Roman times, he seems to have become a scarecrow, a garden bogey-man to frighten away thieves, birds and naughty boys. This is how he appears in Virgil's *Georgics*, book IV: 'let the defence of Hellespontic Priapus, the guard against thieves and birds with his wooden sickle, protect the gardens.' In Columella's poem on gardening, the modest Roman garden is to be protected by the simple statue of the god:

> . . . chuse the trunk of some huge ancient tree;
> Rough-hue it, use no art; *Priapus* make
> with frightful member, of enormous size;
> Him, in the middle of thy garden, place,

L'ᴇʀᴠᴄᴀ chiamata Ruchetta è calda & secca nel quarto grado . La domestica è di maggiore efficacia che la saluatica,e i semi spetialmente si confanno a uso di medicina,& dopo i semi, le foglie. Ha uirtù di consumare e d'incitar il coito . Cotta con la carne ual molto contra la stranguria,la dissuria,& la paralisia . Inoltre cotta in uino,& impiastrata su le reni desta la libidine , posta sul pettignone prouoca l'orina. Il suo seme, & massimamente della saluatica , fa dirizzar il membro uirile.

And to him, as its guardian, homage pay,
That with his monstrous parts he may deter
The plund'ring boy; and with his thret'ning scythe,
The robber from intended rapine keep.

A plant is dedicated to him, rocket (*eruca sativa*), which provokes desire. Dioscorides says that there is a 'wild eruca' whose seed is used instead of mustard. One could try it on hot dogs.

And there is Flora, goddess of flowers. Though not closely connected with gardens, she presided over fertility rites at Rome, the annual *Floralia*. The mainly floral imagery associated with the goddess since the Renaissance, the chaste temples of Flora erected in eighteenth-century gardens, as at Stourhead, beside the lake, and at Nuneham Courtenay, within William Mason's flower garden, and the singing by English schoolgirls of 'Flora's Holiday' represent a puritanical metamorphosis which would puzzle the Romans, if it did not amuse them.

For similar sexual reasons, Aphrodite-Venus is also associated with gardens. Pliny says that Plautus speaks of gardens as being under the guardianship of Venus, though the Roman cult of Venus as goddess of gardens seems to have lapsed by the end of the republic. Goddess of the rose, the flower of purity, desire and passion, her role is like Flora's, though never undergoing so violent a transformation in post-Renaissance times.

Last, the god Terminus should be mentioned, for his statues – *Terms* – served as landmarks, protecting boundaries, whether of a state, or of a rural property. As garden ornaments, to line a walk or to close a vista, they survive until modern times, often becoming confused with statues representing other persons – Faunus, for example, or Priapus.

In Christian times, gardeners found their patron saints – St Phocas and St Fiacre. Phocas lived in the third century near Sinope on the Black Sea, where he cultivated a small garden. Welcoming strangers, he once entertained two visitors who were in fact searching for him to execute him as a Christian. So he dug his own grave in his garden, and led the visitors out to the graveside, inviting them to behead him. Which they did.

St Fiacre, in the seventh century, has a happier story. He was a prince from Scotland or from Ireland who went to convert the Franks to Christianity. Living in a small garden-enclosure in a forest near Meaux, his sanctity was such that no wild animals would enter his garden, and so the legend grew up that his garden was miraculously enclosed.

Neither of these saints ever had the importance of Priapus, nor are they commemorated in gardens. In the Middle Ages, the cloister garden, the *hortus conclusus* or 'enclosed garden' of the Virgin Mary, and the garden of Eden all have immense religious significance, but they are not properly connected with the sacred grove.

THE FARM GARDEN

One obvious source for the garden is the farm which is partly – or completely – developed for pleasure. As with gardens which derive from the sacred grove, it is often hard to say just where the farm turns into the garden; the boundaries overlap, and we should not let this dismay us.

The oldest pictures we have of gardens are from Egypt – paintings of scenes which contain agricultural elements, but which are combined in ways which provide pleasure, and not merely use. The British Museum has a small painting, dated *c.* 1400 BC, showing an ornamental fish-pond in the garden of Nebamun, a 'scribe who keeps account of the corn of Amun', at Thebes. The pond is rectangular, with what looks like a stone border, and within the pond are fish, water-fowl and flowers, probably the Egyptian lotus, while clumps of reeds grow at the edge of the water. Set symmetrically round the pond are fruit trees (date-palms, and possibly vines) and to one side a servant has baskets of fruit, pomegranates or grapes, and a wine-jar. Other Egyptian paintings show activities which are clearly agricultural, such as the

3   The mosque and minaret of the Tekké (above), near Larnaca in Cyprus, are almost hidden behind the surrounding palms and cypresses, while the spring flowers in the foreground create a natural 'flowery mede'

4   The plant rocket (below left) was sacred to Priapus, the god of gardens, and would be planted round his statue

5   Term statues (the one below is a Renaissance version) were set up to mark the boundaries of farms and gardens in Roman times

construction of trellises for vines, and harvest scenes; but this one is, albeit 'useful', decorative and pleasurable as well.

Papyri from much later periods indicate that in Hellenistic Egypt what we should now call 'market-gardening' existed in an elaborate and highly developed form, and we may assume that there was intensive cultivation of fruits and vegetables for consumption in the big cities. The coherent group of papyri which enabled M. Rostovtzeff to write his study, *A Large Estate in Egypt in the Third Century BC* (1922), centred round the estate of a Greek named Apollonius, in the town of Philadelphia in the Fayum, and concerns the plantation of groves of olives, of fig trees and nuts for commercial production, and the despatch of apples, pomegranates, olives, onions and garlic in commercial quantities from Philadelphia to Alexandria. At the same time Apollonius had laurel and garden olives planted in his garden, to give it a Greek character. In the town there was also a grove of trees or park of a pleasurable or religious nature and a fruit garden.

As well as extending the activity of market gardening backwards into Egyptian history, it is fair to imagine that it was common in most stable and populous centres in the Mediterranean and the Levant by the third century BC. By Roman times it had become a sophisticated business, though outside the 'garden' limits of this book. A study by Ludwig Keimer *(Die Gartenpflanzen in Alten Ägypten,* reprint 1967) identifies over forty garden plants in ancient Egypt, whether grown for food, drugs and medicines, for ornament, or for forage, and analyses the extent, nature and period of their use. Apart from some of the more expected fruits, vegetables and herbs – grapes, pomegranates, olives, lettuce, coriander, mint, parsley – the list mentions flowers identified from remains of wreaths, chaplets and posies, such as cornflower, safflower *(carthamus tinctorius)* and *chrysanthemum coronarium,* flowers which we may still see growing freely in the Levant.

Turning to Greece and Rome we find frequent literary examples of farm and villa gardens. In the *Odyssey,* book XXIV, Odysseus returns to his palace at Ithaca, to discover his father, Laertes, expelled from his honoured place in the palace and working as a gardener. When he eventually reveals his identity, Laertes asks for proof, and Odysseus recalls the garden he knew as a small boy,

> I can tell you all the trees you gave me one day on this garden terrace. I was only a little boy at the time, trotting after you in the orchard, begging for this and that, and as we wound our way through these very trees you told me all their names. You gave me thirteen pear-, ten apple- and forty fig-trees, and at the same time you pointed out the fifty rows of vines that were to be mine. Each ripened at a different time, so that the bunches on them were at various stages when the branches felt their weight under the summer skies.

Symmetry, trimness, fertility – more than we would expect from the picture of a farm. The pattern of Laertes' garden reappears, usually in happier scenes, for century after century. In Longus' novel *Daphnis and Chloe* (third century AD), the garden of Lamon is described. It has acquired elements from the sacred grove, as there is a temple in the middle, and from the farm, for its utility, and it partakes of the paradise, since it has a princely character as well:

> A thing of beauty was this garden, a fit pleasance for a prince. It lay on high ground . . . It contained trees of all kinds – apple, myrtle, pear, pomegranate, fig, and olive. On one side was a lofty vine, with ripe grapes mingled with the apples and pears, as if vying with their fruit. There were cultivated trees; there were also cypresses, laurels, planes, and pines. To these an ivy, in place of a grapevine, clung; its berries were large, and in darkness resembled the grapes. The fruit-bearing trees were in the interior, as if under protection; those that bore no fruit were ranged on the outside, like a palisade built by hand . . . The garden was arranged according to a precise pattern, and the trunks were placed at regular intervals. But overhead the branches joined one another and their foliage intermingled; nature itself seemed a work of art. There were also beds of various flowers, some the earth's own sowing, some that man had sown. The roses,

6 Among the earliest representations of a garden, this carving from the tomb of Akhnaton (eighteenth dynasty) shows the plants and trees growing thickly and without absolute order within an enclosure of the strictest symmetry, where the outside walls are matched by the square shape of the pool in the centre. Such formality is a continuing theme in the cloisters of the Middle Ages and in the gardens of Italy and France and is with us still

hyacinths, and lilies were cultivated by hand; the violets, narcissus, and pimpernel were the earth's gift. There was shade for summer, flowers for spring, fruit for autumn, and delight for every season . . . Exactly in the middle of the garden, measuring by length and breadth, was a temple and altar of Dionysos. The altar was surrounded by ivy, the temple with clematis . . .

More simple – but just as important in garden tradition – is the rural retreat, cultivated for utility and for pleasure, simpler than any of the gardens described in this chapter so far, but still clearly cultivated. A model for this is the old bee-keeper's garden in Virgil's *Georgics*, book IV:

> For I remember . . . an old Corycian, who had a few acres of forsaken ground; nor was his land rich enough for the plough, nor good for pasture, nor proper for vines. Yet the planting of a few potherbs among the bushes, and white lilies around about, and vervain, and esculent poppies, equalled in his mind the wealth of kings: and returning home late at night, loaded his table with unbought dainties. He was the first to gather roses in the spring, and fruits in autumn: and when sad winter even split the rocks with cold, and with ice restrained the course of the rivers, in that very season he could crop the soft acanthus, accusing the slow summer, and the loitering zephyrs.

The tradition of withdrawal to the countryside, to a life of rustic simplicity and virtue away from the distractions and vices of the town, is refined by the cultivation of a garden. The Emperor Julian describes such a retreat – a small estate, part farm, part villa – which was his before he succeeded to the throne in AD 360:

> It is twenty stadia distant from the sea, and is therefore undisturbed by merchants and clamorous sailors . . . It can always supply a gasping fish fresh-caught, and an eminence near the house commands a view of the Propontic sea, the islands, and the city; and instead of being disgusted by seaweed, and various other kinds of filth . . . which are often thrown on the beach and the sands, ground-ivy, thyme, and other aromatic herbs will afford you constant delight. When with tranquil attention you have pursued your studies, and wish to relax your eyes, the prospect of the ships and the ocean is delightful.

Curiously, this estate of Julian's on the shores of the sea of Marmora, near Constantinople, is the model for that later 'garden' which Voltaire's hero Candide was to take over, at the end of the novel *Candide* (1759). Voltaire knew of Julian's estate, and he leaves Candide at the end of his adventures to live in a similar small estate in the same part of the world. Candide reflects that the reasonable and practical answer to the ferocity of the outside world is for us to 'cultiver notre jardin'.

Others in the eighteenth century were to think this as well – William Shenstone, in his *ferme ornée*, the Leasowes, near Halesowen, in the early 1760s, and Marie Antoinette and her court, gathering to play shepherds and shepherdesses at the Hameau, the 'model farm' beside the Petit Trianon at Versailles, just before the French Revolution.

THE PARADISE GARDEN

Beside the sacred grove and the farm, the 'paradise garden' provides the main element in later garden history. The word 'paradise' comes from the old Persian *pairidaeza*, meaning an enclosure, and was applied to the enclosed hunting park of the Persian king. The word was taken into Old Testament Hebrew, as *pardes*, to mean simply a garden or park enclosure, and into Greek as *paradeisos*, where, meaning a kingly or sumptuous and extravagant park, it came to influence the later Hebrew sense, extended to cover both the original garden of Eden and the heavenly kingdom, the dwelling place of the saints, the 'celestial paradise'. The spiritual paradise – whether it is the lost home of our first ancestors, or the abode of the blessed – will be a concern of medieval gardens, but the earthly paradise begins much earlier, in the gardens of Prince Cyrus of Persia (d. 401 BC). In the *Oeconomicus*, book IV, Xenophon tells how the Greek envoy Lysander was taken by Cyrus to admire the great king's paradise at Sardis: 'the beauty of the trees in it, the accuracy of the spacing, the straightness of the rows, the regularity of the angles and the multitude of the sweet scents.' He was even more impressed to learn that the planning and much of the labour were the work of Cyrus himself – for husbandry gives both security and contentment.

Parks of this kind were taken over by Alexander when he conquered the Persian empire. Quintus Curtius tells of the 'extensive, charming and secluded parks with groves artificially planted', and speaks of the hunting parks near Samarkand in superlative terms.

Shortly after Alexander's death in 323 BC the Greek Megasthenes visited a part of India and he describes the 'royal residences' in the Gupta empire (near modern Patna), saying that they exceed the magnificence of the Persians. In the parks, he writes,

> Tame peacocks and pheasants are kept, and they [live] in the cultivated shrubs to which the royal gardeners pay due attention. Moreover there are shady groves and herbage growing among them, and the boughs are interwoven by the woodman's art . . . The actual trees are of the evergreen type, and their leaves never grow old and fall: some of them are indigenous, others have been imported from abroad.

These characteristics are repetitive, and lack detail. No contemporary pictures of the parks survive, and we must wait for the Persian pictures of the sixteenth century to see what such parks were like.

In literature, a variation on the 'secluded park . . . with groves artificially planted' appears in the palace and garden of Alcinous, described in the *Odyssey*, book VII. This palace need not concern us, but the royal garden is important:

> Outside the courtyard but stretching close up to the gates, and with a hedge running down on either side, lies a large orchard of four acres, where trees hang their greenery on high, the pear and the pomegranate, the apple with its glossy burden, the sweet fig and the luxuriant olive. Their fruit never fails nor runs short, winter and summer alike . . . In the same enclosure there is a fruitful vineyard, in one part of which is a warm patch of level ground, where some of the grapes are drying in the sun, while others are gathered or being trodden, and on the foremost rows hang unripe branches that have just cast their blossom or show the first faint tinge of purple. Vegetable beds of various kinds are neatly laid out beyond the farthest row and make a smiling patch of never-failing green . . . Such were the beauties with which the gods had adorned Alcinous' home.

This garden, though not large, is *superior* to those of ordinary men, through the perpetual fertility of the fruit trees, the perfection of the fruit, the constant fine weather and the divine patronage. Later paradises may be no larger than this, but are equally distinctive in their luxury.

Obviously these gardens cannot be separated too strictly. Authors, gardeners and kings chose their materials to suit their fancy, their needs and their purses. This kind of garden, being generally large and extravagant, succumbs to time, envy and depredation, and we are left only with the memory, and with vague if superlative descriptions. Such is the case with the 'hanging gardens' of Babylon – the *horti pensiles* looked back to by the Greeks and Romans with awe – luxurious, extravagant, and no longer to be seen. These were built by Nebuchadnezzar (605-562 BC) apparently for one of his wives, who missed 'the meadows of her mountains', the green and hilly landscape of her youth. The best-known description is that of Diodorus Siculus, the contemporary of Julius Caesar and Augustus, who listed the Hanging Gardens among the seven wonders of the world. The gardens have gone, and Diodorus' description may be sniped at by archaeologists – but it is the one which perpetuates the Hanging Gardens of Babylon:

Since the approach to the garden sloped like a hillside and the several parts of the structure rose from one another tier on tier . . . [it] resembled a theatre . . . the uppermost gallery, which was fifty cubits high, bore the highest surface of the park . . . The roofs of the galleries were covered with beams of stone . . . [Over this were layers of bitumen, reeds, brick, lead and then earth] sufficient for the roots of the largest trees; and the ground, when levelled off, was thickly planted with trees of every kind that . . . could give pleasure to the beholder . . . the galleries contained many royal lodgings; and there was one gallery which contained openings leading from the topmost surface and machines for supplying the garden with water.

These descriptions give a slight idea – not an accurate picture, for goodness sake! – of the paradise garden. Luxury beyond the means of ordinary men. Extent, if possible. And delight. Such creations appear spontaneously, expressions of the greatest wealth and extravagance. Persia was to continue an individual form of the paradise garden, while in China a wholly independent tradition of imperial palace gardens existed for at least two thousand years, including the fabulous palace and parks of Kubilai, or 'Kubla Khan', and continuing until the nineteenth century with the 'Garden of Perfect Brightness', the Yuan Ming Yuan, near Peking.

We could find much to separate and distinguish the royal gardens of Nebuchadnezzar, of Henry VIII, of Louis XIV, and the private paradises at the villa d'Este in Italy, at Castle Howard in Yorkshire and at Fonthill in Wiltshire; but all have wealth in common. Petrus de Crescentiis, writing in Italy in the early fourteenth century, remarks of 'the orchards of kings and other mighty lords' that 'those who are rich, thanks to their wealth and worldly resources, have power to satisfy their desires completely, and they lack nothing, except the knowledge and skill to bring their plans to execution.'

THE SMALL AND USEFUL GARDEN

The 'old Corycian' in Virgil's *Georgics* who 'equalled in his mind the wealth of kings' is the model for a continuing theme in garden history: the man of modest means who, shunning extravagance, cultivates a small plot for necessary foods. Virgil says in the *Georgics*, book IV, that he himself has not space to write of horticulture, 'atque aliis post me memoranda relinquo', 'and I leave it for others to treat of after me'. This hint is taken up by Columella in his *De re rustica*, in the short poem (438 lines) which forms the tenth book, entitled 'De cultu hortorum', 'Of Horticulture'. All other parts of his work on agriculture are in prose. The twelfth book repeats much of the horticultural information given in book ten, but in a more sober and fuller form. Columella, writing in the reign of Augustus, may have looked back with approval to the frugal yet varied activities of earlier Roman gardens, in comparison to the large vegetable gardens which existed in his time to feed the vast population of the capital, and in comparison also to the sumptuous, showy and unproductive villa gardens of the wealthy.

In his *Natural History*, book XIX, Pliny the Elder also inveighs against the growing taste for luxury, and regrets the time when 'the kings of Rome indeed cultivated their gardens with their own hands', a time when 'at Rome . . . a garden was in itself a poor man's farm.' Columella, taking up Virgil's unfinished task, describes such a garden, which really was, in its modesty and variety, a 'poor man's farm'.

The garden is enclosed with walls or hedges of thorns, to keep out cattle and thieves. These barriers are strictly utilitarian – not of a labyrinthine kind, as Daedalus might have made – and within, you must not expect to find statues carved by the great sculptors of antiquity. Instead, there is a rough-hewn trunk of a tree for you to reverence, representing divine Priapus, the god of gardens, *terribilis membri*, and armed with a wooden scythe – fecund and protecting.

And you are your own gardener. Columella's poem describes the work, unremitting yet rewarding, that a single man can do. Sometimes he writes as if he himself were the man – 'now is it time for me to dig the sweet soil' – sometimes he speaks as if to the reader, 'eia age', 'Come, get on!', sometimes he describes what the gardener has to do on his own, 'ipse ferens holitor diruptos pondere qualos', 'carrying baskets broken by the weight of manure'.

The round of work goes from autumn to autumn, rich, colourful, demanding, and with its many pleasures. Digging, manuring, watering; sowing seed or planting out seedlings; thinning out, weeding and dealing with snails and caterpillars; and harvesting flowers and vegetables and fruits.

It is a mixed garden – 'numerosus hortus', a garden 'rich in variety' – and so the kinds of harvesting are separately described, and all with enjoyment. When the spring flowers, grown for sale for chaplets or garlands, are ready, then the gardener stuffs his reed basket with dark hyacinths, with roses and fire-coloured marigolds, sells them in the city, and later 'with uncertain step, he returns from the town, his pockets full of cash.'

Vegetables and herbs receive most notice; celery or parsley, leek, beet, parsnip, chicory, lettuce, cabbage, mint, mustard, garlic and onions. Lettuce and cabbage provoke lyrical outbursts: cabbage for its fifteen sorts, and lettuce for its varied sources, shapes and colours. Indeed lettuce, more than any other garden product, represents the type of nature's beauty, usefulness and limitless fertility.

Though the task is never-ending, it is described with satisfaction, often with joy. The Bacchic festival, the rite of spring, the comical appearance of cucumbers and gourds, the man singing up in the fruit trees, as he prunes them: the scenes are vivid and familiar – 'and Gardner in his gardens cloath'd in green'.

A line of later writers are to echo, imitate or unconsciously to parallel Columella's poem – Walafrid Strabo in the ninth century, Jon Gardener in the fifteenth, Thomas Tusser in the sixteenth, and so many more. Often, they are devoted gardeners, rather than masters of the pen. Columella, starting the procession, seems to me one of the best, knowing his garden, describing it well.

THE PRIVATE PLEASURE GARDEN IN GREECE AND ROME

The great pleasure parks, the Persian paradises, are creations on the edge of fable, not exactly described, nor sited in ways which allow us to imagine clearly what they were like.

This lack of detail continues with the first gardens we hear about in Athens – the gardens of the Academy in the fourth century BC, of Theophrastus (c. 370–286), and of Epicurus (341–271 BC).

The first, an enclosed region some distance out from the city, was clearly a form of 'sacred grove'. It was 'named after a certain hero, Hecademus', and a line of verse remains, 'In the shady walks of the divine Hecademus', suggesting a shrine to the dead man, who had bequeathed the region to the citizens of Athens. Plane trees and olives grew there, watered by the river Cephissus. The olives were said to have been reared from cuttings taken from the sacred olive in the Erechtheum. Within the enclosure of the Academy were temples, shrines and tombs – at the entrance, an altar of Love, and, near Plato's residence (a small garden enclosure within the groves of the Academy), a small temple dedicated to the Muses.

Theophrastus' garden is even less documented: we know merely that he owned a garden with a walk, that it was a place for study for his friends and disciples, and that in his will he left the garden to them, so that we may infer that this garden was one where plants were studied, and it may claim, therefore, to be the first botanic garden.

The fame of the 'gardens of Epicurus' has outstripped the little that is known about them. There is here a gap like that between the views and conduct of the historical Epicurus, a man of modest conduct and noble if pessimistic thought, and the common concept of the 'Epicurean', self-indulgent and pleasure-seeking. So Pliny the Elder in the first century AD writes of 'Epicurus otii magister', 'Epicurus, the master of luxurious ease', and in the same vein Voltaire, in a letter of 23 January 1755, exclaims, describing his pleasant, comfortable retreat at Geneva which he was to rename 'Les Délices', 'It is the palace of a philosopher with the gardens of Epicurus – it is a delicious retreat.' The name alone suggests a quality of extravagance which appeals to some, and which others condemn. Contemporary

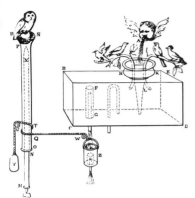

7 An illustration from Bennett Woodcroft's 1851 edition of the *Pneumatica*, showing the Owl Fountain, invented by Hero of Alexandria and set up in the gardens of the villa d'Este in the sixteenth century. 'The figures of several birds are arranged near a fountain, or in a cave, or in any place where there is running water. Near them sits an owl, which, apparently of her own accord, turns at one time towards the birds, and then away from them; and when the owl looks away the birds sing, when she looks at them they are mute'

Greek writings tell us, however, next to nothing about the real gardens of Epicurus. Diogenes Laertius confirms that he owned a garden; that his friends came there and lived a rather frugal life with him, 'content with half a pint of thin wine', and that on his death he left the garden to his disciples, to continue 'the common life in the garden' that they had enjoyed. One disciple, Apollodorus, was known as the 'tyrant of the garden'. But why? The reasons are unknown.

But luxury in the garden, whether stemming from Epicurus himself or not, was adopted by later Hellenistic men of wealth. The most striking example is the garden made on board a sumptuous pleasure-vessel constructed around 235 BC for Hieron II, ruler of Syracuse. On the uppermost deck

> there were a gymnasium and promenades built on a scale proportionate to the size of the ship; in these were garden-beds of every sort, luxuriant with plants of marvellous growth, and watered by lead tiles hidden from sight; then there were bowers of white ivy and grapevines, the roots of which got their nourishment in casks filled with earth, and receiving the same irrigation as the garden-beds. These bowers shaded the promenades.

This garden, so obviously for pleasure, was nonetheless still related to the sacred grove, since on the same deck, next to the promenades, 'was a shrine of Aphrodite'. A vestige of religion is here, but it is a religion of pleasure, with no trace of gloom or foreboding.

Such refined extravagance is curiously matched in the late eighteenth century, when the Duchess of Kingston visited St Petersburg in Russia on her private yacht. Besides the normal crew and her personal servants, she took with her an orchestra, and had the vessel furnished with a gallery of paintings – and a garden.

Hieron's boat, with its garden-beds, its bowers of white ivy and vines, is roughly contemporary with another Hellenistic phenomenon – the invention of mechanical marvels by Hero of Alexandria. In his *Pneumatica*, Hero (*c*. AD 100) describes the working of curious machines and models operated by weights, steam, air-pressure or water. Of interest are the water-machines, which form the basis for the elaborate and ingenious waterworks, fountains and joke-fountains constructed in European gardens from the time of the Renaissance onwards.

The refinement of private gardens in Hellenistic times undoubtedly served as a model for Roman villa-gardens. These private and princely gardens, designed principally or wholly for pleasure, may be contrasted with the simple and useful garden described by Columella, offering a life of frugal happiness. The same contrast may be seen in the agricultural writings of Cato (234–149 BC) praising the simplicity of country life, and of Varro (116–27 BC) in which the sophistication of rich town-dwellers has led to all manner of artificiality, and, incidentally, to an immense elaboration in the art of gardening. To indicate the change Varro says that the Romans of his time 'do not think they have a real villa unless it rings with many resounding Greek names' – for example, *peristylon* (colonnade), *ornithon* (aviary), *peripteros* (pergola), *oporotheca* (fruit-room).

In his treatise (*c*. 40 BC), Varro does not describe a villa-garden in full: for that we must wait until the letters of Pliny the Younger, around AD 100. Varro does however mention in passing several rich and elaborate gardens which existed in his time – such as that of Lucullus near Tusculum – and discusses a particular garden-feature, an extraordinary and sumptuous *ornithon* or aviary.

Most of Varro's treatise is concerned with farming and rural economy. When, in book III, he discusses 'the science of villa-husbandry', he divides this subject into three – 'the aviary, the hare-warren, and the fish-pond' – and he considers the commercial advantages of large-scale exploitation, designed to satisfy the gigantic Roman market. We may be surprised at the creatures he breeds for profit: one group contains 'bees, snails and dormice' – but *chacun à son goût*, and when in Rome . . . There was also a fortune to be made from the skilful rearing of field fares. When he comes to aviaries, he divides them into two – those designed for profit, and those which are 'merely for pleasure', *delectationis causa*. This second kind, which Varro built as part of his own villa near Casinum, is described in minute detail, so that

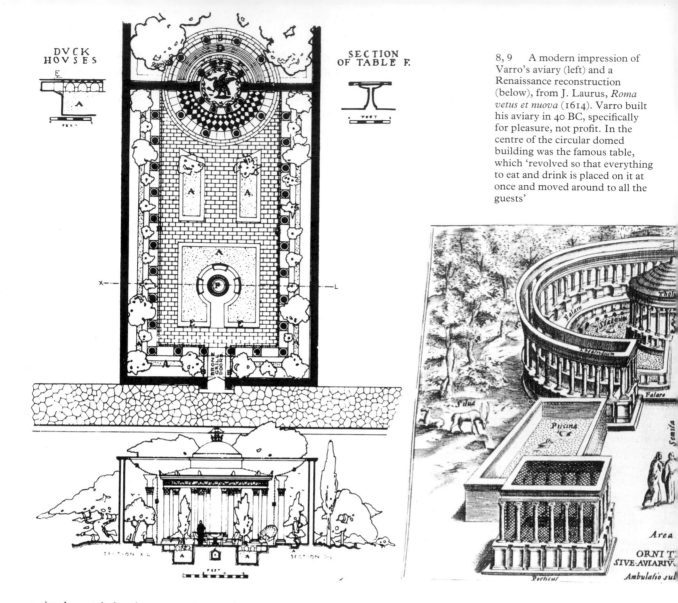

DUCK HOUSES

SECTION OF TABLE F.

8, 9 A modern impression of Varro's aviary (left) and a Renaissance reconstruction (below), from J. Laurus, *Roma vetus et nuova* (1614). Varro built his aviary in 40 BC, specifically for pleasure, not profit. In the centre of the circular domed building was the famous table, which 'revolved so that everything to eat and drink is placed on it at once and moved around to all the guests'

artists have tried to draw or to plan out its appearance (pls 8 and 9). The aviary stands near the bank of a stream, along which

runs an uncovered walk 10 feet broad; off this walk and facing the open country is the place in which the aviary stands, shut in on two sides, right and left, by high walls. Between these lies the site of the aviary, shaped in the form of a writing-tablet with a top-piece, the quadrangular part being 48 feet in width and 72 feet in length, while at the rounded top-piece it is 27 feet. Facing this, as if it were a space marked off on the lower margin of the tablet, is an uncovered walk with a *plumula* [perhaps a façade] extending from the aviary, in the middle of which are cages; and here is the entrance to the courtyard. At the entrance, on the right side and the left, are colonnades, arranged with stone columns in the outside rows and, instead of columns in the middle, with dwarf trees; while from the top of the wall to the architrave the colonnade is covered with a net of hemp, which also continues from the architrave to the base. These colonnades are filled with all manner of birds.

This is the first third of Varro's description. Between these colonnades are 'two oblong fishbasins', and between these a path leads to the far end of the quadrangle, where a round domed building, the *tholos*, is supported on columns. This building serves, by means of divisions made of fine netting, to display the birds, 'chiefly songsters, such as nightingales and blackbirds', and to provide a luxurious dining-

20

area for Varro and his guests. A revolving table bears food and drink, with alternate spouts for warm and cold water, while outside, through the netting and between the columns, there is a view into a shady wood.

Varro's *ornithon* indicates the extraordinary luxury of Roman villa-gardens; it is the earliest full description of a garden feature in Roman literature, and is followed by the famous accounts of two country villas owned by Pliny the Younger (*c.* AD 61–113). These two villas, the Laurentian (near Ostia, on the west coast of Italy), and the Tuscan (inland, at the foot of the Apennines), are described in separate letters (II, 17 and V, 6), dating from roughly AD 100 to 105.

The descriptions are full, though not always clear. A large part of each description deals with the various buildings which make up the villa complex. Since Renaissance times, many attempts have been made to work out the plans, or to draw imaginative reconstructions of the villas and their gardens, and these reconstructions are valuable in themselves as reflecting the artists' conceptions of 'perfection' or 'the height of luxury' in a villa and its garden.

The Laurentian villa is a seaside retreat, enjoying varied marine, mountain and country views. The views are important in all descriptions, and the garden designers of the Italian Renaissance were to seize on this, stressing the need for an extensive hillside view. With the Laurentian villa, Pliny stresses the way in which room after room has, through its folding windows and doors, and its careful siting, not only a choice of view, but also the means either of receiving sunshine at different times of the day, or of excluding the sunshine in hot weather. This brings us to an important refinement of Roman gardens and buildings connected with gardens – the carefully arranged walk or arbour or colonnade, which offers a sheltered, sunny promenade in winter, the refreshment of shade in the heat of summer, and all the while the variety of view obtained as one moves along or round the walk. Let Pliny explain:

> Here begins a covered arcade nearly as large as a public building. It has windows on both sides, but more facing the sea, as there is one in each alternate bay on the garden side . . . In front is a terrace scented with violets. As the sun beats down, the arcade increases its heat by reflection and not only retains the sun but keeps off the north-east wind so that it is as hot in front as it is cool behind. In the same way it checks the south-west wind, thus breaking the force of winds from wholly opposite quarters by one or the other of its sides; it is pleasant in winter but still more so in summer when the terrace is kept cool in the morning and the drive and nearer part of the garden in the afternoon, as its shadow falls shorter or longer on one side or the other while the day advances or declines.

Such an idea goes back to the *peripaton*, the 'walk' or 'promenade' of the Greek garden. Theophrastus had a modest one, mentioned in his will, and the Stoic philosophers were so called because they met, and walked and talked in the great stoa or colonnade, at Athens. The stoa was ornamented with frescoes, and was therefore designated as the Stoa Poikile, the Painted Stoa. It was hardly a garden feature, being set within the city, but the idea of such a walk being associated with philosophy was adapted in a natural and understandable way to the garden, and Hadrian's villa at Tivoli contained the most notable 'walk' of all, the great Pecile, discussed later in this chapter.

The Laurentian villa has several walks of this kind, some of them clearly outside in the garden: for example, 'a young and shady vine pergola, where the soil is soft and yielding even to the bare foot.' Pliny mentions a few plants by name – hedges of box and rosemary, plantations of mulberries and figs – and there is also a 'well-stocked kitchen garden'. He regrets, a little, that there is no running water 'to complete the amenities and beauty of the house', having to make do with wells and springs which lie near the surface of the ground.

We see Pliny's reasons for regretting the lack of running water when we turn to his Tuscan villa. Here, the site is a hillside – 'a vast amphitheatre such as could only be a work of nature' – with mountains, woods, fields, vineyards, meadows and cornfields, and 'everything is fed by streams which never run dry', draining into the Tiber close at hand. These streams feed a multitude of fountains and waterworks throughout

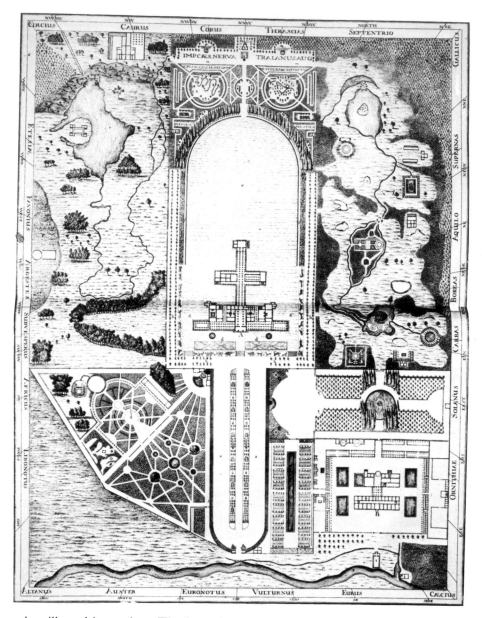

The labels around the border of the plan read (clockwise from top-left corner): CIRCIUS, CAURUS, CORUS, THRASCIAS, NORTH, SEPTENTRIO, GALLICUS, SUPERNAS, AQUILO, BOREAS, CARBAS, SOLANUS, ORNITHIAE, CÆCIUS, EURUS, VULTURNUS, EURONOTUS, AUSTER, ALTANUS, LIBONOTUS, AFRICUS, SUBVESPERUS, ARGESTES, FAVONIUS, ETESIAE.

At the top centre: IMP.CÆS.NERVA TRAIANUS AUG.

the villa and its gardens. The fountains appear within the centre of 'a small court shaded by four plane trees'; 'a fountain plays in a marble basin, watering the plane trees round it and the ground beneath them with its light spray.' Another interior fountain, 'with a bowl surrounded by tiny jets which . . . make a lovely murmuring sound', plays in a room with marble walls and a fresco 'of birds perched on the branches of trees.' Here, by means of the fountain and the painting, the garden has been brought indoors.

Water flows in more elaborate forms: in an 'ornamental pool . . . with its water falling from a height and foaming white when it strikes the marble'; in a choice of swimming baths (these were also mentioned at the Laurentian villa), and most notably in a garden-feature reminiscent of Varro's aviary, set at the far end of an extensive *hippodromus* or 'riding-ground'.

At the upper end of the course is a curved dining-seat of white marble, shaded by a vine trained over four slender pillars of Carystian marble. Water gushes out through pipes from under the seat as if pressed out by the weight of people sitting there, is caught in a stone cistern and then held in a polished marble basin which is regulated by a hidden device so as to remain full without overflowing. The preliminaries and main dishes for dinner are placed on the edge of the basin, while the lighter ones float about in vessels shaped like birds or little boats. A fountain opposite plays and catches its water, throwing it high into the air so that it falls back into the basin, where it is played again at once through a jet connected with the outlet. Facing the seat is a bedroom which contributes as much beauty to the scene as it gains from its position. It is built of shining white marble, extended by folding doors which open straight out among the trees; its upper and lower windows all look out to the greenery above and below . . . the light inside is dimmed by the dense shade of a flourishing vine which climbs over the whole building up to the roof. There you can lie and imagine you are in a wood, but without the risk of rain. Here too a fountain rises and disappears underground, while here and there are marble chairs which anyone tired with walking appreciates as much as the building itself. By every chair is a tiny fountain, and throughout the riding-ground can be heard the sound of running streams, the flow of which can be controlled by hand to water one part of the garden or another or sometimes the whole at once.

Waterworks such as these must have used some of the devices described in Hero of Alexandria's *Pneumatica*, but Pliny's use of fountains owes much also to the practical expertise of Roman water-engineers. The development of the aqueduct is far outside the history of gardens, but the understanding of how to convey water great distances in gently-sloping channels and pipes, set out in extraordinary detail in Frontinus' *De Aquae Ductibus* (*c.* AD 90), was an essential acquisition for the garden designer.

Another recent development in the Tuscan villa is the art of topiary, the training and clipping of bushes and trees into artificial shapes. The newness of this art is referred to in the Elder Pliny's *Natural History,* when he says that 'nowadays' the cypress 'is clipped and made into thick walls or evenly rounded off with trim slenderness', and it is even made to provide the representations of the landscape gardener's work, 'arraying hunting scenes or fleets of ships and imitations of real objects with its narrow, short, evergreen leaf'; and elsewhere, talking of the dwarf- or ground-plane (*chamaeplatanus*) 'produced by a method of planting and of lopping', he adds: 'Clipped arbours were invented within the last eighty years [i.e. about the year 4 BC] by a member of the equestrian order named Gaius Matius, a friend of his late Majesty Augustus.'

In the Tuscan villa, *nemora tonsilia* or works in topiary are a major feature. At the front of the house is a colonnade, before which is 'a terrace laid out with box hedges clipped into different shapes, from which a bank slopes down, also with figures of animals cut out of box facing each other on either side.' Nearby, there is a path 'hedged by bushes . . . various box figures and clipped dwarf shrubs.' On the other side of the house is the 'riding-ground' already mentioned, which has not only tall and short trees and shrubs to protect it and provide shade for the paths – ivy-clad plane trees, box shrubs, laurel bushes, cypress trees and roses – but more box, 'clipped into innumerable shapes, some being letters which spell the gardener's name or his master's'; and 'small obelisks of box alternate with fruit trees.' Then, 'suddenly in the midst of this ornamental scene is what looks like a piece of rural country planted there. The open space in the middle is set off by low plane trees planted on each side; farther off are acanthuses with their flexible glossy leaves, then more box figures and names.'

The unexpected 'piece of rural country' planted among these 'box figures and names' is taken up with enthusiasm by Castell in his eighteenth-century reconstruction – for him, it is an excuse to 'return to Nature'. But we may more reasonably see in this *imitatio ruris* an echo of the 'sacred grove'. Neither temples nor grottoes are mentioned in Pliny's villa descriptions, and this one scene is the only part which can supply such a lack.

The exact sites of Pliny's villas are not known, but the details of Pliny's garden descriptions have been confirmed in a most exciting way in recent years, during excavation of the Roman villa at Fishbourne near Chichester in Sussex (see B. Cunliffe, *Excavations at Fishbourne,* 1971).

From around AD 118 until his death in 138, the Emperor Hadrian built in the foothills below Tivoli, to the east of Rome, not a palace, but a 160-acre complex of palaces – almost a young town – which is oddly termed 'Hadrian's Villa'. Though the remains are still vast, the extent to which we may surely say 'this part was a garden', and add 'and it was a garden of such and such a kind' is disturbingly uncertain. There is little contemporary written comment – Spartian is almost the only writer to guide us, when he says 'His [Hadrian's] villa at Tibur was marvellously constructed, and he actually gave to parts of it names of provinces and places of the greatest renown, calling them for instance, Lyceum, Academia, Prytaneum, Canopus, Poccile and Tempe. And in order not to omit anything, he even made a Hades.' These names are allusive, rather than mandatory – though Renaissance scholars and garden enthusiasts thought otherwise. (The most amazing example of this literal interpretation of Spartian is still to be seen at the villa d'Este, where the feature called the Rometta or little Rome presents, rather like a model village in the twentieth century, a miniature representation of the ancient city of Rome.) In naming a feature or part of his domain Poccile – now Pecile in Italian – Hadrian probably wished to remind visitors of the Stoa Poikile at Athens. There is still a great axial wall left from the Pecile, which offered a lengthy *ambulatio*, a *gestatio* consisting of a single wall roughly 250 yards in length, with a covered colonnade on either side of it. Thus one could walk at ease either on the shady or the sunny side of the wall, according to the season and the time of day.

Nearby is the Canopus. This lake is regular in form – one might call it a 'canal' – and seems to have been closed at one end by a semi-circular arcade, with colonnades continuing down each side of the lake. The colonnades were not exactly regular – on the west side there was a roofed building fronted with caryatids copied from those at the Erechtheum on the Acropolis – and we do not know what plants or bushes were grown. At the far end of the Canopus, the valley closes, and in the steep slope there is a large and impressive apse-like building – a semi-circular arch, leading to an open

11 Venturini's engraving (1675) of the Rometta or 'little Rome' at the villa d'Este. This fanciful model of ancient Rome, made in the 1560s, still exists. It imitated the Roman gardens of antiquity, some of which – like Hadrian's villa – had features which commemorated places or scenes of interest or beauty, such as the river Euripus, the Nile, the vale of Tempe and even Hades itself

'room' with rounded roof and sides. The name Canopus was given to this lake or canal to *suggest* (not to represent) the river Nile, or that branch of the Nile on which the city of Canopus stood, renowned for its luxury, its palaces and its temple of Serapis. Other Roman gardens are known to have had pools or canals named after famous rivers or straits – the Nile, and the Euripus (the narrow, tide-ridden straight between mainland Greece and the island of Euboea). The apse-like building at the far end of the Canopus is less easy to identify – some call it a Serapeum, a shrine to Serapis, some say it is a *triclinium*, a dining-room looking out over the canal, and others suggest a grotto, with water running down the walls in cascades, and flowing out over carvings of marine deities and monsters.

From Spartian's list of 'named' features, the Tempe is conceivably a variant on the idea of the *locus amoenus*, the idyllic or pastoral landscape. We may add to descriptions from Theocritus, already quoted, a passage from Pliny the Elder, which Hadrian could have had in mind when planning his own 'vale of Tempe':

> Part of the course of the Peneus is called the Vale of Tempe, five miles long and nearly an acre and a half in breadth, with gently sloping hills rising beyond human sight on either hand, while the valley between is verdant with a grove of trees. Along it glides the Peneus, glittering with pebbles and adorned with grassy banks, melodious with the choral song of birds.

Varro's aviary and the two villas described by Pliny the Younger provide a full picture of the Roman villa garden. The numerous villas excavated at Pompeii and Herculaneum, the recent excavations at Fishbourne and the vast body of Latin literature confirm many features of these gardens but do not add more. Private pleasure gardens, already established in the first century BC, must have been built around the villas until the declining security of country life in the later years of the Empire made them no longer possible. The last full description of a Roman villa is written by Sidonius, a Gallo-Roman noble living in France in the fifth century. Around AD 460 Sidonius writes a letter – modelled certainly on Pliny's earlier letters – describing his country villa at Avitacum, a spot now indentified as being beside the Lac d'Aydat in Auvergne. The villa, though smaller than Pliny's, has many of the same characteristics in its location – lakeside prospects, pleasant breezes, shelter by shoulders of hilly ground, and fertile countryside around it. The buildings are similar, and the complex of baths includes an elaborate open-air swimming pool. The gardens are not described, though there is a 'covered but open' walk, and many rooms have views of the lake.

Sidonius was a Christian – he became Bishop of Clermont in 469 or 470 – and his faith has led to a simplification, to say the least, of the decoration of his villa. The baths have no suggestive paintings – 'no disgraceful tale is exposed by the nude beauty of painted figures', and there are 'no athletes slipping and twisting in their blows and grips'. Moral, chaste – and so rather hostile to the extravagance and enjoyment we have seen with Varro and Pliny. His remarks on the inscriptions allowed in the baths reveal the change in attitude: 'Only a few lines of verse will cause the new-comer to stop and read: these strike the happy mean, for although they inspire no longing to read them again, they can be read through without boredom.'

The empire was no longer invincible, and warfare swept through parts of Gaul several times in Sidonius' lifetime. Before he died in 479 or 480, Rome had ceded Auvergne to the Goths. In garden history, as in other forms of history, the Middle Ages were about to begin.

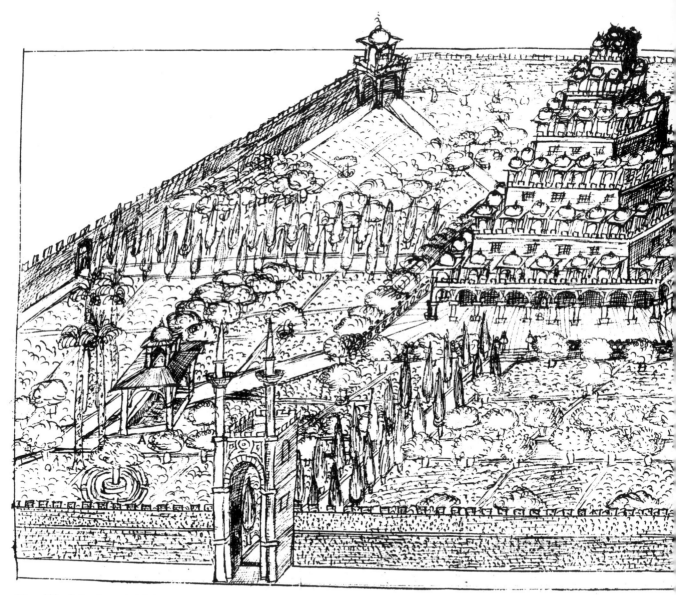

12   Akbar's tomb – a sketch by
the English traveller Peter Mundy
in 1632

2

Persian and Islamic Gardens

PERSIAN GARDENS

'In the beginning' might be said of Persian gardens as truly as of Egyptian or Greek; and their influence continues to this day.

Persian gardens have responded to their surroundings, just as gardens in Italy, France and England have done. These surroundings are so different from those of western and northern Europe that they have produced gardens and attitudes to gardens which are also profoundly different. A great deal of Persia, or Iran as the country is now called, is arid, lacking water and abundant vegetation. It is largely composed of elevated and level country, with areas of barren plain stretching as far as the eye can see, and for much of the year it is extremely hot. Persian or Iranian gardens are a natural and proper reaction to these conditions, and western readers who wish to understand them must first appreciate their surroundings. In reaction to the open and barren wilderness, the garden is enclosed, fertile, and rich with fruit and flowers; in reaction to the drought and heat and unavoidable sun outside, it has water, coolness and shade; in reaction to the hostile vastness of the near-desert, it has order and tranquillity, and is a place where one may sit in the shade, rather than walk in the fierce light of the sun.

I have already quoted phrases from Xenophon's description of the 'paradise gardens' of King Darius the Great (521–485 BC) and Prince Cyrus (died in 401 BC), noted for their ordered planting. These indications are backed up by the excavations of the palaces at Pasargadae, the 'private palace', and the 'garden pavilion', dating from the sixth century BC, where each building is extended by broad porticos or porches, probably with pillars, which look out over a network of straight stone watercourses with small stone pools at exact and regular intervals along the channels. A thousand years later the palace of Khusrau II Parviz (AD 591–628) at Qasr-i Shirin (the 'Imarat-i Khusrau) has similar qualities: the palace is raised on a walled terrace with a roughly rectangular plan, and this space is in turn enclosed within a much larger walled area, clearly a *paradeisos* or hunting park. Between the raised palace enclosure and the outside wall of the *paradeisos* there was an immense pool, probably exactly rectangular and indicating the intention to provide vistas from the palace – or from the arcades of the raised palace enclosure – along the pool.

Not long after the death of Khusrau II (or Chosroes, as western historians used to call him), the Arabs, inspired by the new message of Islam, swept into Persia. Ctesiphon was conquered in 637, and Persia became a Muslim country. Within a few years, the whole of Syria, Egypt, and the entire coast of north Africa had been conquered by the Arabs, while most of Spain and the bulk of Asia Minor, modern Turkey, fell soon after. The dynastic and political coherence of these immense conquests was not to endure, but the religious unity survived (though different sects were also to develop within the body of Islam) and was linked with a general culture absorbed from Persia, and married to the precepts and indications contained within the Koran, particularly those concerning the qualities of Paradise. To apply this statement to all aspects of Islamic culture throughout the Islamic world is to simplify to the point of travesty; yet in terms of gardens, it is true to say that the Persian garden is the source of the Islamic garden, and that with the spread of Islam from Arabia to Persia, further east to India, and west to Turkey, north Africa and Spain, the gardens of Persia were transmitted to every part of the Islamic world. The climatic conditions in the conquered countries had much in common – desert or arid surroundings, burning sun, and little water – and so the model of the Persian garden was readily adopted by the Arab conquerors. These conditions have remained constant, and the nature of the Islamic garden has likewise remained much the same. In temperate climates, experiment and variation in the nature of the garden is possible; in the dry, burning climate of the Islamic world, radical variations would be unlikely, and indeed have not occurred.

When the Arabs conquered Ctesiphon, among the many treasures which they admired was a truly immense carpet made for the Sassanian King Khusrau I (531–579). It was said to be around 450 feet long and ninety feet across, and represented the spring garden of the king. Its plan was that of a *paradeisos*, a royal pleasure park, with beds of spring flowers, and with a broad flowerbed border around the edge. Trees with fruit were shown, and watercourses, all given extra brilliance with jewels and glittering stones. This royal carpet was made in the Persian tradition which went back for centuries and was to continue until relatively modern times, though surviving examples are much smaller. The carpets provide a stylized representation of the Persian garden, which had (the conquering Arabs must have noticed this at once) a singular affinity with the descriptions of the abode of the blessed in the Koran. In the Koran, it is stated that believers go after death to gardens which hold all the delights inhabitants of burning, desert regions would long for. Paradise is enclosed – it has gates and gate-keepers – and the faithful find immortal and beautiful boys and maidens, black-eyed houris, to care for them once they have entered. Fountains are unfailing, while the blessed recline 'upon soft couches'. In the garden, 'They shall feel neither the scorching heat nor the biting cold. Trees will spread their shade around them, and fruits will hang in clusters over them.'

Fountains are often mentioned, and so are rivers: one phrase, 'gardens underneath which rivers flow', or 'gardens of Eden, underneath which rivers flow' recurs many times. In Sura XLVII four rivers of Paradise are mentioned, echoing the four rivers flowing from the Hebrew garden of Eden, but giving them a heavenly quality:

> This is the Paradise which the righteous have been promised. There shall flow in it rivers of unpolluted water, and rivers of milk for ever fresh; rivers of delectable wine and rivers of clearest honey. They shall eat therein of every fruit and receive forgiveness from their Lord.

The fourfold symbolic division of the garden by running water appears in countless Islamic gardens (and it should be noted that 'gardens underneath which rivers flow', and the rivers themselves, provided a part of the inspiration for Coleridge's romantic dream-garden in *Kubla Khan*).

A further fourfold division is encouraged by Sura LV, where *two* gardens, flowing springs, and two kinds of every fruit are promised. This is followed by a further promise:

> . . . besides these there shall be two other gardens . . . of darkest green . . . A gushing fountain shall flow in each . . . Each planted with fruit trees, the palm and the pomegranate . . .

In real Islamic gardens, this division is especially common when a tomb is at the centre, for then the four streams would seem to flow from beneath the tomb, indicating the destiny in Paradise of the person buried there; for example, the tomb of Akbar at Sikandra. Persian garden carpets usually show the same symbolism. The big garden carpet from the Victoria and Albert Museum, shown here, is a good example. It is of Persian manufacture, woven in the seventeenth or eighteenth century, and forms a broad rectangle. Round the edge, a regular, small border of flowers and leaves is followed by a wider one of trees – thin and pointed, resembling cypresses – and shrubs, maybe fruit bushes. Each of these borders is enclosed by a

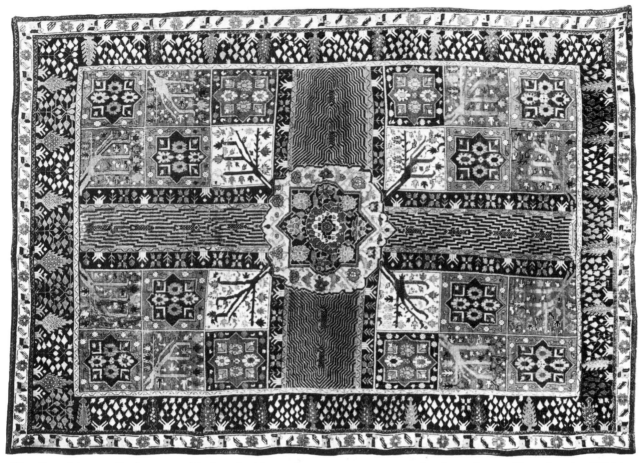

13 One of the great Persian garden carpets, woven *c.* 1700. Within multiple borders of trees and flowers, the garden is quartered by four rivers and subdivided into further regular sections, which we may imagine as being irrigated by lesser channels. The motif in the centre could suggest the pattern of a floral canopy over a *chabutra* or central platform. At the centre-corners of the carpet are four *chenar,* the oriental plane, symbolic of the shade-giving Tuba tree in the Koran

thin band with an abstract pattern, suggesting boundary walls and paths. Within these borders is the garden proper, divided into sections by four 'rivers' with fish in them.

The four quarters are equal in size, each being divided into six squares. They contain alternately flowerbeds, with flowers in square-and-circle patterns, and *chenar* or plane trees, of which four, the most prominent, grow outwards from the central floral design, as if they had been planted at the inner corners of the four sections of the garden. Both the cypresses and the *chenar* have symbolic as well as aesthetic importance: the cypress serves as the symbol for eternity, for it does not lose its leaves, as an earthly equivalent of the Lote tree or 'boundary' tree of the Koran (Sura LIII), and as a poetic symbol for female beauty; while the *chenar* is an earthly counterpart of the Tuba tree, the great giver of shade (Sura XIII). Even the central square-and-circle design, like that of the beds in the smaller divisions of the garden, is symbolic of perfection: it involves the combination of the square with the square to provide a kind of circle, and, more convincing, it is a figure which 'surpasses the number of the seven spheres and is larger than Hell which has only seven storeys, and thus demonstrates the truth that God's mercy is greater than his wrath' (A. Schimmel, 'The Celestial Garden', in *The Islamic Garden*, 1976).

Some Islamic gardens will therefore have eight terraces, or octagonal pools or pavilions. The thirteenth-century Persian poet Saadi's principal work, the *Gulistan* (or rose garden) is properly divided into eight portions, to give it the proportions of Paradise.

At the centre of the garden carpet from the Victoria and Albert Museum there is an elaborate floral design, in which the diversity of flowers, leaves and stems is given order by its inner border, a square-and-circle, reinforced by the eight main flowers around the centre, eight smaller ones being in the outer area of the design. This design resembles nothing less than the carpets which Persian and Mughal rulers would take out into the garden to lay on the ground, or to use as a canopy or awning

against the sun. In the garden carpet, it represents therefore the canopied platform or open-sided pavilion which the ruler would erect over the intersection of the waterways.

Other Persian garden carpets repeat or add to these features – the fourfold division by streams forming a cross, and the central island or pavilion. One of the most explicit is in the Jaipur Museum in India, a carpet woven probably before 1632 with a much longer and narrower shape. It is divided by the four rivers, and has at the centre a domed and highly ornamented garden pavilion, set like an island within a square central pool. The pavilion is open on one side to allow the owner, the king, to sit in the shade and look out along the main watercourse, in which fish, birds and I think dragons sport and swirl. The long garden area is subdivided by water channels

14   One of the most delicate of all Persian garden scenes (left), this is also relatively early. Painted in 1396, it contrasts the 'wilderness' (even though it is sprinkled with flowers) with the high-walled 'paradise', in which flowers, leaves and plants are everywhere apparent. Narrow borders run inside the walls, and a *chenar*, the oriental plane, stands between the gate and the ground-floor window of the pavilion

into eight sections – we may imagine terraces – and the trees and bushes are laden with fruit and flowers, while animals and birds crowd the remaining spaces. Its plan is similar to that of the Shalimar Bagh in Lahore, begun for the Mughal emperor, Shah Jahan, in 1634.

Turn to gardens, rather than carpets. One of the earliest Persian gardens which is described is that of the 'Old Man of the Mountains', the ruler of the fortress of Alamut, some distance from Teheran. Here, according to Marco Polo, whose journey through Persia to China was made in the 1260s, the sheikh set out a garden 'planted with all the finest fruits in the world', and with 'four conduits, one flowing with wine, one with milk, one with honey, and one with water. There were fair ladies there . . . and he gave his men to understand that this was Paradise.'

Polo gives no detail of the planting, and for this we must look at one of the most beautiful of all Persian garden miniatures, painted in 1396 as an illustration to a poem by Kharju Kirmani. The lover – a prince, wearing a crown – arrives outside the enclosed garden in which his lady waits at the top of a pavilion. Though a stream runs past the wall, no water is visible inside the garden, and this is exceptional. But the entire scene is alive with flowers and fruit and leaves. A narrow, bordered bed runs inside the wall, in which lilies are mixed with almond and pomegranate trees, and a *chenar* gives shade. The pavilion itself is covered with floral patterns; even the Arabic script just below the lady's hanging sleeves looks like the twining of stems and tendrils. And birds fly around and in the garden – one perched on an almond tree by the far wall has its beak open to sing. It is surely a nightingale.

MUGHAL GARDENS

Gardens of this kind were a passion with Mughal emperors, beginning with Babur (1483–1530). In his youth he saw the well ordered and irrigated orchards and gardens of Samarkand, formed under Persian influence, and when he began to invade and remain in India (it was a fluctuating, bloody and lengthy struggle), his gardens followed the Persian model. There are many references to his garden-making and love of flowers among the turbulent incidents filling his memoirs, the *Babur-nama* (tr. A. S. Beveridge, 1922). He first invaded the Punjab in 1518, and was eventually proclaimed Padshah in Delhi in 1526. His gardens, whether near Kabul (in modern Afghanistan), which he captured in 1504, or far within India at Agra, survive in dubious and disputed form, but his descriptions remain, and are gloriously illustrated in later manuscripts of the *Babur-nama* prepared in the reign of Akbar (b. 1542, reigned 1556–1605).

The garden he describes most fully is the Bagh-i Wafa, or 'Garden of Fidelity', made near Jalalabad in 1508–9. He calls it a *chahar-bagh*, a fourfold garden, and different illustrations convey this in slightly different ways. One illustration is a double-page miniature, painted in 1589, from the *Babur-nama*.

> In the south-west part of it there is a reservoir, 10 x 10 yards, round which are orange trees and a few pomegranates, the whole encircled by a trefoil meadow . . . a most beautiful sight when the oranges take colour . . .

While the illustration shows a small square tank beneath the four plots, the planting does not fit in with these last phrases and another picture, from a different manuscript of the *Babur-nama*, illustrates this better. Here, the water-tank has in the middle a small fountain-jet (possibly anachronistic, as it seems that these were not introduced into Mughal gardens until the time of Akbar). The chutes are again characteristic – a sloping incline for overflowing water from a pool above, called a *chadar*. This word means 'shawl', and the effect produced on the water is indeed like a white and gleaming shawl, since the slope of the *chadar* is carved with patterns – wave designs, most often – which break up the even flow of the water, making it sparkle.

Babur's tomb is in a garden, the Bagh-i Babur, in Kabul, but this garden is sadly dilapidated, and cannot be identified with any of those he describes in his memoirs.

Another illustration, painted in 1589, shows him holding a garden party in 1528 at

15   A scene illustrating Babur's gardeners at work (above), in the 'Garden of Fidelity' near Jalalabad. Babur's memoirs describe the garden in detail. This scene, including sugar canes and bananas, has 'a reservoir . . . round which are orange trees and a few pomegranates, the whole encircled by a trefoil meadow'. The plantains or bananas appear in the top left and the 'trefoil meadow' in the top right corner

31

Agra. Here, the *form* of the garden is not apparent, but *flowers* are everywhere – embroidered on the carpets, on clothing, on the canopy, and growing out of the ground or from trees. Babur's delight in flowers – he had a passion for tulips, and had the varieties counted, finding thirty-two or thirty-three different sorts – is characteristic of all Islamic garden-lovers and comes, as do the other qualities of these gardens, from the climate. Flowers in the Persian and Indian spring come with a brief, intense and overwhelming beauty. Winter is barely over when the bulbs are in flower: narcissus, tulip and iris; then lilac, jasmine and carnation; and then the rose. A few weeks, and burning summer comes, and flowers are over. 'Alas, that Spring should vanish with the rose!' wrote Omar Khayyam in Persia in the twelfth century. English readers may puzzle over this, forgetting that their climate is kind to roses, and that modern varieties have been bred to bloom over extended periods. I write in late September, and outside in the garden, the roses have been flowering for months on end; the 'last rose of summer' is still far away.

Akbar's tomb at Sikandra near Agra, begun in his lifetime, repeats this *chahar-bagh* in a gigantic form. The water is supplied by eight – the number of Paradise – tanks, two on each avenue, and the immense edifice of the tomb stands square in the centre of the garden. Today, the vegetation is far less luxuriant than it once was, and the appearance of the garden is disappointing. In 1632, soon after the tomb was completed, the English traveller Peter Mundy sketched the general prospect, showing the main divisions of the garden lined with cypresses, and the remainder covered with trees and plants. 'This square garden' writes Mundy

> is againe divided into other lesser squares, and that into other like bedds and plotts; in some, litle groves of trees, as Apple trees (those scarse), Orange trees, Mulberrie treees, etc., Mango trees, Caco [cocoanut] trees, Figg trees, Plantan trees, this latter in ranks, as are the Cipresse trees. In other squares are your flowers, herbes, etc., whereof Roses, Marigolds . . . French Marigolds aboundance; Poppeas redd, carnation & white; & diverse other sortes of faire flowers which wee knowe not in our parts . . .

The diagonal paths in the drawing may not have existed. Mundy's visit was brief and he writes of his sketch: 'The design thereof I have put downe . . . as well as I can remember.'

A year before Mundy's visit to Agra, the favourite wife of the ruler, Shah Jahan (b. 1591, ruled 1628–58, died 1666) had died. She was a Persian lady, Mumtaz Mahal, and Jahan had married her in 1612. Immediately after his account of Akbar's tomb, completed by Shah Jahan, which ends with the admiring 'such a stately gate and such ranges of small Cipresse trees', Mundy goes on with 'This Kinge [Jahan] is now buildinge a Sephulchre for his late deceased Queene Tage Moholl.' Mundy was therefore a witness of the beginning of this incomparable building. The Taj Mahal at Agra is the tomb of Mumtaz Mahal, and it took twenty-two years (1632–54) to complete. Unlike Akbar's tomb, or the smaller tomb of Humayun (Akbar's father) in Delhi, the Taj Mahal has the tomb and its principal adjacent buildings set at the end of the garden, not in the centre. The domed, white marble building with the tomb is raised on a terrace which overlooks both the *chahar-bagh* garden, and the river Jumna on the other side. This *chahar-bagh* is surely the most exactly and carefully executed of all, and matches the greatest formal gardens of Europe for its perfection. In the seventeenth century it must have resembled the formal French gardens more than it does today, for the quarters of the garden and their further subdivisions were filled with flowers. The Frenchman Bernier, seeing the Taj Mahal in 1663, wrote that there were to right and left 'garden *allées* shaded with trees, and many parterres full of flowers'; and they were scrupulously ordered and controlled, not with box edging, as would have been the case at the Luxembourg or the Tuileries, but with a formal edging of stone. In a way, these flowerbeds would have been a preparation for the frieze of marble flowers which adorn parts of the outside walls of the tomb. Bernier noted also that fountains were spaced along the central channel running from the entrance-gate towards the tomb, and that the central avenue was raised high up above the garden, as in the Moorish gardens

16   A plan of the gardens round Akbar's tomb at Sikandra, built in the early 1600s. The gardens surround the central tomb, and a fourfold division, as in the Persian garden carpet, is achieved by broad paths at the end of which water tanks are set. These were once connected by water channels, now dry, and the gardens were originally thickly planted

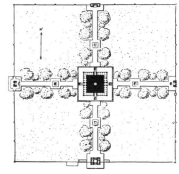

17 An early eighteenth-century miniature of the Taj Mahal, built in 1632-54. The painting shows Europeans admiring the glories of the building; but it is of immense garden interest to see the dense and luxuriant growth of flowers and trees in the gardens, which are today planted much more bleakly. In 1633 the Frenchman Bernier wrote of this scene that it included 'garden allées shaded with trees, and many parterres full of flowers'. This view is taken from the middle of the gardens, which are quartered by four rectangular canals

which have been excavated in the last twenty years – a device which allows irrigation of the flowerbeds, and provides a superb visual effect for the visitor, as if one were walking beside a flowery carpet.

Today, the stone edging of the flowerbeds has been retained only along the main axes of the garden, with designs based on an octagonal motif. The level of the beds has been raised, the flowers have mostly gone, while the thick plantings of trees for shade have been abandoned in favour of more limited planting along the avenues. The present setting may be thought to do more justice to the building, as there is no distraction from the perfect proportions of the long avenue with its extended water vista and flanking paths, and the visitor grasps at once the impeccable placing of the raised central tank of water to reflect the white domes and minarets. The garden is therefore seen as a wonderfully scaled approach to the building, rather than a garden in itself.

TURKISH GARDENS

Turkish gardens are clearly Persian in their characteristics. They are firmly enclosed, and have the same veneration for flowing water in symmetrical basins, for small fountains, for the cypress and the *chenar*, and for the beauty of individual flowers. Most of what we know of them dates from the early eighteenth century, though there are the two garden kiosks in the grounds of the Topkapi palace, both built in the 1570s, which are distinctly 'Persian'. One, the kiosk of Murad III, retains a broad canal, facing the kiosk, which itself stands over a small extension of the canal, and the other, the kiosk of Siyavush Pasha, is raised up like a square island in a square lake, the lake penetrating within the kiosk itself. Elsewhere in the Topkapi palace, there is the 'Marble Terrace' and its tank and fountains, with a small pavilion built out over the water where the sultan could recline.

This desire to situate the viewing place of the garden – be it balcony or pavilion – above water is deeply characteristic of older Turkish gardens. In Turkey, it develops in a special way, encouraged by the proximity of the sea along the shores of the Bosphorus, and by the steeply rising terrain at the back of the sites. While in India and in Persia the great cities were largely inland, in Turkey Istanbul, the one city of importance, was a sea-port. 'Nothing can be pleasanter than the canal', wrote Lady Mary Wortley Montagu in 1718 (*Letters*, ed. R. B. Johnson, 1925), 'and the Turks are so well acquainted with its beauties, all their pleasure-seats are built on its banks, where they have at the same time, the most beautiful prospects in Europe and in Asia.' Their gardens had the possibility of pavilions sited not just over small streams, but actually over the edge of the sea, and this often happened. I think the most exciting of these constructions was the, alas!, now vanished Sultaniye kiosk, built on the Asiatic shore of the Bosphorus by Sultan Suleiman the Magnificent (1520-66), drawn in 1710 by the Dutch artist Cornelius Loos. Here, a causeway was built out into the sea to enclose a tranquil pool in which the kiosk – in Persia we would call it a pavilion – could stand, looking along the varied prospect of the coastline. The kiosk itself was like an island in the pool, connected with the seaward side of the causeway by a narrow bridge. On the side facing the land, the broad leaves of the kiosk were supported on six pillars, giving ample shade, the most sumptuous of balconies, where the sultan would sit and talk or meditate, and watch ships – or the moon. As well as the drawings by Loos, there is an account by the orientalist Antoine Galland, who visited the pavilion twice in 1673. He explains that it was built out in the sea, and adds that 'It is encrusted within and without with most beautiful tiles, which are beginning here and there to come away, since the kiosk is so old; other parts are in marble or porphyry ... A balcony supported by marble, granite and porphyry pillars made this building even more enjoyable.' On his second visit, he noted a verse in Persian: 'This enchanting palace has no equal in the world.'

Much later, built out over the water, there are the kiosks of the Beylerbeyi palace, built in the nineteenth century, and in between, the many houses with gardens overlooking the Bosphorus, such as that of Fathi Ahmet Pasha at Kuzgunchuk (early nineteenth century), where the men's garden has apertures in its seaward wall, and the harem garden has a wall without windows, so that, as Sedad Eldem puts it (*Türk bahçeleri*, 1976) 'it is only possible to sense the presence of the sea, but not to see it.' The ladies' view was from a kiosk raised up over the rear part of their garden, and immediately behind a pool and fountain belonging to the garden itself. Many of these gardens on the Bosphorus also had a delightful feature which other gardens lack – a tiny harbour, an inlet where small boats could enter from the sea through a low archway in the wall, and find themselves literally within the enclosure of the garden. The Turkish gardens are rich in kiosks for sitting and reclining in. All foreign travellers remarked on this. Thévenot noticed it in Syria in the 1660s, where the Turk would sit all day cross-legged on his divan smoking and contemplating his garden. Chardin in Persia a decade later wrote, rather scornfully, that the Persians do not 'stroll in their gardens as we do, but are satisfied with the sight of what they have, and with breathing the air. They sit down in some spot in the garden when they arrive, and stay there until they leave.'

Lady Montagu writes that

18 A crude but revealing drawing (right), made in 1710 by the Dutch artist Cornelius Loos, of the now-vanished Sultaniye kiosk (*c.* 1550). The kiosk was built on piles out over the sea and was surrounded by a sea wall, so that it was sited over a small and tranquil lagoon

19 This detail (below) from a Turkish painting of 1720 shows a party celebrating the circumcision of the Sultan's sons. While the guests watch the ceremony, we may admire the garden-cake, a traditional gift for such occasions. Made of sugar, pastry, marzipan and suchlike, it is three-dimensional and realistic, with four kiosks round a central pond. Fruit trees, cypresses and tulips are regularly planted. Cages with singing birds complete the scene

for some miles around Adrianople [Edirne], the whole ground is laid out in gardens, and . . . fruit trees, under which all the most considerable Turks divert themselves every evening . . . they choose out a green spot, where the shade is very thick, and there they spread a carpet, on which they sit drinking their coffee, and generally attended by some slave with a fine voice, or that plays on some instrument.

Apart from the coffee (unknown outside the Levant until the end of the seventeenth century) this could be a garden scene from Babur's memoirs.

Kiosks are beautifully sited over water, either placid or flowing, in the water garden at Saadabad, in Kagithane, at the end of the Golden Horn. Most of the building dates from 1721, in the reign of Ahmet II (1703–30). A section of river was diverted to form a sequence of three marble-edged pools connected by two shallow ornamental weirs. The channels are of course reminiscent of the water-patterns formed in Italian *cordonata* cascades as at the villa Lante (chapter 6). The upper and lower weirs have these sequences in different order: the upper has cascades followed by channels, so that the central mirror pool is not disturbed by tumbling water, while the lower weir begins with the channels, followed by the splashing cascade. The kiosks enjoy the various levels and appearances of the water – one perched over the water of the central pool seems to float on its surface.

For coolness, fountains were quite often built inside the kiosks: 'What pleases me best', wrote Lady Montagu, 'is the fashion of having marble fountains in the lower part of the room, which throw up several spouts of water, giving at the same time an agreeable coolness, and a pleasant dashing sound, falling from one basin to another.' In a room in one palace there were 'falls of water from the very roof, from shell to shell, of white marble, to the lower end of the room, where it falls into a large basin, surrounded with pipes, that throw up the water as high as the room.' The walls were 'in the nature of lattices', and outside 'vines and woodbines' were planted to 'form a sort of green tapestry, and give an agreeable obscurity to those delightful chambers.'

Lady Montagu was privileged to visit many Turkish ladies in their private quarters, the harem, which European men could not do. These enclosed rooms were often 'painted with flowers', and between the windows were 'little arches to set pots of perfume, or baskets of flowers'. While the rose is the love of Persia, in Turkey the tulip is the flower *par excellence*. Its name, *lale*, has mystical significance, since the consonants are the same as those in *Allah*, and the tulip is a much favoured decorative motif, both in houses and religious buildings. An extraordinary and uniquely Turkish garden record is found in the garden models made in confectionery – sugar, pastry, icing, marzipan – given as presents on special occasions. Mr Eldem's book on Turkish gardens illustrates these from a miniature painting of 1720 which depicts the festivities celebrating the circumcision of the sons of Sultan Ahmet III.

MOORISH GARDENS

While the ancient gardens of Persia are in a ruined state, and those of the Mughals are often strangely misplanted, and while there is virtually no trace of the briefly splendid gardens of Arab-Norman Sicily, a few Moorish gardens in Spain are still tended and loved. The Arabs first invaded Spain in 710, and ruled much of the country for centuries. From 1248 only the Moorish kingdom of Granada survived, but this was not conquered by the Spaniards until 1492, and though fierce efforts were made by the Christian conquerors to eradicate Islamic belief and Arabic learning, aspects of Arabic culture, including the art of gardening, survived.

Literature and archaeology have come together to provide details of these early Islamic gardens. In Cordova, there was a garden, the Hair al-Zajjali, in which the poet Ibn Shuhai'd was buried in the eleventh century, and a later writer, Ibn Khaqan (see J. Dickie, 'The Islamic Garden in Spain', *The Islamic Garden*), said of the garden:

> The courtyard is of pure white marble; a stream traverses it, wriggling like a snake. There is a basin into which all waters fall. The roof [of the pavilion] is decorated in gold and blue and in these colours also are decorated the sides and various parts. The garden has files of trees symmetrically aligned and its flowers smile from open buds. The foliage of the garden prevents the sun seeing the ground; and the breeze, blowing day and night over the garden, is loaded with scents.

This could have served as a 'model' text for Persian gardens earlier in this chapter. The garden is clearly ordered, and the 'files of trees' suggest regular and luxuriant planting within a regular enclosure. The stream 'wriggling like a snake' might be running down an undulating channel, or possibly curving down from level to level – we may think of the later Turkish channels and cascades at Saadabad, and of the serpentine channel in the Chinese garden pavilion, the Liu Pei T'ing in Nan Hai.

Excavations in the Alcázar at Seville have revealed part of an eleventh-century garden with sunken flowerbeds and stuccoed and painted decorations on the sides (this is the patio of the Qasr al-Mubarak). Above and to one side of this site is a twelfth-century garden of the *chahar-bagh* type – four square sections with deeply sunken beds, divided by the 'four rivers'. Also in the Alcázar a section of another *chahar-bagh* garden has been discovered with beds sunk about *fifteen feet* below the surrounding level. This extraordinary discovery is confirmed by a description written by Rodrigo Caro in his *Antigüedades . . . de Sevilla* (1634), a century before the garden was destroyed. Caro called the garden the *Crucero*, 'because it is cruciform in plan', and he describes it as 'a subterranean garden of orange trees, divided into quarters . . . the tops of the trees almost reach the level [of the paths].'

Seville was retaken by the Spaniards in 1248, and much purely Moorish garden building was gradually lost. But in 1364–6, Pedro the Cruel rebuilt portions of the Alcázar, employing Moorish craftsmen. Individual features recall their tradition, such as the low interior fountain, decorated with tiles and the glorious hexagonal tiled basin with its fountain, and shallow watercourse leading to and from it, between

I Painted by Ramdas, probably in 1589, this miniature (right) took the artist fifty days to complete. The picture shows Babur – beneath the canopy – as the host at a party which took place in Agra in 1528 to celebrate the conquest of Hindustan. Flowers are omnipresent – on the woven carpets, embroidered on the clothes, and growing freely on the trees and on the ground

II and III A messenger and his escort must wait – business inside the garden is more important. In this pair of miniatures (overleaf), the emperor himself directs the work in the 'Garden of Fidelity'. 'A one mill stream flows constantly past a little hill on which there are four garden plots', wrote Babur in his memoirs. The planting of the garden is still incomplete. Two men stretch a cord from left to right, parallel to the water channel, while other gardeners dig and another holds up a planting scheme or plan

از زنخ و از سفیده و از سیاه و از رخت و از جنس ساحقها
فرمودم که در پیش من ژیلوچه انداخت شا

خوب می نماید خیلی باغ خوبی طرح شده و در ظرف خوب

کوه سفید سنگهار واقع شده در میان سنگهار و سنگ و سطح

درختهای انار هم هست کردا کرد حوض تمام سه برکزا

جای این باغ همین است در وقت زرد شدن با بجهاند

IV

Round this shaded fountain basin in the gardens of the Alcázar the patterned tiles are bright and shining from the water which constantly sprays over them, while the central pool, level with the hexagonal brim, serves as mirror to reflect the sunlight. The outer border of this fountain is pierced with extra jets – *burladores* or 'jokers' – to wet unwary spectators

an avenue of cypress arches. But these gardens are now heavily overlaid with Renaissance and later European additions – the large labyrinth, the joke fountains, and the scrollwork *broderie* in box.

The best Moorish gardens in Spain are in Granada, in the gardens of the Generalife and the Alhambra. The Generalife, like the Alcázar in Seville, is a complex of gardens built over many hundreds of years, and the upper terraces date from the nineteenth century. The lower sections are, however, Moorish, and excavations have shown the most famous feature, the long rectangular patio de la Acequia, to have had a much more completely Islamic character than it does now. Today, it has planting along both sides of the canal, which is lined with small fountain-jets playing up and over the canal, forming the beautiful and famous water-archway. These jets are not original, but a later Spanish addition, modelled on the exuberant fountains of Renaissance Italy. In 1958 parts of the Generalife were destroyed by fire, and the work of restoration which followed allowed excavation of parts of the patio. It was then discovered that the original garden bedding had been much lower in relation to the surrounding paths, and would have allowed the tops of the flowers to grow roughly level with the paths, and thus give the impression of a flowering pattern within the original glazed green and white tiles bordering the paths, like the flowers within a bordered carpet. The thirteenth-century garden revealed beneath the later one proved also to have had some sort of pavilion, possibly a simple platform like an Indian *chabutra,* or possibly with a dome, set over the central point of the long narrow canal. There are the bases of columns on each side of this crossing, and this indication would make the patio de la Acequia yet another fourfold garden, with paths leading to the central crossing both along the length of the canal, and from the sides. Also of Moorish origin is the smaller patio de los Cipresses, and again its present overarching fountains are a later addition. Enclosed by walls, it contains a pool going round three sides of a square.

Within the Alhambra, close below the buildings of the Generalife, several sections are still clearly Moorish, though overlaid (with the bedding deeply and literally so) with later European features. The fountain pool in the patio de Lindaraja has the eight-pointed circle-with-a-square motif found at the centre of the Persian garden carpet discussed earlier. The patio de la Alberca, also called the patio de los Arragnes (the patio of the pool, or of the myrtles), has an enclosed rectangular pool which in itself could be from any country, but at either end, set within the shelter and shadow of the fantastically decorated Moorish archways, there are shallow fountain-bowls; not for tall and European jets, but for a gentle flow of water, to give the hint of 'gardens underneath which rivers flow'. The patio de los Leones is I think the most purely Islamic of all the surviving Moorish gardens in Spain. This is a *chahar-bagh* in its form, a rectangle divided by water-courses into four quarters. The water rises within the adjacent rooms, as in the Turkish houses described by Lady Montagu, and the fountains then run along and down narrow channels past the slender pillars which line the garden, and form the four rivers dividing the beds. These beds, like those of the patio de la Acequia in the Generalife, were in Arab times at least two feet lower than they are today. Now, they are virtually level with the surrounding paths, and the vile and anachronistic modern planting rises up level with the noses of the twelve lions supporting the central fountain. This patio is one of Spain's most beautiful architectural treasures. Its planting today is a far cry from the orange trees which once used to be there, and which would have risen up from the deeply sunken beds like round coloured cushions. It would not be difficult to restore them.

V

The gardens of the Alhambra have many features which go back to Moorish times. This fountain has the same 'circle-on-a-square' outline which appears in the Persian carpet illustrated in pl. 13. The motif of eight facets or 'corners', or a garden with eight divisions or terraces, is of deep symbolic significance in Muslim art

20 'The Wine Courtyard,
Wind and Lotus' – one of the
'Forty Scenes' depicting the Yuan
Ming Yuan, the 'Garden of
Perfect Brightness'

3

Chinese Gardens

THE SPIRIT

> 'The wise find pleasure in water; the virtuous find pleasure in hills.'
>
> (Confucius, *Analects*)

This phrase contains the essence of the Chinese garden: its intimate association with nature; its striving for movement; its representation of permanence; and its ethical and philosophical preoccupations. Like landscape painting in China, summarized as *shan shui*, or 'mountains' and 'water', the Chinese garden attempts to approach, to display in symbolic form, the essence of nature. This is not a realistic or naturalistic presentation, but one which seeks to find the 'nature of nature'. Landscape painting is closely tied with gardening in China; indeed so much so that the four arts of poetry, calligraphy, landscape painting and gardening are thought of as interdependent, each requiring an understanding of the others, proficiency in each being necessary in order to achieve proficiency in any one.

To round off this linking of landscape painting and gardening, scroll painting in China should also be mentioned. These are not simply extended rectangles of landscape, as one might imagine when seeing the scrolls displayed in western museums. Though vertical scrolls were meant to be hung on the wall, and to be seen at a single glance, the horizontal scroll should be seen section by section, in a slow unrolling from right to left; indeed to see such a painting all at once is to go against its purpose, for nature reveals itself slowly, part by part, moment by moment, and cannot be seen from a single viewpoint. Similarly, the Chinese garden is rarely if ever visible at once, but is discovered scene by scene, one scene leading to the next, which, as it is revealed, replaces the earlier and now invisible vistas which we first perceived.

All this comes back to the pervasive influence of the philosophy of the *Tao*, involving meditation on the unity of the creation, a creation in which nature possesses a hidden yet real order and harmony, and which may be seen, in moments of enlightenment, through intuitive, tranquil receptivity. Gardening, like painting, is an act of reverence, as well as one of delight. Such a concern with the order and harmony of nature is often and clearly at odds with the ways of the world, and the works of men are often considered inferior and distracting. Again and again in Chinese poetry or paintings to do with nature, and in comments on Chinese gardens, we learn that the artist has turned to these subjects after renouncing the false attractions of worldly ambition. Both gardening and landscape painting tend therefore to place man in a subordinate position; present, contemplative, observing, yet only an insignificant part of the natural scene. And the natural scene itself in these works of art, whether paintings or gardens, is a symbolic representation, an essence, an indication, rather than an attempt at realistic re-creation.

Symbolism, whether through rocks, or pools, or the choice and arrangement of flowers and trees, is always present, and always intentional, in a way which is uncommon in most western gardens. In contrast, old Chinese gardens lack elements which westerners would expect to find; in particular, the formal, symmetrical arrangement of the plan (both in its major outlines and in the patterned details of garden bedding and parterres), the artificial manipulation of water in fountains, and the extensive use of grass in lawns. These elements appear occasionally in civic gardens in China today, but these are imitations of western models, and relatively recent in their introduction.

The symbolic treatment of both rocks and trees is found in one of the oldest gardens to survive anywhere in the world, which began as a 'sacred grove', and even today retains something of its first character. This garden, or grove, surrounds the tomb of Confucius, north of the town of Ku Fou in Shantung province, where Confucius spent much of his life. Confucius died in 479 BC and the erection of memorials and temples in his honour began soon after his death.

By a most happy chance, I have had access to a volume of photographs, taken in 1907 or earlier, of the monuments around Ku Fou and around the nearby holy mountain of Tai Shan, both in Shantung province (*Views of the Taishan and Kufou*, compiled and photographed by Tse Tsi Shau, 1907; one of only five copies, this one presented to Col. L. M. Cosgrave, DSO). The monuments appear as they were before the cataclysmic events of the present century, and while the monuments and their surroundings were much as they must have been for many years. Since then, neglect, vandalism, further neglect, and conversion to military, civic and tourist uses have so altered these places that, although many of them still subsist, their air of antiquity has been sadly diminished.

Back in 1907, the sacred grove leading to the tomb of Confucius, approached by an avenue of immemorial cedars, had been untouched for a century or more. The cedars were probably seven or eight hundred years old, as tablets suggest they were planted in the Chin and Yuan periods, between the twelfth and fourteenth centuries. According to tradition, the trees in the grove were brought here by pious disciples, and many, extremely old, are gnarled and knotted, and held together by iron rings. To the Chinese, the writhen, contorted appearance of these old and almost lifeless trunks is worthy of lengthy contemplation, revealing qualities of fortitude and grandeur comparable to the worn yet enduring stones of the mountain-side.

Not so far from Ku Fou is the mountain of Tai Shan, considered the most holy

21   Rocks are essential in a Chinese garden, as in landscape painting, since they suggest the most permanent element of the natural world. This photograph, taken before 1907, shows the massive and extraordinary rock bridge in the mountains near the peak of the holy mountain of Tai Shan. On the western side is the 'Sea Observing' rock, which may be compared with its garden equivalent in pl. 34

22   An aged pine tree – 'green and fresh throughout the year . . . its branches curl like a snake' – giving shade to a part of the Pu Chao temple, in the Tai Yang region (*c.* 1907). Beside the piper and the ancient monk grows a dwarf *bonsai* tree. 'One asks for mournful melodies; Accomplished fingers begin to play' (Yeats, 'Lapis Lazuli')

mountain in China. This mountain has a long, ceremonial approach, beginning with the temple-complex in the town of Tai An, and leading from the town up a broad, winding stairway of seven thousand steps, through gorges and ravines, past temples and monuments, caves and cascades to the highest peak, where further pillars and temples mark the most sacred features. These features include aspects which are typical of the sacred grove, and also essential to the Chinese garden. In the town, the main Tai Shan temple contains a number of large, curiously shaped and to western eyes distorted rocks, prominent in the largest, central courtyard. Rocks of this kind figure in almost every Chinese garden, and I would surmise that only gardens set in a mountainous terrain, and therefore already provided by nature with evidence of mountains, would altogether dispense with such ornaments.

Elsewhere in the Tai Shan complex stand other aged trees, valued both for their antiquity, and for their extraordinary shape: at the Tai temple are six cedars, said to have been planted by Emperor Wu of the Han dynasty (*c.* 180 BC), and in the garden of the Pu Chao temple, outside the town and on the way up the mountain, stands a pine tree from the time of the T'ang dynasty (AD 923-36).

The twisted stone shapes set up in Chinese gardens are in this way related to the grottoes of European gardens, derived in Europe from the caves and hiding-places of rustic and marine deities. Often, set on a pedestal in a courtyard, one of these stones may seem remote from its original inspiration, as do many shell-encrusted fountains displayed in public places in Europe. But in China, the natural mountains and the rocks erected in gardens have always been consciously associated, and their veneration has never been interrupted.

Curious-shaped rocks have always been admired. Both solitary visits to the mountains and the contemplation of a single stone have inspired poems and paintings, and the choice of rocks for gardens has been exhaustively discussed in a Chinese treatise, the *Yuan Yeh* by Chi Ch'eng (1635). (Excerpts from the *Yuan Yeh* have been reproduced in O. Sirén, *Gardens of China* 1949, especially pp. 11-16 and pp. 24-28. No full translation into a European language exists.)

45

The best stones were to be found beneath the water near the shores of Tai-hu lake, near Soochow. When, after centuries of exploitation, the supply dwindled, rich rock-lovers would even take promising rocks from other regions to immerse them in Tai-hu lake, so that several decades later they might be retrieved, beautifully shaped and weathered by the unique action of the Tai-hu waters.

The *Yuan Yeh* describes the qualities of stones from more than a dozen different sites; stones having varied characteristics and degrees of excellence, and serving varied purposes in the creation of a garden. Of the Tai-hu stones, described as 'the most beautiful old stones', the *Yuan Yeh* writes:

> They are solid and shiny. Some have deep hollows, others are riddled with holes, others again are curving or curiously carved. Some are white, others bluish black, while others have a fainter blue-black hue. Their substance is apparent in horizontal and vertical furrows, which stand out and disappear as in basketwork. The surface is full of hollows that have arisen through the hammering of the waves; these are called bullet holes. If one strikes these stones they give forth a faint sound . . . Large stones should be set up in front of big halls. They may be placed under a stately pine or be combined with wonderful flowers. They may be used as mountains set up in a big pavilion out in the garden . . . They have been collected since time immemorial, and are now very rare.

From descriptions like this, from detailed illustrations in painting manuals, from paintings of garden scenes, and from photographs of genuine surviving stones, we may estimate the shape and size of the stones which were most appreciated. They were large (up to fifteen feet in height), pierced with irregular holes, furrowed and gashed with indentations, and often so jutting that they appear to overhang, to be wider at the top than at the bottom. Instructions for setting them up are as detailed as on the original choice of stones. They must appear solidly based, with more beneath the ground than above the surface. When in groups, they should never appear

23 'Chu Suei bridge and Gem Girdle creek' – a scene within the 'sacred grove' containing the tomb of Confucius, north of Ku Fou in Shantung province. The commentary of 1907 says: 'The water and trees look so clean and admirable that travellers reaching there find themselves almost in paradise'

46

symmetrically arranged, and the placing of one or more stones to form an overhanging mountain feature should be contrived to avoid any feeling of instability or artificiality.

Not all these rocks were so large – small ones might be equally attractive, and their irregularities and texture could lead just as well to a contemplation of the natural world. Some stones might be tiny enough to be displayed indoors, on tables. The 'Ling-pi' stones were noted for these miniature qualities: 'they should be selected with an eye to their most beautiful parts and chiselled flat on the bottom, so that they may be placed on a table.' Often enough, these stones were carved and chiselled to look even more mountainous and craggy, and there is only a slight dividing line at this point between the natural stone and the work of sculpture, representing an entire mountain scene. We may remember the passage from Yeats's 'Lapis Lazuli', where such an artefact is described.

Extremes to us – of admiration appear from time to time. In the twelfth century, Mi Fei, painter and stone-lover, had a garden pavilion built for the contemplation of his stones, which included one to which he would bow, addressing it as his 'elder brother'. As a modern writer, Chuin Tung, remarks: 'when stone is endowed with personality, one can find it delightful company.'

The idea of a special place for viewing stones, a *pai-shih* pavilion, was imitated in the late sixteenth century by Li Li-weng, whose pavilion was restored in the nineteenth century by Lin Ch'ing. Some gardens seem to have displayed an overabundance of these contorted rocks – the most notable of these being the Shih Tzu Lin or 'Lion Grove' in Soochow, which still exists. This was laid out around 1350 as part of the garden surrounding a temple, to commemorate a mountain retreat called 'Lion Rock' on the T'ien Mu mountain, and the 'mountainous' character of the garden is indeed overwhelming. A central lake, surrounded by buildings and trees, and crossed by bridges leading to islands and to a stone boat, is dominated by the artificial mountain on which the Hall of the Spreading Cloud stands. This eminence is reached by twisting paths leading through, under and over the massed and fantastic rocks, which seem, with the play of light and shade, and the reflections in the water of the lake, to portray not merely lions but stranger and more alarming monsters. The western eye may find such a collection an extreme in garden art, comparable to the fantasies of Bomarzo. One Chinese writer at least has felt that wildness here has been sought after too eagerly, calling the garden a 'stupendous heap of slag' (Shen Fu, 'Six Chapters of a Floating Life', *Tien Hsia Monthly*, November 1935).

PLEASURE GARDENS

So twice five miles of fertile ground
With walls and towers were girdled round
(Coleridge, *Kubla Khan*)

The royal garden in China began, like all royal gardens, as an enclosure or 'paradise', a hunting park in which first the pleasures of the hunt, and then the pleasures of the palace might be enjoyed.

These palace gardens, alas, survive only in the written records, telling us more often what they cost and how much they were resented than what they were like. The most famous early royal park, the Shang Lin, was that of the Han emperor, Wu Ti or Wu Di (*c.* 160 BC). It was so extensive that it aroused much indignation, and the emperor was forced to allow the land it had consumed to be cultivated once more.

Extravagance is constant, from the earliest enclosures to the last, the Yuan Ming Yuan in Peking. Most famous to the west, and most straightforward to read about, are the great parks described by Marco Polo, visiting China in the last decades of the thirteenth century. Above all, the superlatives echo in our mind – the greatest, richest, fairest, with the most of this and that, rarest, tallest, and superlatively on. In China, he described one old palace garden in the south, and two in the region of

Peking, recently created by the new Mongol lord, Kubilai Khan.

In the south, Polo travelled to Hang Chou, called in his text Kinsai. Until 1267, when it was taken by the Mongols, it was the southern capital of the last rulers of the Sung dynasty. When Polo came there, between 1276 and 1292, the city had fallen to the Mongols, but was still a glittering centre of culture, and his account of the late king's palace is a proof of the well-nigh fabulous delights of a palace garden.

Polo himself admits that his description is of a palace in the past, already falling into ruins, and his account is therefore all the more moving. 'This palace', writes Polo,

is the most beautiful and splendid in the world. No words of mine could describe its superlative magnificence . . . a space of land some ten miles in circumference with lofty battlemented walls and divided into three parts. The middle part was entered through a wide gateway flanked by pavilions of vast dimensions standing at ground level with their roofs supported by columns painted and wrought in fine gold and azure. Ahead was seen the largest and most important of these pavilions, similarly adorned with paintings and with gilded columns, and the ceiling gorgeously embellished with gold . . .

Behind this chief pavilion . . . was a large court, made in the style of a cloister . . . Leading out of this cloister was a long covered corridor . . . which ran right through to the lake at the other end. Communicating with this corridor were ten courtyards on one side and ten on the other, . . . Every courtyard had fifty chambers with their gardens, and these were occupied in all by 1,000 damsels whom the king kept in his service and some of whom used to accompany him and the queen when he went out for recreation on the lake in barges canopied with silk or to visit the temples of the idols.

The other two thirds of the enclosure were laid out in lakes filled with fish and groves and exquisite gardens, planted with every conceivable variety of fruit tree and stocked with all sorts of animals such as roebuck, harts, stags, hares, and rabbits. Here the king would roam at pleasure with his damsels, partly in carriages, partly on horseback, and no man ever intruded . . . Amid this perpetual dalliance he idled his time away . . . And this at last was his undoing, because through his unmanliness and self-indulgence he was deprived by the Great Khan of all his state . . .

The pavilions in front, being occupied by the Great Khan's viceroy, are just as they used to be. But the chambers of the damsels have all fallen in ruin.

Few other records of this palace survive. One supplementary detail of luxury in a Hang Chou palace of the period should however be quoted: this was a 'Pavilion of Coolness', in whose vast courtyard hundreds of vases were filled with jasmine, orchids, red banana-flowers and flowers from rare and exotic trees. These blossoms were fanned by a windmill, so that their perfume was wafted within the great hall of the pavilion. It is an extravagance reminiscent of the King of Paphos in Cyprus, who had pigeons flutter their wings behind him, to cool him while he ate. Marco Polo also talks of two palace-gardens in the north, recently constructed by the Mongol ruler, Kubilai, in his northern capital Shang-tu. The first of these is known to every lover of English poetry, for it is the palace and enclosure Coleridge was to describe in *Kubla Khan*.

Coleridge's poem offers us the ultimate vision of the paradise garden – romantic, natural and exotic. Here, we may read Polo's account, which describes the classic 'hunting park' of a great king:

In this city Kubilai Khan built a huge palace of marble and other ornamental stones . . . [a wall] encloses and encircles fully sixteen miles of parkland well watered with springs and streams and diversified with lawns . . . Here the Great Khan keeps game to provide food for the gerfalcons and other falcons which he has here in mew . . . Often, too, he enters the park with a leopard on the crupper of his horse; when he feels inclined, he lets it go and thus catches a hart or a stag or roebuck . . .

24 A scene from Wen Cheng-Ming's volume (1533) describing the Cho Cheng Yuan, the 'Garden of the Unsuccessful Politician' in Soochow. This picture, 'The Bower adjoining the Rock', shows a man contemplating a small garden stone set on a plain pedestal. The artist's accompanying poem reads: 'Beside the bower is the verdure of a thousand bamboos, And a moss-grown rock from the renowned K'un Shan . . .'

So far, this park is for hunting. But Polo adds:

> In the midst of this enclosed park, where there is a beautiful grove, the Great Khan has built another large palace, constructed entirely of canes . . . It is reared on gilt and varnished pillars, on each of which stands a dragon, entwining the pillar with his tail and supporting the roof on his outstretched limbs . . . The Great Khan has had it so designed that it can be moved whenever he fancies; for it is held in place by more than 200 cords of silk.

A movable yet extravagant palace, set up for the pleasure of the Great Khan in the hot months of summer. In the winter he moved southwards to the new capital, Khan-balik (Cambalu, the modern Peking), and here, within the spacious walled enclosures, further parks were created; a great artificial lake, stocked with fish; and then, from the earth taken up when the lake was dug, an artificial hill, the 'Green Mound', was erected:

> On the northern side of the palace . . . the Great Khan has had made an earthwork, that is to say a mound fully 100 paces in height and over a mile in circumference. This mound is covered with a dense growth of trees, all evergreens that never shed their leaves . . . whenever the Great Khan hears tell of a particularly fine tree he has it pulled up, roots and all and with a quantity of earth, and transported to this mound by elephants . . . In addition, he has had the mound covered with lapis lazuli, which is intensely green, so that trees and rock alike are as green as green can be and there is no other colour to be seen.

I wonder, do we read too much into this description if we imagine it as being one of the earliest forms of arboretum? Which trees, how many, how were they arranged, where did they come from? Collections of herbs, we know, were made centuries BC by Theophrastus, and in medieval monasteries in the west. And the Chinese certainly bred many varieties of flowers. But the collection of trees? Polo's remarks on the 'Green Mound' are tantalizing. Leave it at that.

One aspect of these gardens needs still to be mentioned: the emphasis given to poetic meditation, appropriate in such refined places. This comes out exceptionally well in the long garden-description given in Cao Xuequin's novel *The Story of the Stone*, also known as the *Dream of the Red Chamber*. This novel was written in the 1750s (the author died in 1764) and its garden sections are still wholly part of a continuing tradition.

The story revolves round a young man, Bao-yu, the heir apparent of a noble house. At one point, his elder sister, who has become one of the concubines of the Emperor, is to return to visit her family, and for her honour a garden is created adjacent to the family palace. This garden is quite large and highly complex, and before the Imperial concubine may visit it, each part must be named and given both a poetic title and several lines of poetry, to hint at the sentiments to be savoured there. The head of the house, Jia Zheng, goes round with his courtiers, and remarks: 'All those prospects and pavilions – even the rocks and trees and flowers will seem somehow incomplete without the touch of poetry which only the written word can lend a scene.' Jia Zheng spots his son Bao-yu nearby, and makes him come round on this visit, to help compose the names and verses. The garden is concealed at the entry by

a miniature mountain [with] a great number of large white rocks in all kinds of grotesque and monstrous shapes, rising course above course up one of its sides, some recumbent, some upright or leaning at angles, their surfaces streaked and spotted with moss and lichen or half concealed by creepers, and with a narrow, zigzag path only barely discernible to the eye winding up between them.

The party begin to climb the 'little mountain', and discover 'a white rock whose surface had been polished to mirror smoothness' – a place prepared for a poetic inscription. Then follow suggestions for a name – 'Emerald Heights', 'Embroidery Hill' . . . 'Altogether some twenty or thirty names were suggested', before the son, Bao-yu, is asked for his proposal, and the boy replies: 'I suggest we should call it 'Pathway to Mysteries' after the line in Chang Jian's poem about the mountain temple: "A path winds upwards to mysterious places".'

And so on for twenty pages, with discussions of the merits of this title or that, elaborate literary echoes, and delightful and alarming skirmishes between father and son, as Bao-yu ventures to suggest titles with pretentious or obscure allusions, and the father loses his temper. Even after twenty pages the author does not complete his description. The party is interrupted, and has to hurry back to the palace, and to tantalize us, we are told that they also hurried past

a summer lodge
a straw-thatched cot
a dry-stone wall
a flowering arch
a tiny temple nestling beneath a hill
a nun's retreat hidden in a little wood
a straight gallery
a crooked cave
a square pavilion
and a round belvedere

The following chapter describes the visit to the garden of the Imperial concubine, and the poetic aspect is stressed again – Bao-yu's titles are discussed by the visitor and amended, the beauties of the garden inspire her to write fresh verses, and she asks Bao-yu to write poems commemorating each of the four places in the garden she liked best, 'The Naiad's House, All-Spice Court, The House of Green Delights, and Washbrook Farm'. While he does this, six girls write other poems, and these are all quoted and discussed. For the novelist, the whole episode is one part of the varied background for his study of Bao-yu and his family, but the emphasis placed on the poetic interest of this palace-garden is important for us to appreciate. For the Chinese, a garden without poetry would seem 'somehow incomplete'.

THE POET'S GARDEN

Two years ago, and almost to the day
I swept up leaves: and now again,
My garden much the same.
(Yuan Mei)

I begin this section with the eighteenth-century Chinese poet Yuan Mei, who around 1748 brought a piece of ground in Soochow, believing it was the site of a garden coveted by the poet Li Po, a thousand years earlier. Not satisfied with this, he discovered later that the garden was identical with the one described in *The Story of the Stone*. Though these connections were not really certain, the continuity of poetic attachment to garden landscapes is characteristic of the Chinese garden. No garden, no landscape, without poems and poets.

Yuan Mei in the 1750s is a fair representative of the Chinese poet and his attitude to his garden. The one picture I have found of Yuan Mei's garden, which was called the Sui Yuan, shows how, although it is still extensive, it is altogether more modest than the glittering and costly garden created for the Imperial concubine in the *Story of the Stone* (see pl. 25). And his poems share this self-effacing quality. In his life of Yuan Mei, Arthur Waley translates this piece of verse, which refers to the tall belvedere which the poet had in his garden. He writes to a guest whom he has invited:

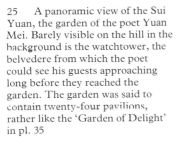

25   A panoramic view of the Sui Yuan, the garden of the poet Yuan Mei. Barely visible on the hill in the background is the watchtower, the belvedere from which the poet could see his guests approaching long before they reached the garden. The garden was said to contain twenty-four pavilions, rather like the 'Garden of Delight' in pl. 35

Don't laugh at my tower being so high;
Think what pleasure I shall gain from its being so high!
I shall not have to wait till you arrive;
I shall see you clearly ten leagues away!
But when you come, do not come in your coach;
The sound of a coach scares my birds away.
When you come do not ride your horse;
For it might be hungry and try its teeth on my plants.
When you come, don't come too early;
We country people stay late in bed.
But when you come, don't come too late;
For late in the day the flowers are not at their best.

Could this belvedere be the small pavilion shown, high up on the mountain, in the background of pl 25?

Yuan Mei's garden was said to have had twenty-four separate pavilions. Such a number of garden-buildings would have varied uses, mostly poetic and reflective. This is clear from an earlier document, dated 1533, by the poet and painter Wen Cheng-Ming (1470-1559), with paintings showing different views of the Cho Cheng Yuan, the 'Garden of the Unsuccessful Politician', in Soochow. With each painting is a poem, commenting on the place, and after the individual views is a prose passage, also by Wen Cheng-Ming, giving an overall description of the garden.

After many vicissitudes, the garden still exists, though much smaller than it was, and it is no longer possible to identify all the scenes Wen Cheng-Ming describes.

The 'unsuccessful politician', Wang Chin Tsz, who began the garden, stated 'I have built this garden as a memorial to my failure in politics.' The site was marshy, with a pond in the centre, and he drained the swampy ground, made islands, raised part of the land into artificial hills, and planted many trees. His friend Wen Cheng-Ming's pictures and poems are redolent of quietness, solitude, and remoteness from everyday concerns. Some of the names are indicative of this: Dreamy Tower, the Place of Clear Meditation, the Elevation for Remote Thought, the Bower of Nature, the Place for Listening to the Sighing Pines. Other names simply refer to plants or flowers or garden features – the Plum Slope, the Peach Tree Banks, the Bamboo Grove, the Lotus Cove, the Birds' Paradise – but the pictures and poems bring out the meditative qualities of each scene. The Fishing Rock, for instance, is not for serious anglers:

The white rock is clear and dustless;
It lies flat on the verge of the water.
I sit there to watch the line move,
And enjoy the sight of swaying bamboos,
My thoughts travel far beyond the rivers and the lakes,
I forget everything and am as quiet as a wren.
You must know that the one who now casts the line
Is not a true lover of fishing!

Another scene, named the Bower adjoining the Rock, begins

Beside the bower is the verdure of a thousand bamboos,
And a moss-grown rock hewn from the renowned K'un-Shan . .

– the rock being one of the famous types listed in the *Yuan Yeh* of 1635. It is fascinating to learn from the appropriate portion of the *Yuan Yeh* that these are small stones – 'they are of very uneven material, full of holes, like hollowed-out rocks, but they are not tall and peaky . . . In their strange hollows one may plant dwarf trees and irises. They may be placed in bowls and used in miniature landscapes; they are not suitable for larger gardens.' This says much about the way in which even small objects and restricted scenes are accepted as means to evoke poetic feelings. The bamboo thicket may be dense, but the K'un-Shan stone is tiny, rather like the tiny trees displayed on a table, outside, in the spacious palace garden painted by Ch'in Ying (pl. 29).

As I have said, the Cho Chen Yuan is now much smaller than it was. Its former spaciousness is clear from an account written in 1747 to commemorate its restoration and extension in the previous decade:

It seemed as though the hills were higher; it seemed as though the pools were deeper; and as though the peaks were more numerous . . . Indeed, it was even more beautiful than before. The place was the old place, but the crooked paths, the curves of the pools all seemed increased and added to . . . The lord of the garden prepared wine, and bade his guests drink; they chanted songs, they chatted, and rejoiced. Their pleasure was very refined, and not in the least coarse.

'The lord of the garden prepared wine . . . they chanted songs' – or rather they wrote poems, often competing one against another. In China, wine and poetry go together, as they do elsewhere, and the Chinese have united them in their gardens

26, 27   Two scenes from Wen Cheng-Ming's volume of poems and paintings of the Garden of the Unsuccessful Politician.

Left   The Bower for Awaiting the Frost:

By the side of the bower are
    some beautiful trees
Their boughs laden with yellow
    fruit
Fit for a tribute to the
    Emperor a thousand li away.

Above   The Elevation for Remote Thought:

When I ascend the elevation of
    a thousand li
My thoughts and eyes are
    filled with freshness.
The leaves are falling, and
    autumn is far advanced;
And yonder across the shore
    the sky is exceeding bright.
The white clouds glide over
    the water;
The hill lies all about under
    the setting sun.

28 'The Pavilion of the Floating Cups', on the shore of the Southern Lake in Peking (from O. Sirén, *Gardens of China*). Built in the eighteenth century, this pavilion stands over a curving channel, through which flows a stream. Each guest would float a wine cup in the stream, and had to compose a poem in the time it took for the cup to sail from one end of the channel to the other. This game was also played in Japanese gardens, and is mentioned as early as the fifth century

more thoughtfully than any other nation. At Nan Hai, the Southern Lake, in Peking, there is a pavilion (or there was: Nagel's *China*, 1977 edition, says of the palace buildings around the Central and Southern Lakes that 'they are closed to all visitors and it is impossible to know what state they are now in') called the Liu Pei T'ing, the 'Pavilion of the Floating Cups'. Here the pavilion stands across a branch of the stream, and the stream itself is channelled in a meandering course across the floor. The pavilion was used for poetic competitions – one had to compose a poem in the time it took for a wine-cup to float from one end of the channel to the other. Although the pavilion may have disappeared, this poem, written by an exiled courtier looking back to a happier time, has survived:

Fallen from favour,
exiled I write to you,
writing, reminding,
hoping these lines will arrive.
Remember.
Red roof, raised on stone pillars, three by three
and round the sides a patterned latticework
hides and reveals, pines, a curve of lake,
the thought of mountains beyond,
white clouds.

Far outside, a peacock cries.

Within, shaded by lacquered eaves and screen
a carved canal winds lazily across the pavilion floor,
dragon's tail coiling and curling,
carrying a small clear stream.

Wine-cups floating
while we compete, composing;
you, in laughter, launching a cup for me,
and in my cup, a pearl.

The date of this pavilion in Nan Hai is not certain, but the tradition of the competitions goes back a long way. The earliest reference is oblique; in Japan 'in the reign of the Emperor Kenso (485-7)' there was 'a sort of literary party held along the winding stream in a garden, after the custom established in ancient China' (Jiro

Harada, *The Gardens of Japan*, 1928). This tradition continues in Japan to the present day, with competitions for the composition of *Haiku*. A similar pavilion still exists in the Koraku-en garden at Okoyama.

In China itself there is a happy reference to these competitions in the *Yuan Yeh*: 'Guests are assembled to take part in the poetical competitions, and by way of a forfeit must empty the cups [i.e. if they could not complete their poems within the prescribed time] . . . In this way innumerable poems are written, and one may imagine oneself to be in the land of the immortals.'

It is sometimes difficult to draw a line between the landscape garden in China, and the landscape pure and simple. Wen Cheng-Ming, the artist who painted and described the Cho Cheng Yuan at Soochow, depicted landscapes which do not differ in their details from the paintings shown here, yet whose general subject is clearly landscape, and not a garden. In between, there are paintings which show pavilions, cottages, small houses, set away in the countryside, or among mountains, which combine the ideal of the humble dwelling, in which tranquillity is possible, with the ideal of rural retirement, enjoying a minute garden beside the cottage, and the vastness of nature round about. For the Chinese, whether actually living in these scenes, or painting them, or looking at the paintings, the enjoyment and fulfilment obtained would be much the same. The same question was to be asked in England at the end of the eighteenth century, when the English landscape garden was thought by some to have 'returned to nature' so successfully that the garden was indistinguishable from the surrounding countryside. To some, this was indeed a triumph – and the Chinese might agree – but to others it was puzzling, and uncomfortable.

Again and again Chinese landscape paintings delight to show, among the rocks, near a torrent, beside a clump of pines or by the lakeside, a pavilion, containing one

29   Part of a sixteenth-century Chinese scroll painting by Ch'in Ying (from O. Sirén, *Gardens of China*). In this scene several characteristic Chinese garden features appear: prominent and varied rocks, some grotesquely pierced and with different colours and textures; the table carrying *bonsai* trees, each in a tiny garden scene of its own; the zigzag fencing, providing an irregular division of the garden; bamboos, suggesting resilience; the crane, symbol of longevity, and the plum tree (*prunus mume*) in blossom, suggesting endurance, with its fragile flowers bursting from the gnarled and blackened twigs

or two figures. In Wen Cheng Ming's painting of his small summer pavilion, the clearing in front is slight, and the bridge across the mountain stream is narrow. The poet-painter sits motionless, looking through his open doorway at the silent scene. Quietly, a friend approaches. Meditation – study – the companionship of a friend – the contemplation of nature. The artist Ch'in Ying, who left the elaborate, lavish scenes of a palace pleasure garden already referred to also painted more tranquil landscapes – 'A Lady in a Pavilion overlooking a Lake', and 'Fisherman's Flute heard over the Lake'. This latter painting is to me similar in feeling to the photograph in pl. 22. In each case, the lake pavilion and the Tai Shan pavilion are subordinate to the overhanging trees, and the musician, listened to from the pavilion, watched by the photographer and by the old temple servant, holds the entire scene in a moment of time.

FLOWERS AND TREES

> I plucked the chrysanthemums beside the hedge
> In calm I found the southern hills.
> (T'ae Ch'ien, or T'ao Yuan-Ming)

One evocative painting of a garden retreat, by Kao Feng-han (1683-1747) portrays a particularly famous Chinese flower-lover, the poet T'ao Ch'ien, or T'ao Yuan-Ming. We see him outside a small country cottage, with pines, plum and bamboo growing informally behind and beside his garden, which is thick with chrysanthemums, and he walks among them, seized with inspiration. He is known especially as an ardent enthusiast for chrysanthemums – he was once offered a high government post, but preferred to cultivate his chrysanthemums, to write poetry, and to drink wine and enjoy the company of his friends. Wine and gardens join again with the chrysanthemums, since a wine was made from their petals.

The chrysanthemum, originating in China, is among the earliest flowers to be cultivated for its ornamental qualities, being described as early as the fifth century BC. The yellow-flowered chrysanthemum is the first to be mentioned, and white and other colours became popular from the T'ang dynasty (618–906) onwards. Specialist cultivation began early, and in the first years of the twelfth century a treatise by Liu Meng records the existence of thirty-five varieties, and soon after the poet Fan Ch'eng-ta wrote that he had seen a collection of paintings which showed more than seventy colours and forms of the flower. By 1708, nearly 300 kinds were described (see H. L. Li, *The Garden Flowers of China*, 1959, from which much of the information in this section is derived).

Because of its autumn and winter flowering, the chrysanthemum came to be regarded as a sign of longevity; medicines were flavoured with its petals and its leaves were recommended in herbal lists. Being associated with the poet T'ao Yuan-Ming, it was also seen as the flower of the recluse, the man who has given up the world for higher – or less demanding – things. As poet and drunkard T'ao Yuan-Ming was committed to both. (In Japan, where the flower was introduced from China around AD 400, the chrysanthemum has a much more public and pompous history, becoming the insignia of the Mikado himself.)

Chinese poetry is rich with references to flowers, which have been admired for their beauty, made use of for food or flavouring or medicines, and have acquired deep symbolic, even metaphysical importance. In the west we ascribe 'meaning' to a few of our flowers – innocence to white lilies, passion to the red rose – and half-remember phrases such as Ophelia's 'There's rosemary, that's for remembrance'; but in China the symbolism is much richer, applied both to single plants or flowers, and to groups. The orchid, the bamboo, the chrysanthemum and the flowering plum suggest the four seasons. This group of plants and trees is also termed 'the four gentlemen' since the qualities linked with them – grace, resilience, nobility and endurance – are the essential ingredients for the ideal gentleman, 'cultured, of pleasing personality and exemplary character' (Mai-Mai Sze, *The Tao of Painting*, 1957).

As with garden rocks, or pools, or gnarled and aged trees, so the flowers are important for their value in bringing wider associations: to see them, to catch their scent or the flicker of their leaves, we are led on to further thoughts.

Only the most important flowers and trees in Chinese gardens can be mentioned here: among flowers, the tree peony, the hibiscus, the lotus; among trees, the peach and plum, the pine, the bamboo, the mulberry and the catalpa.

The tree-peony, *mu-tan*, 'male vermilion' (*paeonia suffruticosa* syn. *moutan*), is thought of as the 'king of flowers' – 'the flowers of the tree peony, that perfect blossom, are naturally different from all the others' (*Tao*). It seems to have been cultivated since the third century AD. During the Sung dynasty (960–1279) there was an enthusiasm for this flower comparable to the 'tulipomania' experienced in the Netherlands in the seventeenth century, especially in the city of Loyang. Many varieties were cultivated, and immense sums were paid for rare and spectacular plants. Their cost is seen in the poem 'The Flower Market' by Po Chu-i (772-846):

> We tell each other 'This is the peony season':
> And follow the crowd that goes to the Flower Market.
> 'Cheap and dear – no uniform price:
> The cost of the plant depends on the number of blossoms.
> For the fine flower – a hundred pieces of damask:
> For the cheap flower – five bits of silk.'

The poet ends with an 'old farm labourer' sighing 'a deep sigh':

> He was thinking, 'A cluster of deep-red flowers
> Would pay the taxes of ten poor houses'.

Over two centuries later, the poet Ou-Yang Hsiu, who also wrote a treatise on moutan peonies, gives a delightful piece of advice to 'Assistant Hsieh planting flowers at the Secluded Valley':

> The light and the deep, the red and the white, should be spaced apart;
> The early and the late should likewise be planted in due order.
> My desire is, throughout the four seasons, to bring wine along,
> And to let not a single day pass without some flower opening.

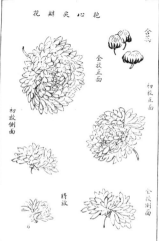

Several forms of the hibiscus have long been cultivated in China: the cotton rose, *hibiscus mutabilis*; the rose of China, *h. rosa-sinensis*, and the rose of Sharon, *h. syriacus*. All three originated in China. *H. rosa-sinensis* is called *fu sang* by the Chinese, and this same name – though it is not clear that it applies to the same plant – is given to the tree of immortality, growing in a faraway land across the eastern sea. In 219 BC the Emperor Shih Huang-ti sent an expedition of 3,000 young men and maidens, led by a Taoist priest, to find the tree and the fruit which would confer immortality. They did not return and the legend suggests that they were the people who became the ancestors of the Japanese. Curiously, the cotton rose, *h. mutabilis*, is called *fu jung*, or 'fairyland flower'.

The lotus (*nelumbo nucifera*) occurs in virtually every Chinese garden lake. In the summer the broad leaves rise well above the water, or float on the surface, while the strongly fragrant pink flowers stand higher than the leaves. The lotus has the symbolic sense of perfection. Chu Tun-ju (*c.* 1080-*c.* 1175) wrote an essay on its virtues in which he says:

> It emerges from muddy dirt but is not contaminated; it reposes nobly above the clear water . . . Resting there with its radiant purity, the Lotus is something to be appreciated from a distance and not to be profaned by intimate approach.
>
> In my opinion, the Chrysanthemum is the flower of retirement and leisure; the Peony the flower of rank and wealth. But the Lotus is the flower of purity and integrity. Alas! Since T'ao Yuan-Ming, few have loved the Chrysanthemum; and none love the Lotus like myself. I could well understand why so many favoured the Peony.

30, 31, 32, 33   Four illustrations from Wang Kai's *The Tao of Painting*, the *Chieh Tzu Yuan Hua Chuan* (1679). This manual of styles in painting shows how objects in nature – rocks, trees and flowers – may be painted to portray the spirit of each. The drawings show a view of a trellis for flowers above a country bridge (top); the chrysanthemum (above), symbol of leisure and retirement; the lotus (top right), symbol of purity, and the orchid (above right), which represents the ideal of delicacy and grace

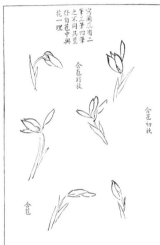

Orchids in China are most highly regarded for their rare and delicate fragrance; a 'virtue' in them symbolic of the 'true friend', a characteristic of the perfect man. The extreme delicacy of the plant represents a spiritual quality admired by the painter: 'in a light mood one should paint the orchid, for the leaves of the orchid grow as though they were flying and fluttering, the buds open joyfully, and the mood is indeed a happy one.'

The peach (*prunus persica*) is associated with longevity. Often, a peach tree would be grown by the door of a house to bring good fortune. It is a tree thought to have mystic qualities, both in its blossom and its fruit. The 'peach of longevity', the *shou t'ao*, is still a standard gift at birthday parties. Even the gum of the peach tree was thought to encourage long life, even immortality, and it was one of the substances favoured by Taoists in search of the elixir. The enchanted, immortal world discovered on the other side of a cave, described in T'ao Yuan-Ming's story, is reached through a valley clothed with blooming peach trees. Though known as the *prunus persica*, the peach is of Chinese origin, having been introduced to Persia, and thence to Europe, at a very early date.

The flowering plum – *mei hua* (*prunus mume*) or Japanese apricot – is one of the most loved, painted and written-about of Chinese garden trees. Together with the pine and the bamboo, it is one of the 'three friends of winter', since its beauty is a winter phenomenon. Not only does it flower at the end of winter, but its delicate, white-pink blossoms contrast with the gnarled, dry, tortuous branches of the tree, which is often of immense age, and venerated as are the cypresses and cedars in temple groves. Age, endurance, dignity – and a frail and graceful vitality.

Countless poems and paintings celebrate this tree. The poet Lin Ho-ching (967-1028), one of many plum worshippers, lived in retirement on an island planted with the flowering trees, in the West Lake near Hangchow. He is famous in China for these lines, which are thought to capture the nocturnal beauty of the plum:

Scattered shadows lie spreading
Over water placid and clear;
At dusk on a moonlit night,
Dim fragrance pervades the air.

The enjoyment of nature by night is much more an accepted part of the Chinese – and Japanese – garden than in the west. We find, it is true, accounts of spectacular firework displays in western gardens, and, from time to time, enjoyment of twilight scenes. But the whole-hearted integration of the night into western gardens has never occurred. In China and Japan it is a reality, with pavilions especially built for 'viewing the moon', and for 'viewing the plum blossom by moonlight'. In *The Story of the Stone*, the young hero composes a set of four poems describing night scenes in the new gardens in the different seasons. 'Night in Winter' brings in superb references to the dark garden and its trees (note that the 'three friends of winter' are present):

Flowering plums and bamboos engulf each other's dreams at the third watch:
But embroidered coverlet and kingfisher-down would still induce no sleep.
Amidst shadows of pines in the courtyard, a lonely crane flaps;
Frost, like pear blossoms, bestrews the ground, though no oriole sings.
The girl with the green sleeves tosses off verses about the cold;
His golden sable pledged for wine, the gay young lord declares it insipid.
Luckily my lord's page is thoroughly adept at blending tea –
Sweeping up the new snow, he makes an instant brew.

Bamboo and pine are indispensable parts of the Chinese garden. Over a hundred species of bamboo were noted centuries ago, during the Sung period. Through its pliant strength, bamboo suggests hardiness and everlasting resilience, one of the four characteristics of the ideal man. When shown in conjunction with pine or plum, the clarity and balance of its outline are often stressed, to contrast with the irregular forms of the other trees. Pines are essential for the impression of age – like garden rocks – and they also stand for silence and solitude. The motif of the pine tree with a crane nearby is a standard symbol of longevity. Li Li-weng, the seventeenth-century artist who built a special rock-garden and rock-viewing pavilion, wrote of the need for pines to complete a garden landscape:

> When one sits in a garden with peach trees, flowers, and willows, without a single pine in sight, it is like sitting among children and women without any venerable man in the vicinity to whom one may look up.

Two other trees should be mentioned – the catalpa, and the mulberry. The catalpa has been used in China as a timber tree from the earliest times: its wood, used for musical instruments and printing blocks, was also prized for making coffins. The mulberry is seen as a symbol of day, since its roots are in the underworld and its crown reaches into the sky, and of human activity, since it is vital for the silk industry. With these contrasting uses, clothing and coffins, the catalpa and the mulberry are seen as 'tending the living and caring for the dead'. In the university hall in Reading where I live, one quadrangle has an old and spreading mulberry tree, the other has a catalpa.

THE GARDEN OF PERFECT BRIGHTNESS

I think it is correct to state that Chinese gardens and garden art hardly changed from the time of Wen Cheng-Ming's description of the 'Garden of the Unsuccessful Politician' until the convulsions of the twentieth century. Many gardens were built, many were destroyed, and much was written about them, but the essential qualities and aspirations which have already been described remain the same.

In 1679 the first version of the *Chieh Tzu Yuan Hua Chuan* (*The Tao of Painting*) by Wang Kai was published. The book is a manual, indicating how objects and scenes – for example mountains, rocks, buildings, trees and flowers – may be painted, with thousands of illustrations showing the different styles of painting, and the different parts of the objects, singly or in conjunction with others, and with a commentary which is technical, practical and poetic. The mixing of colours and the varieties of brush and brush-stroke are discussed as means towards the representation of the *spirit* of the object and of the scene as a whole – for instance, in painting the doorway to a garden, one's aim should be to indicate the quality of tranquillity and isolation such a doorway implies: 'Just by seeing the doorway, you can tell that this is the home of a Taoist philosopher.' Likewise trees and plants – pine, bamboo, chrysanthemum and lotus should illustrate the qualities which such plants embody – longevity, resilience and so forth.

Similarly, the garden and palace complexes built since the late seventeenth century in and near Peking may impress us by their style and splendour (it would be odd if they did not), but in their style there is no sensible difference from what had been made before. Within Peking the gardens around the 'Three Lakes' (Nan Hai, Chung Hai and Pei Hai) had been begun in the reign of Kubilai. This area has since been built over by successive garden-loving emperors, culminating in the additions made by Ch'ien Lung (1736-96) and the Dowager-Empress Tzu Hsi, who died in 1908. In the southern lake, Nan Hai, is the Liu Pei T'ing, the 'Pavilion of the Floating Cups', and many other garden pavilions line the shores of the three lakes.

Far larger and more famous are the gardens of the Yuan Ming Yuan (the 'Garden of Perfect Brightness', or the 'Perfect and Brilliant Garden') and the associated gardens of the Ch'ang Ch'un Yuan (the 'Garden of Everlasting Spring') and the Wan Shou Yuan (the 'Garden of Innumerable Years'), some distance to the north-west of Peking. This area, even larger than the great park of Versailles, was first treated as an imperial garden in 1709, in the reign of the Emperor K'ang Hsi (1662-1723), and enlarged and superbly embellished by his son Yung Cheng (1723-36) and his grandson Ch'ien Lung. The most extensive and ambitious building was undertaken from 1737 onwards, and a series of forty paintings was begun in 1744 by T'ang Tai and Shen Yuan to record the most beautiful views in the gardens. These were repeated in a series of forty woodcuts, adorning a literary work mainly written

34 'The Double Mirror and the Sound of the Lute' – another of the 'Forty Scenes' depicting the Yuan Ming Yuan. While the scene of 'The Wine Courtyard, Wind and Lotus' (pl. 20) has intoxicating allusions, to a famous inn beside the lotus-covered West Lake at Hang Chou, the scene here is set for poetic meditation, with the cliff-top pavilion and the musical sound of the cascade beside the Lake of Happiness. Both engravings are from Le Rouge's *Jardins Anglo-Chinois*, which showed the gardens to Europeans only forty years after their creation in the 1730s by the Emperor Ch'ien Lung

by Ch'ien Lung himself, the *Pictures and Poems of the Yuan Ming Yuan*. The emperor's contribution included poems, commentaries and descriptions of the many scenes. The 'Forty Scenes' became known gradually to Europeans, and were copied by the Swedish garden architect F. M. Piper, and also reproduced with reasonable fidelity by G. L. Le Rouge in his *Détails de Nouveaux Jardins à la Mode: Jardins Anglo-Chinois* (1774-86). A long description – though not the pictures – reached Europe soon after the gardens were complete, as the Jesuit missionary J.-D. Attiret wrote a flowery report of them in 1743, which was published in the *Lettres Edifiantes*, vol. xxvii, in 1749, translated into English, and republished several times. From his letter, Europeans would have derived general impressions of lavish, exotic and irregular scenes which, without pictures, must have seemed so extravagant as to be improbable. But when Attiret's text is compared with the illustrations, it does not seem so exaggerated, and his aim of describing a paradise garden in order to indicate its many differences from Versailles can now be understood. His first points concerning the gardens of the Yuan Ming Yuan are vital:

> They are situated in a vast domain in which mountains, between twenty and sixty feet in height, have been raised by hand, so forming an infinite number of little valleys. Canals of clear water flow along the beds of these valleys and come together in several places to create ponds and lakes, on which one may travel in beautiful vessels.

The area had in fact been given its well-nigh infinite variety by means of immense excavations – the digging of lakes and stream-beds, and the creation of artificial hills and slopes from the soil and rocks dug out in the process. The largest lake, Fu Hai (the 'Lake of Happiness'), was two miles in circumference, and contained several small islands, some round the edge linked by bridges and causeways, and a group of three, the 'Isles and Green Terraces of the Immortals', which were connected to each other, but were far out in the middle of the lake. Attiret writes:

> The real jewel is an island or rock, rough and desolate, rising six feet above the water in the middle of this sea. A little palace is erected on this rock, which has, however, over a hundred rooms. It is four-sided, and is of indescribable beauty and elegance. The view from it is remarkably fine – one sees all the palaces, one after another, along the shore, and beyond, the mountains, canals, and bridges over the canals, the pavilions and the triumphal arches decorating the bridges, and the clumps of trees which screen or divide the palaces so that those living in one may not overlook those in another . . .

Attiret was one of several French and Italian Jesuit missionaries established in Peking, and closely connected with the emperor's gardening activities. Others – Giuseppe Castiglione, Benoit and d'Incarville in particular – were ordered by Ch'ien Lung to design and supervise the building of a series of palaces and garden features along the northern side of the Ch'ang Ch'un Yuan. The inspiration dated from 1747, when the emperor noted pictures of *fountains* among some illustrations of European scenes which Castiglione had painted. Fountains were a novelty to the emperor, and he commanded the Jesuits to demonstrate them. Benoit was commissioned, and was so successful that Ch'ien Lung insisted on other European buildings and gardens being built. Between them, the Jesuits made a 'small Versailles', with little palaces, clipped hedges, ornamental flowerbeds, geometrical pools, scores of fountains, and an extraordinary maze, with divisions made of carved brick walls standing almost to head-height.

These palaces and gardens were always seen by the Chinese as a curiosity, and had no influence at all on traditional Chinese garden practice. They were an amusement, not to be taken seriously, rather like the religion which the Jesuits endeavoured to introduce to the emperor's court. It was tolerated, but not embraced: in 1760, some years after the gardens were complete, Ch'ien Lung acquired a new concubine, the Muslim princess Hsiang Fei, the 'Perfumed Concubine'. To please her, the emperor equipped one area in the gardens with painted scenes (executed in part by the Jesuits) to represent the streets and houses of a Muslim town, and he made the Jesuits convert one of the buildings, the gazebo called Fang Wai Kuan, 'Look Abroad Hall', into a mosque. It was hardly the ending these Christian missionaries had planned.

Ch'ien Lung died in 1796, and the Yuan Ming Yuan then declined, though remaining the most lavish gardens in the world. In 1860, for reasons of revenge which we may understand, even if we do not accept them, French and English soldiers broke into the gardens, looted the palaces, and burnt them to the ground. Today, virtually nothing of the Yuan Ming Yuan remains, though a few miles to the south-west the I Ho Yuan, the 'New Summer Palace', likewise partially destroyed in 1860, was reconstructed by the Dowager Empress Tzu Hsi in traditional forms. Several features round and to the north of the lake, K'un Ming Hu (the 'Western Lake', for centuries so famous that it even reappears, in symbolic form, in the garden of the Ginkakuji in Japan), still remain, either built by Ch'ien Lung, or rebuilt on his foundations: the Jade Belt Bridge (sometimes called the Camel's Hump Bridge), the Mirror Bridge, the Bridge of Seventeen Arches, the covered walk, half a mile in length and painted with landscapes and flowers and scenes from history and mythology, running in gentle curves along the northern shore – and the marble boat, begun by Ch'ien Lung and refashioned by Tzu Hsi, who added the curved stone 'paddle wheels' on each side. She had diverted funds meant to build up the Chinese navy but used by her to rebuild these gardens. The marble boat was her sole contribution to the fleet, an extravagance as great as any of the earlier boats in garden history.

35 The 'Garden of Delight', Ai-yuan t'u, painted by T'ang I-fen in 1826. This garden is similar in intention to the Sui Yuan of Yuan Mei (pl. 25), with pavilions, bridges, rocks, viewing-places and shelters set round the shores of an irregular lake. The visitor would proceed thoughtfully, observantly from spot to spot, composing poems, meditating, pausing to admire the chrysanthemums or to rest with a companion, paint a picture, watch the moon or just drink wine

Besides the wonders of Ch'ien Lung's gardens, and those of Tzu Hsi, smaller and equally traditional gardens were still being made. In 1826 the artist T'ang I-fen (1778-1853) painted a scene of the Ai-yuan t'u (the 'Garden of Delight') which could indeed illustrate the Cho Cheng Yuan, the 'Garden of the Unsuccessful Politician', or the old Sui Yuan bought by Yuan Mei in 1757. Like these, it has an irregular walk round a central and branching lake; like these, it is the subject of poem after poem. There are about twenty architectural features – bridges, pavilions and shelters – scattered through the scene. Some areas are fenced with bamboo, and small plants stand in pots on a table; elsewhere, other tables support *bonsai* trees or contorted rocks, and chrysanthemums grow in a raised bed.

Calmness, contemplation, the forms of nature leading to poetry, as in the lines by Chen Tchou (1427-1509):

Serene the path to the faraway garden,
My garden-house lapped round with calm;
Tender the thin mist, poems in the air,
A year's leaves rest on the autumn stream.

36   A dry landscape in the
entrance court of the Daitokuji
temple in Kyoto

4

Japanese Gardens

CHERRY-BLOSSOM, WINE, POEMS AND MOONLIGHT

In the fifth century AD, the Emperor Richiu was once happily viewing the blossom of the wild cherries along the shores of a lake near his palace, while being rowed round the lake in a pleasure-boat. As he passed close to the steep bank beneath the overhanging trees, petals fluttered down, some of them falling into the wine cup held in his hand.

This image of perfect pleasure may serve as a beginning for the history of gardens in Japan. From that moment, we are told, began the custom of wine drinking at the time of cherry viewing, and there is still a popular saying, 'Without wine, who can properly enjoy the sight of the cherry blossom?'

Such celebrations were not only bibulous, but poetic and often profoundly contemplative occasions. Some of the earliest Japanese poetry is to do with the fleeting beauty of the cherry blossom, or of other flowers, and the composition of poems while viewing these flowers in bloom was from the beginning, and remains today, a pastime taken up with utmost delight and deepest sensitivity. In the fifth century, in the reign of the Emperor Kenso, a literary party was held along the banks of a stream, with courtiers floating wine-cups down the stream, composing poems as the cups drifted from one point to another. This occasion, called a *kyoku-sui-no-yen*, was modelled on the Chinese competition already described and was continued until recent times. At Okayama, in the Koraku-en gardens, created in the late seventeenth century, there was a long pavilion, called Kyoku-sui-En-no-Chin built over a stream. The length of the channel within the pavilion was some thirty feet, and one had to compose a poem in the time it took for one's wine-cup to float along this channel.

Though flower-viewing has become a national pastime, it was at first the pleasure of the aristocratic élite, who refined it in ways which must leave western flower- and garden-lovers feeling uncouth and awkward. By the ninth century, the ladies of the court had already devised a code of dress which enabled the colours of their kimonos to suit the flowers or foliage they would be viewing.

Such love of blossom and foliage – willow and maple in spring, and maple again in autumn – led naturally to the planting of bushes and flowers near the houses of the nobles, and this too was refined and perfected at an early date. In the *Tale of Genji*, written in the eleventh century, we hear of several gardens in and around the capital, Kyoto. The hero, Prince Genji, has gardens created round the apartments of his ladies to suit their inclinations, and each of these reflects one of the seasons. The Spring Garden, for Lady Murasaki, has 'a profusion of early flowering trees', with 'cinquefoil, red-plum, cherry, wistaria, kerria, azalea, and other such plants as are at their best in springtime.' Lady Akikonomu's garden 'was full of such trees as in autumn-time turn to their deepest hue'; clearly a display of foliage, rather than flowers, for 'here indeed was such beauty as far eclipsed the autumn splendour even of the forests near Oi, so famous for their autumn tints.' The summer garden was created for the 'Lady from the Village of Falling Flowers', having 'hedges of the white deutzia flower, the orange tree "whose scent reawakens forgotten love", the briar-rose, and the giant peony.' The winter garden was made for Lady Akashi, with a 'close-set wall of pine-trees planted there on purpose that she might have the

63

pleasure of seeing them when their boughs were laden with snow; and for her delight there was a great bed of chrysanthemums', to be enjoyed 'when all the garden was white with frost.'

The description of the April outing to Lady Murasaki's Spring Garden is vivid with the freshness of blossom. Prince Genji has boats, 'built in the Chinese style', set on the lake, and the excursion proceeds by water:

> The lake . . . seemed immensely large, and those on board, to whom the whole experience was new and deliciously exciting, could hardly believe that they were not heading for some undiscovered land. At last however the rowers brought them close in under the rocky bank of the channel between the two large islands, and on closer examination they discovered to their delight that the shape of every little ledge and crag of stone had been as carefully devised as if a painter had traced them with his brush. Here and there in the distance the topmost boughs of an orchard showed above the mist, so heavily laden with blossom that it looked as though a bright carpet were spread in mid-air.

The experience is totally absorbing – 'here, like figures in a picture of fairyland, they spent the day gazing in rapture' – and inspires more poetry: 'When the wind blows, even the wave-petals, that are no blossoms at all, put on strong colours; for this is the vaunted cape, the Cliff of Kerria-Flowers.'

This tradition of joyous and poetic garden-viewing is – as the phrase about the boats, 'built in the Chinese style', suggests – something which has its parallel in the garden history of China, and this very visit in *The Tale of Genji* may be compared with the later, fuller account of the inspection of a Chinese garden in the *Story of the Stone.*

One did not always go out to view cherry or plum blossom. The rich and the powerful, like Prince Genji, would plant groves of these trees, and to do this would buy, beg or plunder good trees as best they could. The process was taken seriously, like the finding and collection of garden-stones described in the next chapter. Owners of fine specimens did not like to give them up, and feelings of resentment, frustration and guilt were at times intense. Once, in the fifteenth century, the shogun had been presented with some choice plum trees, and one of them was damaged, losing a large branch as it was being transported from the original garden to its new site. As a result, 'three of the gardeners were imprisoned, and five young knights, who evidently were responsible for the accident, were ordered to be arrested. Three of them fled into exile, and two others committed suicide.'

In Japan, as in China, almost as much delight is experienced in the *night-time* aspect of a garden as during the day. Again and again poems recall the scent of barely-visible blossoms, moonlight on the flowering cherries, the rustle of leaves in the darkness:

> The hazy Springtime moon –
> That is the one I love,
> When light green sky and fragrant blooms
> Are all alike enwrapped in mist.

This poem, from Lady Sarashina's *As I Crossed a Bridge of Dreams,* a poetic autobiography written in the eleventh century, is wholly characteristic of her gentle, elegiac, often nocturnal musings. Her brief attendance at the Heian court in Kyoto was undistinguished, since she was timid and reserved. She writes: 'I was so used to staying with my old-fashioned parents at home, gazing hour after hour at the Autumn moon or the Spring blossoms, that when I arrived at Court I was in a sort of daze and hardly knew what I was doing.' Her romantic hopes remain unfulfilled, moonlit yearnings for a prince who might one day share her delight in the calm beauty of flowers and trees.

On one occasion, she describes a moon-watching vigil with her sister (who will die soon in childbirth), when the moon 'shone brightly, lighting every corner of the earth':

At about midnight, when the rest of our household was asleep, my sister and I sat on the veranda . . . Presently a carriage approached . . . and the passenger ordered his attendant to call for someone, 'Oginoha, Oginoha!' ['Reed Leaf', a girl's name] cried the man, but there was no reply from inside the house and presently he gave up. The gentleman played his flute for a while in a beautiful, clear tone; then the carriage moved away . . . We sat there all night, looking at the sky; at dawn we went to bed.

The pleasure of moonlight was savoured even more fully from 'moon-viewing' platforms and pavilions, where one might enjoy the moon's progress over one's garden: at the Katsura Imperial Palace, built in the 1620s, there is a broad wooden platform jutting out from the palace buildings, allowing a superb night view over the lake, bridges and islands. This custom may well be inherited from Chinese models, as is the love of shadows cast by moonlight:

Harvest moon:
On the bamboo mat
Pine-tree shadows.

But the Japanese take the art a stage further by creating features which, beautiful by day, may be even more so in the light of the moon, and which reflect the moon's radiance on to nearby objects – the use of white sand. The most famous of these features is at the Ginkakuji, or Silver Pavilion, at Kyoto, created in the 1480s for the Shogun Yoshimasa, probably with the advice and help of the garden-designers So-ami and Zen'ami. Here beside the pavilion are two features of white sand; one, nearer to the pavilion, a steeply rising, symmetrical cone, five yards across at the base and some six feet tall, with a flattened top, and the other stretching away for many yards, a flat and spreading 'sea' of sand, roughly lozenge- or tear-shaped, two or three feet thick, and with its surface crossed by fourteen parallel ridges. What these mysterious features represent remains a puzzle, as does their origin and even the date of their creation. Today, they are called the 'Moon-facing Height' (Kogetsudai) and the 'Silver Sand Sea' (Ginshadan), and are often said to suggest the cone of Mount Fuji and the Western Lake (Si-hu) near Peking, with its waters patterned with ripples or waves. One recent writer claims that 'they came there, apparently, by gradual chance', explaining their initial appearance in the gardens to the fortuitous presence of piles of left-over builder's sand. Visitors, readers, garden-lovers must judge: in practice and in reality they are given to the moon. Yoshimasa, the creator and owner of the Ginkakuji, himself wrote a poem in 1487 on the viewing of the moon, describing his expectation as the moon's disc rises higher and higher behind the hillside horizon:

My lodge is at the foot
Of the Moon Waiting Hill –
Almost I regret
When the shortening hill shadow
At length disappears.

As I have said, such occupations were first the privilege of the aristocracy. Today, four favourite 'traditional' occupations of holidaygoers in Japan are flower-viewing, shell-gathering, mushroom-picking and moon-viewing. Snow-viewing counts as a form of flower-viewing, being the 'floral display' of winter, and often enough the pictures we see of Japanese gardens show them in winter, with ice-encrusted lakesides and bridges and rocks mantled in snow.

Though the viewing of blossoms remains as popular as ever, it has tended to be excluded from most types of Japanese gardens since the sixteenth and seventeenth centuries, when the thoughtful and austere attitudes of Zen Buddhism and of the related tea-ceremony came to influence garden art. Nowadays, unless there is a wish to incorporate Western features, few flowering plants are made use of in the landscape garden. The massed groves of cherry or plum trees so admired for their flowers are kept in separate parts of the landscape, or are admired as they grow wild on the hillside. The early gardens were changed by the banishment of many flowers, thought to be frivolous, and in their place evergreen shrubs and trees were cultivated, as representing eternal rather than transient beauty. Garden flowers were restricted to areas close to the house, often in enclosures between buildings, or were cultivated separately for display indoors; for example, the chrysanthemum and the peony, which are cultivated with assiduity and passion even, are not found in the Japanese landscape garden. The Japanese garden as we see it today is most often a monochrome one, in which moss, grasses, shrubs and trees present both subtle and wide-ranging gradations of green, grey and silver tones. Among the flowers or flowering shrubs commonly employed are the iris, the azalea, the hagi or sweet clover *(Lespedeza bicolor)*. The iris is restricted to the edges of streams or slightly marshy areas, while the azalea is of course an evergreen, apt to be clipped into close, rounded and almost rock-like shapes – how profoundly different from its present use in western countries as a flowering shrub!

RULES

'Very rare flowers, however beautiful, are not considered desirable material for gardens, the scarce and unfamiliar being favoured only by vulgar and ignorant persons' (Joseph Conder, *Landscape Gardening in Japan*, 1912). Such flowers, driven out of the garden, remain a vital part of Japanese culture, and their growth and arrangement indoors, like that of commoner garden plants, has an immense and historic lore of its own, related to the proper, auspicious and aesthetically satisfying presentation of nature in miniature. In the art of *rikkwa*, or 'erect flower arrangement', for example, landscape terms such as 'valley' and 'grotto' indicate the interstices and openings in the pattern of leaves and stems. Better known than *rikkwa*, which may use up to twelve different species in a single arrangement, is the art of *ike-bana*, or flower arranging, simpler, and more subtle since it uses fewer

37   The proper placing of the stones in the Japanese garden is essential, since their appearance and qualities should indicate their use and position, and since the garden, however small, must contain appropriately sited features, most of them involving arrangements of stones. The *Sakuteiki*, which codified the rules for laying out gardens in the eleventh century, states that if the rules are broken 'the owner of the garden will sicken unto death, his residence shall also be laid waste, and shall become as the dwelling-place of demons'

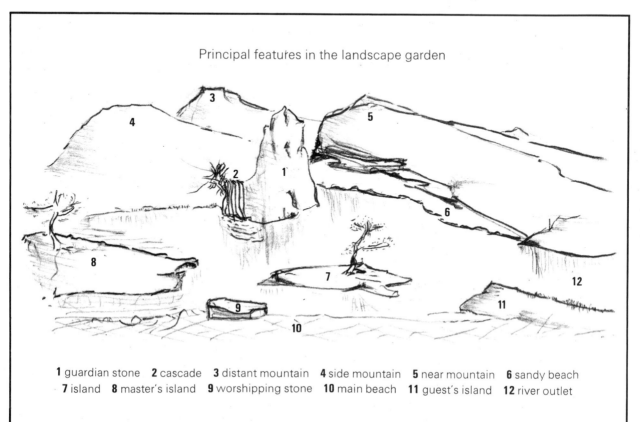

Principal features in the landscape garden

1 guardian stone   **2** cascade   **3** distant mountain   **4** side mountain   **5** near mountain   **6** sandy beach   **7** island   **8** master's island   **9** worshipping stone   **10** main beach   **11** guest's island   **12** river outlet ingredients. In addition to these arrangements of *cut* flowers, stems and branches, there are the more permanent forms of miniature landscape: the *hako-niwa*, or box-garden, being a landscape in miniature; the *bon-kai*, or tray-garden, which uses mud or peat, and sand within a tray of bronze, stone or porcelain; the *bon-seki*, which creates a landscape in a black lacquered tray using stones and sand; and the *bon-sai*, best known to the west, the cultivation of dwarf trees no more than a few inches in height.

These tiny gardens invite us to stillness, to contemplation. The earliest gardens in Japan, as elsewhere in the world, were part of temples and of palaces – sacred enclosures, and paradises. Near Kyoto, the most sacred spot in the whole of Japan is the Ise shrine, consecrated to the sun-goddess, supposed ancestress of the emperor. This shrine is a small and simple building, surrounded by a bare expanse of shingle, round which rise tall forest-trees. The Ise shrine dates from the fifth century, and its open pebble enclosure is called *yuniwa*, a 'purified space of ground'. Today, the Japanese word for garden is *niwa*, related to the *yuniwa* of Ise, and meaning a space of ground 'set aside for special purposes', which could be religious, or political, and so we find that the courtyard of the Shishin-den, the ceremonial hall of the old Imperial Palace in Kyoto, is called *oniwa* when it is used for state ceremonies, *yuniwa* when used for religious ceremonies.

Ceremonies involve ceremonial, and gardens are not excepted. The raked gravel before the Shishin-den, just like the pebbles round the Ise shrine, is subject to rules. It is sacred, and neither ordinary folk nor ordinary plants are allowed. Only two trees stand there, a mandarin orange and a single Imperial cherry, the *sakon-ne-sakura*, each having propitious associations. Nearby, the gravelled courtyard of the Seiryo-den has only two plants – two clumps of bamboo, closely controlled in wooden frames. In the eighth century a second word, *shima*, or 'island', came also to suggest a garden, for the Japanese 'paradise' garden (of the sort described in the extracts from the *Tale of Genji*) had as its distinguishing feature a lake with islands. This seems to have been as a result of Chinese influence, with the idea that paradise or the Happy Land was found in three remote islands, Horai, Hojo and Eishu, and so, to suggest the idea of this paradise, symbolic islands, or island-hillocks if the garden was a dry one, were created in the gardens of the aristocracy. To supplement the auspicious nature of the Islands of the Blessed, islands suggesting the shape of a tortoise or a crane – symbols of longevity – were made, and pine trees – the tree of longevity – were planted on the island.

These auspicious tokens – island, tortoise, crane – are part of the paradise garden in its Japanese form. The sacred grove likewise presents religious themes, using stones to represent the Buddha and attendant saints and disciples. These stones include a trinity at the centre, with Shakyamuni or the Buddha in the middle, and the saints Monja and Fuken on either side. The hagiography is extended sometimes to include sixteen disciples, and Conder gives a numbered diagram showing the related positions and names of no less than forty-eight Buddha- or saint-stones in a temple garden. But this open symbolism was soon replaced by a broader approach, encouraged by the spread of Zen Buddhism, in which direct 'one-for-one' symbolism was superseded by the view that the Buddha was omnipresent, and that the contemplation of any and every object could lead to wisdom. The stones, once 'named' for the Buddha or saints which they represented, became carefully controlled means of suggesting, of hinting rather than stating outright.

Suggestion is a key word in the Japanese garden, an art-form already infinitely sophisticated while we in the west were still in bearskins chasing wild beasts or wild neighbours. By the eleventh century, the art of gardening in Japan had been codified, in the *Sakuteiki*, a treatise on the making of gardens, written most likely by Tachibana no Toshitsuna, who died in 1094. This book (alas! not yet published in English) reveals that for several generations the Japanese had accepted strict rules – one might say taboos – for garden-design. The author refers to painters of the Yamoto-e or Japanese, as distinct from the Chinese, school in the ninth and tenth centuries who were also expert in the disposition of garden rocks. This expertise was not simply aesthetic, but was also related to the understanding of what was propitious or objectionable. Water therefore should flow in a certain direction – east, then south, and to the west – and not otherwise, to avoid ill-fortune of one or several kinds. The *Sakuteiki* draws up immensely detailed instructions for the treatment of water, as for stones and other garden features. The movement of water is studied, and ten different forms are described, flowing, for example, 'from the sides towards the centre', 'among rocks', 'over rocks', 'to one side', and so on. *Cascades* – the fall of water – are also classified, and their use is strictly controlled to suit the quality of the lake and garden in which they appear. They should not be too wide, since that would dwarf the lake; and their source should sometimes be hidden by bushes or branches, to lend mystery, and to give the feeling of greater height to the cascade. Cascades naturally fall over, beside and on to stones, and stones are in Japan, more than in any other country, the most important element of a garden. In China they play a major part, and no doubt this influenced the Japanese; but the material, size, proportion, placing, relationship and grouping, the setting upright or slantwise or horizontally according to the qualities of the stone, these matters have been codified in Japan in a way which is unknown elsewhere, and astonishing in its complexity.

The rules in the *Sakuteiki* are dictated by several considerations. They are practical – e.g. to prevent land from being worn away by the stream – and aesthetic, both in relation to the garden as a whole, large stones being unsuitable in a tiny garden, and *vice versa,* and in relation to the stones themselves. Stones which look water-worn should be used in water-scenery, while rugged, mountainous rocks should be used in mountain-scenery. Some stones are simply not suitable, because of their bent or distorted form, and are called 'diseased stones', while stones with a naturally vertical character should not be laid flat, since they will look as if they have been accidentally overturned – such stones are 'dead stones'. If the stones are placed in a vague, unintelligent, purposeless way, they are 'poor stones'.

Later treatises elaborate the rules and system laid out in the *Sakuteiki*. There is the *Senzui Narabini Yagyo No Zu,* 'Depictions of Mountains, Water and Landscape', dating from 1448, and the aesthetician and garden designer So-ami (died 1525) wrote the *Tsukiyama Sansui Den,* 'On Hill Gardens'. This was the basis for a much-reprinted work by Kitamura Enkin, *Tsukiyama Teizoden,* 'Creating Landscape Gardens' (1735), which illustrates styles and categories of garden arrangement which are still referred to in modern texts, though not always fully accepted. In particular, the categories of hill garden and flat garden are set out; *tsuki-yama* or 'artificial hill', and *hira-niwa* or 'level garden', and the three degrees of elaboration which may be discerned, *shin, gyo* and *so: shin* the fullest and most elaborate, *gyo* the intermediate, and *so* the most simple and purified. These degrees of elaboration are applied to other arts, like calligraphy, painting and flower arrangement.

With the *tsuki-yama,* 'artificial hill' garden, there is an enumeration of the basic components which is repeated from text to text, and which includes twelve or more basic features and then a sub-division into *shin, gyo* and *so* styles. The illustrations given in Harada's *Gardens of Japan* are the clearest. Similar pictures and texts exist for the *hira-niwa* or 'level garden'. This has been further subdivided with the development of the *cha-seki* or tea garden, which has yet more distinctive features and rules.

The *shin-gyo-so* classification is applicable not merely to gardens as a whole, but to the components of a garden – for example, to the kind and use of stones, or to the style of gateways, bamboo fences, walls and water basins, lanterns or stepping-stones. With stepping-stones, for example, there is the general distinction offered by Ito: 'those with little space between them are deemed *shin,* and the stones themselves are artificially cut. The arrangement of either cut or natural stones with a bit more space between is *gyo,* and natural stones with a maximum of space is *so.*' Going beyond this, however, Conder gives both text and illustrations to elaborate the idea, using the terms 'finished' for *shin* and 'rough' for *so.*

Shin and *gyo* and *so* are useful terms, indications which Japanese garden critics have used to give their opinions of the character of this garden or that, though in the fifteenth and sixteenth centuries, when gardens were created which may now be described as *shin* or *gyo* or *so,* it is probable that such categories were not consciously in the minds of the creators.

VII The 'borrowed scenery' of mountains and countryside extends beyond the long dyke of the upper garden at Shugaku-in, near Kyoto. This imperial garden, created in 1656-9, is considerably larger than Katsura, begun forty years before, and has a more spacious atmosphere. The lake, though appearing natural, is formed by the damming of streams in a branching valley, and has affinities with the lakes made in European 'landscape gardens'

38, 39   A photograph and a plan (right) of the *kare sansui* or 'dry garden' in the monastery of Ryoanji, Kyoto. The garden, which measures some thirty by seventy feet, is the most famous of all the 'abstract' gardens in Japan, and was designed in the 1480s – one of the fifteen stones bears the names of two garden workers known to have been active in Kyoto in 1489 and 1490. No plants grow in the enclosure apart from patches of moss on the big stones. The fine gravel is carefully raked in a lengthwise direction. The photograph, a view of the garden from the veranda or viewing platform of the enclosure, shows four of the five groups of stones indicated in the plan. The fifth is further to the left

VIII   Nasedera, Kyoto (top left), with blossom so close that it shades the tree. While the traditional gardens of Kyoto mostly eschew the display of flowering plum or cherry trees (Sambo-in is a famous exception), the viewing of blossom has been a passion, festive, poetic and contemplative, since earliest times, and the flowering cherry has become the national flower of Japan

IX   Snow covers the grassy slopes by the lake at Rikugi-en (left), in Tokyo. This garden was completed in 1702 for Yanagisawa Yoshiyasu, a famous samurai and political figure of the period, and has been faithfully maintained in a state close to the original. Gardens seen in the snow are deeply admired in Japan, and 'snow viewing' counts as a form of 'flower viewing', since the snow gives the gardens its special beauty, comparable to that of spring flowers, or the light of the moon

The earliest Japanese garden treatise, the *Sakuteiki*, defines certain gardens as *kare sansui* or 'dry gardens', and this type has become for many westerners the Japanese garden *par excellence*. In the tenth and eleventh centuries, these *kare sansui* gardens may have been crudely imitative, in the same way that some islands in paradise gardens may at first have been shaped more obviously like tortoises than they were in later centuries. Zen Buddhism brought a broader view of nature, in which every part of the creation was a part of the Buddha, and in which the simplest stone could convey the universality of Buddha and the essence of reality.

The temple garden of Ryoanji (*c.* 1490) is classed by later writers as *so*, or one which is so simplified as to be almost purely symbolic. It is severely rectangular, with temple buildings on two sides, and walls on the other two. From the temple side, one views the garden from a covered veranda, and the visitor should sit to contemplate the scene. The Ryoanji garden is some thirty by seventy feet in size, and its level surface is covered with a uniform bed of pebbles, raked in an unobtrusive but consistent lengthwise direction. In this large expanse (let us keep to abstract, rather than physical terms) fifteen stones are set, in five groups of 5, 2, 3, 2 and 3 stones respectively. Close round the stones a little moss grows, but there are no plants, flowers or trees. What does this mean? Several writers repeat a pallid story, that the rocks are *islands*, across which a tigress and her cubs are fleeing for safety. Rubbish: this is a story for parties of schoolchildren, to keep them quiet. (Maybe, though, there is some truth in it – *Hamlet*, after all, has a rattling good 'story'.) And it is almost as much rubbish to suggest that these rocks are islands in the sea. They are, at one and the same time, *rocks* and the *universe*. They are what they are, and through their own nature, they suggest *le tout*. Ryoanji is, more than any other garden, an exercise in *reductio ad perfectionem*. It is a garden perfect, just as the garden monument, the Altar of Good Fortune, designed by Goethe at Weimar in 1777, the cube surmounted by a sphere, is the monument perfect. The form has been reduced to its ultimate limits, and so, in our contemplation of it, our thought may then expand infinitely outwards. Among European gardens I can think only of Aislabie's

40 The sand and rock composition at Daisen-in, within the temple of Daitokuji, before the striking modifications made to the gardens in recent years. Here, the view is unimpeded as towering rocks and greenery descend towards a flowing expanse of moss-grown shingle and sand in the foreground. Today, this view is virtually bisected by a screen, and every scrap of moss on the sand has been removed

moon-ponds at Studley Royal (*c.* 1725) to match this abstract perfection, with a pure two-dimensional composition of water and lawn, framed in a wooded amphitheatre. In Japan, there are many other abstract gardens, mostly formed of stones set in raked gravel or sand (for example, the gardens of Shinju-an and Myonshin-ji in Kyoto), or beds of moss growing in an expanse of sand (e.g. to the side of the Sambo-in, in the Daigoji temple). Quite often, the abstraction is tempered with *suggestions*, as at the entrance court at Daitoku-ji, where the stones, set in sand, are flanked with bushes and trees, and, at the far end of the garden, a miniature 'mountain range' and 'cascade' diversify the dry landscape.

To return for a moment to Ryoanji. This garden is, above all others in Japan, a garden for contemplation. No one walks on the gravel expanse, except, occasionally, the trained gardener with his rake. We do not even saunter round the garden, but stop to meditate. A sixteenth-century Zen priest called Tessen Soki wrote a garden book *Ka Senzui No Fu*, in which he speaks of 'reducing thirty thousand miles to the distance of a single foot', and another Zen priest, Shinzui, said of a similar creation 'one can never tire of looking at such a garden', and became lost in thought, forgetting the passage of time. These attitudes fit Ryoanji, a masterpiece by an unknown creator. Tessen Soki may himself have been the designer, or So-ami, the writer of the *Tsukiyama Sansui Den;* we do not know.

Not long after this *kare sansui* garden, another was created in a small L-shaped area (130 square yards) round two sides of the abbot's residence at the Daisen-in in Kyoto. The Daisen-in garden, dating from around 1513, and possibly designed by So-ami (who painted landscapes within the building) is surrounded by building or garden walls. Like Ryoanji, it is for contemplation, and is so arranged that one may look at it from a veranda along the 'inside' of the L-shape, or from either end of the two arms of the garden. The corner of the garden formed at the juncture of the two arms is crowded with jagged and upward-jutting rocks, which dominate the garden in the manner of a mountain-range. Small bushes, ferns and moss behind and between them give the impression of forest and verdure, while between these soaring peaks slips a motionless 'cascade', a dry spreading watercourse of pebbles and sand. Near the mountains, a slim horizontal stone supported at either end gives the feeling of a 'bridge', and half-way along the main arm of the garden another horizontal stone seems to suggest a broad yet shallow check to the flow of the water; after which the river of sand moves on more calmly, bearing on its surface a 'boat-shaped' stone, a cargo-junk which 'floats' serenely onwards.

Rightly and understandably, the Japanese consider this garden to be in the *gyo* style, less simple, less austere than the *so* of Ryoanji, but not as full, as realistic, as complete as the *shin* style we shall see at Katsura. Two differences in attitude to the presentation of Daisen-in, each with practical repercussions, illustrate the difficulties which an unlearned western observer must experience in trying to appreciate a garden of this kind.

The first difference is related to the use of moss. Recent pictures of the Daisen-in show the mountains, islands and the 'cargo-junk' contrasted with a neat and, as it were, spotless river and sea of sand, white, impeccable. Recent writers, L. Kuck among them, approve of this appearance, which dates from 1954, when radical spring-cleaning techniques were applied to the garden. In contrast, earlier writers such as Harada comment with approval that this now white river of sand was then 'covered with beautiful thick moss', and plates 49 and 128 in Harada's book show the broad, calm estuary of the river with the cargo-junk floating in just such a sea of moss. A greater difficulty (for moss, I imagine, can grow again) comes with the addition, or restoration, in 1961, of a wooden bridge which is now thought to have passed across the centre of the sand (or moss!) river, so effectively cutting the dry landscape into two parts: a mountain, cascade and tumultuous river section, and a placid, estuary-like river. This wooden bridge, partition is a truer word, has a window in the centre, allowing a spectator at the far end of the 'river' to glimpse the mountain-scenery from which the river originates. Which interpretation is right – a full landscape, or a bisected one? To echo Montaigne: 'Que sçais-je?', 'How should I know?'

FROM PARADISE TO TEA TO PARADISE

While the early Japanese pleasure-gardens, the background for the *parties folles* of the *Tale of Genji*, could be visited on foot or by boat, the austere stone gardens of the fifteenth century, such as the Daisen-in or Ryoanji, were contemplated by a sitting visitor. Our thought may soar far away, but we remain in a single spot. Even the sea of silver sand at Ginkakuji, the Silver Pavilion, is best viewed from the pavilion itself, while we sit, waiting for the moonrise.

Contemplation need not however be so static. Beside the enclosed dry landscapes I have described there were many temple gardens of a more extensive kind – still subject to the prescriptions of manuals like the *Sakuteiki* – in which the garden served as a suggestive extension of the religious atmosphere of the temple. The most famous of these larger temple gardens is the Saiho-ji at Kyoto, possibly first formed in the eighth century, but developed and given its distinctive character by the Buddhist priest Muso Soseki, or Kokushi (1276–1351), in 1339. This garden, called also Koke-dera, or 'Moss Garden', since it is the most richly carpeted with mosses of any garden in Japan – fifty kinds have been identified there – now covers several acres, including a 'lower' garden with a *kare sansui* stone and dry cascade composition. The garden is viewed from winding paths among the trees, over the bridges, and past undulating oceans of moss, pierced by rugged yet peaceful stone-arrangements. At Saiho-ji all these features are intended to offer brief glimpses – suggestions – of eternity. Though modern visitors may experience keen pleasure in viewing the garden, its purpose was without doubt a religious one, and the varied, quiet circuit which it offers is to provide matter for meditation and prayer. As Ito writes, 'it is not man but Buddha who walks about in this "paradise" which represents *Sanzen-sekai* or "the whole world". No matter how a stroller might enjoy this garden, it was not made for his apprehension but for the Buddha'; and it is with this spirit, rather than a feeling of poetic extravagance, that the tortoise island, signifying longevity (which may at the same time represent Mount Shumisen, the Buddhist paradise), and the double lines of stones suggesting vessels moored at night, waiting to sail to the Islands of the Blessed, should be appreciated. There is also the Yogoseki stone, the temple's guardian stone, where the deity came to rest and observe Muso Soseki in his task of creating the garden; while the stone cascade in the upper garden, created by Muso Soseki, is close in spirit to the groupings of Buddha- and saint-stones I have already mentioned. They suggest the ultimate permanence of the divine, glimpsed through nature's most durable forms. Contrast these symbols of eternity with the jagged, soaring peaks of the Daisen-in: there, we stationary humans are invited to a *voyage* of thought, upwards and out into the wider sea of the imagination.

At first Saiho-ji was also renowned for its cherry-blossom and for other flowers; a cherry-blossom viewing was held here in 1347. Today the only brightly coloured vegetation is the crimson flash of autumnal maple, with azaleas in the late spring. The stillness, the ever-present carpet of moss propose an eternal tranquillity, as in the line 'Green moss growing thicker each day, but without a particle of dust'. Europe can hardly match this, except in England, in the Savill gardens near Windsor.

At Saiho-ji there was a main hall, the *shariden,* which was to be imitated or echoed both for its elegance and for its setting in two later buildings in garden-parks in Kyoto; the Kinkakuji or 'Golden Pavilion', and the Ginkakuji or 'Silver Pavilion'.

The Kinkakuji was begun in 1397, and the lake and garden around it were consciously modelled on those at Saiho-ji. Though the present building is a replica (the original pavilion was burnt in 1950) the lake and islands still contain features which the Japanese think symbolic, and which were to enhance the idea of this garden as a 'land of happiness', surrounding the palace of paradise. The pavilion stands directly by the shore, and immediately to one side are the four stones that represent ships moored at night, soon to set sail for Horai. On the other side of the pavilion, the tortoise and crane islands each bear pine-trees to enrich the thought of longevity. This pavilion has both religious and secular purposes; the second and first floors are dedicated to Kannon, the goddess of mercy, and house Buddhist relics, while the ground floor was used for poetry competitions, flower-viewing and viewing the moon. Aesthetic enjoyment has come into the religious garden. Elsewhere in the Kinkakuji gardens were other buildings, including one for snow-viewing, the Kansetsu-tei.

The Ginkakuji, or Silver Pavilion, was begun in 1482, as an imitation both of the Golden Pavilion, and of its original inspiration the *shariden* or central hall at Saiho-ji. We have already considered the Silver Pavilion for its cone and sea of silver sand, objects to be viewed by moonlight from the pavilion. These were for static contemplation, but the other parts of the Ginkakuji garden – the lake and islets on the other side of the pavilion, and the upper garden on the wooded slope of the hill behind – were clearly to provide a changing and stimulating series of glimpses and views. The Silver Pavilion is smaller, simpler than the Golden Pavilion, but similar in having both.

To return to the period of Saiho-ji, the small garden of Tenryu-ji outside Kyoto, another temple garden thought to have been redesigned by Muso Soseki, can be mentioned here. The garden is barely an acre in size, and the walk which one can enjoy is much more constricted than at Saiho-ji. The path round the small lake is therefore one which lacks both the many surprises and changes of perspective of the moss garden, and also much of its exceptional tranquillity. Tenryu-ji is however still a temple garden, and the many stones around the lake, the cascade and the Horai island are all related to the same religious symbolism; but the garden is somehow less meditative, more 'pleasurable'. Reverence has acquired a more worldly delight in the picturesque and immediately beautiful scene, either in the course of walking round the lake, or in static contemplation from the porch of the temple building, looking out over the sand beach, past a superb stone peninsula lined with 'shore-protecting stones' to the lake, and trees on the further side.

As in China, garden stones of quality were sought after with eagerness and determination. Often they were plundered like lovely plum trees from other people's gardens. The general and garden-lover Hideyoshi, a century after the creation of Ryoanji, was a noted seeker of stones, and his rebuilding, from 1598 to 1618, of the garden of the temple of Sambo-in (first set out in the twelfth century), where more than seven hundred stones were brought together, made this the most varied and *sumptuous* of all the stone gardens in Japan. In this clearly *shin* garden rocks, bushes, bridges, lanterns, cascade, streams and lake are combined to achieve the utmost variety. Hideyoshi first thought to remodel this garden in 1597, on the occasion of a cherry-viewing party, and the decision to proceed was taken in early 1598, shortly before another formal cherry-viewing visit by Hideyoshi on 15 March 1598. The garden still retains cherry trees – unlike many old gardens in Kyoto, which have lost the flowering trees which were once theirs.

As so often in this juggernaut history, my simple path from one garden to the next leads over a muddle of cultural, historical and religious developments. We cannot reasonably proceed from the paradise (religious) to the paradise (secular yet aesthetic), from Saiho-ji in the fourteenth century to Katsura in the early seventeenth century, without discussing the tea ceremony and its related garden.

The tea ceremony is one of the contemplative arts special to Japan. Though the main Japanese interest in the tea garden dates from the seventeenth century, the tea ceremony was first developed in the fifteenth century, in the garden of the Silver Pavilion, or Ginkakuji, by Murata Juko (1423–1502). To begin with, the idea was to create a small, distinct garden area leading to the tea room in the pavilion. Soon, the ceremony was seen to need a separate building, a tea house apart from the residence, for which a separate garden was equally necessary. Simplicity was always essential – a small tea house, simply furnished, with interior dimensions limited to the area of four and a half *tatami* mats (the mats used for floor-covering, some 6ft × 3ft in size); and a simple garden approach, containing at first no more than a single willow or maple tree.

This development was codified by the most famous of the Japanese tea-masters, the poet, aesthetician and garden-lover Sen no Rikyu (1522–91). Under his influence, the design of the tea house became austere, with a single window, enough to provide light but no distracting view, and a small doorway for entry. A veranda for garden-viewing was eliminated. As if to compensate for this severity, the garden approach was elaborated as a temporal, as well as a spatial, means of preparation for the ceremony within the tea house. The tea garden, the *cha-niwa*, was a passage-way to an event, a space through which the visitor – you, reader, or myself – should proceed physically, aesthetically experiencing the gradual shedding of the world's concerns, while proceeding towards the tea house.

The tea garden again demands *suggestion*. Sen no Rikyu is famous in Japan for the episode where, preparing his *cha-niwa*, he had swept and tidied the garden, and then, dissatisfied with its too-perfect appearance, he shook the maple tree which grew there, so that just two or three flaming leaves fell on the mossy ground. What he had endeavoured to do was not true enough to nature: the *natural* fall of the leaves was needed to complete the aesthetic effect. Another anecdote is related to morning glories, which he had grown for the entertainment of his guests. When the guests arrived, they found the *cha-niwa* bare of flowers. Puzzled, they entered the tiny tea house, to find displayed one single morning glory, serving to suggest the perfection of all such flowers.

Though Sen no Rikyu did not recommend the display of flowers in the *cha-niwa*, since there would normally be a flower-arrangement within the tea house itself (our appreciation would be diminished by a previous display), other elements in the tea

garden were permitted, indeed necessary, and they were most carefully studied. For Sen no Rikyu, and later for Furuta Oribe (1543–1615), another influential tea-master, the uniqueness of the garden effect was a guiding principle, as in the 'once-only' nature of the two anecdotes. This principle was applied to the garden designs, where they tried to achieve variety of effect in the placing of trees, and in the design of gates, lanterns, water-basins and stepping stones.

Stepping stones, unconsidered trifles in many western gardens, mere means of avoiding the mud, assume sudden and extraordinary significance in the Japanese tea garden. Not only do they indicate our path, but their spacing and grouping dictate our pace and attitude. If the stones are small and placed close together, we may, for example, walk carefully, giving our attention to the stones themselves; if we reach a large, broad stone, we may stop to look up and admire the new prospect which is before us. One name for the tea garden is *roji*, which has several meanings which may be applied to the garden; 'a narrow path or alley', 'on the way', 'while walking', and lastly 'dewy ground' or 'dewy path'. The last meaning has a religious sense, coming from a passage in the Buddhist sutras which tells of such a place, 'a dewy path' where one is reborn after escaping from the furnace of worldly desires. The tea garden offers 'rebirth', but it is not specifically religious, but rather spiritual and aesthetic. The rebirth of the tea ceremony, the *cha-no-yu*, is consciously prepared by means of the stepping stones in the tea garden: Sen no Rikyu recommended that their arrangement should achieve a proportion of three-fifths walking, and two-fifths viewing and appreciation of the scene. Later, Furuta Oribe was to reverse this, suggesting two-fifths emphasis on walking, the functional aspect, and three-fifths looking. The rules for laying out these stones are of immense complexity, since the different features in the tea garden – gate, waiting-bench, well, washing-basin and so forth – require appropriate stones for their approach, which in turn govern the setting and spacing of the lesser stones. And, naturally, the size, texture and colour of the stones become immensely important, since they form the physical basis of the *roji*, the 'dewy path', and are in a literal sense so constantly before our eyes.

41   An aerial view of the imperial palace and garden at Katsura, completed in 1659. The visitor follows the paths round the lake, crossing several bridges and passing tea houses, a temple and the varied buildings of the palace. This garden covers nearly fourteen acres, and the spirit of its design may be matched with that of certain European landscape gardens in the eighteenth century – compare this view with the plan of Shenstone's Leasowes (pl. 137) or the engraving of Stourhead (pl. 134)

42　One of the many paths, outlined with stepping stones, in the grounds of Katsura. Part of the lake can be glimpsed on the left. The stepping stones, as in the smaller setting of a tea garden, are so arranged as to suggest not only the general direction of your walk, but also your pace, and hint even at the mood or attitude you might adopt – pausing to look round or walking carefully and observing the quality, texture and placing of the stones themselves

The early seventeenth-century garden of Katsura, which crowns the gradual development of the large contemplation garden, from Saiho-ji onwards, brings into the garden almost as its most important feature the hundreds of stepping stones which lead round the garden and to and from its several tea houses. Work on the imperial palace and garden at Katsura was begun in 1620 and completed in 1659. The garden covers nearly fourteen acres, and its design may have been the work of Prince Toshihito, or of the great tea-master Kobori Enshu (1579–1647). To use an Elizabethan phrase, it is a garden of 'incredible sumptuousness', not in gold and silver, but in the richness and variety of the unfolding scene.

In its extravagance, Katsura may be compared with the gardens of the Italian Renaissance. Kobori Enshu, when asked if he would design the gardens, is said to have accepted on three conditions: 'no limitation as to the time of its completion, no interference, and allowance of unlimited expenditure.' In its tranquillity, its reverence for nature, its slow unfolding of views, and its literary allusions (*The Tale of Genji* is said to have been the *livre de chevet* of Prince Toshihito, the owner and possibly designer of the garden) it may be compared with the English landscape gardens of the eighteenth century.

Much of the peacefulness of Katsura comes from its several tea houses and their related features, which are introduced to us in different ways by their stepping stones. The Katsura garden is not merely an extended 'dewy path' leading to tea houses – the awkward term 'stroll garden' is occasionally found to describe the quiet perambulation involved – but was elaborately conceived to satisfy many needs, aesthetic, spiritual and recreational. There is a small temple, Onrin-do, and a lawn and other areas for sport; a kind of football called *kemari*, archery and riding. The lake is large enough for boating parties, as in the *Tale of Genji* itself, while within the palace there are residential rooms, and others for entertaining guests, or for music. In front of the palace is the open moon-viewing platform, Tsukimi-dai, and moon-viewing was also a special activity at Geppa-ro. From the platform, one could observe the rising moon. From Geppa-ro, one saw the moon's reflection in the lake.

LATER GARDENS

Katsura, though seemingly inexhaustible in its controlled variety, is well under ten acres in area: its scale is small, and can be threatened when too many visitors appear at once. A much more spacious sequence of gardens, built like Katsura by imperial command, is connected with the detached palace of Shugaku-in, near Kyoto. The area of the lower, middle and upper gardens is near sixty acres, and the most famous part, the upper garden, covers half the total. The upper garden was designed and built in 1656–9 for the ex-emperor, Gomizuno. A tea house, the Rin-untei, already stood on an elevated slope in the grounds, to take advantage of the spectacular landscape view across the city and to the mountains beyond. Gomizuno had a great dyke thrown up between two spurs of ground, to enclose a valley in which a lake could form from the accumulating water of the mountain streams. It is a large lake, well over 300 yards in length, and 150 yards wide, with three islands and a shore-line which curves into small bays and creeks in the most 'natural' manner, and extends for two thirds of a mile. In eighteenth-century England, such a lake (made artificially by damming a stream in a valley, but looking 'natural' since the rising waters followed the original contours of the ground) would be thought to be in the best manner of Capability Brown; but this lake is in Japan.

The garden of Shugaku-in is imitated by many other large pleasure gardens in Japan. Like Katsura and like Shugaku-in, these gardens are formed round an irregularly-shaped lake, with a wandering path roughly following the curves and twists of the shore-line, to offer as much variety and interest as possible. As at Katsura, the mood is varied by allowing sudden prospects of distant scenes: gardens in the Edo region, built from the seventeenth century onwards, often include the most famous of all Japanese landscape prospects, the view of Mount Fuji, as does, for example, the Fukiage garden, built in 1705 within the grounds of Edo castle, or the Toyama-so (1670), or the Hama Goten (1670). Alternatively, they may allow views across the lake to buildings, bridges, groups of stones or striking trees, which are perceived in new perspectives. These gardens remained strongly poetical, with

43 A celebrated view across the lake in the garden of Kenroku-en, Tokyo, showing the remarkable stone lantern. Garden lanterns and lamp posts in Japan have been elaborately classified according to their shape and purpose. The lantern here is famous, not for its mushroom-shaped top (which is to keep the snow out of the 'firebox'), but for the daring and graceful use of legs of unequal length, which hold the lantern out over the water

44   The Ritsurin-en gardens at Takamatsu, in Kagawa Prefecture, were created in the eighteenth century and are much larger than the earliest landscape gardens, emulating, rather, the pleasure gardens of Shugaku-in. There are six ponds in Ritsurin park, cleverly divided by islands and winding channels, while mountains provide a memorable background of 'borrowed scenery'

scenes which a cultured man would find allusive. Just as the scenes at Katsura were meant to recall the *Tale of Genji,* so the appreciation of the garden of the Koraku-en, built in the late seventeenth century, assumed knowledge of both Japanese and Chinese classical literature, and the garden of the Rikugi-en (1702) alluded to each of the canonical eighty-eight most famous scenes in Japan. Often these clues or hints could be slight, minute – to the unlettered visitor, so faint as to be inaudible. In the lower garden of the Shugaku-in, there is a tiny waterfull, a foot high, a foot wide, with a roughly triangular stone above the top of the fall. Westerners, like peasants, may think: 'It's a waterfall. Very pretty'. But the Japanese visitor should be aware that this is a reminder of the Shiraito-no-Taki, the waterfall of 'white threads' at the foot of Mount Fuji–the stone at the top *suggesting* the cone of the volcano.

Such gardens have been created in Japan even in the twentieth century. In 1917, the garden of Hekiunso was made near Kyoto, designed by Nomura Tokuhichi. Like Katsura, Hekiunso has a prominent central lake, and like Shugaku-in, the garden makes use of 'borrowed scenery', here the towering forest-ridge beyond the lake. To my mind, the most beautiful feature of the garden is the boat-house on the lake, in which a boat is moored. A curving plank takes you from the shore to the deck of the boat. Its bows rise up, reflected in the quiet waters: your voyage may begin. But here, the voyage is made by the human spirit, for the boat is a tea house, and within its small cabin the tea ceremony (prepared by the tranquil approach among rocks and trees) still has the simplicity and strength which masters like Sen no Rikyu or Kobori Enshu could evoke: 'One room, a vase, a single morning glory.'

45 An illustration from a late
fifteenth-century manuscript of
Petrus de Crescentiis' *Opus
ruralium . . . commodorum*

5

Medieval Gardens

THE HERB GARDEN

With the collapse of the Western Roman Empire, gardens and garden art dwindled to such an extent that we may say, without exaggeration, that they virtually disappeared.

Great gardens are unheard of in the west for seven or eight hundred years, except in fantasy, where, as we shall see, writers and artists quite often used the garden as a focus for their imaginative presentation of either spiritual or worldly delights; and it is not until the later Middle Ages or the early Renaissance that real gardens begin to be built with such fantasies as a model.

Practically nothing is known of western gardens from the time of Sidonius Apollinaris until the reign of Charlemagne, when three documents appear in a way which garden historians find particularly convenient, since they provide a convincing outline of garden practice at the time. First, around 795, there is a section in the *Capitulare de villis vel curtis imperii* (regulations for the administration of the towns in Charlemagne's empire) which lists seventy-three plants and fruit-trees which must be grown.

The second document is the plan of a monastery and its related buildings which is preserved in the monastery of St Gall in Switzerland. Its date is probably around 816, or a little later, and though it has been disputed whether the plan is for a 'real' or an 'ideal' community, it is remarkably detailed, and three separate gardens are distinctly indicated, while we may assume that a fourth may also have been made within the square cloister which lies beside the church and occupies a central position in the plan. The first three gardens are all to one side of the monastery, and were probably contained within the general outside wall. They are rectangular, and each has a particular purpose. One, the *herbularius* or physic garden, is next to the infirmary, and has sixteen separate beds, each for a different plant. The second is the *hortus* or vegetable garden, and has eighteen beds, set out in two rows of nine, each for a different plant, and between the rows is a hexameter: 'Here in beauty the garden's tender plants grow green.' The third garden has a double function: it contains thirteen trees, mostly fruit trees, and they are spaced evenly among the fourteen rectangles – the graves of monks who have completed their earthly pilgrimage.

The third document is a Latin poem, *Liber de cultura hortorum*, commonly referred to as the *Hortulus*, or 'little garden', written by a monk, Walafrid Strabo (809–49), and dedicated to Grimald, the abbot of St Gall, who had earlier been Walafrid's teacher while in Walafrid's nearby and related abbey of Reichenau. The *Hortulus* is a poem of 444 lines, and though it deserves to be considered in its own right, it can be seen as a descendant of Columella's poem on gardening, with a similar first-hand knowledge, understanding and delight in the work, the plants and the produce.

Walafrid's poem begins (lines 1-75) with general remarks: a gardener's life is a quiet one, but needs hard work. Gardening begins for him with the coming of spring – and *nettles*. 'Quid facerem?', he asks, 'what should I do?', and digs up their tangled roots – several times. He is, in this opening section of the poem, describing the making of a small garden from scratch, for he goes on to explain that, to stop the soil from being washed away, it has to be edged with planks, and raised up in rectangular beds higher than the level of the ground. The Roman writer on agriculture, Palladius, already advises raising or lowering the beds in one's vegetable garden, depending on the drainage *(Opus agriculturae*, book I), but the planks are new. This detail, coming in a poem written around AD 840, is fascinating, for once manuscripts or early printed books begin to show pictures of gardens, their flower and vegetable beds always have raised edges, usually of planks, and in Europe the practice of making 'raised beds' in formal gardens continues until the early eighteenth century.

Walafrid plants from seed or from cuttings, and he waters them 'drop by drop', and, most convincing detail, literally 'with my own hands', i.e. 'letting the water run through my fingers', so that the seeds are not disturbed by the rush of the water. His garden, within the monastery, has high walls, and so some parts are shaded, and others receive little rain.

Nearly all the rest of the poem consists of twenty-two sections describing the appearance, quantities and uses of plants which he grows. I give the Latin name used in the *Hortulus,* and the most probable English name for the plant he describes: *salvia*/sage; *ruta*/rue; *abrotanum*/lad's love, southernwood; *cucurbita*/gourd; *pepones*/melon; *absinthium*/wormwood; *marrubium*/horehound; *feniculum*/fennel; *gladiola*/iris; *lybisticum*/lovage; *cerefolium*/chervil; *lilium*/lily; *papaver*/(opium) poppy; *sclarega*/clary; *menta*/mint; *pulegium*/pennyroyal; *apium*/celery; *vettonica*/betony; *agrimonia*/agrimony; *ambrosia*/tansy; *nepeta*/catmint; *rafanum*/radish and *rosa*/rose. A handful of others are mentioned: for example the nettle, as a weed; the Indian pepper and the pomegranate, as 'foreign' products; the poison aconite; and the apple and the peach which grow in his teacher Grimald's garden – and he may have cultivated some which he does not name. Those which he does are mentioned first for their herbal, medicinal properties, and second for their appearance – beautiful, interesting, curious or comical. Sadly for ourselves, he says nothing of how to sow, plant, thin out, prune, or graft after the first general section – except that, implicitly, the smaller plants are sown in rows – the radish, 'rafanus', appears in 'the very last row', before the rose, which presumably grows by the walls of his garden. But both the radish and the rose are described in terms of their usefulness, their value, not horticulturally.

He lists some plants which we might consider to be purely ornamental – the iris, the lily, the rose – but this is a misconception. In Walafrid's time these plants all had culinary, herbal or medicinal uses which fully justified their place in a small garden. For centuries plants were credited with medical or, we might say, miraculous powers, which we have now forgotten. In Walafrid, the lily (*lilium candidum*) cures snake-bite, the iris quells 'saevum . . . dolorem vesicae', and helps starch the washing, and the rose, as he has told us, has innumerable uses. It has been suggested that Roman legionaries commonly used madonna lilies as a corn-cure, since there is an otherwise incomprehensible correlation between the sites of legionary camps all over the Roman empire and the spots where such lilies are to be found growing freely today (see Alice M. Coats, *Flowers and Their Histories,* 1968).

'But', as Burton says in the shortest sentence of the *Anatomy of Melancholy,* 'I digress.' Walafrid's plants are grown for their usefulness. He has hardly any vegetables, as these would have been grown in the fields. In his garden, the rose, the lily and the iris appear, as they do in the gardens of the *Capitulary* and the St Gall plan. They are the only 'flowers' to be cultivated, but their beauty, their ornamental qualities are the least important. At the end of his poem Walafrid writes eloquently of the symbolic, mystic value of the lily and the rose, and there is no doubt that these flowers would be used to decorate the church and that roses and other flowers in their season would be used for chaplets and garlands regularly worn by the clergy on festival days until the Reformation.

Walafrid's list overlaps convincingly with the plants and trees named in the St Gall plan, and these in turn overlap in a tolerable way with the much longer list in the *Capitulary*. The three documents provide a composite picture of the state of gardening in western Europe around AD 800 – simple, restricted, utilitarian and just surviving.

46   In this detail from pl. 45 the lady is weaving sprigs of greenery (possibly rosemary) round the framework of a double crown. The larger framework to the right represents a ship. By the middle of the fifteenth century Giovanni Rucellai's garden in Florence contained a variety of figures made from plants grown round such frameworks or from clipped bushes – topiary work – and this was to become a characteristic of the Italian Renaissance garden

MEDIEVAL GARDEN FEATURES

After Walafrid, it is a long while before another group of texts on gardens occurs. Lists of plants appear, in encyclopaedic or linguistic works; references to gardens, or illustrations, are scrappy, almost accidental, and we must bring together the glimpses and passing comments to form an overall picture. It is sensible, therefore, and necessary to discuss the different features of medieval gardens.

THE SQUARE, ENCLOSED GARDEN

The shape of the medieval garden comes from the square or rectangular shape of the cloister. In religious houses a walled garden had of course a special Christian symbolism, for it was the virgin bride of Solomon's *Song of Songs,* and by implication the Virgin Mary. 'A garden enclosed is my sister, my spouse; a spring shut up, a fountain sealed.' When medieval paintings show Mary, the mother of Jesus, in a garden, she is almost always in a garden which is enclosed with a wall, a fence or a paling, and often the means of enclosure is the most carefully depicted part of the background. In secular gardens walls were just as necessary, and the areas enclosed were roughly square or rectangular, or composed of rectangular sections, from the proximity of other town houses of rectangular plan. Even the spacious gardens of kings should be 'enclosed with high walls'; this is recommended by the Italian Petrus de Crescentiis, whose *Opus ruralium . . . commodorum,* completed *c.*1305, contains one of the first accounts after Walafrid of gardens and garden theory, 'de viridariis'.

Within the walls the subdivisions of the gardens were again square or geometrical, with cross-paths between rectangular beds or garden areas of similar shape and size. This square or rectangular plan of the garden and its subdivisions, and its relationship to the walls of the house joining the garden, forms the basis of all subsequent formal gardens in Europe, being reinforced later by the influence of the foursquare Persian garden.

HEDGES AND TRELLIS WORK

If the garden was not surrounded by walls, then thick tall rectilinear hedges, or wattle or paling fences were used. Small country enclosures are quite often shown with wattle fences going round the area in a rough circle, possibly because the artists found it simpler to portray. Defining a garden for people of moderate wealth, Crescentiis (c. 1305) says first that it should be enclosed with ditches, and hedges made from thorn bushes and roses. In hot regions there should be pomegranate hedges, and in colder ones hedges of nut, plum and quince. And then, 'in the most suitable places, one must make trellis work and tunnels in the shape of houses, tents or pavilions.' In noble and royal gardens this idea is extended: he recommends 'a palace with rooms and towers made uniquely from trees, where the lord and his lady . . . may go in fine dry weather.' Trees should be planted, several years in advance, where the walls are to be, and trained and clipped to form roofs and divisions. The work can be done more quickly with poles fastened together, and grown over with vines planted alongside.

The practice of making trellis work arbours, wooden pergolas and the like goes back without interruption to Roman times, where numerous wall paintings, as in the villa Livia, show garden scenes with trellis work. But so far as I know it is not specifically mentioned in medieval writings as a garden feature until Crescentiis' text, nor does it appear in any earlier paintings or miniatures as part of a garden, though agricultural treatises show vines on trellis work. In the fourteenth and fifteenth centuries, references are frequent, and elaborate trellis work of this kind, known in English as 'carpenter's work', was a distinctive feature of the gardens. But trellis work or carpenter's work is one of the most ephemeral features of an art which is nothing if it is not transitory. Thomas Hill, in his *Most Briefe and Pleasaunt Treatyse* (1563) explains exactly how such a 'herbar . . . may be framed with Ashen poles, or the Willow', and how 'the branches of Vine, Mellon, or Cucumber, running and spreading all over, might so shadow and keep both the heat and Sun from the walkers and sitters thereunder.' He adds that 'If they be made with juniper wode, you nede not to repayre nothyng therof in ten years after: but if they be made with willow poles, then you must new repayre them in three years after.' Repairing the arbour comes under 'January's husbandry' in Thomas Tusser's *Five Hundred Points of Good Husbandrie* (1573) – if you don't, it will fall apart:

> For rotten and aged may stand for a shew
> but hold to their tackling there do but a few.

GRASS

Within this enclosed space, the earlier medieval gardens had beds, to which we shall return, and expanses of grass: there is little difference between the idea of a 'meadow' and the 'flowery mede' of medieval times, and early descriptions and pictures show that the grassy section of a medieval walled garden is meant to be similar to the classical *locus amoenus*, the 'pleasant' and entirely natural spot out in the country.

The earliest instructions for making a grassy lawn come in the *De vegetabilibus* of Albertus Magnus (1193–1280), written around 1260, in an entire section to do with gardens, 'de plantatione viridariorum':

> Nothing refreshes the sight so much as fine short grass. One must clear the space destined for a pleasure garden of all roots, and this can hardly be achieved unless the roots are dug out, the surface is levelled as much as possible, and boiling water is poured over the surface, so that the remaining roots and seeds which lie in the ground are destroyed and cannot germinate . . . The ground must then be covered with turves cut from good [meadow] grass, and beaten down with wooden mallets, and stamped down well with the feet until they are hardly able to be seen. Then little by little the grass pushes through like fine hair, and covers the surface like a fine cloth.

These instructions are repeated, word for word, by Crescentiis in the early 1300s, and again and again until the seventeenth century. It would be fascinating to know whether (as is likely) Albertus Magnus in the 1250s drew his method from an earlier writer, and whether in the 1600s gardeners still took this advice seriously when making a 'greene plot'.

TURF SEATS
Here and there in the garden, at the side of the grass, around a tree or along the wall there would be raised banks, covered in turf, for sitting on. The depiction of these is so frequent that there can be no doubt that the practice was widespread, even if we today might think it a damp one. Albertus Magnus is again the first to mention this feature: 'Between the beds and the grass a raised turf section must be set up, filled with delightful flowers, and nearly in the centre, suitable for sitting on, where the senses may be refreshed and where one may rest with pleasure.' They were held up with boards, like raised flowerbeds, or with woven wattle, or even with bricks. Illustrations sometimes show such seats with flowers growing in the grass. In literature, the most beautiful, and easily the most flowery of turf seats is Titania's in the *Midsummer Night's Dream* (II, ii):

> . . . a bank whereon the wild thyme blows,
> Where ox-lips and the nodding violet grows:
> Quite over-canopied with lush woodbine,
> With sweet musk roses, and with eglantine:
> There sleeps Titania sometime of the night . . .

TREES
The elaborate and fanciful grafting of trees was a medieval enthusiasm which we have now lost. Crescentiis writes 'It is also a great beauty and pleasure to have in one's garden trees variously and marvellously grafted, and many different fruit growing on a single tree.' This interest led to credulous ideas that through grafting one could produce fruit of a new or compound kind. The *Ménagier de Paris* (1393) tells the reader: 'If you would have grapes without pips, take at the waxing of the moon in the time when vines be planted . . . a vine plant with its root, and slit the stock right through the midst unto the root, and draw out the pith from each side . . .'

THE MOUNT
In the later Middle Ages gardens might have a mount, or small hill, either in the middle, or more often to one side against the wall, as a vantage point from which the attractions of the garden might be seen, and where a summer-house or arbour might be built. The origin of the mount may go back a long way, when a country property needed a look-out, in England a 'toot-hill', to observe the approaches round about; but the idea of looking *outwards* from one's garden does not gain favour until the late Renaissance.

In England few mounts survive except in the gardens of the Oxford and Cambridge colleges, where they have been partially preserved within later gardening schemes. A successful modern mount is in Lord de Ramsey's garden at Abbots Ripton, where the mount provides a view over the fairly level East Anglian terrain, and itself offers an interesting variation of contour.

Mounts were sometimes round, sometimes square in plan. The castle of Wressel, in the East Riding of Yorkshire, once had at least two round ones, described by John Leland in his *Itinerary* in the 1530s: 'in the orchards were mountes *opere topiario* [i.e. with topiary work growing on them], writhen about with degrees like turnings of cockilshilles, to come to the top without payn.'

RAISED BEDS
Walafrid Strabo shows already that beds were raised above the level of the ground, and edged with planks. He doesn't say how high above the ground, and later pictures vary enormously in the impression they give. The practice survives into the second half of the seventeenth century. The 1652 edition of Thomas Hill's *Gardeners Labyrinth* (first published in 1577) still echoes Palladius: 'In a moist and watry

Garden plot this skilful Neapolitaine willeth, that the beds . . . be reared two foot high . . . But in a dry ground, the edges of the beds raised a foot high, shall wel suffice.' The first edition of John Rea's *Flora* (1665) reduces the raising to a minimum, with plank edges, fastened to posts, which could be seen in many sensible vegetable gardens to this day.

PLANTS

Within the beds the medieval garden had a limited number of plants, compared with today's international abundance. In small gardens, herbs would be the main plants, as with Walafrid; then vegetables and fruit trees, and last flowers. There are lists compiled in medieval times of plants, and some are divided into groups, such as 'for potage', 'for sauce', 'for the coppe', 'for a salade', but little to tell how or where they were grown. Albertus Magnus does not go into details: 'the grass shall be so proportioned to allow behind it, in a rectangular area, all kinds of scented plants, such as rue, sage, and basil to be planted, and flowers, such as violets, columbine, lilies, roses, iris and the like . . .', and Crescentiis echoes Albertus.

Two late medieval documents discuss the growing of plants, the *Ménagier de Paris* of 1393, and the English poem 'The Feate of Gardeninge' by Jon Gardener, written in the first half of the fifteenth century. The Ménagier or 'Goodman' mentions only a few plants in his garden but discusses the gardening work each requires, beginning his year at All Saints, the first of November: thirteen herbs; a dozen vegetables; five fruit trees and bushes (vine, raspberry, currant, cherry and plum), and five flowers (violet, gillyflower, peony, lily and rose). His treatise deals most thoroughly with housekeeping, and in the cookery section other herbs, vegetables and fruit are mentioned. Apart from a preoccupation with regulating one's sowing, planting and grafting according to the state of the moon, which is common to most medieval – and even Elizabethan – gardening instructions, his advice is solidly practical: '*note* that in rainy weather it is good to plant but not to sow, for the seed sticketh to the rake.' When planting beans 'plant them . . . at divers times, so that if some be taken by the frost others be not.'

Herbs and vegetables are his main concern, but we know that he approved of flowers for chaplets. The book is written as a manual for his wife, and he remarks: 'I am pleased rather than displeased that you tend rose trees and care for violets and make chaplets and dance and sing.' His one extravagance with flowers is with roses – to have them out of season. He writes: 'If you would keep roses in winter, take . . . little buds . . . and leave the stems thereof long, and set them within a little wooden cask . . . without water. Cause the cask to be well closed and so tightly bound up that naught may come in or out thereof, and at the two ends of the aforesaid cask tie two great and heavy stones and set the cask in a running stream.'

Jon Gardener's 'Feate of Gardeninge' lists nearly a hundred plants, and like the Ménagier the poet gives seasonal advice.

Compared with the limited practical advice in Albertus Magnus or Crescentiis, his short poem (196 lines, printed in full in *Archaeologia*, vol. LIV, 1894) is comprehensive. It has sections on the growing of trees, on their grafting, on the growing of vines, the setting and sowing of seeds, the sowing and setting of worts, a special section on parsley and one on other herbs, and a section on saffron. Flowers are not treated separately, though he names several, including 'Peruynke violet cowslippe and lyly' and 'Rose ryde, rose whyghte, foxglove and pympernold.'

For Jon Gardener these are still 'herbs', pretty ones maybe, and used in garlands and chaplets, but needed for cooking and medicine – useful, as is all his advice. On parsley he is typical. Sow it in March, and cut it as it grows:

Let hym never too hye go.
To lete hym grow too hye hyt is grete foly,
For he wul then blest and wanchy [sicken and grow sickly]
His kinde is nought to be sette [planted]
To be sow is al-ther best.

And then Jon Gardener concludes: 'Now hereof let we be.' Enough.

Sses y ferv et
surtar
Et maintessoie
le escoutar
Se le ovoir seane mille ame
Le touchet qui estoit de charne
Ille ouuir vne pucellette
Oui asse estoit coince et nette
Cheueils eur blonc con vng bassi
La cher plus tendre qunni vonssin

front reluisant souref voultie
Lentreuil si nestoit pas vetie
Aneput asse mians y mesme
Lonis eut bien fait a droiture
Leeveuist eut vne come faulsante
Pour faire amic atone siome
Doulce a same eut et sauouree
La face blanche et consouree
La bouche petite et grossette
Et au menton vne fossette

XI   The idea of the *verger* or
'orchard' as a form of the ideal
garden continues throughout the
Middle Ages. This miniature
painting, from a manuscript of the
fifteenth-century *Songe du
Vergier*, shows such an enclosure,
with interwoven trees all round,
to give safety, and a meadow
scattered with trees and flowers. A
stream rises in the bottom left-
hand corner, rather like the
'fontaine' of Narcissus which
bubbles up in the Roman de la
Rose (pl. 49)

FANTASY GARDENS

All the elements I have described from real gardens reappear in medieval imaginative literature and its illustrations. Like the real gardens, those of fantasy begin simply and become more ambitious, colourful and extravagant. This is seen in Biblical illustrations, where the earliest portrayals of the garden of Eden or of Paradise are stark and crude, but become ever more detailed and elaborate, in the poetry of epics and romances, and in the illustrations made of these for such poems. The earliest surviving French play, the *Mystère d'Adam* (*c*.1150-60), has Latin stage directions which explain the stage set for the garden of Eden:

Paradise is set up in a high place . . . there will be scented flowers and leaves; there are in Paradise various trees and fruit hanging from them, so that it appears a most pleasant place [*amenissimus locus*].

This bareness is paralleled in early romances. In Chrétien de Troyes' *Erec et Enide* (*c*.1165-70) there is a magic open garden, with a spell which protects it as if with an enclosure. Flowers and fruit grow there all year round, all pleasing birds sing there, and all useful herbs and spices grow there abundantly; but Chrétien gives no details. Again his romance *Cligés* tells of a 'grafted tree' filling most of a walled pleasure garden. It bears flowers and fruit, including pears, and the branches have been trained to give close shade over the grass, even at midday. Not a rewarding description.

In the early thirteenth century the details begin, as they do in the *De vegetabilibus* of Albertus Magnus. The first part of the *Roman de la Rose* was written by Guillaume de Lorris between 1220 and 1230. Well over a century later it was translated into English verse by Geoffrey Chaucer and others, Chaucer now being allowed to have translated as far as v. 1705 of the *Roman*, which happens to be the section of the poem with most garden references.

In his dream the narrator comes to a great garden (in French a *verger*) behind an embattled wall, and is let in through 'a wycket small' by Lady Idleness, wearing (for our instruction!) a chaplet 'of fyne orfrays' – gold embroidery – and above this 'a rose garlande', who accompanies him through the garden. They enter by a little path 'Of myntes ful, and fenell greene', i.e. a path with fragrant herbs both to walk on, and at their sides. The garden belongs to, and was made by Sir Mirth, who also wears 'a rosen chapelet'. Mirth and his friends are busy dancing on 'the grene grasse', and several of them have garlands or chaplets of roses. The god of love has many-coloured flowers on his clothing, arranged in a marvellous pattern – roses, broom, violet and periwinkle.

The trees in the garden were brought 'fro the lande of Alexandrine', i.e. from the East, and the garden is the most delightsome place in the entire world, 'so fayre' that 'it seemed a place espyrituell', a 'paradyse erthly'. It is therefore an *ideal* garden which Lorris means to portray. In Chaucer's English, which is most satisfactorily accurate,

The garden was, by mesurying,
Right even and square in compasyng.

It contained many trees, all bearing fruit; pomegranates, nutmegs, almonds, figs and dates. These are exotics – more so in Chaucer's England than in Lorris' France – and others follow, bearing spices; clove, licorice, ginger, cardamom, cinnamon and turmeric. Then come native fruit trees, then laurels and pines, cypresses and olives, and tall timber trees 'in assyse', that is equally spaced in rows, and trained across in arches – 'And every braunche in other knet' – to stop the fierce (French and marvellous) sun from scorching the tender grass. Squirrels, does, roebuck and rabbits run freely, and countless birds sing endlessly. In the springs, the water runs clear and bright: no frogs, no stagnant water that Bacon will come to grumble about in his essay 'On Gardens', for this is an ideal, a magic garden. Beside the streams the grass is tender and green, and 'much amended' by flowers.

The earlier illustrations do not match the fantasy, for the year 1220, of the verse; but successive presentations of particular scenes show immense advances in subtlety. The first illustrated manuscript, *c.* 1300, shows the garden with a couple of crude trees, trunks with bunches of leaves, and later miniatures, forgetting the 'haut mur bataillié', tend to show a modest, even mean enclosure with low walls or a wattle fence. This applies to the earliest woodcuts also, where the 'development' of the garden can hardly be noticed beyond the change from a woven wattle to a paling fence. But the superb general view from the Harleian MS (pl. X), with the complex garden scene set in a border of tendrils, flowers and butterflies, takes us beyond the earlier illustrations, and beyond Lorris's text itself – and, in a particular way, beyond that of Chaucer's English version of around 1400.

The view, painted by a Flemish artist around 1500, contains much that is appropriate to the garden in the poem and shows three linked moments from the text (lines 630–730 in the French). It not only depicts all the features mentioned in the poem, but adds all sorts of extra details: raised beds, a clipped bush within a circular frame, a raised turf seat, and, most interesting, a carved nine-sided fountain, gushing water from nine gargoyle-heads down into a circular stone-rimmed basin, from which the surplus water runs into a carved stone channel.

This fountain is not in Lorris' poem. In the French, Lorris writes several times of 'fontaines', springs of water, which were 'clear' and 'fresh', without 'frogges', and pleasantly shaded by the trees; and of 'petiz ruisaus', small streams which had been made to run, babbling and sweetly, through channels. When Chaucer comes to translate 'fontaine' he does so each time with 'welle'; both with the various

47, 48   The first printed texts of the *Roman de la Rose* were illustrated by woodcuts which show the development of garden styles from the late Middle Ages until the early Renaissance. The earliest of the three woodcuts shown here and on page 93 dates from about 1481. It shows the Lover reaching the Rose in a crude garden surrounded by a wattle fence, a common feature of medieval gardens. The next (right), which dates from about 1494, shows him within a rectangular enclosure made of palings and with a bush clearly resembling a rose

'fontaines' or springs found in the garden, and with the particular 'Fontaine d'Amors' into which Narcissus and the lover gaze, where the water

> . . . welmeth up with waves bright
> The mountenance of two fynger hight.

It is a natural spring, and so too are the other 'fontaines' in Lorris's poem. The *fountain* in the painting is a – beautiful – anachronism. For the water to pour out of its raised spouts means raising the head of water higher than the level of the spouts, and this, in Lorris' time, would have been unlikely, as it would in Chaucer's England, though Boccaccio's Italy, in the 1350s, was beginning to think of such effects. By 1500 they were no longer rare. Late Gothic and early Renaissance illustrations often show fountains of this kind, and they are only a short way behind fountains which squirt their water *upwards,* defying gravity and reversing the natural order of things. The fountain in this illustration to the *Roman de la Rose* is a foretaste of the Renaissance, whose gardens will turn the fantasies of the Middle Ages into reality.

Many other late medieval works describe dream adventures set in similar 'pleasant places', for example the *Dit du Vergier* by Guillaume de Machaut (*c.* 1300–77) and the *Songe du Vergier* by P. de Maizières (1378).

In the middle years of the fourteenth century Giovanni Boccaccio began the *Decameron*. This work stands between the Middle Ages and the Renaissance, as do its gardens. The band of aristocratic story-tellers, who leave Florence and stay in various pleasant country villas to avoid the plague raging in the city, are pictured in several rural and garden scenes. Two in particular deserve attention: the garden described in the introduction to the Third Day, and the meadow described in the conclusion to the Sixth Day. The latter, the 'Valley of the Ladies', is an unfrequented, almost secret 'flowery mede'. It is so regular a valley, 'perfectly circular in shape', surrounded by hills of roughly similar size which descend in 'a regular series of terraces . . . like the tiers of an amphitheatre', and the trees on the plain and on the slopes (fruit trees facing south, and timber on the north-facing slopes) are 'so neatly arranged and symmetrically disposed' that the entire scene looks both designed by men, yet created by nature. Beneath the trees on the plain there is a 'continuous lawn of tiny blades of grass interspersed with flowers, many of them purple in colour.' As are all good 'flowery medes', this valley is crossed by a stream. It flows along 'a neat little channel to the centre of the plain', forming 'a tiny little lake like one of those fish ponds that prosperous townspeople occasionally construct in their gardens.'

While this scene is still medieval, with its quasi-hidden quality, its flower-strewn

49, 50   Two miniatures from the *Roman de la Rose*: Narcissus at the fountain (below), and the Lover, smitten with longing for the Rose, standing in front of the god of Love (right). The latter picture shows many details of a late-medieval garden – on the left, the arbour of carpenter's work, entwined with red and white roses, and on the right, behind the tree, a long turf seat, supported by a low brick wall. Behind this turf seat is a trellis framework for more climbing flowers, and an ornate fountain appears on the far side

51 In this woodcut from a 1529 edition of the *Roman de la Rose*, the fence has acquired a much more ornamental look than in earlier versions. The Lover's quick gesture belies the slow pace of the poem – it takes 12,000 lines to reach this point

grass, its encircling trees, the walled garden described in the introduction to the Third Day looks forward to the gardens of the Renaissance. Boccaccio's fancy suggests that, though walled and enclosed, and formal in its plan, it contains tame, free-running animals in abundance – 'as many as a hundred different varieties' – and twenty kinds of birds. This, with the claim that 'if Paradise were constituted on earth, it was inconceivable that it could take any other form', echoes past gardens of an ideal kind. But the rest of his description is, I think, as much forward-looking as imaginary. The garden was 'surrounded and criss-crossed by paths of unusual width, all as straight as arrows and overhung by pergolas of vines', fragrant, since they are in flower, and the paths 'along the edges of the garden were almost entirely hemmed in by white and red roses and jasmine.' The middle of the garden was a lawn, 'dotted all over with possibly a thousand different kinds of gaily-coloured flowers', and in the centre of the lawn, behold! 'a fountain of pure white marble, covered with marvellous bas-reliefs. From a figure standing on a column in the centre of the fountain, a jet of water, whether artificial or natural I know not . . . gushed high into the sky . . .' The water then passes to 'finely constructed artificial channels surrounding the lawn on all sides'. This gushing fountain, with its bas-reliefs, its column, its 'figure' and its surrounding 'artificial channels' could be found in many a Renaissance garden, constructed for pleasure and the delight of the senses. It is not impossibly far from the villa gardens, modelled on those of ancient Rome, which Alberti will recommend at the end of the fifteenth century.

52   A view over the fountain of
the lamps at the villa Lante,
designed by Vignola in 1564

6

The Renaissance Garden in Italy

For the gardens of the early Italian Renaissance, we must still turn to texts and to paintings rather than to real gardens. We are fortunate that texts are from this point frequent and explicit; though sometimes they suggest kinds of departure from medieval patterns and processes which may not have been imitated in fact. It is human enough that the ideas, the ideals, wishes, fancies and fantasies should outstrip men's sober, more cautious putting-into-practice; though sobriety is hardly a watchword in this most joyous and exuberant age.

For the basic pattern of the early Renaissance garden we may look to the writings of Leone Battista Alberti (1404–72). Alberti was among the first and most remarkable of the 'complete men' of the Renaissance. His life, his writings, his interests and sympathies seem to go the entire round of life, revealing an energy, a curiosity, enthusiasm and delight which are characteristic of his time. After listing Alberti's activities as an athlete, a musician, an artist, an architect and a writer, Jakob Burckhardt adds 'but the deepest spring of his nature has yet to be spoken of – the sympathetic intensity with which he entered into the whole life around him.'

Alberti's love for the Italian landscape appears in his *Del Governo della Famiglia*, in his praise of rural life, as lived in the country villa, with its gardens still enclosed, but sited on sloping ground, so that over the walls and from the loggias and porticoes of the building the landscape could be seen, surveyed and enjoyed: 'There you may enjoy clear, brilliant days and beautiful prospects over wooded hills and sunlit plains, and listen to the murmuring of fountains and of running streams that flow through the tufted grass.'

Is this so different from the pleasant retreats described a century earlier in the *Decameron*? But Boccaccio wrote no architectural treatise to back up this atmospheric, delightful idea. In Alberti's *De re aedificatoria*, he explains how a country house should be planned, and how its gardens and general setting should be designed and chosen. Looking at his phrases, it is obvious that Pliny is his guide. Alberti, loving the Italian countryside, not unreasonably loves also the Italian, the Roman past.

Most important, the site should be on sloping ground, to provide views, prospects – how important this idea was to be in succeeding centuries! – over the surrounding countryside. One's house should 'enjoy all the Pleasures and Conveniences of Air, Sun, and fine Prospects', so that you have 'a View of some City, Towns, the Sea, an open Plain, and the Tops of some known Hills and Mountains'. The garden still has walls (this is 'a very proper Defence against Malice or Rapine'), but with the slope one can see both inside and outside, having the 'Delights of Gardens, and the Diversions of Fishing and Hunting' close under one's eye. Although Alberti writes often enough about the *enclosed* nature of the garden, in a spacious courtyard with its portico, it is nonetheless open to sunshine and cooling breezes, and the courtyard and portico are to partake of the freshness and delight of the gardens. The pavements are to be stained 'in Imitation of the Bellflower weed, with its Branches twining about very beautifully', or inlaid with mosaic 'in Imitation of Garlands and Branches of Trees', while the walls are adorned with bas-reliefs and pictures. If your house is a grand one, maybe these pictures will show the 'memorable Actions of great Men', but for the more modest 'Pleasure-House and Gardens', you will have 'Pictures of pleasant Landskips, of Havens, of Fishing, Hunting, Swimming, Country Sports, of flowery Fields and thick Groves'. And, for perpetual refreshment of the eye, one should have 'Pictures of Springs, Cascades and Streams of Water'.

Nature, then, is brought inside, or at least into the portico of the villa; but Alberti is not advocating any wild rush to the jungle, for the villa itself extends reciprocally out into the garden. The garden is to be 'well-disposed', i.e. planned and ordered with care, echoing in its straight lines and curves 'those Figures that are most commended in the Plans of Houses, Circles, Semicircles, and the like', while the trees 'ought to be planted in Rows exactly even, and answering to one another exactly upon straight Lines'; a recommendation going all the way back to Xenophon's description of the gardens of Cyrus. From Pliny's *Letters* he takes the idea of topiary, with 'box shrubs clipped into innumerable shapes, some being letters which spell the gardener's name or his master's.'

Grottoes, too, he recommends, and again because the 'Ancients' had them. 'The Ancients used to dress the Walls of their Grottoes and Caverns with all manner of rough Work . . . and some I have known dawb them over with green Wax, in Imitation of the mossy Slime which we always see in moist Grottoes.' Grottoes must always have been popular in warm, often excessively warm countries, for refreshment and solace in the burning summer midday hours. They form a recurrent feature of the Italian garden, and sometimes, in a small garden, the gushing fountain set in a shaded recess is the *raison d'être* of the entire composition. Graced with statues of water-nymphs or river-gods, the mossy, rough-hewn stones become a setting hallowed by mythology, favoured by the Greeks and Romans. The nympheum, with nereids, Tritons, Oceanus, Neptune, dolphins, Tiber or Old Nile – classical precedents surge up from the sea and river and stream justifying a grotto in every garden.

Before passing on to the gardens which were created in Italy following Alberti's treatise, one more point must be mentioned. As we have noted, a villa garden should have a sloping site, and views over the countryside; but these views are not to be equally evident from every part of your garden; instead, there is to be the element of *surprise*, achieved if possible by siting the villa itself high up in the estate, so that one climbs gently but steadily up through the garden, and then, reaching the villa, discovers all the glories of the view. Of the siting of the villa, Alberti writes: 'I would have it stand pretty high, but upon so easy an Ascent, that it should hardly be perceptible to those that go to it, till they find themselves at the Top, and a large Prospect opens itself to their view.' This is particularly true of the villa Medici and the villa d'Este, but applies to some extent to many other Italian gardens, so often are they sited on hillsides. Montaigne in 1581 was to note the natural advantages which this gave to Italian gardens. Writing of Roman gardens, which were 'of singular beauty', he adds 'and here I learnt to what an extent art is aided by a hilly, steep and irregular site, for they [the Italians] derive advantages from this which cannot be matched in our level gardens, and they make the most skilful use of this variety in the terrain.'

THE DREAM OF POLIPHILUS

Beside the exuberant opening-out of the garden recommended by Alberti, there is in the Italian Renaissance a fantasy element which takes gardens far away from the mystery of the Christian religion into a pagan and hedonistic realm.

Some time after 1467, the monk Francesco Colonna (1433–1527) wrote his *Hypnerotomachia Poliphili*, which was published in Venice in 1499. It was translated into French in 1546, and a part of the book was translated into English in 1592 as *The Strife of Love in a Dreame*.

This work describes the dream-vision of Poliphilus, who in his dream passes through many fantastic scenes, driven by his love for the beautiful Polia. Wild forest, ruins, an enormous stepped pyramid, a dragon, enigmatic sculptures, colossal and perplexing statues, lavish palaces, and many pastoral and garden scenes are

described, and illustrated with precise and evocative woodcuts. The book had an immense influence on sixteenth- and seventeenth-century writers, artists and architects – for example, Rabelais, Spenser, Shakespeare, Bernini – who echoed, borrowed or pillaged the ideas and images in countless ways.

The gardens and garden-features described involve strange and exciting flights of fancy. Like Boccaccio, Colonna was delighted by flowers, whether wild or cultivated. The book contains the perfect description of a 'flowery mede', and we should remember that Colonna is the contemporary of Sandro Botticelli (1445–1510), whose 'Primavera', both in the actual grass and lawn where the figures tread so lightly, and in the breathtaking, unforgettable dresses belonging to these figures, at once recreates and perpetuates the old concept of a grassy field, scattered with springtime flowers. Poliphilus stands by a pool, 'hedged about with a fence of sweet roses and jessamine', and looks out at

> the plaine fieldes. It was wonderful to see the greens thereof, powdered with such variety of sundry sorted colours, and diverse fashioned flowers, as yellow Crowsfoot or golden Knop, Oxeye, *Satrion*, Dogges stone, the lesser Centorie, Mellilot, Saxifrage, Cowslops, Ladies fingers, wilde Chervile, or shepeardes Needle, *Navens* Gentil, Sinquifolie, Eyebright, Strawberies, with floures and fruites, wilde Columbindes, Agnus Castus, Millfoyle, Yarrow, wherewith *Achilles* did heale *Telephus*, and the rust of the same speares head that hurt him. Withe the white Muscarioli, bee floures and Panenentes in so beautifull and pleasant manner, that they did greatly comfort mee (having lost my selfe) but even with the looking uppon them.

Colonna was obviously intrigued by ruins as a background for reflection: he is, I think, the first modern European to indicate their appeal as a feature of the landscape. Early in his book he describes two colossal figures, of a man and of a woman. The man, although surrounded by 'a heape of ruinated, broken and downe-fallen marbles', is still above ground, and Poliphilus is able to enter the hollow colossus and explore the threescore paces of his outstretched frame, finding 'every part of man's body having upon it written his proper appellation in three ideomes, Chaldee, Greeke and Latine, that you might know the intrailes, sinews, bones, veines, muscles and the inclosed flesh, and what disease is bred there: the cause thereof, the cure and remedy.'

He describes an elaborate series of gardens round a palace. These, like medieval gardens, are still enclosed. But they are conceived with extravagance. The first 'greene Closure' is notable for the 'curious twisting of the branches and their green leaves . . . so artificially twisted and grown together, that you might ascend up by them, and not be seen in them, nor yet the way where you went up.' Another arbour is illustrated in the *Hypnerotomachia*, and conveys the idea of a combination of plants and architecture. This is 'a fine arbour of sweet jessamine in all to be painted and decked with the pleasant and odoriferous flowers of three sorts commixt.' A reconstruction of this very arbour has been made in England at Bowood, in Wiltshire.

Within the palace the garden continues in the long and lofty gallery, 'the roof whereof was all painted with a green foliature, with distinct flowers of folded leaves, and little flying birds.' How many galleries have been decorated in such a way! Certainly we read about them in Alberti's treatise, and even earlier. But the surrounding galleries and rooms with their roofs painted to resemble leafy arbours, vines or tree houses date from the Renaissance, and they are one of the most delightful signs of the way which villa and garden in Italy became truly a part of each other. Colonna's gallery has its contemporary equivalent in the Sala delle Asse in the Castello Sforzesco in Milan, where a painted ceiling of intertwined branches was probably the work of Leonardo da Vinci.

Leaving the palace, Poliphilus is shown a series of gardens which become more and more fantastic. One has golden wire and gold and silver creations, not living plants; another has topiary work, not in box or in yew, but in spun glass. Poliphilus passes on to view a giant maze; yet not with paths which one follows on foot, for it is a

53   A woodcut from the *Hypnerotomachia Poliphili* (1499). To the left, the narrator Poliphilus stands with his mistress Polia, looking on a scene of tumbled classical ruins. Colonna is one of the first writers to appreciate the aesthetic appeal of ruins in a landscape – a theme which reached its fullest expression in the landscape gardens of the eighteenth century. In the early years of the Renaissance, such fantastic sights were still a feature of the city of Rome, where medieval buildings stood amid the gigantic debris of the past

water labyrinth, and the seekers must travel by boat. Then comes an enclosure where 'the boxes and Cyprus trees' were all 'silk' and 'the leaves, flowers, and outermost rind were of fine silk, wanting in store of pearls to beautify the same.' Round the closure were seats of 'marvellous and incredible sumptuousness', covered over with 'histories of life and venerie' and within the garden 'leaves, grass, and flowers of silk like a fair sweet meadow; in the midst whereof, there was a large and goodly arbour, made with gold wire and overspread with roses of the like work, more beautiful to the eye, than if they had been growing roses.'

Rabelais too echoes Colonna's garden, in his *Cinquiesme Livre* (1563) where Pantagruel and his friends visit the land of satin, in which the 'trees and herbage never lose their leaves or flowers, and are all damask and flowered velvet. As for the beasts and birds, they are all of tapestry work.' But Rabelais is not enchanted – the birds don't sing, and when the narrator plucks the fruit, hanging from a piece of tapestry, 'the devil a bit I could chew or swallow; and had you had them betwixt your teeth, you would have sworn they had been thrown with silk; there was no morsel of savour in them.'

The English translation of the *Hypnerotomachia*, *The Strife of Love in a Dreame* (1592), stops rather less than half way through Colonna's book. Yet the second half of the book contains the most elaborate description of a 'perfect' garden ever written. Poliphilus eventually reaches the island of Cythera, the home of the goddess of love, and this entire island is conceived as a garden. Curiously, it is set in level ground, so that there are not the hillside views characteristic of the Italian Renaissance garden. The climate is constant, with no storms, and the garden-realm is itself exactly circular, with a tinier circular island and palace at its centre, set in a circular river. Twenty radial walks lead out like spokes from the centre, and these are cut into at regular intervals by circular walks. The hedges, topiary-work statuary and colonnades which divide up the sections, and the filling-in of the sections with intricate knots are described, and involve fantastic elaboration and extravagance. Woodcuts support the complicated explanations of the text, from the overall plan to the fiddly and bizarre topiary figures which stand at the corners of the beds. One of the most extreme conceptions is the giant carrying two castles above his shoulders, yet this no stranger than the topiary which actually existed in the garden of the villa Quaracchi in Florence, built around 1459 by Giovanni Rucellai: 'spheres, porticoes, temples, vases, urns, apes, donkeys, oxen, a bear, giants, men, women, warriors, a harpy, philosophers, Popes, Cardinals.'

The Isolotto of the Boboli gardens in Florence, an oval island, decked with orange and lemon trees, and set in an oval lake surrounded with regular hedges of clipped bay is powerfully reminiscent of Colonna's island of Cythera. Guide-books may hint that the Isolotto was inspired by the circular island in Hadrian's villa at Tivoli. Maybe; both are of similar shape. But the Isolotto is first and foremost a garden island, not an architectural one, and in this it is derived from Colonna's Cythera, where the architecture is always subordinate to the idea of the garden. The twin entrances to the garden island of the Isolotto, pairs of pillars crowned with the capricorn symbols of Cosimo I, and flanked by Triton fountains, could come from the pages of the *Hypnerotomachia*.

THE VILLA MEDICI

After writing of so many gardens which no longer exist, it is a perplexing delight to write of the gardens of Renaissance Italy; scores of them exist, many are superb, and the difficulty is in choosing which to describe. The villa Medici in Rome is an excellent beginning, since its plan is still medieval, while its detail is of the Renaissance. The villa was begun in 1544, and the garden laid out at the same time by Annibale Lippi. In 1580 it was bought by Cardinal Ferdinand de' Medici, who brought here in 1584 a collection of sculptures and reliefs which were incorporated in the garden façade of the villa or set in the garden. On the outside this villa is not ornate, but from the garden side its encrustations of sculpture and porcelain give it great richness. Extending to one side of the villa is a terrace supported on columns, with arched recesses in between, to form an arcade for the display of classical statues.

54, 55 Woodcuts from Colonna's *Hypnerotomachia* (1499), illustrating the adornments of the circular garden-island of Cythera: top, a giant in topiary work; above, an intricate knot pattern

56   A detail (right) from Falda's
view (1683) of the gardens of the
villa Medici, showing a round
mount, encircled by tall trees,
probably cypresses, and
approached, from the left,
through a closely planted wood.
The figure '4' indicates the long
terrace looking down on to the
main gardens, further to the left.
To the right are smaller knot
gardens, while the villa itself
stands overlooking the main
gardens, beyond the bottom left-
hand corner of this view

57   Term statues guard the
stairway which leads to the mount
at the villa Medici. The ascent,
now thickly shaded with ilex,
leads up to a small pavilion, a
belvedere. While climbing the
steps, the visitor is prevented
from seeing far to left or right,
and so the spectacular view at the
top, out over the city of Rome, is
all the more enjoyable

The fountain in the courtyard has a copy of Bologna's 'Mercury', and an Egyptian obelisk stood in front of the terrace. This much could come from the *Hypnerotomachia*, but the plan of the main garden is in no way advanced from the assemblage of squares characteristic of medieval gardens. But the garden does incorporate a feature which fulfils Alberti's requirements to the letter. From the top of the long terrace, backed by a grove or *bosco* of ilex, we look down into the main garden. If we turn round, a heavily shaded walk leads through the trees to a stairway flanked by Terms. The stairs take us steeply up to the top of a circular mount, with the evergreen ilex thickly grouped round its sides. At the summit there is a belvedere, a gazebo, and from it we see the domes and turrets and rooftops of Rome. In the whole world of gardens I know of no more beautiful 'surprise'. When Evelyn saw the mount in 1644, he thought it represented a 'fortress', but in Falda's views of 1683 it is called a 'Mausoleo', and this is a more likely intention, since there is in Rome the cone-shaped 'mausoleum of Augustus', which was converted to a garden by one of the Soderini family, and had trees growing round it in a similar way – Du Pérac's *Vestigi dell' Antichità di Roma* (1575) calls it 'un bellissimo giardino'.

THE VILLA D'ESTE

No garden in the world is more exuberant than the great water-garden of the villa d'Este at Tivoli. It was begun around 1550, and completed in the 1580s, to the design of the architect Pirro Ligorio (*c.* 1520–83). Ligorio was commissioned to design the villa itself and the garden in 1550, when Cardinal Ippolito II d'Este was appointed Governor of Tivoli by Pope Julius III. Ligorio was principally an architect, but was, like Alberti, a man of many other interests – artist, garden designer, antiquarian – and this alliance is apparent in the gardens of the villa d'Este, where the overall conception is geometric and architectural, where sculpture and mosaic are extremely important in the details of the fountains, where landscape design is involved in the wide views over the Campagna towards Rome, and where paintings indoors of country scenes match the landscape outside.

Ligorio's interest in classical antiquity is apparent in several ways, principally his acceptance of Alberti's precepts concerning the siting and layout of the garden. The villa d'Este enjoys views 'that overlook the city, the owner's land, the sea or a great plain', and the plan of the garden is so arranged that one should enter at the bottom, and follow 'gently rising paths towards the house', culminating after many a delight in 'astonishment at the view when one arrives at the top.' Within this framework, classical antiquity reappears in the Rometta or Little Rome, the models, in stone, of buildings and monuments representing ancient Rome. This harks back to the *topia* of the Roman garden, as does Ligorio's Ovato fountain, which is thought, in this garden of rich and splendid and spectacular fountains, to be the most beautiful of them all. The Ovato fountain (named after the egg-shaped motif), flowing out in a great rounded cascade beneath a giant statue of the Albunean Sibyl, was designed by Ligorio after examining the *triclinium* of the Canopus at Hadrian's villa.

The terrace of the Hundred Fountains, now crumbling and thick with moss, used to have between its sculptured eagles, ships and fleurs-de-lys a series of terracotta bas-reliefs, telling the stories of Ovid's *Metamorphoses*. Another fountain related to the revival of learning is the Owl fountain, designed by Giovanni del Luca and executed by Raffaello Sangallo. Its idea comes directly from the *Pneumatica* of Hero of Alexandria, a text written in the first century AD but not printed until 1575.

The villa d'Este is the most complete water garden in the world, with infinitely varied water spectacles, from the majestic Organ fountain to the tiny rivulets and cascades along the climbing ramps leading to the villa, the hissing central jet of the Dragon fountain, the extravagant multiplicity of jets and sprays and streams of the long, breathtaking Hundred Fountains, and the quiet and most marvellously comforting reflections of the tranquil fish-pond pools.

Water, the life of the garden, is openly linked with the idea of fertility. Now set in the lower boundary wall of the garden, but originally at the centre of the Organ fountain is the joyously fecund statue of Diana of the Ephesians – many-breasted, larger than life, with streams of water gushing from each nipple. This fountain may startle us with its frankness, but the garden of the villa d'Este is characteristic of the Renaissance in its jubilant credo of delight. High upon the ramps leading to the villa are two small female sphinxes, each spurting water from large and handsome breasts. This is the public statement of enjoyment, pleasure, entertainment: through the sight and sound of water gleaming and splashing; through the sensual appeal of these statues; through amusement, both scholarly, with the models of the Rometta, and simple and ingenious, with the trick water effects which used once to wet unwary visitors and with the acoustic devices in the fountains producing the sounds of music, trumpets, birds and cannon.

The delight of the villa d'Este is aristocratic – no poor man, and no uneducated man, could create this paradise – and though the garden is open, ascending the hillside to claim domination over the countryside spread before the windows and balconies of the villa, it is a garden which combines ostentatious public spectacles with moments of surprise and variety. Visitors gazing at the Ovato fountain may not notice the cool, shaded stone dining tables set in the far corners of the enclosure, where select and courtly parties might appreciate, in tranquil privacy, the fountain's inexhaustible grace and power.

The villa d'Este has known countless visitors, and these visitors have seen it in its early glory, in its years of decay, and in its present tidy, splendid, yet unmysterious and overcrowded state. Montaigne in 1580s had never seen its like outside Italy, and thought it marvellous; Frenchman in the early 1700s, comparing it with the vastness and arrogance of Versailles, were often contemptuous, and in the 1760s both Fragonard and Hubert Robert were moved to admire, and to sketch and to paint its melancholy decay. A century later the composer Liszt stayed there, and his 'Jeux d'eau à la Villa d'Este' and 'Cyprès de la Villa d'Este' evoke something of this rich sadness.

Today the garden is a part of the age of *son et lumière*, and a million people come each year. It is great and glorious, triumphant and beautiful. But the mystery has gone.

THE VILLA LANTE

Today the villa Lante, Bagnaia, is the most perfectly kept of all Renaissance gardens, since it was extensively and faithfully restored in 1954. It must be visited if the nature of the greatest sixteenth-century gardens is to be understood. Not to visit it, is to neglect one of the rarest masterpieces of garden art.

It was designed and begun in 1564 by Vignola (1507–73), who died before work was completed in the 1580s. His first patron was Cardinal Ottaviano Riario, followed by Cardinal Giovanni Francesco Gambara. After Gambara's death in 1587 the building was brought to completion by Cardinal Alessandro Montalto. Beside the villa d'Este, the villa Lante is small. It has a slim rectangular garden, descending in terraces down a wooded slope, with a watercourse directed down the central sloping axis, from a grotto at the very top towards the square pool in the lowest garden area. The villa is in two parts: a pair of identical casinos built one on each side of the central axis, and a little more than half-way down the garden. This exceptional procedure gives the garden an importance in the composition which it rarely has elsewhere. At the villa d'Este, the casino is not given so much attention, though it is large, since the garden is so demanding; but one is never in any doubt that it is there, and that sooner or later in one's marvelling ascent, it will be reached; but at the villa Lante the two buildings are silent. Even their identical appearance suggests the modesty of Montaigne's scepticism, 'ny l'un ny l'autre'; and while they wait, elegant yet undemanding, the garden is there to be enjoyed.

Entirely to one side and barely noticeable from the formal garden is a much larger *bosco,* designed as a hunting park, but with several fountains and a maze. The maze has gone, but the fountains, including the lovely Pegasus fountain, remain.

The villa Lante is a quiet water garden. Nowhere is there the roar of Este's Organ fountain, but water trickles or splashes or sprays on every terrace. From the rough grotto at the top it falls through moss and ferns to a pool (this grotto, like that at the villa Aldobrandini, suggests the rustic origin of gardens), reappears in the carved and angular fountain of the Dolphins (the natural stream has been tamed) and then flows, between hedges and overshadowing trees, down the *cordonata* or chain cascade – a device and a movement and a sound of incomparable life and elegance. Beside this cascade, the 'ordinary' step cascades or water stairways of the villa Aldobrandini or Chatsworth or Caserta may go hang. They are bigger, grander, and duller – by far. There is another *cordonata* cascade at Caprarola, but when I saw it, it was dry. Only the *chadar* of the Islamic garden can approach this delight of water falling yet controlled, murmuring yet smooth. The garden of the villa Lante acquires elegance, control and order as it descends. From terrace to terrace the garden widens, with balustrades extending to either side, and allowing each time a fuller and a further view across the countrysida˙ Between the fountains of the Giants and of the Lamps, which control the central terraces, the watercourse wells up inside a long dining table of stone, filling its central trough to cool the cardinal's wine (a device taken no doubt from the one in Varro's aviary). At the villa d'Este, such *al fresco* dining is to one side, for the middle of the garden is too public; but here, even on the central axis, in the shade of plane trees, all is on a scale which is to the measure of enjoyment, not grandeur. At Schloss Hellbrunn, near Salzburg, the stone dining table (with its water jokes, soaking the diners between one course and the next) is modelled on this one at Bagnaia; but it lacks Lante's modesty.

At this level the balustrade overlooks the lowest and most formal part of the garden, with the casinos well back on either side. Beyond is the town, beyond that the plain, as Sitwell says, 'stretching out mile after mile, league after league, day's journey after day's journey, until at last the purple distance melts at the world's edge into a silvery gleam of sea . . .' Here at the villa Lante the details of the Campagna are different from those seen from the hillside villas of Frascati, or from Tivoli, or from the secret garden at Caprarola; but the principle and the effect are essentially the same.

When Montaigne saw the villa Lante in 1581, only one of the casinos had been built, but the square formal garden was almost complete. At the centre there was a pyramidal fountain, now replaced by a fountain-star and the Montalto crest, held aloft by Bologna's four 'Moors'. The fountain is on a circular island joined by four bridges to the shores of a square lake, with a little stone island or boat in each quarter, and round this square lake are the formal knots, in box and yew and gravel, with lemon trees to give variety to the corners. (In the eighteenth century the four beds along each side were combined to make two scrollwork parterres, with a happy lengthening effect on the composition as a whole.) Montaigne's description could apply, more or less, today:

> There is a tall pyramid which casts out water in several different ways: here it shoots up, here it falls. Round the pyramid are four small fair lakes, clear and pure and brimming with water. In the middle of each is a little stone boat, with two men carrying arquebuses in each, who draw up water and shoot it at the pyramid; there is a trumpet in each boat which likewise draws up water. Round this pyramid and the lakes are the most lovely walks, with stone balustrades carved with great art.

THE GIARDINO SEGRETO

While the villa Medici and the villa d'Este are gardens which are 'public' throughout, there is in the Italian Renaissance a tradition of private gardens, *giardini segreti*, hidden or discreetly tucked away. The extent of their privacy varies – some are by no means 'secret' – but the intention is the same, to provide an intimate area where garden and water delights may be enjoyed away from the full gaze of other visitors. At the villa Lante, even though the scale of the garden is not overwhelming, such a *giardino segreto* exists, to one side of the grotto, at the top of the watercourse; a minute space which the unknowing visitor passes by in his eagerness to discover the pleasures of the grotto and fountains beyond. In Rome, the villa di Papa Giulio, begun in 1550, contains a – more or less – secluded and sunken area, the

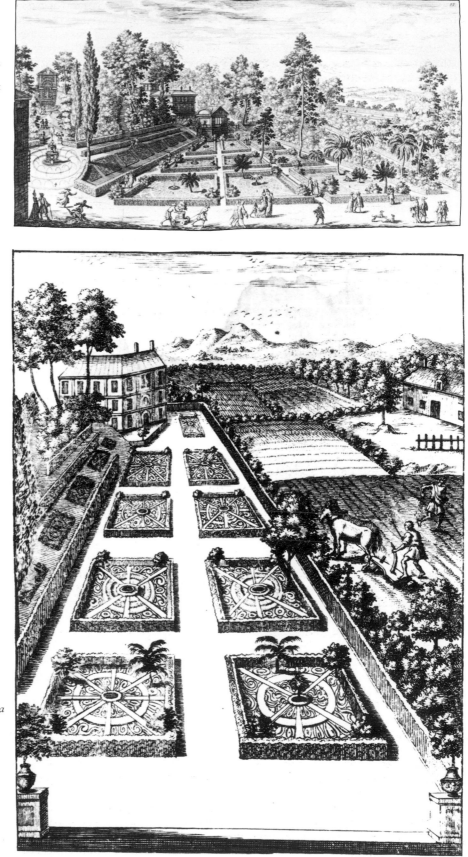

58   The villa Pia, within the gardens of the Vatican, from Falda's *Giardini di Roma* (1683). This view shows the seventeenth-century formal garden outside the villa Pia. The garden building was designed by Pirro Ligorio in 1560 as a private retreat for the Pope. It enjoyed a view over the knot garden, while maintaining considerable privacy within the oval vestibule between the two buildings in the centre of the picture

59   Timothy Nourse's *Campania Foelix* of 1700 imitates Falda's view of the villa Pia, but the details have changed. The patterns of the knots and the planting of individual trees remain the same, but the house has become English, like the surrounding countryside. Nourse's frontispiece hovers on the edge of Addison's phrase of 1712: 'a Man might make a pretty Landskip of his own Possessions'

nymphaeum, set in the centre of the garden, and yet not visible from the principal courtyard. Looking from the main entrance one sees right across the courtyard, through a colonnade, and *over* the nymphaeum to a further garden on the other side. Here, as Sitwell says, 'one may dine in a watery saloon, surrounded by running streams and bubbling fountains.' This cool and shaded, sculptured and be-fountained semi-circle, adored with mosaic, and approached down curving stairways from the upper level of the gardens, responds to the grottoes of the ancients described by Alberti: part mossy cave, part treasury of sculpture, part house, and yet part garden as well. The architects and artists are not certain: Michaelangelo, Ammanati and Vignola were involved, and Vasari himself claims to have taken part. At the upper level of the nymphaeum the inner walls were once faced with painted landscape scenes, bringing the 'countryside' into the enclosure. In the same way, the main courtyard of the villa has a sumptuous open colonnade which is still decorated with frescoes of trellis, vines and birds, to bring the 'garden' within the building.

Among secret gardens the most beautiful is at Caprarola, not far from Viterbo. Here in 1547–9 a palace (pentagonal, with the shape and massive proportions of a fortress) was built by Vignola for Cardinal Alessandro Farnese. Behind two sides of the palace, beyond a moat, were set a pair of formal gardens, and then, decades later, Vignola designed a *giardino segreto* around a smaller building, the villa Farnese, which was not completed until 1587, fourteen years after his death. This private garden is far removed from the giant splendours of the palace, through thick concealing woods. It is approached up a sloping causeway, between high walls, and with a *cordonata* cascade which should lisp and whisper, flash and gleam down the central incline. At the top, reclining river gods support a fountain, and beyond and above this is the casino. The garden itself is invisible until the summit of this incline is reached; and then, walking to left or right of the fountain, the visitor steps up into the first half of the garden: an area of box hedges, watered by fountains, and with the most marvellous open wall in existence. This garden, raised up among the surrounding trees, is enclosed on three sides with a low parapet, along which are spaced a line of lofty *canephori*, stone statues bearing urns upon their heads.

Behind the casino is a further garden, raised up and reached by steps lined with spouting fish, fountains and shells. This garden is the most private place, with trees all round, yet the elegance and extravagance are as great here as in the open splendours of the villa d'Este. The flowerbeds, now desolate, are bordered with sculptured stone, and were each set with fountains, while the paths were adorned with mosaic patterns in coloured pebbles. Today, the one remaining fountain plays with a solitary grace Vignola did not intend. The villa Farnese is now more secret than any cardinal could have imagined; yet no less beautiful.

Two other gardens must be mentioned for their privacy: within Rome, the garden of the palazzo Borghese (begun in 1590, designed by Flaminio Ponzio), and in the country, the *giardino segreto* of the villa Ruspoli at Vignanello (*c*. 1600). The first, in the heart of the city, is small, tightly enclosed by high walls, but richly clothed with creeping plants, and alive with the music of fountains. Evelyn admired it in 1644. At the villa Ruspoli, beside the broad and noble garden of box hedges, there is a narrow lower terrace, which is invisible from the village below and accessible only from a concealed staircase. This terrace has the appeal of a forbidden country – glimpsed, desired, yet beyond our reach.

THE VILLA ALDOBRANDINI

The Renaissance garden enters a new stage at the villa Aldobrandini in Frascati. Suddenly, and this appears to have no specially convincing garden precedents, the villa is set, tall and spreading, in the very middle of the garden, in the most commanding spot, with the dominant view. While there are many other ways of seeing, visiting and enjoying the garden, there is only *one* supreme view; that from the house itself. Indeed, the view is only superlative and absolute from one point in the house, to which we shall in due course return.

The villa and the gardens were both begun in the last years of the sixteenth

XII   Diana of the Ephesians (right), many-breasted goddess of fecundity. This openly pagan fountain-statue at the villa d'Este typifies the joyous exuberance which pervades the gardens. She once stood in the centre of the Organ fountain, but has been removed to a quieter spot in the lower section of the garden

XIII   The Hundred Fountains (far right, top) at the villa d'Este stretch almost the whole width of the gardens. The main sculptured motifs are eagles, boats and fleurs-de-lys, spouting delicate threads of water, which fall and flow into the lines of downward-pouring jets

XIV   Inspired by the outdoor dining tables described by Pliny and Varro, the stone dining table at the villa Lante (far right, bottom) has a long water-filled trough running down the centre for cooling the wine. Plane trees provide partial shade, while fountains splash nearby, and the view extends over the village rooftops and across the Campagna

60   This detail (below) from M. Greuter's panorama of 1620 shows a bird's eye view of the villa Aldobrandini. The villa itself stretches from left to right across the steeply sloping garden

XV Princely privacy – a view of the *canephori* in the *giardino segreto* of the villa Farnese, Caprarola (left). Wholly hidden from the fortress-like palace and its formal garden, this elegant and perfectly formed Renaissance retreat would have been appreciated by Pliny as sharing many qualities of a Roman garden – statues, fountains, clipped hedges, shaded and sunny walks, and a villa which enjoyed all these as well as the distant view

century, created for Cardinal Pietro Aldobrandini in 1598–1604. They are the work of Giacomo della Porta and Carlo Maderno, while the frescoes within the villa are by the Cavaliere d'Arpino. Much visited, much commented-on, the villa Aldobrandini is the best known of the cluster of hillside villas and gardens at Frascati, and although its gardens are now partly overgrown, and a sad restraint lies on its fountains and waterworks, its arrogance and beauty can move us still.

As with so many Italian gardens, that at the villa Aldobrandini is on a hillside – a steep one, with as superb a view as any. The garden begins (like that at the villa Lante) high up on a wooded slope, with a grotto from which the central source of water flows, proceeding downwards in a variety of falls, cascades, jets and rills, following the central and sloping axis directly towards the middle of the façade of the villa. After five or six stages – not far different from those of the villa Lante, though steeper and therefore more boisterous – the tumbling stream reaches the water theatre, a vast and lofty semi-circle of wall, recessed with niches and statuary, facing the villa across a spacious courtyard. In its course downwards from the grotto to the water theatre, we can follow the water through a rough and rocky cascade, a simple, sloping channel with narrow sides, a broad yet steep water stairway, and among the

61 A detail from one of Falda's views of the villa Aldobrandini shows how the water flows down the central axis towards the 'water theatre'. This view is taken from the commanding viewpoint, from the upper and central section of the villa itself: while the many visitors below are obviously entertained with the spectacle of sculptures, fountains and water jokes, they do not enjoy the whole view in the way that the master does

most extravagant and lavish of all the Renaissance water features to survive anywhere in Europe – a pair of tall stone pillars, flanking the water stairway. The water spurts from the top of these pillars, to race headlong down their sides, following channels which coil round and round the sides of the pillars like helter-skelters. At the bottom of the final cascade the water splashes and sprays over and down into the many sections of the water theatre, at the centre of which stands Atlas, bearing a watery globe upon his shoulders.

As at the villa d'Este, all the water-works at the villa Aldobrandini are fed from the central stream, coming from so high up on the slope of the hill that its gravity feed is adequate even for the towering pillars of the helter-skelter. This feature looks pale, dull even, when dry, but with the water bursting from the top, and coursing down and round the sides, the pillars are among the proudest marvels of garden architecture.

Beneath, on each side of the water theatre, the walls open into shady rooms which contained water-marvels once much admired, though now vanished. Evelyn wrote in 1645 of 'an artificial grot, wherein are curious rocks, hydraulic organs, and all sorts of singing birds, moving and chirping by force of the water.' The rooms are now empty, and we must rely on the comments of past travellers, and the handful of engravings by Falda and Venturini which survive.

Significantly, the villa itself is the main object which visitors in the gardens see as they follow the water downwards from its source. The view is hemmed in by the tall, straightly clipped ilex *bosco*, and only the master himself, from his exalted vantage-point, could see both the garden and the views of the countryside beyond. For the villa, though it stretches right across the gardens, is very narrow, with a depth of a single spacious room or two smaller ones. The master had but to turn round to be able to look downwards across the Campagna from the other side of his gallery.

This second view, from the *front* of the villa, passes today over the most superb, indeed arrogant clipped ilex hedges I have seen. They extend between the main gates of the villa and the beginning of the curving ramp which leads to the front of the villa itself. Early engravings show these hedges as having fairly modest proportions, and serving partly to guide the eye towards the villa from the entrance gates, and partly as a screen to hide the fruit trees and knots and smaller divisions of the front garden area. But today they have grown to a prodigious height, and have been trained to arch right across the *allée* leading to the villa, so that one massive and autocratic line of hedge sweeps up towards the villa.

The villa's unique and commanding situation, enjoying the *spectacle* of the gardens as from the central and best vantage-point in a theatre, is a development which leads accurately and significantly towards the garden art of the seventeenth century. Many gardens in the 1600s remain, naturally enough, firmly and beautifully planned in the spirit of delight of earlier Italian gardens, where surprise, variety and individual enjoyment are as important as a sense of overall unity. We may think of the villa Garzoni, at Collodi in Tuscany, or the villa Massini at Massa di Carrara. But the main developments will follow what is done at the villa Aldobrandini in the direction of control, so that gardens will come to show (and be clearly seen to show) the authority of the owner, whose power extends from his house, and characteristically from the principal and central viewpoint of his house, out over the gardens and countryside. But this development belongs essentially to France and to the seventeenth century, when the delight, serenity and more human glories of the Italian Renaissance garden have already reached their joyous and unmatched perfection. 'Chacun à son goût': myself, I know of no gardens to equal those of Italy.

BOMARZO

The grounds of the villa Orsini at Bomarzo are the Zimbabwe of gardens. Created for Vicino Orsini in the 1560s, there is a brief reference in 1564 to the 'Teatri, e Mausolei' of Bomarzo, but scarcely any other known references to them in contemporary records, and they were not commented on by travellers or garden enthusiasts until this century. The grounds are separated from the fortress-villa

62 This enigmatic statue smiles across the indecipherable garden of Bomarzo. No plan or description survives from the 1560s, when the gardens were created, and the modern visitor sees the strange statues, carvings and buildings at Bomarzo in a setting of trees and paths which has little connection with the original scene

Orsini by several hundred yards – there is no villa or dwelling-place of any kind in the grounds, nor does it appear that there ever was one – and the arrangement of the many garden features over the sloping and rocky site seems capricious and perplexing. Scattered up and down the hillside are some twenty, at least, huge statues of human beings, gods and goddesses, animals and monsters; a leaning house; an amphitheatre; an open colonnade rather like a forum; a temple; a fragment of a colossal ruin, and other stone features, for the most part carved directly from rocks which protrude from the sloping ground.

Practically all these objects are 'fantastic', in size, in detail, in conception, and in juxtaposition one with another, and present an unexplained, continuing puzzle. The architect, designer and sculptor are unknown. The plan of the whole is no longer clear: there may once have been a sequence, an order for viewing these giants, monsters and weird animals, but it is not known, and the meaning of many of the carvings is also obscure. The *atmosphere* of the place is certainly reminiscent of Colonna and the *Hypnerotomachia*; but no written evidence exists to support either this, or any other suggested inspiration for the garden.

The enormous tortoise, carrying a tall, stately female figure on its back, is relatively easy to appreciate: a presentation of Fame, moving slowly but firmly forward. But why should this carving be set aside in a quiet and unnoticed part of the grounds? And the dragon, rending a smaller animal (maybe a lion-cub), or the war-elephant, little less than life-sized, and crushing a soldier with its trunk?

'Elephanti leoni orsi orchi et draghi' states one of the inscriptions. For us today, more of a mystery than in the mid-sixteenth century. The modern trees, dense round these silent carvings, add to the secrecy of the place, for they have no regular order, follow no avenues or axes, and thin out unexpectedly to show us a line of giant pine-cones, or, between the monsters and the *tempietto*, the three-headed, watchful Cerberus, and at last open to the central glade in this *sacred wood*, where the small and perfect temple stands. This may have been built as a mausoleum for Orsini's wife; but it has no Christian symbolism. It is a jewel in stone, but a jewel whose dedication is unknown, inscrutable.

Our journey through the garden of Bomarzo may not be as dreamlike, as fearful, as fantastic as that of Poliphilus; but this garden shares the spirit of Colonna's strange *Hypnerotomachia*.

THE VILLA GARZONI AND THE VILLA GASPERO MASSINI

There is no end to the delights of the Italian garden: fine examples can be found in Florence, in the Boboli gardens, or outside, at Pratolino; further north, near Venice or along the Brenta, and at Milan and Genoa. They continue to be made into the eighteenth century, though suffering from French influence; and suffering again, alas!, from the simplifying tendencies associated with the English landscape garden.

In the mid-seventeenth century three Italian gardens should be mentioned: the villa Garzoni, near Collodi in Tuscany; the villa Gaspero Massini, outside Massa di Carrara, and the garden-island of Isola Bella in Lake Maggiore. This last garden is discussed later, as it forms the concluding flourish of Renaissance garden fantasy.

Work on the gardens of the villa Garzoni began in 1652. They are large, on a steep hillside with splendid views, and the firmly geometrical plan, with a central axis down which water spouts, spurts and flows, and with walks and avenues at right angles to this axis is reminiscent of the villa Lante. So too is the progression from simpler to more formal effects, from a tiny grotto to fountains, a water staircase, terraces with sculpture, and a final large formal garden at the foot; and so is the unobtrusive nature of the villa, sited high up on one side of the gardens. But the resemblance is more in theory than in feeling. The gardens here are bustling and open and brash: the central complex of stairs coping with three terraces in a single architectural feature is one which demands a throng of visitors; while the immense yew hedges, which cross the garden and are pierced with embrasures to hold the busts of emperors and to allow lesser mortals to peep out to the magnificence below, cast regimented blocks of shade, not the dappled patterns which come from the plane trees at the villa Lante. It is a different mood, less intimate, though still intriguing: the maze and the delicious hedge theatre to the side are hidden, and the long hedges are closed with statues, most often in terracotta, whose details, be it of dwarf, peasant, Turk or naked philosopher, still enchant. The greatest difference from the villa Lante is in the main formal garden; two circular pools, with fountains, the bedding of great intricacy. Allowing for the present planting, which is happily anachronistic, it has a cheery and theatrical opulence, which would make it a fit setting for an opera. At the villa Lante, the mood is more delicate, glowing and shaded, quiet and sparkling by turns: one would expect poetry, or madrigals.

At the very end of the century the terrace garden of the villa Gaspero Massini was built on the outskirts of Massa di Carrara, at that time the capital of a tiny principality. The villa was then the country pleasure house of the prince, who had a palace in town, and a medieval castle on the mountain above.

The villa is backed by a hill, and looks over towards the town, and up to the distant castle, outlined against the sky. Joined to one side of the villa is a sequence of terraces, approximately L-shaped in plan, with a small garden enclosed between the villa and the right angle of the terraces. The terraces themselves rise up in four stages, with an ever-widening view across the countryside. They are open, spacious colonnades facing outwards, some roofless like pergolas, and others covered and arcaded with recesses for sculpture and urns, and connected by easy staircases to allow a long and varied promenade, keeping in the sun or in the shade as the season suggests. It is like a tiny land-locked section of the terrace gardens at Isola Bella, rising up and up like the poop of a ship; or rather, it is like such a section from Isola Bella, had that wonder fallen into decay. Today these inland terraces are crumbling, and a jungle of creepers and thorns and weeds spreads among the plaster mouldings, tilting the urns, choking the promenades; but the garden is genuine, and its sculptures have not yet been packed off to newer and less lovely homes. Built in the

63   At the villa Garzoni, begun in 1652, the steep central axis leading to the formal area at the bottom of the slope is rather like that of the villa Lante. But the balustraded terraces and stairways are much more prominent, and give a feeling of bustle and activity far removed from Lante's repose

64 The wildly overgrown terraces of the villa Gaspero Massini, just outside Massa di Carrara in Tuscany. The complex series of terraces, backing on to the steep hillside, was built at the end of the seventeenth century and has views over the town of Massa and up towards the late medieval fortress on the mountain opposite. The extravagance of the repeated arches and columns, the urn-topped balustrades and lavish statuary are a continuing part of the sheer enjoyment of the Renaissance garden

1690s, it has a curious literary importance, for Massa di Carrara, Voltaire tells us in *Candide*, almost became the home of the 'vieille', the old woman who looks after the heroine Cunégonde. In her youth she was betrothed to a 'Prince of Massa di Carrara'; but on her wedding-day, he was poisoned by a jealous mistress, and so . . .

* * *

The Italian Renaissance garden did not die when the French formal garden achieved such fame in the 1660s, but subsided for a while. Italian architects were still employed – as at Wilhelmshöhe near Kassel, where the great cascade was begun in 1701 by the architect G. F. Guerniero – and gardens of a distinctly Italian style were still created, one of the most beautiful outside Italy being in Sweden, at Sandemar, begun around 1700. Here the site is barely sloping, but the view leads out to an arm of the sea near Stockholm, and Alberti would not condemn it. It has, like all gardens of an Italian stamp, prominent hedges and sculpture, giving fine vertical strength to the scheme, rather like the monumental yews in the English Victorian garden at Biddulph in Staffordshire or the less massive, but more consciously Italian hedges of Sir George Sitwell's garden at Renishaw, in Derbyshire. Colour and variety come from the contrasting greens of hedge and grass, from the pale gravel, and the gleaming white of the painted (and so jaunty) wooden statuary; and its scale is exactly that of the true Italian garden: no arrogance, no bleakness, but always enjoyment. The visitor is not overawed, not ignored, but courteously received: *Come in, and welcome.*

65   Water jokes at the villa
Mondragone, at Frascati, from
Falda's *Fontane di Roma* (1675)

7

Jokes and Puzzles

THE JOKE FOUNTAIN

Fountain *joyeusetés* go well back into the Middle Ages, but they have a new and invigorating popularity in the Renaissance. Unwary spectators were wetted in much the same way as they had been for centuries, but in the new Italian gardens, they were wetted more often, with more delight, and with an added sprinkling of classical learning.

Colonna's dream vision gives a fine introduction: Poliphilus is taken by maidens to a bath, at one end of which are sculpted two nymphs, supporting an 'Infant holding his little Instrument in both his hands,' who 'continued pissing into the hot water, fresh cool water.' One of Poliphilus' guides then says to him

Take that Crystal vessel and bring me some of that fresh water! I intending to do so went to the place. And I had no sooner set my foot upon the step to receive the water but the pissing Boy lifted up his pricke, and cast sodeinlye so colde water upon my face, that I had lyke at that instant to have fallen backward. Whereat they so laughed, and it made such a sounde in the roundness and closeness of the bathe, that I also beganne to laugh that I was almost dead. Afterwards, I founde out the concavitie, and perceived that any heavy weight, being put upon the moveable stepping, that it would rise up like the Key and Jacke of a Virginall, and lift up the Boyes pricke, and finding out the devise and curious workemanship thereof, I was greatly contented.

Colonna's explanation is clear, though there is not any exact detail. But such tricks, and much more complicated than this, were fully described in the text of Hero of Alexandria's *Pneumatica*, known in manuscript in the 1550s, printed in a Latin translation in 1575, and in Italian in 1589. This work, written in the first century AD, explains how to construct scores of mechanical contrivances, many of which were obviously for use in temples, rather than gardens: for example, the 'Sacrificial Vessel which flows only when Money is introduced', or 'Temple Doors opened by Fire on an Altar'. But the gardens and grottoes of the Italian Renaissance made good use of these tricks as well, with 'A Bird made to whistle by flowing water', with 'Birds made to sing, and be silent alternatively by flowing water', and with various water-powered organ and trumpet devices.

Tricks and toys of this kind were fairly widespread in Renaissance gardens, and were remarked on with more or less approval by many visitors, and imported into cooler and less favourable countries. Many of Hero's devices are re-described in Salomon de Caus' *Raisons des Forces Mouvantes* in 1615, and were installed in gardens in France, England and Germany throughout the seventeenth century.

Today the best-preserved water jokes are to be seen, and experienced in Austria, at Schloss Hellbrunn near Salzburg, where the Prince-Archbishop of Salzburg, Markus Sittikus, had them installed during his rule from 1612 until 1619. As well as the stone dining table which squirts water up through the seats, and paths, stairs, archways, floors, roofs and walls which do the same, there are subtler drenchings from antlers fastened to the wall, and many water toys which perform charming and innocent tricks. In England, crude jokes are depicted in John Worlidge's *Systema Horticulturae of 1677* (the illustration, pl. 68, needs no comment), and in Robert Plot's *Natural History of Oxfordshire* (1677), where the description and numbered illustration of Thomas Bushell's grotto and joke fountain at Enstone, built around 1630, tells every dripping state (pl. 67). The text for numbers 9, 10, 11 and 12 gushes with punishment:

> *The streams of* water *from about* 30 pipes . . . *that sportively wet any* persons . . . *which most people striving to avoid, get behind* the Man *that turns the* Cocks, *whom he wets with* 10. *A* spout *of* water *that he lets fly over his head; or else if they endeavour to run out of the* Island *over the bridge, with* 11, 12, *which are two other* spouts . . . 11 *strikes the* legs . . . 12 *the* reins *of the back.*

Some water toys were sweeter: Colonna, in the *Hypnerotomachia*, tells of a weather-vane trumpeter on a rooftop, whose instrument sounds when the wind blows into the back of the trumpeter's head, and Thomas Nash tells in *The Unfortunate Traveller* (1594) of an Italian garden where the rainwater made music. Elsewhere, in an Italian 'summer banquetting house', Nash saw a tree with 'enchained chirping birds, whose throates being conduit piped with squared narrowe shels, and charged with searching sweet water, driven in by a little wheele for the nonce, that fed it a farre off, made a spirting sound, such as chirping is, in bubbling upwards through the rough crannies of their closed bills.' Nash may not have known, but these 'chirping birds' came from Hero of Alexandria.

In Italy, trick fountains were everywhere. At the villa d'Este, one area, leading to a statue of Venus, seems to have been devastatingly wet (pl. 69). At the villa Aldobrandini unsuspected jets spurted out from the walls and stairs, and at the villa Mondragone, also at Frascati, there was a special set of hose-pipe attachments in one courtyard, for jolly visitors to play with. These are described by the French *philosophe* Charles de Brosses who visited Frascati in 1739, many years after the gardens had been created. De Brosses was travelling with several youthful French companions, and had a very wet day of it. They began

66, 67, 68, 69   Joke fountains in fiction and in fact. Colonna's 'pissing boy' (above), of 1499, 'lifted up his prick, and cast sodeinlye so colde water upon my face, that I had lyke . . . to have fallen backward.' Equally embarrassing was John Worlidge's idea (top right), in the *Systema Horticulturae* of 1677, of a 'Statue of a Woman, that at the turning of a private Cock, shall cast Water out of her Nipples into the Spectators Faces.' Real joke

at Mondragone, around a polypriapic pool: i.e. where the edge of the basin is fitted all round with hose-pipes, made from leather, and with copper nozzles at the end. These pipes were lying there, idle and innocent, when – after the tap had been turned on – these fine creatures began to stand up in the oddest way, and, as Rabelais says, began to piss fresh water non-stop. Migieu grabbed one of these weapons and squirted it straight in Lacurne's face; he shot back, and we all joined in this excellent sport, and went on for half an hour until we were drenched to the skin. You'd think winter was not the best season for this little game, but the day was so mild and fine we couldn't resist the temptation.

We went back to our inn to change all our clothes, and then guess what happened: we were sitting, behaving ourselves, by the Belvedere at the villa Aldobrandini, waiting to hear the centaur blow his trumpet [another water device], and didn't notice a hundred treacherous little pipes distributed between the joints of the stones, which suddenly went off in jets over us. Well: we had no dry clothes left after the games at Mondragone, and so we plunged boldly into the wettest corners of the palace, where we spent the rest of the evening playing the same sort of tricks. There is an especially good little curving stairway where, as soon as you are part of the way up, the water-jets shoot out, criss-crossing in every direction, from above, below and the sides. At the top of these steps, we got our revenge on Legouz, who had been responsible for the wetting by the Belvedere. He had intended to turn on a tap to squirt water at us, but the tap was designed to trick the tricker – it shot out a torrent of water, thick as your arm, and with ferocious force, straight into Legouz' stomach. Legouz bolted off, his trousers full of water, guttering down into his shoes.

We all fell over with laughing, and that was enough. But the end wasn't as funny as it had been in the morning: we had to stay in with nothing to wear but our dressing-gowns, eating a vile supper, while they dried our clothes.

THE VERDANT PUZZLE

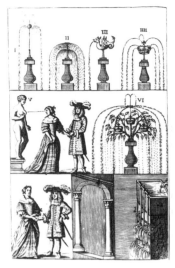

In the sixteenth and seventeenth centuries, few large gardens in Europe were without a maze, variously called a maze, labyrinth, 'house of Daedalus' or 'Dédale', sometimes 'Troy-town' or 'The Walls of Troy'. Few survive, and we may now be inclined to think of them as oddities of garden art. Those that remain – for example, in England at Hampton Court, Hatfield and Chatsworth; the Alcázar in Spain; Sturefors in Sweden, and Weldam in Holland – tend to be of much later date, and with hedges of a head-high sameness.

The hedge maze, formed most often from clipped yew, box, or privet, was one of several forms of outdoor maze which appeared in gardens in the late Middle Ages and in the Renaissance. Before the fifteenth century, mazes certainly existed but nothing suggests that they were incorporated into gardens before this time. A word of explanation is necessary.

The concept of the labyrinth goes back many centuries BC, as an architectural idea to express the elaborate, tortuous windings of palaces, prisons and catacombs. Such creations – in Egypt, near Lake Moeris, where the sacred crocodiles were buried, and at Knossos in Crete – definitely existed, and the latter, connected with the legend of the Minotaur kept by King Minos in the labyrinth designed by Daedalus, appears in simplified, symbolic form on Cretan coins.

This Cretan pattern, linked with the legend of Theseus seeking the monstrous Minotaur at the centre of the maze, forms the basis of later European maze designs.

In Greek and Roman gardens no mazes appear to have been constructed, though at Pompeii there was a mosaic labyrinth on the floor of a small room, perhaps a study or library, with a representation of Theseus attacking the Minotaur at its centre. Another house in Pompeii has a tiny labyrinth pattern crudely scratched on the plaster covering of a pillar, with the caption LABYRINTHUS HIC HABITAT MINOTAURUS – a forerunner of our SLIMEY LIVES HERE (see E. Breton, *Pompeia*, 1853).

In the Aeneid, book V, a labyrinth game or dance is mentioned, the *lusus trojae* or 'Game of Troy', performed by soldiers as a drill or exercise, and apparently played also by Roman children. Patterns for such exercises were cut out or marked out on

fountains were made in the 1630s at Enstone (bottom left), in England, by Thomas Bushell (here, '*the* Man *that turns the* Cocks' is crouching in front of his diabolical controls) and at the villa d'Este (bottom right) in the 1560s. Venturini's engraving of 1675 shows a multitude of jets moistening – or drenching – the visitors. The Este eagle and the fleur-de-lys adorn the walls, as they do the Hundred Fountains (pl. XIII)

70　A detail of a view by Falda (1675) of the villa Aldobrandini. In 1739 Charles de Brosses wrote of this scene: 'There is an especially good little curving stairway where, as soon as you are part of the way up, the water-jets shoot out, criss-crossing in every direction, from above, below and the sides'

tessellated floors, and possibly on the Campus Martius in Rome.

These labyrinths are still a long way from garden mazes, but they are the beginning. The Church took over the idea of the labyrinth as representing the tortuous path the believer must follow to reach his spiritual goal, and the Cretan labyrinth pattern was depicted in many churches, painted, carved or executed in mosaic or tiles; as at Lucca, where a small labyrinth is carved on one of the piers in the cathedral porch.

Labyrinths on the floor, forming part of the pavement, seem to have encouraged believers to accomplish a miniature voyage of penitence. They became known as 'Chemins de Jerusalem'; such paths could stand either for the terrestrial pilgrimage to the Holy Land, or the spiritual one towards the Heavenly City.

Here the maze approaches the garden, for in England these 'Chemins de Jerusalem' were frequently created in the open air, cut in shallow tracks in the turf outside the church. (Did such mazes exist on the Continent? I have found no reference to them, in spite of the fact that many existed *within* churches, either on the walls or on the floor.) Curiously, the story of the Trojan soldiers and their martial exercise reappears, for often the mazes outside the village church were on the village green, and acquired a secular, holiday quality, becoming known as 'Troy-towns', 'Troy-walls' or the 'Walls of Troy'. Shakespeare refers to the abandonment of these

71, 72 Two English turf mazes: the 'mizmaze' (top) at Breamore in Hampshire still exists in just such a rural setting, while the plan is all that remains of the curious maze (above) at Pimperne in Dorset. It was ploughed up in 1730. Though extensive and complicated at first sight, both mazes have a simple, single track

mazes in his time in *Midsummer Night's Dream*, II, ii, with:

> The nine man's morris is fill'd up with mud;
> And the quaint mazes in the wanton green,
> For lack of tread, are undistinguishable.

Still existing are the maze at Breamore, near Fordingbridge in Hampshire; at Wing in Rutland, and at Troy Farm, Somerton, in Oxfordshire. One, at Pimperne in Dorset, had an unusual heart-shaped form, and the wildly winding path led to a heart in the centre – a lover's maze. This appears in John Hutchin's *History and Antiquities of the County of Dorset* (1774), with a folio plate in which the path of the maze is shown by a double line. The text explains 'this maze at Pimpern was formed of small ridges about a foot high, and covered near an acre of ground. It was entirely destroyed by the plough about 1730.'

At this point (and it is as if we were in a maze with no apparent solution) we must jump into the garden. I know of no clear reference to a garden maze in the Middle Ages. Rosamund's bower at Woodstock, built by Henry II, was almost certainly 'labyrinthine' in its architectural intricacy. Though set in a park, it was a building, not a hedge maze. The nearest to a garden maze I can find are sketchy references to a 'Maison de Dédale', a 'House of Daedalus', in the fourteenth and fifteenth centuries. Charles V of France (1364–80) had a labyrinth, a 'Daedalus', in his palace garden at the Hôtel Saint-Paul in Paris, and when this was destroyed by Bedford, the English regent, in 1431, the hedges of this feature were taken down to make room for nearly 6,000 elms and many kinds of fruit and ornamental trees. Rather later, King René of Anjou is said to have included 'dédalus' among the features of his gardens, both in the 1450s near Angers, and later at Aix-en-Provence, in the gardens of Baugé and Reculée. But those mazes may still have been architectural, buildings with intricate divisions of rooms and passages, set within a garden, rather than garden features in their own right.

The maze as a *garden ornament* comes into being in the late fifteenth century, and rather as a misunderstanding than as part of a long-continued tradition: in Renaissance Italy the maze was thought of as an element in the villa gardens of the Romans, and therefore to be included as a feature in the new gardens, inspired by the models of antiquity, which were created in Tuscany and in Rome. The error is Alberti's, who says in his *De re aedificatoria*, book IX, that 'the Ancients stained the Pavements of their Porticoes with Labyrinths, both square and circular, in which the Boys used to exercise themselves.' Alberti was probably thinking of the passage in Virgil's *Aeneid* already referred to. Again, in Colonna's *Hypnerotomachia* a most

73 A section of the turf maze at Troy Farm, Somerton, near Oxford, showing the shallow divisions cut in the turf. Such mazes, made for amusement and dating from the sixteenth century or earlier, are now exceedingly rare and are derived from the labyrinths laid out in some churches in England and on the Continent for miniature voyages of penance

117

elaborate water labyrinth is described: 'a Garden of a large compasse, made in the forme of an intricate Laborynth allyes and wayes, not to bee troden, but sayled about, for insteade of allyes to treade uppon, there were ryvers of water.' This might be imagined as similar in scale and grandeur to the great maze in Tintoretto's painting, now at Hampton Court, that is to say a fantasy, not a portrait of any existing or indeed feasibly buildable labyrinth. Colonna does not say how tall the divisions of the maze were – merely 'the water being envyroned upon either side with roses, trees and fruits.'

At all events (a useful phrase, when the evidence is weak – the silence here of other garden historians is a sign of ignorance), Renaissance gardens suddenly abound in mazes. Italian gardens, like the villa d'Este, the villa Lante and the villa Garzoni are peppered with them, and in the 1500s they appear in France. Leonardo da Vinci, in the 1490s, has two characteristic and appealing memoranda in his *Notebooks*, first 'repair the labyrinth' – set among reminders concerning 'ruler–very sharp knife–spectacles–slippers–clothes from the excise man' – and then again 'to repair the labyrinth', in a similar collection of knots in his handkerchief. In 1534, the Abbey of Thélème in Rabelais' *Gargantua* has 'le beau labyrinte' in the middle of 'le beau jardin de plaisance'. And the plans of French gardens in du Cerceau's *Les Plus Excellents Bastiments de France* (1576, 1579) have many mazes and maze-shapes, simple, complex, single or in pairs.

'Le beau jardin de plaisance', 'the fine garden of delight', Rabelais calls it. We should remember this *delight*, which helps to explain why most of these mazes had low, rather than high, divisions or hedges. The delights they offered were more subtle than the simple confusion we experience in the head-high yew and privet labyrinth of Hampton Court, which was not built until the 1690s.

Hyssop, thyme and cotton lavender, which were used in the early mazes, are small – they grow, at the most, knee-high. Mazes made with these are therefore to be surveyed as well as walked in. Their colour should be remembered, with box and yew also recommended: these were invaluable in winter as evergreens, in an age when flowers more or less came to an end with hollyhocks, not to begin again until the snowdrops and aconites of earliest spring. Tudor England, and seventeenth-century Europe as a whole, still lacked chrysanthemums, just as they lacked the autumnal, flaming maple, and their winter gardens were dull without these grey and silver evergreens. And they were also for *smelling*. Charles Estienne in his *Agriculture et Maison Rustique* (1570), recommends the cultivation of many rows of scented herbs, 'both for the reserve for your scented garden, for your hedges, and for your winter stews'; for example sage and hyssop, thyme, lavender, rosemary, marjoram, costmary, basil, balm, 'and one bed of camomile to make seats and labyrinths, which they call Daedalus.' In the first English version of this work, translated by Richard Surflet in 1600, we are told to grow one bed 'of cammomill, for to make seats and a labyrinth', and later that 'these sweet herbes, and flowers for nosegaies shall be put in order . . . and some of them upon seats, and others in mazes made *for the pleasing and recreating of the sight*.' Estienne's plan of a maze doesn't show us the height of the divisions, but camomile is to be trodden on and may be used for a 'lawn' or bank.

Most of the many sixteenth-century mazes were low; travellers who saw them comment with surprise if they are high. Paul Hentzner, the German, at Theobalds in Hertfordshire in 1591, speaks of 'labyrinths made with a great deal of labour', and in 1603 James I came there and 'recreated himself in the meanders compact of bays, rosemary and the like overshadowing his walk.' Now bay may grow to twenty-five feet, and rosemary may reach a floppy seven or eight, but both are happier at shoulder or waist height. In this period the only clear reference to a high maze I know is William Lawson's suggestion in 1618 that 'Mazes well framed a mans height, may perhaps make your friend wander in gathering of berries till he cannot recover himself without your help.' But this is late. Earlier, the Swiss traveller Thomas Platter, viewing Nonsuch in September 1599, remarks I think with surprise that 'I came into a labyrinth or maze, which was set round with high plants so that one could neither go over or through them.' On the next day he came to Hampton Court, where he found

74, 75   From Thomas Hill's *Most Briefe and Pleasaunt Treatyse* (1563). The patterns of these two mazes are repeated in roughly the same form for at least a century. They are similar (though not identical) to those in du Cerceau's view of the great knot garden at Gaillon (pl. 81). The divisions would have been made with low-growing evergreen plants – hyssop, thyme, cotton lavender or marjoram – or, from around 1600 onwards, with box

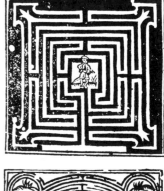

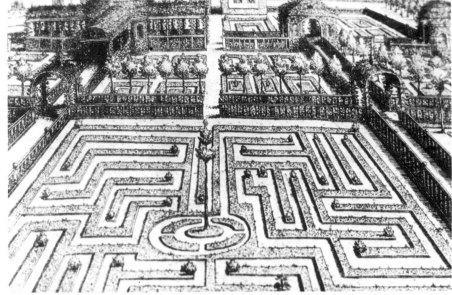

76 This view, from Vredeman de Vries, *Hortorum viridariorumque formae* (1583), not only illustrates the low divisions of the garden maze in Renaissance times – probably no more than knee-high – but shows several arbours in carpenter's work, grown over with climbing plants. Although the artist aims to present an overall view, it is clear that this garden is divided into many small and separate sections

a maze with painted divisions and fruit trees, and adorned with two marble fountains, so that one could not spend much time there without getting lost; for one was distracted, not only by the delights of taste, scent and sight, but also by the ravishing song of the birds and the lisping of the streams which entertained one's ears. It was indeed like an earthly paradise.

The painted divisions (*gemelten Gewegsen*) he saw were no great physical impediment. His perplexity came from the confusion of enjoyments which the maze could offer.

The surviving mazes are later, taller, and less subtle in their pleasures. Hampton Court's present maze, set out *c.* 1699, with its high hedges of yew, is an amusement for children, like that at the villa Garzoni, made in the 1680s, or the maze at Schönbusch, near Aschaffenburg in Germany, laid out in 1829. The Schönbusch maze is the prettiest of the later labyrinths, being in field maple and delightfully light in colour, and with an attractive gingko planted in the middle. But the scents, the flowers, and the Renaissance conceit of being 'lost' in a puzzle only knee-high have gone. The *labyrinthe* at Versailles, designed by Le Nôtre, had high hedges, it is true, but there it was enlivened by thirty-nine statues and fountains, each illustrating one of La Fontaine's fables; all destroyed in 1775. In the Netherlands, two worthwhile mazes have been made within the last century: at Weldam, around 1900, and in 1927 at Tjaarda, in Oranjewoud.

Of the mazes made, and vanished, since the Renaissance, I regret most that at Peking, within the grounds of the Yuan Ming Yuan, designed for the emperor by Jesuit missionaries around 1750 and destroyed with the rest of the 'Garden of Perfect Brightness' in the nineteenth century. No more un-Chinese garden ornament can be imagined. How curious the moment must have been, when the emperor and his companions came to see this maze! They would be able to write a poem while watching a wine-cup float along a carved channel; what lines would they have composed as they puzzled their way through this most artificial of all garden inventions?

77   The topiary garden at
Levens Hall, established at the
end of the seventeenth century

8

The Renaissance Garden in France and England

The gardens of the late Middle Ages and those of the sixteenth century in France, England and the Low Countries have much in common. The features of medieval gardens continued – foursquare enclosures, regularly divided, with beds raised up higher than the paths, and tunnels and arbours made of trellis work – but were overtaken by the excitement of the Renaissance, and like the gardens of Italy became converted to enjoyment and extravagant display. Often the Italian attitude and skills were directly imported, with patrons in France or England hiring Italian designers and craftsmen to work for them; beginning with the employment of Pacello de Mercogliano by Charles VIII of France at the end of the fifteenth century, fifty years or more before the great villa gardens of Tivoli, Frascati and Rome were created. By the 1530s, Italian craftsmen were working at Hampton Court.

Virtually nothing is left of these gardens: often they were framed in quickly perishable materials, like the wooden 'carpenter's work' which lasted at best for a decade; and if they were more solidly built, the changing fashions still had them destroyed, and we must turn to written or pictorial sources to find what they were like. While manuscripts, and the miniature paintings which illuminate them, come to an end, printed books begin, both of older garden writers, like Petrus de Crescentiis, and of new writers, particularly in England, where Thomas Hill's *Most Briefe and Pleasaunt Treatyse* was printed in 1563, being the first book in English to deal solely with gardening. In other countries, classical writers on agriculture and horticulture were printed from manuscript sources, and in Italy and France the texts of Columella and Palladius, for example, were both printed in Latin and ruthlessly pillaged to supply material for 'new' texts and compilations, usually in the vernacular. Both Hill's *Treatyse*, and the *Praedium Rusticum* of Charles Estienne (1554), a comparable early French farming and gardening text, rely heavily on older writers, and in each case the authors' later works – Hill's *Proffitable Arte of Gardening* (1568) and *Gardeners' Labyrinth* (1577) and Estienne and Liébault's *Agriculture et Maison Rustique* (1570) – draw away from these sources and become more original with each of their many subsequent editions. Improvements in techniques soon permitted fine details to be reproduced, and mid-century works on architecture, such as Sebastiano Serlio's *Architettura* (1537) and Jacques Androuet du Cerceau's *Les Plus Excellents Bastiments de France* (1576 and 1579), show plans of gardens or garden features with an accuracy not previously possible. A further corroborative source appears in surviving tapestries and embroideries, made in the Low Countries or in France, and sometimes in England, in which gardens, or glimpses of gardens, appear.

As a starting point for the English sixteenth-century garden, I can think of no better illustration than the tiny vignette from the title-page of Hill's *Treatyse* of 1563 (pl. 78). Though enclosed, like a cloister garden, and divided into regular sections, it has a degree of openness – the countryside surrounds it. It has an arbour of carpenter's work (on the right) which could be found in earlier gardens, but the central fence of lattice is supported by squared ornamental pillars, each with a carved bust on top, like crude Term statues. Though primitive in execution, they were undeniably a part of the Renaissance revival of classical motifs. They are the country cousins of the caryatids of the villa di Papa Giulio, or the *canephori* of the villa

Farnese at Caprarola. Within this enclosure, the beds are most formally divided, beyond the needs of vegetable economy, and in the centre there is a knot which, from its formal shape, can only have contained flowers. Hill's other illustrations show gardeners at work, digging, planting, watering, and repairing an arbour; rather like the busy scene in Peter Breughel's painting of *Spring*, many times copied, imitated and engraved. Hill's first vignette is paralleled in a contemporary Flemish embroidery (pl. 79) of a moated manor house and its garden, and in a later painting, *c.* 1622, by one of Joost de Momper's pupils (pl. XVI), showing another walled and moated garden. In each scene, the tunnels and arbours allow views of the garden and of the country outside, and in each a boat is moored by the water-gate. Though enclosed, the gardens are a part of the countryside.

If Hill's picture or the embroidery are in any way unrepresentative, it is because they lack extravagance. They are both gentle and modest, while the garden details of du Cerceau are not. Du Cerceau wishes to show that the 'new' French buildings and gardens of his time are magnificent. Looking back from the twentieth century, we can see that more often than not they are formed round castles or mansions built in the Middle Ages, with features that are unsymmetrical, Gothic, and an embarrassment to someone excited about the discoveries and improvements of the Renaissance. If we examine du Cerceau's detailed picture of the *deambulationes*, the nobly proportioned 'galleries de charpenterie' or carpenter's work at Montargis (pl. 80), we might imagine a glorious wooden extension of the colonnade at the villa di Papa Giulio. These walks, 'now covered in ivy', are the most sumptuous – to judge from the scale of the tiny yet swaggering figures within – of any in the Renaissance, and can fairly be compared with those of Weldam. But du Cerceau's other plates of Montargis show that the castle is truly medieval (a keep within an irregular outer wall), with the gardens almost entirely on the outside: a band of square beds, varied with a couple of mazes, a few tunnels of trellis work, and the one masterpiece of carpenter's work I have described. Beyond all this, the vineyards.

GAILLON

The numerous drawings of the château and gardens at Gaillon, Eure, best support du Cerceau's suggestions of French pre-eminence. Gaillon was built by the Cardinal d'Amboise at the very beginning of the sixteenth century. It is a château, part-medieval in its irregular shape, part-Renaissance in its pretension to symmetry and in its glorious fountain in the centre of the courtyard. Outside the château is the pleasure garden, with knots which were in 1510 of a fanciful and late medieval representational kind, like those in Colonna's *Hypnerotomachia*. This pleasure garden was entirely separate both from the château and from the large and rectangular *potager* or vegetable garden, but still surrounded by walls so that it would have little or no view of the country round about. This garden is drawn in exceptional detail (pl. 81), so that we may see just how it does or does not advance. Above all, it is extravagant. The beds or knots – twenty-four small square ones and two large mazes – are ingeniously varied with pleasingly curved patterns within their rigid outlines. In du Cerceau's bird's-eye view they are bordered with low hedges and planted with vaguely pyramidal shrubs at the corners. At the centre is an ornate wooden archway standing over a fountain. This much goes beyond any medieval garden, yet its nature, essentially enclosed and separate from the house and countryside, remains far behind the prescriptions of Alberti.

Away to one side of the château and its gardens, along a narrow path through the trees, is a small remote area, containing the garden, hermitage and 'white house', illustrated separately (pl. 82). This secluded garden may never have been finished: du Cerceau's text of 1576 says that the Cardinal de Bourbon, who controlled Gaillon in the 1550s, 'is at present adorning it with buildings', and that in this area 'the cardinal is having a Charterhouse built, furnished with all delights.' No other record of it exists, and no trace of it appears on later plates of the Gaillon estate; but it is to my knowledge the unique instance of a *giardino segreto* in a French garden at the time of the Renaissance, and it is singularly similar in spirit to the remote, yet luxurious villa Farnese at Caprarola, built in the same period. The little 'hermitage et maison

XVI   A moated garden in the Netherlands (right) – a detail from a landscape (*c.* 1620). As in pictures 78 and 79, the corners are places from which both the garden and the countryside may be surveyed

XVII   A flower-lover's paradise in 1694 (bottom right) – the frontispiece to Johann Walther the Elder's volume celebrating his patron Johann of Nassau's botanical collection in his garden at Idstein

78, 79   The title page of Thomas Hill's *Most Briefe and Pleasaunt Treatyse* of 1563 (below) shows well what an English version of an Italian Renaissance garden might have been like, while the Flemish version (bottom), from an embroidery of about 1590, echoes its formal divisions and surrounding arbour of carpenter's work, and also echoes strongly the garden in pl. XVI

80, 81, 82 Three scenes from
Jacques Androuet du Cerceau's
*Les Plus Excellents Bastiments de
France* (right). The splendid
deambulationes or 'galleries' of
carpenter's work in the gardens of
Montargis (top) have now, alas!,
vanished, as has every
contemporary specimen of
Renaissance carpenter's work.
The formal knot garden at Gaillon
(middle) had existed since the
early 1500s, and the first knots
had included representations of
heraldic devices, but du Cerceau's
engraving shows abstract
patterns. The two mazes in the
foreground are divided by low
hedges, probably no more than
knee-high. The bird's eye view of
the hermitage and *maison blanche*
at Gaillon (bottom), shows the
'white house' apparently
surrounded by water, like the
Sultaniye kiosk on the Bosphorus

blanche' of Gaillon remains a minor mystery, a paradise of pleasure and austerity; at
one end of the canal, the ornate moated palace, and at the other, the jagged caves of
the hermitage. Around this time, Montaigne set out his credo of uncertainty, 'que
sçais-je?', and these two buildings at Gaillon might express similar doubt about the
absolute rightness of sensual or spiritual values. Is it too fanciful to see the peculiarly
shaped pond in the foreground as a balance or scales, with equally weighted pans on
each side?

KNOTS AND CONCEITS

This strange pond, like the rest of the *giardino segreto* at Gaillon, is characteristic of
the sixteenth-century love of fantasy, which they might broadly term the 'conceit',
puzzlement, obscurity, double use or meaning, or simply intricacy of design or
execution, which we find at every stage of garden art at this time. The love of
intricacy is at its most evident in the elaborations of the knot, the ornamental garden
bed, laid out within the enclosed garden in patterns of low evergreen bushes, with
the gaps filled either with other herbs, or flowers, or inert coloured materials, such as
sand or brick-dust. The edging would usually be in scented herbs; lavender, thyme,
or rosemary, sometimes thrift or cotton lavender, less often box. If the garden was of
any size, the plants within the knots would probably be divided into two groups,
those for the 'nosegay' garden, and those for the herb garden.

XVIII   Walther's detailed
painting of the grotto at Idstein (it
can be seen halfway down the
garden in pl. XVII, on the left),
shows it to be far removed from
the gloomy caverns of the next
century. More flowerpots with
choice plants are arrayed on either
side

Almost always the knot would be set out in a square framework, with the flowers
or herbs grown within the edging of low bushes, though sometimes in the following
century the beds themselves would be given strange shapes, like those in the garden
at Idstein near Frankfurt-am-Main, painted in 1654 by Johann Walther, which are
shaped like fruit and leaves. Sometimes the flowers seem to have been grown within

83 The frontispiece of the *Hortus floridus* of Crispin de Passe. The garden, meant for the display of rare and tropical flowers, is surrounded by an arbour of carpenter's work

these patterns in an indiscriminate manner, and sometimes they are in groups of one kind or another, while the most intricate patterns may have had only coloured sands or gravel in between the lines. If an interwoven pattern of an embroidered or 'strapwork' kind was made – by planting contrasting 'threads' or lines of different plants – this would be called a *closed* knot, while a simpler design without interwoven lines, and with the square area merely divided into sections, was called an *open* knot. For the closed knot, Markham (in *The English Husbandman*, 1613) advises the gardener to study the design:

> Then precisely note the several passages of your knot, and the several thrids [threads] of which it consists . . . in one thrid plant your carnation Gilly flower, in another your great white Geli flower, in another your single-coloured Gilly flower, and in another your blood-red Gilly flower . . . [or] your several coloured Hyacinths . . . your several coloured Dulippos [tulips] . . . [and then, oh happy gardener!] if you stand a little remote from the knot, and any thing above it, you shall see it appear like a knot made of divers coloured ribans, most pleasing and most rare.

The wealthy or curious gardener would often strive to achieve the most complicated 'closed' patterns of the sort Colonna had already described in the *Hypnerotomachia Poliphili*. In 1520, Cavendish praises the extravagance of the gardens at Hampton Court, where he marvelled at 'The Knots so enknotted it cannot be expres't.' And, as at Gaillon, *each* square knot-pattern would be different from the next, so that the visitor would be continually surprised by the variety of the patterns, deliberately counterfeiting the patterns used in embroidery or leather-work, plaster ceilings or wooden panelling, or tiles upon the floor. The aim was to provide pleasure: as the owner walked the paths of his garden, he would both 'diligently view the prosperity of his herbs and flowers', and at the same time achieve 'the delight and comfort of the wearied mind, which he may by himself or fellowship of his friends conceive in the delectable sights and fragrant smels of the flowers.'

THE BOTANIC GARDEN

In the sixteenth century new plants and trees begin to flood in to Europe from the East and from the newly-discovered Americas. We tend to think of potatoes (in England 1585 or 1586), tomatoes and tobacco (in the 1570s) as the great American novelties of the sixteenth century, but this is a pathetic underestimate. A list of a score of plants and trees which came to Britain between 1500 and 1700 indicates the wealth of foreign imports, which we now think of idly as having grown in Britain from time immemorial:

Year introduced	Vernacular name	Botanical name	Source
c. 1500	Holm oak	*Quercus ilex*	Italy
c. 1500	(red) Mulberry	*Morus nigra*	Persia
1547/48	Bear's breeches	*Acanthus mollis*	Italy
before 1548	Strawberry tree	*Arbutus unedo*	Mediterranean and Ireland
1548	Stone pine	*Pinus pinea*	Italy
c. 1550	African marigold	*Tagetes erecta*	Mexico, via Africa; from Africa to Spain c. 1535
c. 1580	Crown imperial	*Fritillaria imperialis*	Turkey, via Vienna 1576
c. 1580	Hyacinth	*Hyacinthus orientalis*	Turkey, via Padua
c. 1578	Tulip	*Tulipa gesneriana*	Turkey, via Holland
c. 1582	Oriental plane	*Platanus orientalis*	Persia, via S.E. Europe
1593	Yucca	*Yucca gloriosa*	Central America
before 1596	Laburnum	*L. anagyroides*	S. Europe
before 1597	Laurustinus	*Viburnum tinus*	S. Europe
before 1597	Sunflower	*Helianthus annuus*	Western North America, via Peru, via Spain
before 1597	Marvel of Peru	*Mirabilis jalapa*	Southern Central America
before 1597	Nasturtium	*Tropaeolum minus*	South America
before 1627	Lobelia	*Lobelia cardinalis*	North America
before 1629	Passion flower	*Passiflora*	Central America
1637	Horse chestnut	*Aesculus hippocastanum*	Balkans
1640	Swamp cypress	*Taxodium distichum*	North America
before 1648	Golden rod	*Solidago*	North America
by 1659	Cedar of Lebanon	*Cedrus libani*	Lebanon

84   An evergreen bottle tree (*sterculia rupestris*) in the Botanic Garden, Sydney – a noble survivor from the original wood. The trunk bulges out into a rounded mass which contains a large reservoir of water. In 1842 this botanic garden was described as 'literally a walk through Paradise'

These plants were more often than not grown as 'curiosities' in plant collections rather than as regular garden adornments, or kept in pots (sometimes large and ornate), ready for special admiration and ready also to be carried within the shelter of early forms of greenhouse in the winter. The systematic study of plants in western Europe may also be said to begin again at this time, after a pause of over a thousand years. In 1545, the first university botanic garden was laid out in Italy, at Padua, and others soon followed, for example at Leiden, Leipzig and Heidelberg. In England, the first was at Oxford (1621). These botanic gardens were specifically for the collection and study of plants, and their design was functional rather than aesthetic. At Padua, the area was circular, divided into beds in which the different plants were grown in groups according to their categories; useful for study, but not necessarily ensuring a beautiful garden. Indeed Jakob Burckhardt pointed out that the classifying and collecting urges which inspired the design of early botanic gardens were a retarding influence in garden design, as may still be seen in the intriguing and instructive collections displayed in classified groups, and set out in symmetrical beds in certain institutions, as in a part of the Cambridge botanic garden, for example, or in a section of the herb garden at Fulham Palace in London. Botanic gardens have generally followed the example of Padua, though most have achieved some degree of compromise: at Leiden the original rectangular beds are accompanied by other more spacious and imaginative planting, but other botanic gardens, such as Uppsala in Sweden, where the modern garden is some distance away from Linne's, were too small to allow transformation.

In the nineteenth century, botanic gardens were founded in countries where no previous institutions existed to control or limit what might be set up: in particular, Australia is notable for the variety and beauty of its botanic gardens, principally at Sydney and Melbourne. The garden at Sydney has a spectacular site, overlooking and running down to the sea, and as early as 1842 J. Hood (*Australia and the East*) writes of it as 'literally a walk through Paradise . . . in position the finest in the world'. The botanic garden at Melbourne (1845) enjoyed the difficult but brilliant

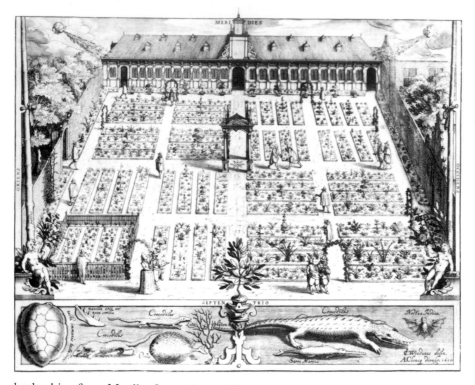

leadership of von Mueller from 1857 until 1873, and then the more sensitive control of William Guilfoyle, whose shaping of the landscape still survives. The botanic garden at Darwin, founded in 1872, is interesting as an early example of a botanic garden responding to exceptional climatic conditions, as does, later still, the Californian botanic garden at Santa Barbara, founded in 1926. In Australia and in America these gardens deal with collections of tropical and of desert plants respectively, as the proper and natural flora to display, and the gardens, each in their different ways, treat such flora imaginatively, with attractive open-air settings which one could not emulate in more temperate regions. The new botanic garden designed by Franz Joseph Greub and actually under construction at the university of Düsseldorf has a remarkable and imaginative combination of the formal bedding necessary for instruction, and of areas of garden excitingly designed to represent the natural terrain – rocky, fertile, dry, moist, shady, or exposed – in which different kinds of plants and trees will grow.

As well as the botanic gardens, royal and private collections of plants were begun in the sixteenth and seventeenth centuries. Many were soon dispersed, but often enough they have been recorded in the herbals and flower-books written and illustrated by or on behalf of the owners. Some writers, like Fuchs (1501–*c.* 1570), or Dodoens (1517–85), or Clusius (L'Ecluse, 1526–1609), or de l'Obel (1538–1611), were scientists who endeavoured to study and classify the plants they described, and others, such as John Gerard *(The Herbal,* 1597), John Parkinson *(Paradisi in sole*

86 The plan of the new botanic garden (left) designed by Franz Joseph Greub for the university of Düsseldorf. To the right, areas of open or wooded parkland provide space for visitors to relax; in the centre is an area of formal bedding for instruction, near to the handsome hemispherical cupola containing the university's collection of South American plants. On the left, the garden is skilfully designed to allow widely different kinds of planting in natural situations, with the terrain divided between several lake and hillside scenes

Paradisus terrestris, 1629), and Sir Thomas Hanmer (his *Garden Book* was written in 1659 but not published until 1933), vary from devoted collectors and classifiers to amateur gardeners with a love of individual flowers. For their part, the artists had more or less botanical knowledge to supplement their eye for the characteristic shape, texture and colour of the plants they portrayed. Among the more famous artists in the period are:

> Jacques Le Moyne de Morgues, d. 1588 (his water-colours, *c.* 1570, of flowers and fruit are in the Victoria and Albert Museum, London)
> Pierre Vallet, *c.* 1575– (*Le Jardin du roi très chrestien Henri IV*, 1608)
> Crispin de Passe, b. 1590 (*Hortus floridus*, 1614)
> Basil Besler (*Hortus Eystettensis*, 1613)
> Johann Walther (his two volumes depicting Johann von Nassau's collection at Idstein, *c.* 1654, are in the Victoria and Albert Museum)

THE FANTASTICAL GARDEN

Though the new plants and trees tended to remain 'collector's items' and to be kept in separate gardens – like the 'medicinal garden' in Olivier de Serres *Théâtre d'Agriculture* of 1600 – the extravagance of the sixteenth century must have been as amazing and delightful in the now-vanished gardens of England, France and the Low Countries, as it was in Italy. Palace-like constructions of carpenter's work were run up for court pageants, or to welcome the English or the French monarchs on their tours through their domains; fantastic topiary adorned the trellis work and figures of men and beasts, castles or heraldic devices were created either upright, in climbing plants, or across the ground in patterned knots, as they were at the villa Quaracchi in Florence, or in the pages of Colonna's *Hynerotomachia Polyphili*. To match the woodcuts in Colonna's text is the illustration from Gervase Markham's enlargement of Estienne's *Maison Rustique*, showing the carpenter's work, topped with wooden birds and a wooden ship, ready for plants such as jasmine or honeysuckle to climb up and adorn them. Sir Hugh Platt's *Garden of Eden* (1655) has a variation on this: 'Birds, beasts, pyramids etc. do grow speedily'; you make a hollow, three-dimensional model in wood or burnt clay, and stuff the holes in it with thyme, hyssop or rosemary.

A simplified plan for a garden appears in William Lawson's *New Orchard and Garden* (pl. 89). This book, re-edited again and again until 1683, refers back to gardening in the 1570s, for Lawson in 1618 writes of his garden labours of 'forty and

89 This illustration (left) from William Lawson's *New Orchard and Garden* shows a late Elizabethan garden. A mount 'M', at each corner, overlooks both the delights of the garden and the countryside beyond it. 'N' is a still house. The horse and man under 'A' are topiary figures, while 'C' stands for garden knots

eight years'. The plan and the text of the book certainly hark back to the Elizabethan period: the six square sections of his plan fit into an overall rectangular shape, divided into three levels or terraces; a mount stands at each corner, and a fountain plays at the crossing of two main walks. But each of the six garden sections is as 'curious' and as diversely interesting as the more lavish knot gardens in the plans of du Cerceau. Topiary and knots indicated on the plan are backed up in the text with other delights: mazes, for example, 'well framed a man's height', and 'a Bowling Alley, or rather (which is more manly, and more healthfull) a payre of Buttes, to stretch your Armes.' If you are tired, then he recommends as 'seemly and comfortable' raised 'banks and seats of Camomile, Penny royall, Daisies and Violets', and for sport of a restful kind, he writes: 'I could highly commend your Orchard, if either through it or hard by it, there could run a pleasant River with silver streams; you might sit in your Mount and angle a peckled Trout, sleighty Eel or some other daintie Fish.'

90 The garden of Apolidon (below) from the French version of book IV of *Amadis de Gaule* (1543). This garden is an ideal of Renaissance extravagance, from the parterre above the castle, with its agate statue of Venus, to the maze-cum-lighthouse in the upper centre of the plan

But fantasy built, or wished to build, stranger gardens by far. Like the medievals, the sixteenth- and seventeenth-century gardeners tried their hands at fantastic graftings of many fruits on a single stock – the anonymous *Country-man's Recreation* of 1640 has a sweetly-limping couplet to acknowledge the importance of this art:

To God be praises on hie in all our Worldly Planting,
And let us thank the Romaines also for the Art of Graffing and Gardening.

One of the 'conceits' described by Sir Hugh Platt in his *Floraes Paradise* (1608) was the retarding of cherries from ripening. He tells of Sir Francis Carew's entertainment of Queen Elizabeth at Beddington, and of how 'he led her Majesty to a cherry-tree, whose fruit he had of purpose kept back from ripening at least one month after all cherries had taken their farewell of England: he had done this by putting on a canvas cover and keeping it damp . . .' On the grand scale, the royal or noble palaces of Hampton Court, Nonesuch, Theobalds and Kenilworth in England, or Anet, Fontainebleau and the Tuileries in France had wonders and to spare: mounts with banqueting houses on top (as at Hampton Court), statues and grottoes, knots of endless variety and infinite complexity, and the mazes and water-jokes which I have already discussed.

Turning to gardens of an imaginary kind, it is fascinating to see how the seventeenth century turns into reality what – or part of what – the sixteenth had dreamed. In 1543, the fourth book of a French version of *Amadis de Gaule* was published, enlarged and with new illustrations. This well-nigh interminable late-medieval romance, attributed without much confidence to a Spanish writer, Acuerdo Olvido, was given a seasoning of the new Renaissance when it was turned into French. In the fourth book, which is all that concerns us here, the sumptuous palace and garden on 'L'Isle Ferme' built by the prince-magician Apolidon has two illustrations and is fully described (previous texts had spared only a few lines).

The description and picture of the palace itself are reminiscent of the new palaces and châteaux being built in France, and also echo the hyperbolic descriptions of the Abbey of Thélème in Rabelais' *Gargantua* (1534). At Thélème, the gardens are the only part to be treated skimpily, but in *Amadis* the illustration of the garden is detailed, and responds accurately to the text: 'One entered within a garden or parterre of the same area as the building described above [i.e. the palace]. The garden was planted with all the kinds of flowers and good herbs one might desire.' This is like the gardens of Estienne or Olivier de Serres, for nosegays and for herbs, while the design is much like that in Hill's title-page vignette.

The statement that it was 'un jardin ou parterre' is one of the first ever to use 'parterre' to mean a garden. Here it means simply 'a regular or foursquare garden', a 'garden where the beds are well-ordered'. The unique sense which it was to have in the seventeenth century does not yet apply.

At the centre there is a fountain, but it is a special one: the water spurts

from the nipples of a Venus carved in agate, mounted on an emerald pillar, and holding in her right hand the apple given her by Paris [the *selfsame* apple of discord, clearly acquired through Apolidon's magic power], and pendant on her left ear the noble pearl which Cleopatra had so long in her possession, after she had consumed the other in the presence of Mark Antony.

Round this parterre – the word is used again – run painted galleries, with hunting scenes on the ground floor and scenes of battles above. Outside is the park, with a wood set on the side of a mountain, planted with pines, cypresses, laurels, free-standing ivies, palms and turpentine trees.

The lower part was set aside for an orchard, so pleasant and delectable that nature seemed to have done all in her power to make it rare and exceptional: for there you saw an infinite number of orange, pomegranate, lemon and myrtle trees, all planted in rows . . . and another part [in the centre of the illustration] was a meadow, watered by an infinity of little streams . . . with tender green grass and violets, marguerites, pansies and other scented flowers.

Magical, rare and wild creatures came here: the phoenix, once a year, a couple of unicorns; the beaver, bathing its tail, with civets, a pelican, stags, roes, squirrels, hares and rabbits. And other birds; 'it was heavenly to hear them warbling, especially the nightingale, the canary, and the solitary lark.' On an island in one of the streams, there was a 'Daedalus or maze, four acres in area, planted with the rarest balm of Engady, and customarily guarded by two snakes of the kind which once watched over the golden apples in the garden of the Hesperides.' And at the centre of this maze stood a gilded colossus of bronze, bearing aloft a crystal lantern with an ever-burning rod inside ('with which Prometheus had guarded the fire he once stole from heaven'), so bright that it served as a lighthouse for sailors passing by.

Fantasy, foursquare – a wall with battlements runs all round. Only the river, too big to tame, flows in an untidy diagonal through the woods, the meadow and the orchard, like the river Nadder through the real formalities of Wilton.

A similar richness of formal fantasy comes in the description of the garden of Eden in du Bartas' poem on the creation in the *Seconde Sepmaine* (1578), lines 459-520. This poem was translated by Joshua Sylvester as *The Divine Weeks*, and the garden description is both accurate and picturesque. Du Bartas does not give square walls to Eden, like the garden in *Amadis*, but the details are still characteristic of the period. Adam strolls in a rose garden 'which (one would think) the Angels did daily dresse in true love-knots, tri-angles, lozenges.' When he walks along a 'levell lane', the trees are exotic and proper for Paradise – plane, orange, lemon, and citron – and the fruit trees yield abundantly without artificial attention, for they are 'un-graft Trees'. But they are all arranged with architectural symmetry: the fruit trees' 'leavie twigs, that intricately tangle,/Seem painted walls whereon true fruits do dangle'; and they are planted 'in checker round and square'. The jewel-strewn river is crossed by 'natural' and extravagant bridges:

> . . . rocks self-arch'd by the eating Current:
> Or loving *Palms*, whose lusty Females willing
> Their marrow-boyling loves to be fulfilling
> (And reach their Husband-trees on th'other banks)
> Bow their stiffe backs, and serve for passing-planks.

Adam wanders through 'crooked walks', which are seen in terms of formal labyrinths, and to complete the rich formality of Eden, these paths are not 'simply hedgèd with a single border Of Rosemary', but are fantastical,

> . . . cut-out with curious order,
> In *Satyrs, Centaurs, Whales,* and *half-men-horses,*
> And thousand other counterfeited corses.

It is a fascinating thought that while du Bartas wrote of this wholly formal

91   The countless
representations of the Garden of
Eden are not really the business of
this book; yet the paradise garden
is a recurrent ideal, and Holbein's
woodcut of 'Adam and Eve in
Paradise' is characteristic of a
superior sixteenth-century
presentation of an un-formal
Eden, anticipating John Milton's ·
description a century later

Paradise, some sixteenth-century painters – Holbein, Breughel and Savary for example – were concerned to show our first parents in scenes nearer a jungle or a zoo than a garden. The same fantasy appears in a late sixteenth-century Flemish valance showing a young zooful of exotic animals, roaming round a moated summer-house a little like a kiosk or *chabutra* in an Islamic garden!

SIR FRANCIS BACON

In the early 1600s, Sir Francis Bacon was involved both in the theory and fantasy and in the reality of gardens. Born in 1561, he had had forty years' experience of Elizabethan life when he inherited his father's estate at Gorhambury in Hertfordshire in 1602. He gardened here extensively, and his notes outlining a scheme to make a four-acre water garden exist in the British Museum. It was to have 'a fair rail with images gild round about it, and some low flowers, especially strawberries and violets', and between the 'fair rail' and the water 'a fair hedge of timber work till it touch the water, with some glasses coloured for the eye.' I imagine that this carpenter's work was a tunnel, running beside the lake, and the 'glass coloured for the eye' would have been set high up on the top of the hedge to be seen from outside, and from across the lake. In the lake were several islands, each with different features: one had an arbour of hornbeam, another an 'arbour of musk roses set out with double violets for scent in autumn', and the 'Middle Great Island' had 'a house for freshness, with an upper gallery open to the water, a terrace above that and a supping room below that'; in principle rather like the 'maison blanche' in the small *giardino segreto* at Gaillon, though less ornate. Later in the century John Aubrey described it as a 'curious Banqueting House of Roman architecture, paved with black and white marble', which supports the suggestion. But the 'house for freshness', and the islands round it have now gone completely. Around 1680 Aubrey noted that the ponds were untended, but that Bacon had had them 'pitched at the bottoms with pebbles of several colours, which were worked into several figures, as of fishes, &c.' This was 'in his lordship's time', when the figures 'were plainly to be seen through the clear water' – 'now overgrown with flags and rushes.'

Bacon's garden has gone; but his essay 'Of Gardens', published in 1625, a year before his death, remains as a delightful monument to his enthusiasm, though not to the clarity of his presentation. The separate parts of this essay – literally an 'attempt' to set down thoughts on and around a subject, like the earlier *Essais* of Montaigne – are fascinating and instructive, but it is hard to draw a convincing plan of the garden he describes, and as hard to say that Bacon has a coherent and unflawed body of ideas on the subject. Later readers have chosen to look in Bacon's essay for confirmation of their own views – approving the wild, or the formal, the plain or the intricate garden – rather than seeing how his variety of interest is characteristic of the late Elizabethan age. Better, and more profitable, is to see and to enjoy the parts, as one was intended to do in a sixteenth-century garden. This essay, written after a lifetime's experience, describes the ideal. Near the beginning, he says 'I do hold it in the royal ordering of gardens, there ought to be . . .'; i.e. he is discussing gardens designed on a grand and princely scale.

Bacon, like all those of his time who were sensitive to unpleasant smells, responded eagerly to pleasant scents, and especially to 'the breath of flowers in the air (where it comes and goes, like the warbling of music)', so he devises a fragrant series of plants whose scents rise up in the air, like violets, or 'strawberry-leaves dying . . . a most excellent Cordial smell'; and best of all, burnet, wild thyme, and water-mints to tread on: 'therefore you are to set whole alleys of them, to have the pleasure when you walk or tread.'

He imagines a 'prince-like' garden, of thirty acres, with a 'green in the entrance', 'a heath or desert' on the far side, and a 'main garden in the midst'. This main garden is to be square, and with a 'stately arched hedge . . . of carpenter's work' all round, arched and adorned with cages of birds, and 'over every space between the arches some other little figure, with broad plates of round coloured glass gilt for the sun to play upon' (like the 'glasses coloured for the eye' in his lakeside hedge at Gorhambury).

92   Another Flemish
embroidery, *c.* 1590, of a paradise
garden. From the central
viewpoint, a man and a woman
look over the moat to a menagerie
of animals, from a unicorn to a
gigantic toad, which roam in the
surrounding grounds

Inside the 'great hedge' of the main garden, he wants a relatively simple garden. Knots with 'divers coloured earths . . . be but toys: you may see as good sights many times in tarts'; elaborate topiary, 'images cut out in juniper or other garden stuff . . . be for children', and fountains may be a 'great beauty and refreshment; but pools mar all, and make the garden unwholesome and full of flies and frogs.' The fountain jokes and devices – 'of arching water without spilling and making it rise in several forms (of feathers, drinking glasses, canopies, and the like)' – are all very well, 'pretty things to look on', 'but nothing to health and sweetness'. So we may imagine he has few knots, but rather broad walks and hedges clipped soberly, 'round like welts [or borders], with some pretty pyramids', and in the centre, 'a fair mount, with three ascents, and alleys, enough for four to walk abreast'; this last resembling the 'cockleshell' turnings of the mount at Wressel Castle, 'to come to the top with pain'. At the centre, maybe beside the mount, or maybe at the top, 'some fine banqueting-house' is to be built, and we may think of the 'house for freshness', with its 'supping room', which he made on the 'Middle Great Island' at Gorhambury.

Bacon's 'heath' is to show 'a natural wildness', but this does not mean the sublime wildness of the eighteenth century. It is a scene of flowers; more like a medieval 'flowery mede' than a twentieth-century 'wild garden', though it is hard to be sure. The flowers grow 'here and there, not in any order', but they are, or so I read the text, 'set' in separate and tidy clumps, raised in 'little heaps, in the nature of mole-hills', and some clumps, of pinks, daisies, violets, sweet-williams, red roses and others, are to have taller 'standards' or bushes at the centre, kept in order 'with cutting that they may not grow out of course.'

And at the corners of the complete garden, he will, like William Lawson, have a mount 'to look abroad into the fields', and no doubt to look in and over the garden itself.

SALOMON DE CAUS AND JOSEPH FURTTENBACH

The 'royal ordering of gardens' was put into practice at the time Bacon wrote his essay in ways which run parallel to this work; indeed, Bacon might have heard of the wonderful gardens begun at Heidelberg, and illustrated in the *Hortus Palatinus* of Salomon de Caus. This slim volume of plates, published in 1620, is one of the most moving of all monuments to the fragility of gardens, however great. Caus had designed and supervised the creation of this Renaissance marvel, built on an intractable site beside the castle, high above the town and the river Neckar. The text of his book is an *au lecteur* of only three pages, in which he speaks of the 'delay to the work' which has occurred. He writes: 'Thus with much work and expense we have now, in November 1619, arrived almost to the completion of the whole design. And had it not been for the present wars, the whole would have been completed in six months or so.' Further on he adds that a large pavilion which had been planned 'has still remained incomplete, because of the wars of Bohemia.'

These wars, and other wars beyond, raged round Heidelberg well past the time of Salomon de Caus. His work was never finished, and what had been built was soon abandoned. But the 'Scenographia' (see endpapers) and the lesser plates illustrating the details of the garden remain to show how vast, how extravagant the conception was. It had delights within and without – Alberti could not complain about the view – and the intricacy and variety respond to the magnitude of its scale. In the eighteenth century, the debased successors to the formal gardens at Versailles will be grand, but empty. At Heidelberg, every section is 'curious', with the excitement in detailed work which inspires the sculpture of the fountains in the palazzo Borghese in Rome, or the knots in the garden at Gaillon.

We can see such love of detail in the other book published by Salomon de Caus, *Les Raisons des Forces Mouvantes* (1615, second edition 1624). This is a book of fountains, and of related matters, such as grottoes with fountains, mounts with grottoes, orangeries with fountains, water toys and jokes, and crude fire engines. One is that of the 'owl and birds', which was installed at the villa d'Este, and which Caus acknowledges as coming from Hero of Alexandria's *Pneumatica*. The edition of 1624 has towards the end the 'design for an orangery', with a note adding that

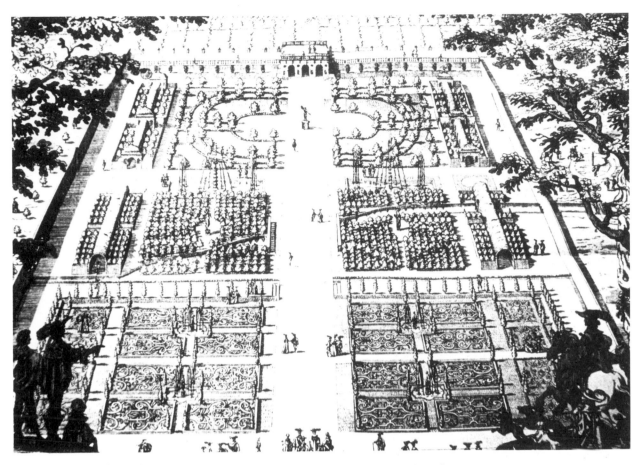

93   Wilton (this picture dates from 1640 or earlier) was the first great formal garden in England. It was executed from designs by Isaac de Caus, the son or nephew of Salomon de Caus who designed the even more stupendous and extravagant gardens at Heidelberg in 1619, shown on the endpapers to this book. The plan at Wilton has a striking general unity, with its firm central avenue, and division into matching areas of knots and trees. As at the villa Aldobrandini, Vaux and Versailles, the principal view is from the mansion

Caus 'had built four of this kind at Heidelberg.'

An Isaac de Caus, probably Salomon's son, went to England and designed another of the great late Renaissance gardens, at Wilton in Wiltshire. Whether son, brother or nephew, he certainly knew of Salomon's work, for two of the designs for carpenter's work at Wilton in Isaac de Caus's *Wilton Garden* correspond with designs in Salomon's *Hortus Palatinus*. The view of Wilton (pl. 93) is like the Heidelberg 'Scenographia' for the detail of the bedding in the foreground, the carpenter's work running along the sides, and the grotto-pavilion at the far end, though its general shape, with the irregular course of the river Nadder through the centre, is nearer to that of the garden in *Amadis de Gaule*. All three gardens are vast: Wilton, the smallest, was a thousand feet long and four hundred wide. Caus shows in his comments that this garden was designed to be surveyed not only from within, but from viewpoints in the house itself, looking towards the nearer and more detailed part of the garden, and from two raised terraces, one at the end of the first section of 'Platts' or beds (a 'little Terrass rased for the more advantage of beholding those Platts') and one at the far end of the garden. This idea that a garden needs to be seen from a special viewpoint, and the eventual designing of the garden to be seen best from one such viewpoint, is a particular development of the seventeenth century, and was to become increasingly important in the design of formal gardens in the French manner.

For a few years Wilton survived in this glorious form – once 'the noblest in England', Evelyn suggested – and was then changed and changed again. Soon after Salomon and Isaac de Caus had worked at Heidelberg and Wilton, the two remaining Renaissance fantasy gardens were conceived. One remained a plan in a book, while the other, Isola Bella, was eventually built. The first is in the *Architectura Civilis* of Joseph Furttenbach, published in 1628, and is, like Bacon's essay, a proposal for a princely garden, though it is grander, more fantastic and more detailed than Bacon's scheme. Furttenbach has designs for other smaller gardens in this book, and more again in his *Architectura Recreationis* of 1640. They are all enclosed, and those of any size are actually within fortifications, like the princely garden of 1628. But this largest garden is so vast that it is a countryside in itself. It is interesting to see that the text which refers to the raised viewpoints on walls and terraces, e.g. numbers 3, 20 and 21 on the plan, speaks only of views inward into and over the garden itself. The outward views are only for sentries. Within, all is richness and variety: such complicated knots, edged with box and filled with flowers, such elaborate carpenter's work, fishponds, fountains, aviaries, walks lined with statues, an orangery, a great grotto, and beyond a hunting park – and in this 'a small Pallazotto, standing in the wilderness', where the prince may read or relax. It is an oddity, easier in the drawing than the execution, but not, I think, any more wilful or spendthrift than others we have seen. Make its walls less fortress-like, and its affinities with Bacon, with the villa Lante and its *bosco*, with Caprarola, with Gaillon and with the garden of *Amadis de Gaule* are clear.

THE GARDEN–GALLEON OF ISOLA BELLA

The garden of Isola Bella (originally to be Isola Isabella, named after the wife of Count Carlo Borromeo) was made from an island in Lake Maggiore. Work began around 1630, and the gardens were completed in 1671, though the palace was never fully built as originally planned, and the island itself did not receive the narrow

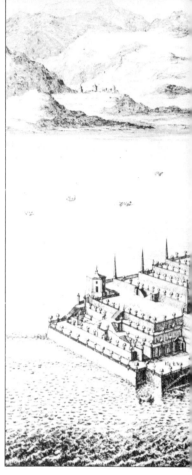

94   Joseph Furttenbach's project (1628) for a princely palace and gardens (left). One of the last great Renaissance garden designs, it is comparable with Caus' gardens at Heidelberg (see the endpapers to this book). The walls are for defence and to allow a view inwards, in the manner of a medieval mount. Though there is a 'progression' from the elaborate gardens in the foreground – knots, statuary, arbours, aviaries, fishponds – to the distant wilderness for hunting and meditation, there is no single overall view of the gardens, any more than there is at the villa d'Este

95   Isola Bella (above), from Fisher von Erlach's *Entwurff Einer Historischen Architektur* (1721). This shows the island-garden as it should have been, with a jutting point to the right representing the prow of the great galleon. Though this prow was never built, easily enough of the gardens was made by 1671 to convey the feeling of this most extravagant boat of stone, whose stern rises up in terrace after terrace encrusted with carvings, adorned with sculpture and always green flowering plants and citrus trees

pointed end, lined with cypress or poplar trees, which is represented on the early engravings. The aim was to convert the rocky and irregular island into the shape of a tremendous stone ship, a superb garden-galleon anchored in the lake, with all the seclusion of an island, but with the total luxury of varied and limitless views of water, coastline, countryside and mountains, endlessly changing with the seasons, the weather and the time of day. Edward Gibbon had the rarest visit to Isola Bella: when he went in May 1764, the rain was 'so very heavy' that the island could not be seen from the boat at all! Though the 'prow' of the vessel was not built, easily enough was completed to convince us of the overall design. At the 'stern', terrace upon terrace rises up like the poop of a galleon, adorned with sculpture and manned by the statues which crowd the niches and balustrades.

The island-garden and the boat-garden have fascinated gardeners since the beginning – most of all, I think, because of the richness and variety of the idea, the compression of opposites into the single, and often quite small expanse. Isola Bella is the most extravagant of all these boat-garden-islands. They are still being built; at Vizcaya in Florida, and in the last ten years in the Persian Gulf. The new mosque of Sultan Omar Ali Saifuddin at Bandar Seri Begawan is surrounded on three sides by a broad crescent of water, and here a costly stone boat is moored, with pointed prow and overhanging stern, and summerhouses whose raised roofs counterfeit lateen sails.

96   A diagonal view across the
main axis and the transverse canal
at Vaux-le-Vicomte

9

The Formal French Garden

The formal French garden begins to distinguish itself from the gardens of Italy around the year 1600. In 1600 Olivier de Serres published his *Théâtre d'Agriculture*, a work which not only repeats much information to do with gardening in the sixteenth century, but expresses confidence in the superiority of new French gardens: 'One need not travel to Italy or elsewhere to see gardens finely set out, since our own France has won the prize from all other nations . . .'

In the chapter on 'The use of plants and flowers for borders and compartments', de Serres writes of the intricate designs of knots which can be seen in French gardens and of the plants used in terms which seem appropriate for Elizabethan England: designs of 'letters, patterns, figures, coats of arms, men and beasts, buildings, vessels, boats' set out with evergreen or verdant plants such as myrtle, lavender, rosemary, box, marjoram, thyme, hyssop, sage, camomile, mint and even parsley. And then he adds that because of the frailty of most of these plants,

> it has been resolved to make [the compartments], or nearly all of them, out of box alone, so that the compartments of the parterre may endure longer. The beauty of the foliage of box remains the same, whatever the weather, even ice and snow. Its hardiness gives it a long life and makes it easy to maintain. For this reason, disregarding its strong and unpleasant odour, box is used for the most delicate work in the parterre.

Though it has other important features, the formal French garden has at its centre the parterre, and the parterre is distinguished from the knot by being laid out almost always in box. It is distinguished also by its relationship to the overall design of the garden, and its relationship to the house, palace or mansion for which this garden is designed. While the knots of Elizabethan gardens – or those in France illustrated by du Cerceau – had no special resemblance one with another, the parterres of the formal French garden were designed as part of a unified and general plan. Furthermore, this overall plan was related to the house itself in a manner which was new. De Serres indicates this in the same chapter, though not as forcefully as he does when declaring the new supremacy of box. In 1600, French gardens are still far removed from the uniformity of style which they were later to acquire.

> These plantings of box . . . will not be made in a confused manner . . . so that the compartments remain uniform . . . We should note that, just as the painter endeavours to make one side of his design match the other, so the gardener will do likewise . . . for example, if on the right you have a design of a scroll, a square, a circle, an oval . . . then on the left this must reappear without addition, subtraction, or any other variation . . .

So much for the balance of the halves, or quarters, of the overall design (we may reflect, looking forward a century, that this very *balance* is what Pope finds so offensive in the formal garden, in his 'Epistle to Lord Burlington'). The garden as a whole is then to be seen from the house. The word parterre means 'on' or 'along' the ground, and in the seventeenth century it came to mean a section of the garden which was best appreciated from a higher position; in particular, from the house, and best of all, from the central and commanding position in the house, in other words the great room on the raised first floor, the *piano nobile*. Here the master would receive and dazzle his guests with the magnificence of his possessions, and from the windows of this room the ordered elegance and extent of his gardens would be seen. This idea is foreshadowed in the arrangement of the villa Aldobrandini, and is brought to its arrogant conclusion in the châteaux of the seventeenth and eighteenth centuries.

De Serres writes that 'for reasons of perspective . . . you must make those further away more extensive than those which are nearer. On the other hand, the nearer they are, the closer together they should be . . .'

Two paragraphs later, de Serres mentions that 'M. Claude Mollet, gardener to His Majesty', has been responsible for some of the parterres which he admires. This Claude Mollet (*c.* 1563–*c.* 1650) is one of a dynasty of Mollets who are at the very heart of the French formal garden. His father Jacques Mollet was the head gardener of the Duc d'Aumale at the château of Anet in the 1580s, and Claude Mollet worked there with him as a young man. In 1582, the architect Etienne du Pérac (d. 1601) returned from a visit to Italy, and was employed by the Duc d'Aumale. Du Pérac taught the young Mollet

> how fine gardens were to be made: so that an entire garden did not, and could not be other than a single compartment, divided up by the principal walks. And so these designs looked far more impressive than those which my late father, and other gardeners of his time, would have made. These were the first parterres and compartments of *broderie* ['embroidery', looking like brocade] which were made in France, and this is why I have since then always made them in the grand manner . . . so that I have no longer been content to make compartments in little squares, one of one sort, and the next of another.

This quotation is from a manuscript by Claude Mollet (see E. de Ganay, *Les Jardins de France*, 1949), and its sentiment is reproduced both in Claude Mollet's *Théâtre des Plans et Jardinages* (published posthumously in 1652), and in several other books published in the first half of the seventeenth century. Already in the 1570s, some of the plans drawn by du Cerceau – in particular that of Charleval, a garden which, like the château, was never executed – hint at a wished-for *overall* unity of house and garden which earlier French châteaux did not have. The *Raisons des Forces Mouvantes* of Salomon de Caus (1615) contains the design of a mount (with a watery grotto beneath) with the comment: 'There are several fine and excellent gardens situated on flat ground, so that one cannot see their form, nor the parterres which they contain, and it seems to me that the finest view of a garden is to be seen from above', therefore, readers, 'make this mount'; and the *Traité du Jardinage* (1638) of Jacques Boyceau de la Barauderie takes Claude Mollet's ideas a stage further by insisting on the need for an overall proportion of the parts of the garden, coupled with a desire for variety, which he solves by introducing curves and arabesques into the design of parterres.

A year before Claude Mollet's posthumous work was published, his son André Mollet's *Jardin de Plaisir* appeared (1651). André, who worked for Louis XIII, had become the head gardener of Queen Christina of Sweden, and the book was published in Stockholm. This work codifies the concept of a formal garden. The drawings of gardens, and the particular details of the *parterres de broderie*, all fulfil the requirement of a unified plan, conceived with a principal viewpoint situated in the house itself. The text accompanying these designs includes the following paragraph, which is nothing less than a summary of the arrangement and ingredients of a French formal garden:

> To the rear of the house [i.e. facing the garden front], the *parterres de broderie* must first be set out, so that they can be seen and enjoyed from the windows, without any obstacle in the form of trees, fences, or other high objects which might interrupt the view.

XIX, XX Designed by Le Nôtre, the gardens at Vaux-le-Vicomte were laid out in 1657-61, and restored to their present state, closely resembling the original gardens, at the end of the nineteenth century. The principal vista is from the château over the *parterre de broderie* and along the main axis to the arcaded grotto, beyond which the terrain slopes up to the statue of Hercules, outlined against the horizon. The general symmetry of the gardens is repeated in particular details, and gives them remarkable unity, with the château as the centre and source of control

97 At the side of the Luxembourg in Paris, the *parterre de broderie* lives on, the essence of a tradition nearly four centuries old. In 1644, John Evelyn admired Boyceau's parterres here – 'the embroidery makes a stupendious effect' – and although the original area of *parterre de broderie* has been simplified, much survives. The photograph shows the laying out of a new parterre, with the ground divided into squares to correspond with the master plan

XXI Courances (top left) is today one of the most beautiful examples of the French formal garden. Designed in the 1690s, possibly by Le Nôtre himself, it fell into disrepair, and was faultlessly restored three centuries later by Achille Duchêne. The exact symmetry of the horizontal plane is relieved by the billowing shapes of the chestnuts enclosing the lawn and pool

XXII The formal French garden was recreated in England as well as in France. Here, the fountain garden at Blenheim (left) was designed in the present century by Achille Duchêne, consciously echoing the *parterre d'eau* at Versailles

Beyond the said *parterre de broderie* will be set the parterres or compartments of turf, as well as the *bosquets*, walks and various fences in their proper places; so contrived that most of the walks are always terminated by some statue or fountain; and at the end of these walks you should erect fine scenes, painted on canvas, so that you may take them indoors in bad weather. To complete this design, statues should be erected on pedestals, and grottoes built in the most appropriate places. According to the quality of the site, the walks should be raised on terraces and one should not neglect aviaries, fountains, water-works, canals and other such ornaments. When these have been properly established in the right places, you have made the perfect pleasure garden.

Half a century has passed between de Serres' book of 1600 and André Mollet's *Jardin de Plaisir* of 1651. It took this long for the idea of the formal garden to gain wholesale acceptance. In the 1640s it is seen both in England and in France: in the overall unity of the gardens at Wilton, designed by Isaac de Caus, and in the beautifully proportioned gardens of the Luxembourg, designed by Boyceau (who also designed the now forgotten gardens of early Versailles for Louis XIII), and observed, with perspicacity, by John Evelyn in 1644. As an Englishman, still used to knots laid out with many plants, he writes: 'The parterre is indeed of box', and then continues 'but so rarely designed and accurately kept cut, that the embroidery makes a stupendious effect to the lodgings which front it.' Evelyn sees the essential: that the parterre is related to the house, and that its success and effect depend on its proper association with the proportions of the house.

This principle is accepted by other members of the Mollet dynasty; by André's brother Claude, who worked for James I of England, and by Gabriel, who worked for Charles II on the design of St James's Park in London. It was also accepted by the great André Le Nôtre (1613–1700), himself the son and grandson of notable gardeners, and by most of Le Nôtre's disciples, well into the eighteenth century. The principle of the subservience of the parterre to the house is so firmly established that the patterns of the parterre can become incomprehensible when seen from the 'wrong' viewpoint: the engraving of the eighteenth-century parterre at La Muette, from Le Rouge's *Détails des Nouveaux Jardins à La Mode*, shows this to perfection (see pl. 98).

In the French formal garden, both the *parterre de broderie* and the further sections of the garden are to be seen and enjoyed first and foremost from the house, since the house is the symbol of authority. The garden is an area where nature, elsewhere unruly and irregular, has been tamed, and made to follow the dictates of the owner. The irregular growths of bushes and trees have been trained into geometrical and symmetrical shapes, either as hedges, clipped into green but clearly architectural forms, or as elements of *broderie*, straight or curving lines of box, punctuated by cones and pyramids of clipped yew; and the fountains in the formal pools obediently squirt and spout their jets in balanced and symmetrical patterns.

André Le Nôtre, who began his gardening career at the Tuileries gardens in Paris

some time before 1649, succeeded his father Jean Le Nôtre, who had worked for a while under Claude Mollet. The Tuileries already had a fine garden, and Le Nôtre worked there in a subordinate position for some while, his designs for the Tuileries (his own favourite garden) not being executed until he was well established. His greatest garden still survives, at Vaux-le-Vicomte, Seine-et-Marne, created between 1656 and 1661 for Nicolas Fouquet, Louis XIV's ambitious and powerful finance minister. Probably because it was a creation begun from scratch and brought to completion in such a short period, and achieved with the friendly cooperation of the architect Le Vau and the painter Le Brun, who were in charge of the building and its decoration, Vaux is a garden composition with an immediately perceptible unity, like the unity of the Mughal garden of the Taj Mahal, of the same period. The gardens which surround the château on all four sides are clearly *appropriate*, as an approach, at the front, as flanking ornaments, and as a great embellishment and extension of the château at the rear. Everywhere at Vaux there is a sensation of control, and it is a control which emanates from the château, saying in so many words: 'I, Nicolas Fouquet, am in command.' From the steps looking over the main *parterre de broderie* or, better still, looking out from the first floor of the château, the gardens appear as an immense gesture of power, where the elements of nature have been tamed, disciplined and brought together to serve as parts of a human scheme. The parterre is, as it were, a carpet laid out before the château, an extension of the elegance and richness to be found within. As the visitor proceeds down the main *allée*, the fountains, clipped bushes and statues confirm the sense of discipline. In a subtler way which is Le Nôtre's triumph, the masterly arrangement of the different levels of pool and canal and grassy slope beyond contrives to give superb reflections and reminders of the symbols of power and control: the symmetrical fountains, the symmetrical arcade and balustrade of the grotto, the towering statue of the Farnese Hercules at the end of the vista, and as one turns round to look back up the main *allée* – following the gaze of the colossal Hercules – the vision of the château itself, both real and duplicated in the pool at the foot of the great parterre.

The gardens of Vaux are still wonderfully close to their state in 1661, when they were completed. Fouquet was disgraced (this is discussed in the following chapter) and the gardens gradually fell into disrepair. Much of the sculpture was removed, and it was not until the very end of the nineteenth century that the gardens were restored under the direction of the architect Laîné, followed by Henri Duchêne (1841–1902), the father of the more famous Achille Duchêne (1886–1947), who restored many classical French gardens and designed others in the same style – for example the water parterre at Blenheim in England.

It is appropriate to mention here the gardens of Courances, Seine-et-Oise, made in the middle of the seventeenth century (Le Nôtre's name is associated, but without proof), and like Vaux-le-Vicomte allowed to deteriorate. Achille Duchêne was called in to restore the garden early in the present century, and the *parterre de broderie* is now in a state of perfection which Le Nôtre would approve. The main garden, like the principal vista at Vaux, is designed to be appreciated first and foremost from the château, and the view of the slightly rounded, yet symmetrical *bassin* beyond the parterre, with a plain framework of lawn and billowing chestnut trees, is one of the most beautiful garden prospects in the world. Le Nôtre himself would not, I am sure, have countenanced such gentle greenness: the chestnuts would have been

clipped back, tall and straight (or rather, hedges of hornbeam would have been planted in their place) to reveal the statues which are now half-hidden in the shade, while the edge of the *bassin* would have been outlined with bright gravel paths. In the same way, the lovely twin canals which run beside the drive leading to the front of the château would not be overhung and shaded as they are today. Or would they? At Trianon, Le Nôtre's favourite area was his *bosquet des sources*, a small region through which springs of water trickled in the shade of trees planted in an irregular pattern.

Unlike Vaux-le-Vicomte, many of the other gardens which Le Nôtre worked on, such as Fontainebleau or Chantilly, were already partly or wholly built when he began to transform them, and have since undergone further changes, so that they do not represent Le Nôtre's conception in its purest form. The idea of the unified parterre, intimately related to the situation and proportions of its château, was not fully accepted in France until Le Nôtre's time, and outside France it was received with far less conviction. The *Théâtre d'Agriculture* of Olivier de Serres in 1600 certainly gives the parterre the emphasis which it is to hold in France for the next 150 years, but the book also contains a chapter on the importance, content and design of a medicinal herb garden, centred round a circular or square mount.

While the designs of Boyceau and the two Mollets, André and Claude, show the new unified gardens, other books, even French ones, do not. The volume of designs by D. Loris, *Le Thresor des Parterres de l'Univers* (1629), is divided into *parterres allemands*, *parterres françois* and *labyrinthes*, but far from reflecting the new fashions in the French designs, Loris' patterns are throughout exactly square in their overall proportions, and are patently knots rather than parterres.

In England, writers such as John Evelyn, Sir Thomas Browne (1605–82), and Sir William Temple (1628–99) all reveal an awareness of French influence, but none of them admits French supremacy in garden matters. It is not until the remodelling of the main garden of Hampton Court in 1689 that the formal French garden is really established in Britain, and its dominance will last only twenty or thirty years before the effects of the new interest in 'nature' and the 'landscape' begin to be felt.

102   A view over the Latona
fountain down the Grand Allée,
towards the Apollo fountain and
the mile-long Canal

10

Louis XIV and Versailles

THE BIRTH OF VERSAILLES

The garden-front of the château of Versailles faces west, extending north and south for over six hundred yards. Stretching westward from the centre of this façade are the gardens, whose central, east-west axis is well over a mile in length. This axis begins with water parterres in front of the château, then passes through the Latona fountain and down the grassy Allée Royale to the Apollo fountain. Beyond the Apollo fountain begins the great Canal, running westward along the central axis of the gardens for a mile. The Canal is cross-shaped, and its south and north arms lead to the Menagerie and to the gardens of the two Trianons. The area of gardens between the façade of the château and the Apollo fountain is called the Petit Parc, and is crossed by subsidiary *allées* mostly running parallel to the central axis, or crossing it at right angles. Most of the Petit Parc, which is thickly wooded, is therefore divided up into geometrical sections, which contained the various *bosquets* – the Labyrinth, the Three Fountains, the Colonnade, the Water Theatre and so forth. Some of these features have been destroyed but many still survive. Immediately before the garden-front of the château, in front of the northern and southern wings, are the Parterre du Nord, the north parterre, and the Parterre du Midi or south parterre. Further beyond the Parterre du Midi is the Orangery, and then a large lake, the Pièce des Suisses, and to the north of the Parterre du Nord are more *bosquets* and the Neptune fountain. Though not very elevated, the château stands at the highest point in the gardens, and the ground slopes gently away towards the west, and also to the north and south.

South of the Pièce des Suisses is yet another garden: the enormous formal *potager*, the fruit and vegetable garden designed and directed by Jean de La Quintinie (1626–88), whose *Instructions pour les Jardins Fruitiers et Potagers* (1690) was translated by John Evelyn as *The Compleat Gard'ner* (1693). The *potager*, a subject in itself, must be passed over in favour of the king's far greater and even more impressive pleasure gardens.

The château and gardens of Versailles began, we know, in the reign of Louis XIII, when that king acquired the park for hunting and built himself a house of moderate size as a necessary residence – a superior hunting lodge, one might say – with unassuming gardens on one side.

But their spiritual beginnings – much more important – are elsewhere, at Vaux-le-Vicomte, and we may date them to the day: 17 August 1661. This was the date of Nicolas Fouquet's sumptuous reception, offered to Louis XIV and his court, at Vaux. In modern terms, we could call it a 'house-warming', for the entire château – the building, the interior decoration and the surrounding gardens – was just complete. It was a memorable date, for Fouquet, for Louis XIV and, though neither would have thought so at the time, for garden history.

The poet La Fontaine, a great friend of Fouquet's, was one of the guests, and five days after the party he sent a long description to another friend, Maucroix, who was away in Rome. Almost all the festivities took place in the gardens, which we must imagine peopled with several thousand guests for the whole of a summer's afternoon and evening. 'The king, the queen mother, the dauphin and dauphine, and many princes and great lords were there. There was a magnificent dinner, a fine comedy, a

103 A simplified yet revealing engraving of the principal vista at Versailles. Published in 1733, this view had already existed for well over sixty years and is much the same today. The overall symmetry of the gardens, their immensity, and the architectural control over the elements of nature are immediately apparent. The tiny human figures are absorbed in this vast landscape, where the great Canal stretches into the distance, while the Menagerie and Trianon are hidden at the extreme ends of the left and right arms of the canal

delightful ballet, and an incomparable firework display.' Beginning with a 'promenade', all the court walked round the gardens to view the fountains. Then to dinner, and after that the comedy, Molière's *Les Fâcheux*, performed outside in a theatre set up in the *allée* of the pines.

This was followed by a ballet, after which came a firework-display. Then a roll of drums, for the musketeers were present to accompany the king to his palace at Fontainebleau for the night. The guests therefore walked back through the gardens towards the château to conclude the evening with a collation. Suddenly, 'when no-one expected anything more, the sky was in an instant hidden by a terrifying cloud of rockets . . .' This surprising climax to the entertainment had an unfortunate effect: a pair of horses, harnessed to one of the coaches, took fright, fell into the moat and were killed. La Fontaine adds, 'I would not have thought that my account should end in so tragic and pitiful a way.'

The ending was to be far more tragic. On 5 September 1661, less than three weeks after his great reception, Fouquet was arrested by Louis XIV. It was indeed a party to end all parties: the king himself was envious to the point of enmity. Fouquet was never to be released, and his long years in prison made him an unhappy legend, perhaps the 'man in the iron mask'. For his part, Louis XIV was never to forget the challenge to his supremacy which Vaux represented, and the château and gardens of Versailles as he made them are the direct and real result of his visit to Vaux. For forty years, from 1661 until the turn of the century, the gardens of Versailles, of Trianon and Marly are created in the shadow of Vaux, and in their extent and splendour, variety and extravagance they emulate and endeavour to surpass the model of Vaux, both in its formal details and in its arrogant aesthetic of command.

Swiftly the king took Fouquet's team of artists – Le Vau, the architect, Le Brun, the painter, Le Nôtre, the gardener – and set them to work at Versailles. Their talent henceforth was employed to declare *his* glory, and the château and gardens at Versailles were to be the creation which *he* could demonstrate to the world, as Fouquet had demonstrated Vaux in August 1661. Louis XIV did not however do this just once, as did Fouquet, but innumerable times, and for over half a century, from the early 1660s until his death in 1715.

THE ROYAL ITINERARY

Indeed, the gardens rather than the château are what visitors were expected to admire, and from journals, travel accounts, memoirs and biographies one could cull a young bookfull of anecdotes concerning the visits which people made to the gardens, guided personally by the king, or in his suite, or going round with his representatives; making the whole tour, a partial tour, or inspecting a single feature in the gardens. The king himself was indefatigable – when young, he would walk or go round in a coach, while in his old age he would be taken round in his *roulette*, a small three-wheeled chariot pulled and propelled by two or three footmen. We see him aged sixty-two, in his *roulette*, with Le Nôtre, aged eighty-eight. Saint-Simon writes of Louis' affection for Le Nôtre:

> One month before his death, the king, who liked to see him and to talk with him, took him round his gardens. Since Le Nôtre was so very old, the king had him go round in a chaise pushed beside his own. When this was done, Le Nôtre said 'Oh, if my old father were only alive to see me now – to see his son, a poor gardener, going round in a chaise beside the greatest king in the world – then my happiness would be complete.'

What a promenade that must have been: the gardens at the moment of their greatest glory, truly one of the world's wonders, and visited, inspected, reviewed by the two men who had done most to create them – one the most powerful king, and the other the greatest gardener of the age.

It would have been especially fascinating to know what *itinerary* they took, what route through the gardens, to see which parts, which features? Did they go the complete round, visiting Trianon and the Menagerie (which would take them most of a day); did they visit the Petit Parc alone, the *allées*, *bosquets* and features nearest to the palace? Or was this visit remarkable also for its spontaneity – did Louis, or did Le Nôtre, decide *en roulant*, as it were, what they would go to see? Silly questions, you may think, and virtually impossible to answer. Unanswerable, yes; but I believe not silly at all, for Louis XIV had himself written an itinerary for viewing the gardens, entitled *La Manière de Montrer les Jardins de Versailles*, which not only indicates a route round the gardens, but tells, indeed commands the visitor to view them in a certain order, and to look at them in a certain way (see *Garden History*, I, 1 September 1972, where I have edited and translated the texts). Several manuscript versions of this document exist, the earliest dated 1689, the latest 1705, while a map published in 1714 reproduces the stations of the itinerary in full, bringing the history of this composition to the close of Louis XIV's reign (he died on 1 September 1715).

La Manière de Montrer les Jardins de Versailles evolves with the gardens it describes – the earlier texts refer to features which are later altered or destroyed and new features take their place. For example, the first texts refer to the Marais at one point, where the later texts refer to the Bains d'Apollon. The Marais, or the 'Marsh', was a rectangular pool containing a metal tree in the centre, which spouted water from its branches, while at each corner of the pool clumps of metal reeds, or bullrushes, spouted water in a similar way. The Marais was created for Mme de Montespan, Louis' mistress in the 1670s. When she fell from favour, the memory of her garden influence was erased, and in 1704-5 a new feature, the Bains d'Apollon, the 'Baths of Apollo' was quickly set up in its place. The continuing evolution of the gardens in Louis' reign can in fact be seen as well in the history of this spot as anywhere. Prior to the Marais, the site was covered with trees. The Marais lasted for forty years, and when it was destroyed in 1704, the statuary for the new Bains d'Apollon was obtained from another feature which had also been destroyed, the Grotte de Tethys. The Grotte de Tethys was near the palace, approximately on the site of the present chapel. This grotto, with elaborate rock and shell ornamentation, sumptuous statuary, and a profusion of hydraulic effects – fountains, a water-organ

104, 105   Two versions of *La Manière de Montrer les Jardins de Versailles*. The earliest (top) is headed 'On the 19th July 1689: at six o'clock in the evening', and was specially arranged for the ex-queen of England, the wife of the exiled James II. The written version (above) is in the impatient handwriting of the Sun King himself. Louis XIV wrote this between 1699 and 1704. Its manner is abrupt and autocratic: '1. Leaving the Château by the vestibule which is below the King's chamber, go to the terrace. Stop at the top of the steps to consider the . . . garden . . . 2. Then turn to the left . . .'

149

and many water jokes – was one of the first of Louis' garden developments at Versailles, and had a boisterous quality strongly reminiscent of Italian Renaissance gardens, which came to jar with the severer, more dignified character of later parts of Versailles. It is interesting that two of the major works which were rejected at Versailles during Louis' lifetime – the Grotte de Tethys and Bernini's noble equestrian statue of Louis XIV – were strongly un-French in their qualities. The joke features of the grotto lacked dignity, while the surging impetuosity of Bernini's sculpture – surely one of his greatest works – was wholly foreign to Louis' need for superbia. When Louis first saw this statue, he was so disgusted with it that he ordered it to be destroyed, but it was preserved after slight modification by the French sculptor Girardon, and eventually set up at the far end of the Pièce des Suisses, the lake of the Swiss guards, where few visitors, then or today, were likely see it. 'The Daughters of Tethys Watering the Horses of Apollo', a group of statues by Girardon – had been part of the sun-god mythology of Versailles in the Grotte de Tethys. (Tethys, or Thetis, was a sea goddess in whose palace Apollo, the sun god, rested after his travels across the sky.) After the destruction of the Grotte, the sculptures were set up for a few years as the Bains d'Apollon in a separate part of the gardens, and then in 1704 removed to the site of the Marais, which became the new Bains d'Apollon and was inspected by the king in October 1705. These sculptures remain approximately where they were placed in 1704, though they now form part of the late eighteenth-century grotto built by Hubert Robert.

The full itinerary of *La Manière de Montrer les Jardins de Versailles* must have taken visitors most of a day. Starting from the centre of the palace, visitors were told, in numbered sections, to proceed systematically through the gardens, moving gradually via the Orangery, the Labyrinth, the Ballroom, the Girandolle and the Colonnade towards the great Canal. When reaching the fountain of Apollo (driving his chariot – not to be confused with the Bains d'Apollon) at the head of the Canal, the itinerary warns: 'If it is wished to see the Menagerie and Trianon the same day, go there before viewing the rest of the fountains.' In other words, the full visit takes a long time, for the Menagerie and the palace of Trianon were each away at opposite ends of the cross-arms of the Canal and privileged visitors would be taken there by boat. By boat or on foot, a fair way to go, and once there, a fair tour of inspection to be made. After this, they would return to the head of the canal, near the fountain of Apollo, and continue through the remaining *bosquets,* visiting for example the 'Domes', the fountain of Enceladon, the Council Chamber, the Water Mountain, the Marais, the Three Fountains, the Dragon Fountain, Neptune and the Triumphal Arch. In this way the visitors would cover every feature in the Petit Parc, and eventually work their way back to the front of the palace, where they had begun their tour some hours before.

I think it is fair to say the visitors 'were told' what to do, and that they 'worked their way' through the gardens. The *Manière* is written in an autocratic style which is far removed from the normal style of a guide book. The relationship between writer and reader is different. Whereas the usual writer of a guide or description (Félibien, for example, or Mme de Scudéri) writes to invite the reader to *share* his experience of the place to be visited, creating an imagined intimacy between the writer and the reader, Louis XIV writes as a supreme director, explaining to his subordinates how to show visitors what there is at Versailles. None of the manuscripts of *La Manière de Montrer les Jardins de Versailles* speaks directly to the visitors, who are – as it were – outsiders.

There is not even any intimacy apparent in the instructions given by Louis to his subordinates – they exist to do his command: 'Leaving the Château . . . go on to the terrace. You must stop at the top of the steps . . .'

The earliest text was drafted on the occasion of a visit to the gardens on 19 July 1689 of the ex-queen of England, Marie d'Este. In 1689, the Stuart king, James II, had fled to France, preceded by his queen, while William of Orange became the new king of England. James, exiled in France, was to become known as the Old Pretender. According to the *Journal* of the Marquis de Dangeau, the queen had remained in poor health, and was sad at the prospect of permanent exile. On Saturday, 16 July, 'the King went to Saint-Germain to visit the Queen of England,

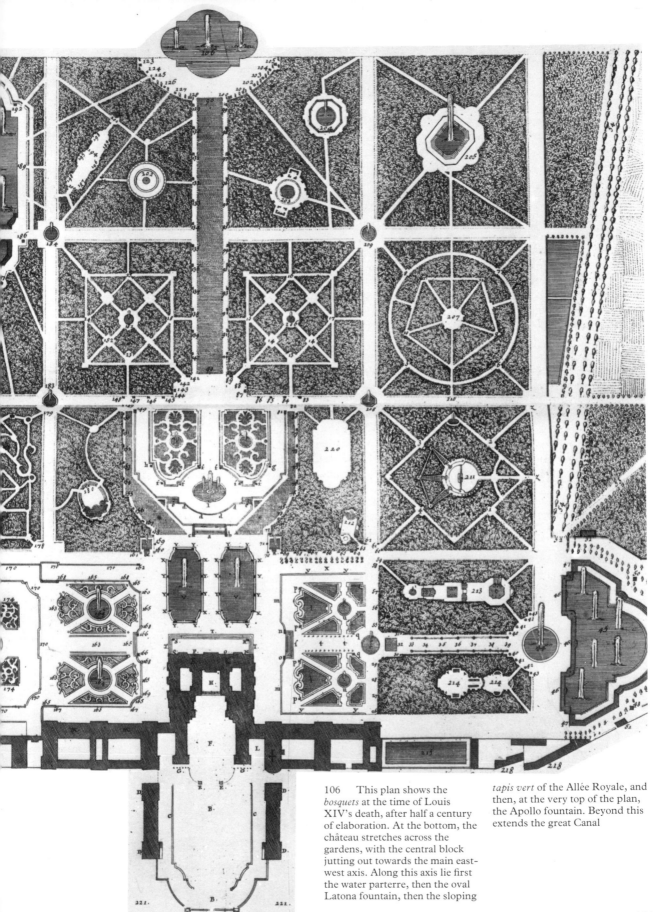

106   This plan shows the *bosquets* at the time of Louis XIV's death, after half a century of elaboration. At the bottom, the château stretches across the gardens, with the central block jutting out towards the main east-west axis. Along this axis lie first the water parterre, then the oval Latona fountain, then the sloping *tapis vert* of the Allée Royale, and then, at the very top of the plan, the Apollo fountain. Beyond this extends the great Canal

151

who had intimated to him that she would like to come to Versailles to speak with him.' And on Tuesday, 19 July, Dangeau reports from Versailles:

> The Queen of England came here to see the fountains, of which she had only seen the smallest part before. While waiting for her, the King had his musketeers drill in the courtyard; there was a large collation at the Marais, and yet another at the Three Fountains. Monseigneur was present with her on this promenade until eight o'clock . . . The Queen of England left at the fountain of Neptune, and did not have occasion to see Madame la Dauphine . . .

The text of the itinerary and Dangeau's commentary correspond exactly. This visit was clearly a major diplomatic occasion, in which the principal figures were Louis XIV himself, the Dauphin, and the Queen of England, on her first visit to this section of the Petit Parc at Versailles. We can understand the 'fruit and ices' served at the Marais, the additional ices served at the Three Fountains, and the relative shortness of the itinerary – beginning at six, and ending about eight o'clock with the departure of the Dauphin, and including the two collations – when we know that the queen had already seen a small part of the gardens, and that she was still in a depressed state. Compared with the massive itinerary of the full *Manière* her two-hour visit represents a genuine effort on Louis' part to avoid over-tiring his royal guest.

THE GLORY OF VERSAILLES

Versailles was vast. The physical exhaustion which may result from a full visit is in part the effect – almost a wished-for effect – of the inexhaustible treasures displayed by the owner, director and dictator Louis XIV. When the Englishman Martin Lister went to Paris in 1698, he wrote in a general way of the unusual size of French gardens – 'These vast riding Gardens are unknown to us in England, and *se promener à cheval, ou en carosse*, is not *English*. We cannot afford to lose so much Country as those Gardens take up' (*A Journey to Paris in the Year 1698*, 1699). His remarks had a certain truth in the seventeenth century, when France was the strongest nation in Europe. The conspicuous use of land to adorn one's residence, without any return of crops or fattening of cattle was a sign of power, and a proof of wealth – English landlords, and even the English monarch, could not afford this ostentation. Yet in the eighteenth century this was to be reversed: the spacious garden landscapes created in England by the wealthy aristocracy were to be beyond the pockets of the – by then – straitened French, and English visitors in the 1750s and after were to laugh at the ineffectual imitations of their gardens attempted by the French.

Lister did not know what the next century would bring, and Versailles impressed him as a superb phenomenon, outside his English experience. Both the size and the rich detail of the gardens amaze him: 'In a Word, these Gardens are a Country laid out into Alleys and Walks, Groves of Trees, Canals and Fountains, and everywhere adorned with ancient and modern Statues and *Vasa* [urns] innumerable.'

Versailles in the 1690s was, as much as the pyramids in Egypt, a gesture of arrogance, appreciated, accepted or resented in Louis' own time. Félibien, the royal historiographer, writes succinctly of the use throughout the château and the gardens of the sun-motifs, linked with that of Apollo: 'It is proper to point out that, since the Sun is the king's device, and since poets identify the Sun with Apollo, there is nothing in this superb edifice which is not linked to this divinity.' There is in the gardens of Versailles an extraordinary and intended emphasis on the Apollo-sun-god allegory: not only are there many features related to different aspects of the mythology connected with Apollo, but they dominate the gardens, from the statues of Apollo and Diana set by the central window of the Galerie des Glaces to the group of Apollo and his chariot at the head of the Canal, and the Latona fountain midway between the château and the Canal (Latona or Leto was Apollo's mother). The east-west axis of the gardens, marked by these memorials of the sun god's power and progress, seems to be united to the axis of the sun itself, as it rises beyond the château, and sets at the far end of the great Canal. It is curious that at Versailles the

107 The statuary at Versailles is still spectacular, though not as glorious as in Louis XIV's day. Gods, goddesses and heroes support and enrich the single theme of the Apollo myth, sun god and classical forebear of Louis himself. Here, at the end of the Allée Royale, the statues cluster round the great Bassin d'Apollon, where the god steers his chariot and plunging horses into the ocean, having blazed his day-long course across the sky

108 The Petit Trianon was not built until the second half of the eighteenth century, long after Louis XIV's death. Its atmosphere, leafy, even rustic at times, is profoundly different from that of the main gardens at Versailles – less arrogant, less exacting, less single-minded. Here, the temple de l'Amour, given a lake and woodland setting, offers an alternative deity – not the sun-king, but the gentler god of love

temples of love, friendship, music, wisdom and the like, so frequent in great gardens from the Renaissance onwards, just are not there. They would have been a distraction from the Apollo-sun-Louis symbolism, an impertinence even. Versailles is firmly dedicated to this one cult, and we may see the *entire* complex of château and gardens as a kind of temple, in which the living god-king, Louis XIV, himself resided. The most immediately convincing evidence of this is in the chapel, where only the king faced the altar, and all other worshippers faced the king. But this is well known and drifts from the gardens.

A part of the arrogance of Versailles is common to much seventeenth-century thought concerning the relative status of man and nature. When Saint-Simon in his *Mémoires* accuses Louis XIV of spending inexcusably large sums on the gardens of Versailles and Marly, in levelling, digging canals and installing fountains, and in many times moving and re-moving vast numbers of well grown trees to make fresh *bosquets* and avenues, he sums it up as 'ce plaisir superbe de forcer la nature' – 'this proud pleasure in compelling nature'. To Louis, as to most of his contemporaries, whether in France or elsewhere in Europe, the natural world of trees, stones and water, forests, hills, and the sea, was not in itself beautiful or admirable, but lacking in beauty, proportion and harmony until man had brought it under control, and imposed on it his man-centred order, balance and symmetry. From the 1660s until the mid-eighteenth century, general views of Versailles are alike in stressing the transformation of the 'natural' aspects of the scene into geometrical and architectural components. The free growth and movement and direction of plants, water and terrain are subordinated to human – and royal – control. Whether it is the great panorama of Versailles painted by Pierre Patel in 1667, when the gardens are still in their early state, or later views, painted or engraved by Le Pautre, Perelle, Allegrain or Silvestre, when the gardens were complete, the symmetry of the fountain-jets, the clear-cut vertical outlines of the hedges and the ruler-straight direction of the *allées*, often stretching out and away as far as the eye can see, all these affirm the triumphant extension of the king's power over nature.

THE FOUNTAINS

This is seen most impressively at Versailles in the use of *water*. Versailles was in Louis' reign a water garden, one of the great water gardens of the world, much more obviously so than it is today. Nowadays, the *grandes eaux* at Versailles are a spectacle restricted to certain days in the year, and the remaining fountains are vastly less numerous, less elaborate and often less powerful than they were. But to follow Louis' own itinerary, one would in fact proceed through the gardens from one fountain feature to another, and would never lose sight of water or fountains throughout the visit. Louis continually urged his garden architects – Le Nôtre himself, Claude Desgots, Le Nôtre's nephew, the Francinis, father and son, and Claude Denis, the *fontainier du roi* who succeeded the Francinis – to design and build bigger and better fountains and to arrange adequate supplies of water for them. His most memorable demand was that they should play 'à gueule bée': 'full-throated fountains' were required.

The most varied, if not the largest, was the Théâtre d'Eau, the 'Water Theatre', created in 1671, and destroyed in the 1770s. In this 'theatre', the 'action' was provided not by actors, but by a multiplicity of water-jets, tall, short, thin, broad, curving, vertical, single, multiple, playing in a total of ten combinations, and using several hundreds of separate jets. 'And all', writes Denis, 'perform these many different things, to show obeisance to the king of kings.' And if we look at the engravings of this period, the fountain-jets are invariably shown balanced, symmetrical and controlled – controlled by the authority of the king.

The king's itinerary is not alone in revealing the importance of the fountains – other visitors show it in their accounts. In 1687 Nicodemus Tessin, the Swedish architect and garden designer, went round the gardens with Le Nôtre and wrote a long and detailed account of his visit. It is dominated by the theme of fountains, beginning with the description of the 'machine de Marly', raising water from the Seine to an aqueduct leading to Versailles, and then continuing with the different

153

fountains to which this water was distributed throughout the gardens. Naturally the fountains are set in stone, of varied colours and design, and adorned with statues in marble or in bronze, and round these are paths, hedges and metal or wooden trellis work; but the fountains themselves were for Tessin the most most important part.

In the same way, Martin Lister in 1698 writes that on

> May the 17th the Waters were ordered to Play for the Diversion of the English Gentlemen. The Playing of the spouts of Water, thrown up into the Air, is here diversified after a thousand fashions. The Théâtre des Eaux, and the Triumphal Arch are the most famous Pieces . . .'

Lister does not mention the Three Fountains, a feature built in 1677 and destroyed a century later. The Three Fountains, designed by Le Nôtre, is especially interesting since its conception is attributed to the king himself, and since of all the fountain-*bosquets* of Versailles it is the most wholly devoted to water. Whereas other fountains have again and again a mythological or historical reference, from the statuary which they incorporate, the Three Fountains seems to have been a purely abstract composition using water as a fluid yet firmly controlled medium, extending the solid geometrical forms of the stone steps and *bassins* in further geometrical and symmetrical designs. Tessin admired it greatly:

> This *bosquet* is universally applauded, and is indeed the most renowned for the quantity of its fountains; the Sheaf is the greatest which has ever been constructed [it had 140 jets], and the great Shell at the lower end of the *bosquet*, with its fine jets, sheets of water and cascades, is marvellous; in short, it is all worthy of M. Le Nôtre's genius.

Strangely, in this great water garden, water was always, then as today, in short supply. Unlike the foaming, throbbing fountains of the villa d'Este, those of Versailles could never play unceasingly, drawing on the endless flow of a nearby mountain torrent. Part of the arrogance of Versailles lies in the very assurance that the many dominant horizontal planes of this un-Italian terrain – the interminable *allées*, the long, straight walls of clipped hornbeam, the forbidding breadth of the château, even the far-distant view of the great, mile-long Canal beyond the Petit Parc – will all be relieved by the soaring, delicate force of the fountain-jets. To achieve this masterly effect – and those who have seen the *grandes eaux* in their majesty will know that it is achieved – the fountains had to be displayed in careful groups, corresponding to the king's progress around the gardens. Amid his more solemn financial and political duties, Colbert devised an itinerary which ran parallel to the king's, but 'secretly' with a system of whistle-blasts, and with boys running ahead and signalling with flags, to indicate the whereabouts of the king's party, and whether or not it was 'safe' to turn off this or that group of water-effects. In a more wholesale way, water had to be supplied in ever-increasing quantities and from a considerable distance, to meet these demands. The 'machine de Marly' already mentioned was completed in the late 1680s to pump up water from the Seine towards Versailles, and its fourteen massive waterwheels and elaborate accessory equipment made it then and for well over a century one of the world's hydraulic marvels, matching in its size the immensity and wonder of the gardens it served. Other schemes to pipe rivers of water to Versailles were considered and set in motion – in particular one to connect the waters of the river Eure to Versailles was given much attention, though never completed – and it should be remembered that in the enormous extent of the palace-buildings at Versailles, one considerable section to the north is still called the Reservoir.

A last indication of the dimensions of Versailles comes with the great Canal, cross-shaped, a mile in length, which was in Louis' reign equipped with several sizable sailing-ships: yachts, a frigate, a galley, and also two sumptuous gondolas sent as presents to the king by the republic of Venice. To man these ships, which were used for pageants and mock-battles, and as ferries between the head of the Canal and the gardens and palace of Trianon near the northern cross-arm of the Canal, a contingent of Venetian sailors was maintained at Versailles, living in quarters near the Bassin d'Apollon, and commonly called the Petite Venise. While the king and his party would sail or be rowed in one ship, another would follow to provide music. Félibien writes of this as part of an evening entertainment: 'Deep in the silence of the night could be heard the violins, following the king's ship. While these ships floated gently forwards, one could glimpse the water glistening round about, and hear the

109 'These gardens are a country', wrote Martin Lister in 1698, overawed by their magnificence, variety and extent. When Louis XIV's visitors made the *full* tour of the gardens which the king himself prescribed, they were warned, 'if it is wished to see the Menagerie and the Trianon the same day', to travel by boat from the head of the canal, just beyond the Apollo fountains at the bottom of the grassy slope in this photograph

155

rhythmic splashing of the oars, as they left silvery furrows in the dark surface of the canal.' The Canal and surrounding gardens have here become the setting for a scene of fantasy, as many gardens have done before and since. Fountains by day, fireworks by night, with music, ballet, and endless theatrical inventions to dazzle and entertain – we cannot calculate the extent or the extravagance of Louis' response to Fouquet's one evening at Vaux-le-Vicomte in 1661. The most famous entertainment was in 1664, when he presented a lavish pageant called 'Les Plaisirs de l'Ile Enchantée'. It lasted seven days, with jousts, opera, comedy, ballet and fireworks, and virtually all taking place in the gardens, in various *bosquets* and on the Canal. Here at Versailles, the king remains the master, director, principal actor and hero, and the gardens are an immense theatre, with an infinity of lines of perspective centring on the monarch, and radiating out from him again – the sun-god, centre of the universe he himself illuminates.

TRIANON

To find some relief from the public display of Versailles, Louis created not one, but two lesser palaces and gardens – Trianon, close to the château of Versailles, at the head of the northern arm of the Canal, and Marly, four miles to the north of Versailles. In each case, work began from scratch in the late 1670s; in each case artists, painters, sculptors, architects and designers were commissioned from the team employed at Versailles, and in each case the gardens have many features which at three centuries' distance seem common to both and to Versailles, and seem to mark them as gardens in the same family, even if their size and details show considerable differences. They both extend symmetrically on one side or other of a château, with geometrical parterres near to the château, straight *allées* extending beyond, and the geometrical and human control of the natural scene reinforced by clipped hedges, and by skilful juxtaposition of horizontal bands of grass and gravel and straight lines of trees, leading to richly gilded or enamelled buildings, or imposing statues in marble or bronze.

I stress these similarities before discussing the individual qualities of the two retreats. Trianon – later to be known as the Grand Trianon, to distinguish it from the Petit Trianon built in the second half of the eighteenth century – is of course far smaller than Versailles. A first palace and garden were created for Louis' mistress Mme de Montespan, the palace being known as the Trianon de Porcelaine, since it was adorned on the outside with glazed tiles to help give it an 'oriental' air. This palace lasted only a few years: when Mme de Montespan fell from favour, it was destroyed (like the Marais in the Petit Parc) and replaced by a new palace, the Trianon which we know today, built in 1687-8 for the new favourite, Mme de Maintenon. Here Louis would retire with selected courtiers from the busier, public scenes of Versailles to a smaller and more intimate setting.

Trianon was distinctive among Louis XIV's gardens for its flowers, and was at first referred to as the Palace of Flora. The smaller scale of the parterres, and the enclosed nature of the garden as a whole seem to have encouraged this: it did not have any vast perspectives leading out from the palace, nor any large expanses of water to lead the eye away into the distance. Instead, the *allées* were closed in with tall trees, and often overshadowed, so that there were remarkable contrasts of light and shade within the garden – 'point out the darkness of the wood [l'obscurité du bois], the great jet of water and the sheet of water, on the other side of the shade', reads this part of the king's itinerary. Generally, Le Nôtre is thought to have disliked the use of flowers in gardens, following Saint-Simon's statement that Le Nôtre 'said of parterres that they were only good for nursemaids, who, since they could not leave the children in their charge, gazed out longingly at them from the second floor, and walked out there in their imagination.' But parterres would not normally have been composed with flowers, but with box and coloured stones and gravel. Tessin makes a somewhat extreme, but enlightening statement about this when he comments that at Versailles (as distinct from Trianon) 'there are only about twelve assistant gardeners [valets], the rest are all day labourers, since for the most part they have only to rake the *allées*.' (He should have added 'and to clip the hornbeam hedges', but his statement is still valuable in showing how unimportant flowers were in the main garden.)

Exceptionally, however, the parterres at Trianon were made with flowers, 'parterres de compartiment de fleurs', and were famous for the fact. A painting by Cotelle shows the parterres in front of the palace stuffed to overflowing with flowers, and with fragrant orange trees standing up among them. On the other side of the palace, the small Jardin du Roi was also a flower-garden. There was a large nursery at Trianon devoted solely to the supply of flowers – in Tessin's words 'une furieuse pépinière', 'a fantastic nursery', 'where there are many close frames containing nothing but flower pots, to the total of 200,000.' To support this, Saint-Simon commented on 'a prodigious quantity of flowers, in pots which were set in the flowerbeds, so that they could be changed, not just every day if it was wished, but even twice a day if desired'; while Le Nôtre himself in 1694 remarked that there were 2,000,000 flower pots used continually for these changes in every season. And he added that at Trianon 'you never see a dead leaf, nor any plant which is not in flower.'

As well as Le Nôtre's claim that there were 2,000,000 pots, there is a plan for the planting of flowers at Trianon, dated 3 August 1693, which not only shows the order and arrangement of the flowers in the beds, but names them in three groups (bulbs, perennials, large perennials), and gives the quantities required, totalling 96,000 items for this section of bedding. The flowers named are tulips, narcissi, hyacinths, rocket, speedwell, sweet william, rose campion, campanula, gilly flowers and heartsease. Several of those on Le Nôtre's plan are fragrant, and Trianon was renowned also for its quantities of orange trees, of jasmine, and of tuberoses. Tuberoses flower most readily in the late summer, and Saint-Simon said that at Trianon on one occasion, he had 'seen the king and all his courtiers leave the gardens because of the overpowering fragrance of the tuberoses.'

One other feature at Trianon should be mentioned – the Bosquet des Sources, the Springs. This *bosquet*, on the north side of the main buildings of Trianon, was designed by Le Nôtre, and seems to have been not only retired and shady, like so much of Trianon (the part of the buildings nearby was called Trianon-sous-Bois, or Trianon-beneath-the-Trees), but also *irregular* in a way which is uncharacteristic of Le Nôtre and virtually unknown in the classic *jardin français*. It was a modest and roughly triangular area, shaded with many trees. Sloping gently from the apex of the triangle, the whole area was crossed by small water channels. Le Nôtre himself wrote in 1694 that here the streams 'meander without order, and turn in the open spaces around the trees, with fountains irregularly spaced . . .'

Visiting this *bosquet* in 1687, when it must have been very new indeed, Tessin describes the water as flowing 'as the big trees allowed', and running in grass-lined channels, with occasional waterfalls to make a splashing sound. This little garden was destroyed in the early 1800s, and there are, so far as I know, no early pictures of it to show whether it could possibly be considered a genuine 'reaction' to the formality of French gardens.

MARLY

Marly, though not as vast as Versailles, was much bigger than Trianon. Work began in 1677, with Louis XIV looking for another 'retreat' where he could have a greater degree of privacy than even Trianon allowed. It was to be, in Saint-Simon's mocking word, a 'hermitage' (how different from the ideal of the rustic hermitage which was already forming in England and in Germany). But once the site at Marly was chosen, gardening-fever seized the king, and he was to prove as impatient and as passionate a perfectionist at Marly as he was elsewhere. It is right to talk of Louis XIV, rather than Le Nôtre, at Marly. Though Le Nôtre was almost certainly involved – he possibly drew up the first plans – there is no documentary evidence to connect him with Marly before his death in 1700, and much of the elaboration of the gardens was not undertaken until the late 1690s, and continued until 1714. From a 'hermitage' Marly became a sumptuous palace garden, using an entire valley with its symmetrical arrangement of water, buildings, avenues and *bosquets*. The palace was small – or relatively so – and central. Down towards the palace, from the head of the valley, flowed a steep and immense cascade, La Rivière, ending in the Petit Parterre, while on the lower side was the Grand Parterre, a balanced and imposing series of fountains and *bassins* extending gently downwards and out along the valley. On either side of these *bassins* was a row of six painted and gilded *pavillons*, residences for the favoured gentlemen (on one side) and ladies (on the other) who were invited to attend the 'Marlys' held here by the king. Behind these twelve *pavillons* were the *bosquets*; on the side leading to Versailles, the Bosquets de Louveciennes, on the other side, the Bosquets de Marly. To provide a view out over the countryside towards the river Seine, heroic excavations were undertaken in 1699 to extend the valley, which had originally been somewhat enclosed.

Unlike Versailles, Marly was a garden palace, a place devoted to luxury and relaxation. The scale was immense, yet the pleasures were – as far as they could ever be for Louis XIV – of a private kind. In 1699, near the top of the Rivière, where the valley was steep, the king had a track, La Ramasse, set up for the *roulette*, a sledge-shaped vehicle which carried several passengers and which ran on wheels between wooden rails like a modern roller-coaster. A little further uphill was a large reservoir for the fountains, and when this froze in winter it was used for skating. Two separate courses were laid out for the game called 'Mail', an early form of golf. Near to the château was the Place de l'Escarpolette, where a large swing seating three or four people at once was set up. No doubt games and amusements took place in other royal gardens, but at Marly they have an exceptional prominence which is tied to the private and pleasurable nature of the gardens.

Marly was as much a water and fountain garden as Versailles. Water was relatively abundant, and the steeply sloping head of the valley allowed spectacular fountain and cascade effects, in particular the great axial step-cascade of the Rivière, and a second cascade, the Cascade Champêtre, built at the upper end of the Bosquets de Louveciennes. The Rivière had fifty-three steps from top to bottom, made from coloured marble, and ended in a series of broad, stepped pools before the château. The entire composition, like that of the Cascade Champêtre, was modified several times, acquiring gorgeous red marble and gilded sculptural fountains at the foot. In 1706 two sculptured groups were set at the top, 'Neptune and a Triton', and 'Amphitrite with Three Sirens', and it was also intended to erect there a huge rock, spouting water in all directions, but this plan was never carried out. 'I was watching while Abbé Anselme stood at the foot of the cascade, he was almost in ecstasy', one courtier wrote to the king. Louis noted at the side 'It shows his good taste.'

The Rivière was the greatest cascade of its time. Others had been made in French gardens – at St Cloud for example – outdoing their Italian predecessors in the extravagance of their ornament. The Rivière did more. Its height, breadth and length left the Italian cascades far behind, and I have no doubt that this was a part of the king's intention.

Not only was Italy outdone. As at Versailles, the countless sculptures showed the king as the greatest patron of the arts in the whole of Europe, and the order and symmetry of the gardens as a whole showed the completeness, the assurance of his control over the physical world. Among the detailed plans of the *bosquets* at Marly some show the degree of perfection of the topiary work: arbours, galleries, porticoes and colonnades all formed from living trees and shrubs, trained and clipped into architectural forms, and stretching sometimes for scores of yards through the gardens. Raw nature is here converted into green architecture; artificial, yes, but also dignified, and since many of the plants used in these arbours were scented, such as jasmine and honeysuckle, delightful as well.

Louis was himself the principal agent in designing and developing Marly. His last changes date from 1714, and his last visit to Marly was on 9 August 1715. He died on 1 September.

After Louis' death Marly was not used as a royal residence for many years, and the gardens fell into decay. The Rivière, symbol of the vitality of Marly, was abolished in 1728 and replaced by a sweeping *tapis vert*, a long expanse of lawn. Many statues were taken away to adorn other royal gardens, and when, in the middle of the eighteenth century, Louis XV came to stay at Marly fairly frequently, the gardens

XXIII   The Rivière or cascade at Marly, seen in 1714. Created in the 1690s, it was destroyed in 1728. The Duc d'Antin was here in 1708 with his acquaintance, the Abbé Anselme. He wrote to the king: 'I was watching while the Abbé Anselme stood at the foot of the cascade, he was almost in ecstasy.' 'It shows his good taste', commented Louis XIV

XXIV   La Fontaine de la Nymphe – one of the many small *bosquets* at Marly, seen in 1713. This illustration shows the elaborate perfection of the topiary; the trees and shrubs are treated as green architecture, to be shaped and controlled as part of a wholly formal scheme

LA RIVIERE.

FONTAINE DE LA NYMPHE

110　Fun and games – with royal spectators. This sketch (right) of the Place de l'Escarpolette at Marly shows vividly the pleasurable nature of the gardens. Three or four children could sit in the swing, while others watched. Trellis screens shelter the enclosure, and a part of the small but extravagant palace buildings shows beyond. Elsewhere at Marly was La Ramasse, a railway track for a kind of royal roller-coaster

XXV　The Bains d'Apollon (top left) at Versailles. Not all Versailles remained formal: in the 1770s Hubert Robert – painter, architect and garden designer – refashioned this *bosquet*, using sculptures by Girardon, which had been given a formal setting a century earlier. The 'Baths of Apollo' is a romantic conception, a green and shady grotto, irregular and 'natural' in its shape and planting

XXVI　'Point out the darkness of the wood, the great jet of water and the sheet of water, on the other side of the shade' – part of Louis XIV's instructions for viewing the gardens at Trianon. Though the fountains in this photograph (left) were remodelled in the early nineteenth century, the effect of sunshine and shade must be close to what the king – and Le Nôtre as well – admired

were maintained in a much less splendid style. The English traveller Thomas Pennant visited Marly in 1765, and noted 'both house and gardens much neglected', though there were still 'some good waterworks and beautiful arbors'. At the Revolution the furniture, buildings and gardens were sold, and the château was demolished. Today the area of the gardens has become a public park, and the great skeleton of the principal *allées* remains as it was, while the *tapis vert* (which had been the Rivière) and three *bassins* mark the central axis down the valley. Louis XIV would certainly remember the outline.

111   The enormous formal
garden at Drottningholm, outside
Stockholm, designed by
Nicodemus Tessin the younger

11
The Development of the Formal Garden in Europe

Versailles was to exercise an enormous influence over garden design, not just in France but throughout Europe, though at the same time it would be silly and wrong to maintain that the picture in the late seventeenth and early eighteenth centuries was one of wholesale French domination of garden aesthetics. Beside gardens which are both designed by Frenchmen and look like French formal gardens, there are a multitude of others which, though sometimes attempting to rival or outdo the extent and grandeur of Versailles, stem aesthetically from the Italian Renaissance tradition. This survived in Italy itself, in Vienna and other parts of the Empire, and in Switzerland and the southern German states generally; while in Holland a garden style which had evolved – like the Italian, French and English – from the small and foursquare gardens of the Middle Ages continued somewhat separately from the French because of the extraordinary uniformity of the flat terrain intersected by straight, low dykes and canals. As the eighteenth century advanced there was not only the radical opposition to the French formal garden which began in England, but the softening, weakening and variation of the French formal rigidity and seriousness which we call rococo, and which appears in almost all European art of the period, not least in the gardens. Within the rococo, the most characteristic forms are those of chinoiserie, and these are likewise important in gardens.

THE SHADOW OF VERSAILLES

Remembering these reservations, it is still true to say that Le Nôtre's gardens, and those of his disciples, Desgots, Marot, Le Blond, Tessin, Van Vittel, London and Wise and a score of others, were to triumph for most of a century, and the aesthetic of Versailles was to be repeated in France and all over Europe. Even in colonial America, in centres such as Williamsburg and in estates such as Middleton Place near Charleston, gardens were made which repeat the symmetry and control of the French formal garden. A little Versailles or a big one, a mansion or a palace, a single parterre or an entire estate, the size would vary, but the wish to emulate, or even to out-do, was certain.

BRITAIN
In 1689 the newly-established William of Orange was doing this at Hampton Court. Evelyn noted in his *Diary* for 16 July 1689: 'I went to Hampton Court about business, the Council being there. A great apartment and spacious garden with fountains was beginning in the park at the head of the canal.' The great semi-circular parterre, with its fountains and complex *broderies*, was being made. It lasted less than twenty years, since Queen Anne, who succeeded William in 1702, disliked the smell of box, and had the *broderies* removed. The outline is still there, but is so simplified, and so obscured by the monstrous green toadstools of clipped yet overgrown yews that Versailles is altogether forgotten. British noblemen had palaces and gardens made in the spirit of Versailles: Vanbrugh's Blenheim, for the victorious Duke of Marlborough, and Castle Howard, and Stowe. Smaller mansions and gardens were made: Caversham Park, near Reading, and Shotover near Oxford, with its arrogant and beautiful rectilinear canal, the longest of its kind in Britain; while great mansions

163

which already existed had their gardens re-made in the manner of Versailles, at Chatsworth and Longleat and Badminton. And once, the gardens were made without waiting for the mansion to be extended to match their symmetrical grandeur, at Melbourne in Derbyshire. Here, London and Wise produced the main formal plan 'to suit with Versailles', as one of them wrote to the owner, Thomas Coke, around 1696, but the house was never extended sideways to make its façade align properly with the central axis of the gardens. Many, many gardens in Britain imitated the model of Versailles, as can be seen from the engravings of John Kip and Leonard Knyf in the volumes of *Britannia Illustrata*, beginning in 1708. The *allées*, the hedges, the parterres, the fountains, all were imitated from France; and most have gone. At Chatsworth the outlines of the plan remain, as does the splendid cascade, made by the Frenchman Grillet in 1694–5, enlarged in 1702–3, and modelled on the Rivière at Marly; but the west parterre, by London, begun in 1690, and the Great Parterre to the south, by London and Wise (1694), have gone. Aerial photography of the site, taken in dry weather, has shown the patterns striking up through the grass. In the great drought of 1976, an air balloon was sent up to photograph traces of the long-vanished parterres at Stowe.

The most intriguing and the most fully described parterre in Britain was at Nottingham, and made around 1705–6. Let Defoe, who mentions it in the third volume of his *Tour thro' the Whole Island of Great Britain* in 1727, explain. He speaks of the 'beauties of *Nottingham*' among which are 'the Garden of Count *Tallard;* who in his confinement here as Prisoner of War taken by the Duke of *Marlborough* at the great Battle of *Blenheim*, amused himself with making a small but beautiful *Parterre*, after the *French* Fashion.' The plan is illustrated and analysed in an appendix to George London and Henry Wise's *Retir'd Gard'ner* of 1706. Apart from areas of grass, the only growing things were 'Pots and Plants', though two lesser parterres had 'Pyramid-Plants', 'Standard Ever-greens', a 'Hedge' and 'Borders . . . for Flowers'. All other effects and details in the complicated *broderie* were achieved with inert materials: red sand or brick dust; 'the slag of Pit-coal fine beaten'; yellow sand; 'Spar that comes from the Land-Mines, or Cockle-shell beaten very fine'; gravel – 'bright . . . &c as the Country affords.'

Defoe concludes his reference to Tallard's garden with a laconic 'but it does not gain by *English* keeping.' In 1727 the tide had begun to turn, and the parterres made in England would soon be obliterated.

In Britain, however, many formal outlines survive, and were created alongside the new 'natural' gardens of the eighteenth century. One of the world's greatest formal gardens was made between *c.* 1720 and *c.* 1760 at St Paul's Walden Bury, in Hertfordshire. The designer is not known. Here there are no parterres, though these may have existed where the lawn now extends from the house. St Paul's Walden Bury is in essence a garden of grassy, hedge-lined walks, which stretch straight and far into the distance, to terminate in temples, statuary, or glimpses of the wings of the house. One walk leads the eye to the village church, but otherwise it is largely a self-contained garden, interest and variety being maintained by the changing levels of the terrain, and by the surprise effects at the multiple intersections of the walks.

Hidden behind the hedges in one large 'island' or woodland is the most successful *giardino segreto* in the British Isles, the oval enclosure of the 'Running Footman', rising in plain terraces from the statue of the Discobolos, the 'Running Footman', past a formal pond and up to an open rotunda at the top. The deep appeal of this part of the gardens comes from its private and tranquil nature – from outside its existence is unsuspected, and yet its generous grassy slopes inspire a feeling of spaciousness and repose – and from the contrast of its rounded outlines with the ruler-straight directness of the main walks.

FRANCE

In Britain, St Paul's Walden Bury is a rare and beautiful survival. In France, gardens of a wholly formal nature were made right up to the Revolution in 1789, to patterns which Le Nôtre himself might have overseen. The plates illustrating 'Agriculture–Jardinage' in the *Encyclopédie* were published in 1762. The plans are entirely formal, a succession of parterres with more or less elaborate *broderie*, while

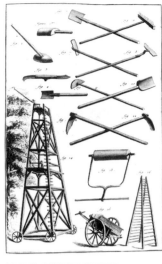

112, 113 Published in 1762, the plates on 'Agriculture, Jardinage' for the *Encyclopédie* look back with approval on 150 years of French formal gardening. This giant ladder on wheels, big enough to be a siege tower, was used for clipping hedges to a great height. The photograph, taken at Villarceaux in 1971, lends authority to the engraving of 1762. The height of the ladder can be judged from the continuing row of trees on the far side of the pond, where human figures indicate the scale

the tools which two plates illustrate are those needed to maintain the gravel, hedges and borders of a formal garden – clippers, sieves and riddles, the line, and a mobile platform, like a Jacob's Ladder on wheels, for trimming hedges vertically to a height of twenty-five or thirty feet. Until the Revolution scores of gardens such as that at the Hôtel de Pompadour near Fontainebleau, or Villarceaux (Seine-et-Oise), Limpiville near Dieppe, La Mogère (Hérault), or the urban Jardin de la Fontaine at Nîmes were continuing the formal tradition of Versailles, and books of appropriate designs were published, both for new gardens, and to illustrate gardens recently made in the formal style. The theory and details of the French formal garden were set out fully and firmly in 1709, in *La Théorie et la Pratique du Jardinage* by A. J. Dézallier d'Argenville, which was many times re-issued, the last French edition being in 1760. The most detailed and elaborate designs for formal trellis work ever published are in P. Roubo's *L'Art du Treillageur* of 1775, and the long series of *cahiers* of G. L. Le Rouge's *Détails des Nouveaux Jardins à la Mode (Jardins Anglo-Chinois)*, published in twenty-one sections between 1776 and 1787, has beside its plans and views of 'English' and 'Chinese' gardens, both real and fantastic, almost as many details of formal gardens, large and small, real and projected, in France or elsewhere on the Continent. Similarly Jacques Delille's long and placid poem, *Les Jardins* (1782), while praising the landscapes of Kent and Brown, still approves with equal firmness the 'prodigies' of Versailles.

In France the most intriguing example of the survival of the formal parterre is related by a Mrs Cradock, who travelled on the Continent in the 1780s with her husband. In her journal – it now exists only in a French translation, *Journal de Madame Cradock . . . 1783–86*, tr. O. D. Balleyguier (1896) – she describes a visit to the property of a Jewish merchant some miles outside Bordeaux (3 July 1785):

> This house and the garden round it are absurd. [The garden is] a small piece of ground surrounded by a narrow border adorned with some two hundred blue and white flower pots perched on frames. In the middle, no doubt representing the Tables of the Law, is a design in box, cut excessively low, to look like an inscribed scroll of paper: the interstices are filled with different colours of sand, to imitate *broderies*. Since this area cannot be covered over, it has to be repaired after every shower of rain. It is hard to understand that the French are rapturous about this folly, and that they exclaim 'C'est magnifique!'

Her husband, Joseph Cradock, gives a similar description, ending 'This really was one wide waste of abomination.'

SWEDEN

The Swedish architect and garden designer Nicodemus Tessin came to Versailles in the 1680s, met Le Nôtre, discussed and noted the details of the gardens, and on his return to Sweden designed in the French style both for the king and for himself. Near Stockholm there is the royal palace of Drottningholm, with a huge garden whose spreading *allées*, whose parterres and fountains immediately remind one of Versailles, while in the city itself there is the small and beautiful box parterre in Tessin's own garden. Noblemen elsewhere in Sweden built similar gardens to the king's, if smaller – such as that at the castle at Sturefors, where the main axis, still geometrical, now bears the imprint of succeeding styles, but where the best view is obtained, as it should be in a garden of this type, from the elevation of the *piano nobile*, and from the central windows of the owner's principal rooms. The plans for the original *parterres de broderie* at Sturefors still exist, though the bedding today has no connection with what was then designed.

RUSSIA

In Russia Peter the Great took back with him after his European voyages not only the scars of Evelyn's holly hedges at Sayes Court, but the inspiration of the gardens at Versailles. So powerful is the memory for British readers of Peter's rough behaviour at Deptford in 1698 – he was, for amusement, wheelbarrowed backwards and forwards through the holly hedge of Evelyn's garden, and Evelyn presented a bill for £150 for the damage to this and to other parts of his property – that we forget his residence in France, where for a while he lodged in the Trianon at Versailles, behaving even more outrageously (he filled the little palace with prostitutes) and came to admire the gardens. Soon after his return to Russia he began work on the new city of St Petersburg, and on the creation nearby of the palace and gardens of Peterhof. These were designed by the Frenchman Le Blond in 1713 and were completed by about 1725. Immediately in front of the palace, steps descend past powerful fountains, gilded statues and tumbling cascades, and out to a great canal (reminiscent of the Canal at Versailles), which stretches far out towards the Baltic.

GERMANY AND AUSTRIA

In Germany and the Austrian Empire many rulers, great and small, tried to make their own Versailles. The most enormous was at Vienna, where the palace and gardens at Schönbrunn continue to impress by their scale. The architect Fischer von Erlach proposed an even greater expanse of parterres and *allées* in 1721, but the effect is one of dispersion. The lesser, but still enormous gardens of Nymphenburg and Schleissheim in Munich were both designed, wholly or in part, by Frenchmen – Charles Carbonet in 1701 changing Nymphenburg from its earlier Italian form, his work being continued and enlarged by Dominique Girard from 1715. Girard was an engineer, and employed by the ruler, Kurfürst Max Emanuel, to enlarge the elaborate water and canal system at Schleissheim, which had already been linked in 1702 with Max Emanuel's other garden at Dachau six miles away, and which he hoped, but in vain, to join to the garden at Nymphenburg. Nymphenburg has since been modified by the addition of landscape garden features, but its main water axis still stretches straight and far beyond the palace. Schleissheim is flatter, and is surrounded with waterways in the Dutch manner, which Max Emanuel had seen in the Netherlands. Schleissheim remains much as it was when Girard and Enrico Zuccali, who drew up the plan of the garden, were alive. When F. L. von Sckell, the German landscape gardener, came to work at Schleissheim in 1801, he agreed not to tamper with the earlier design, and Girard's parterres are still there.

Girard worked in other German gardens, producing designs in the French style, notably for the garden of the Augustusburg at Brühl, where he cooperated with François Cuvilliė. On the south side of the castle, an elevated U-shaped terrace embraces the top section of an ambitious and beautiful parterre and water garden, which is, to increase the attraction of the terrace view, set slightly lower than the surrounding terrain. The parterres were obliterated in the second half of the century by P. J. Lenné, who replaced them with an 'English garden'; but in 1946 the original parterres were restored with full fidelity to their plans of 1750, and their *broderie* is now unsurpassed by any in France.

Another Frenchman, Nicolas de Pigage (1723–96), was the principal designer of the formal gardens at Schwetzingen, where he was engaged in 1749. It is a happy thought that Voltaire, staying at Schwetzingen as the guest of the Elector Carl Theodor, was in the midst of heroic and continuing cultivation, for one of the legends surrounding his novel *Candide* (published in 1759) was that it was written day by day and chapter by chapter during his stay at Schwetzingen, and read out by Voltaire chapter by chapter and evening by evening, as an entertainment for his host. It is a good story, even if unlikely; and Schwetzingen had a good 'French garden', now rather bare, but still worthwhile. Pigage was later active with F. L. von Sckell in designing and supervising the making of the 'English garden', with its Chinese bridge, its mosque, its Roman water tower, and the enchanting *trompe l'oeil* Ende der Welt – a strange alliance between the formal and the landscape garden.

In 1755, shortly before Voltaire's visit to Schwetzingen, Pigage had visited Schloss Benrath, on the Rhine, and had been appointed 'Ober-Bau-Direktor' for the 'gardens, *allées*, promenades, waterworks, cascades, parks &c.' He supervised the building of the gardens at Benrath in the years that followed, and then in 1777 the ruler Carl Theodor became ruler of Bavaria, and soon after took his court from Mannheim to Munich. Although parts of the garden to the west were changed to the 'English' style early in the nineteenth century, by M. F. Weyhe, the main *allées*, and the *bassins* on each side of the castle have hardly been altered since Pigage set them

114   The vast symmetrical garden at Karlsruhe was begun by Karl Wilhelm von Baden-Durlach in 1715. As its name 'Charles's repose' suggests, it was meant to be yet another retreat from the busy world, a 'Hermitage', a 'Solitude', such as were intended at Trianon, Marly, Bayreuth and Stuttgart. The *allées* through the woods and the avenues through the town radiate from a central tower like the thirty-two points of the compass, allowing a view back to the tower from every crossing. A botanic garden founded by Karl Wilhelm still forms part of the gardens

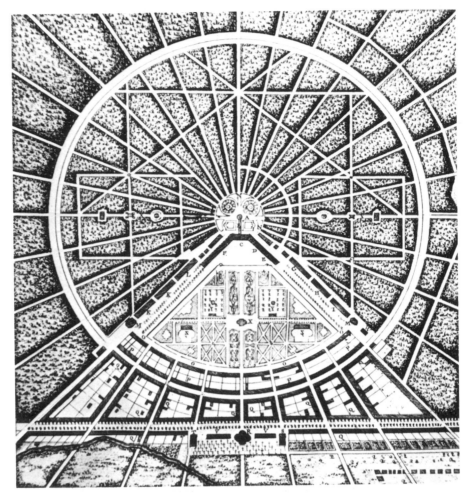

out. To the north the semi-circular *bassin* remains, to the south the long mirror-canal, the Spiegelweiher; to the east the 'French garden,' impeccably formal, with cascades and a glimpse of a higher pool beyond; and to the south-west, beside the Spiegelweiher, the great square of the *bosquet*, now thick with beech trees in their tallest prime, with walks which run diagonally from one corner to the other, meeting at the central *rond-point* or *Stern*.

Benrath has lost the details of its first French style – the walks in the vast *bosquet* were once lined with hedges or with trellis work, there was once a labyrinth – and the recent bedding between the castle and the long canal is thoughtlessly crude. But these same walks have the grandeur one would hope to find at Versailles; the proportions are right – nature here, though overgrown, though neglected, is still subordinate to human design. Man, in the person of Carl Theodor, though he died in 1799, is still in control.

The avenues at Benrath have the moving grandeur of a creation which, at its most noble moment, can only decline; they are like the old and incomparable plane trees at the villa Lante – our wonder is tinged with melancholy. But the Hofgarten of the Residenz at Würzburg is now in its first perfection of recreation. Begun in 1744 by Johann Prokop Mayer for the Prince-Bishop of Würzburg, and stopped in 1778 when there was a change of patron, so that Mayer's full plan was never executed, it was largely destroyed in World War II. Since then the garden which Mayer had built, to the east of the palace, has been restored, and it is my opinion that the clipped hedges, arbours and trellis work are the best examples of this formal work in existence. Mayer's task was not easy – the half-moon of ground is hemmed in between the Residenz and the city walls, rising up as a genuine barrier between the garden and the space beyond – but by means of multiple stairways, terraces at different heights and constantly shifting perspectives he has succeeded in giving this simple and rigidly restricted area a wonderful feeling of variety. The modern parterres of roses are not what Mayer intended, and the cascade and fountain which were once in the upper centre of the plan have gone; but the arbours climbing up beneath the curving walls of the fortifications and the trellis work arcades beneath these arbours are marvels of design, which correspond both to Mayer's original plan, and to the ideal requirements of the Platonic formal garden.

SPAIN AND ITALY

In the south of Europe two other gardens in the French manner must be mentioned. In Spain the large fountain and water gardens of La Granja at San Ildefonso were made in the 1720s for Philip V, and slightly later the even greater – one could say megalomaniac – landscape of the gardens at Caserta, near Naples, was made for the king, Charles III (the son of Philip V of Spain). Here the designer was Luigi Vanvitelli (originally Van Vittel, a Dutchman) and in the 1750s he made the stupendous step-cascade which tumbles down and down in many steps and stages and extends through a mile or more of the landscape. At Caserta the cascade is without rival as the most memorable feature. Its scale is gigantic, so much so that the park which surrounds it leaves the visitor not so much impressed as stranded, and so far from the palace, down below in the flatter part of the terrain, that the essential idea of human control, of the domination of the landscape by the extended architecture of the palace, and hence by the ruler himself, is dissipated. The cascade at Caserta emulates the Rivière at Marly, and outdoes it easily in size. But size on its own is not enough, any more than it suffices at the Venaria Reale, the giant garden-cum-hunting-park begun near Turin in 1740 by the French designer Bernard for Vittorio Amadeo II, Duke of Savoy, to adorn Juvara's palace of Stupinigi, begun in 1729. For the really vast gardens, wherever they may have been planned, or begun, or completed, vast resources are needed. Vast talents. And a tolerable site. At Caserta, the resources were finite, the talent was mediocre, and the site misused. Had the palace been set higher up, and thus dominated the view . . .

From the vastness of Caserta, which fails, turn to a modest and successful detail within a finished garden from another age – the villa Lante at Bagnaia. Here, in the square expanse of the formal garden which lies at the foot of the central axis, the square subdivisions on either side have been most beautifully modified in the eighteenth century into rectangular *parterres de broderie*, scrolls of box against red gravel. Today, these are a trifle ragged, but the subtle value of the change is real and apparent – from the windows of the two halves of the villa looking out and down into this garden, the *rectangular* shapes give a length and direction to the *square* expanse which complements the central appeal of Bologna's fountain, and which continues the downward motion of the central axis.

THE DUTCH GARDEN

Parallel to these gardens in the French style are others in diverging and different styles. In Holland, alas!, the splendid gardens made in the late seventeenth century have gone, and only engravings and paintings can, for the moment, remind us of the past. The baroque splendours of Het Loo, the palace and gardens built by William of Orange between 1684 and the end of the century – with gardens designed by the French *émigré* Daniel Marot – are now in process of restoration, with ample contemporary documentation available to ensure accuracy. Het Loo was, at first glance, much like a formal French garden, but had three features which are more characteristic of Dutch gardens; lavish plantings of tulips, division of the garden area into somewhat smaller beds, even in the parts which are distant from the house (a tradition carried over from the gardens of the sixteenth century), and a framework of small, narrow canals bordering the outer sections of the garden. The flanking canals, necessary for drainage in many parts of the Low Countries, are imitated in gardens as far apart as Schleissheim in Munich, and Herrenhausen in Hannover. Herrenhausen, like Schleissheim, was designed by a Frenchman, Martin Charbonnier, who worked for the Electress Sophie from 1682. She had taken over a smaller

115 Het Loo – the palace and gardens, engraved by R. de Hooghe. The gardens were principally designed by Daniel Marot, a Huguenot émigré who worked for William of Orange. Het Loo, begun in 1686, was considerably enlarged in 1692, to emulate the extent of Versailles, just as William enlarged the gardens of Hampton Court from 1689 onwards. Long neglected, the gardens of Het Loo have been magnificently restored

garden on the site in 1680, and gave herself wholly to the task of creating a noble garden. She spoke proudly of 'le jardin de Herrenhausen, qui est ma vie', and died in the garden in 1714. Though she spoke in French, and though her gardener was trained in France, Herrenhausen was closer to Het Loo than to Versailles.

THE ITALIAN TRADITION

The Italian tradition continued in Dutch and German gardens throughout the seventeenth century, and into the eighteenth. While J. Van der Groen's *Neder-landtsen Hovenier* (1669) gives a few plans of contemporary Dutch gardens – Rijswijck, and Honselaersdijck, and the Huis ten Bosch – in which parterres with curving and unified designs of *broderie* appear, these gardens have a Dutch, and un-French squareness of plan, and the remainder of his book illustrates details of garden plans which reveal no overall subordination to a principal design. Page after page of knots appear in a confusing juxtaposition one with another, followed by details of trellis work and sundials which could easily have been an appendix to J. Vredeman de Vries' *Hortorum viridariorumque . . .* of 1583, or the *Hortus floridus* of Crispin de Passe of 1614. Apart from the French *broderies* in the main plans, nothing seems to have changed. The same applies, and with extraordinary force, to the two great volumes of J. C. Volkamer's *Nürnbergische Hesperides* (1708-14), in which the many plates depicting the citrus fruit and trees collected by Volkamer and his friends have detailed vignettes of the gardens of worthies in the city and neighbourhood of Nuremberg.

One may say in an absolute manner that all the gardens illustrated by Volkamer are formal: though published when the 'wind of change' was just beginning to blow in England, there is no slightest whisper of would-be wildness here. Quite a few of the gardens have *broderies* of a curved French style, and several have plans which

pretend to a certain symmetry. But the majority are still exquisitely formal gardens of a Renaissance style, with topiary, sundials in box, joke fountains, arbours in carpenter's work, and even mounts – and the view of the 'Spalliergang in Herrn Seuters Garten' ('the hedge walk in Mr Seuter's garden') even has the unmistakable shapes of turf seats, four of them, set round the circular pool at the intersection of the walks. These small gardens, perfectly formal, are like those of Vredeman de Vries, or that in the frontispiece of M. Merian's *Florilegium renovatum* of 1641, showing the garden of Herr Swindius. Volkamer's own garden, 'viridarium suburbaneum Iohan: Cristofferi Volckameri in Norimberga', with the date 1695 outlined on his box sundial, is filled with curiosities and 'conceits'. Le Nôtre and his disciples would have despised it – and yet it survived.

116 This broad view of J. C. Volkamer's garden (1714) retains a Renaissance enthusiasm for detail, for the antique, and for a garden in which the separate parts are important in building up a general impression. As at Heidelberg (see the endpapers) the intricate details are not strictly subordinated to the overall design. Volkamer's formal garden contains vegetables, choice flowers, *broderies*, hothouses, an

elaborate sundial, an obelisk, and a structure with four columns showing the distance from Nuremburg to other cities

BETHLEHEM AND SANSPAREIL

Stranger things were to be seen in Germany within a year or two. Around 1717, Graf von Sporck, who was a deeply devout Roman Catholic, set up his two hermitages in the region of Kukus, in the rocky woods of Neuwald in Bohemia. The foundations are described in 1720 by G. C. von Stillenau, in his *Leben . . . Grafen von Sporck*, who explains that Sporck had three years previously endowed these hermitages to enable worthy people to turn away from the vainglory of the world and contemplate their Creator. The two hermitages were dedicated to noted Christian ascetics, St Paul and St Anthony, and Stillenau adds that the forest surroundings are so peaceful that 'here disturbance itself would find tranquillity'. A third hermitage was dedicated to St Bruno, and set up beside a bare and rock-ringed pool.

After a short while, Sporck's hopes were deceived, as the three hermits were accused of heresy and tried in the local episcopal court. Sporck promptly sacked them, and in the 1720s he commissioned a sculptor, Matthias Braun, to carve the numerous outcrops in the forest with the figures of saints and penitents. Sporck named this region 'Bethlehem', and most of the sculptures, which are of large and even gigantic proportions, still lurk in the thickets of Neuwald. Though Sporck's Bethlehem had a religious purpose, he had created a 'landscape with hermitages' which is on the edge of garden history, and at a time when in England the perennial attraction of a tranquil life, the rejection of worldly pleasures in favour of rustic seclusion was once more making itself felt. John Milton, a Protestant if ever there was one, could still write in 'Il Penseroso' (1632):

And may at last my weary age
Find out the peaceful hermitage,
The hairy gown and mossy cell . . .

Milton, and other Englishmen after him – Abraham Cowley, Timothy Nourse, Alexander Pope, William Kent and William Stukeley – would all have felt a certain sympathy with Sporck's Bethlehem, and a great deal of interest.

In the 1740s a rock and forest wilderness was converted to a garden landscape in ways which correspond much more closely to developments in English gardening, and yet which seem to have had no direct impulse from English garden practice. This was at Sanspareil, near Bayreuth in Bavaria, where the Margravine Wilhelmine von Bayreuth (the sister of Frederick the Great of Prussia) transformed the mountainous forest into a sequence of scenes – cliff and cave and grotto – related to the adventures of Telemachus, the hero of Fénelon's prose epic *Télémaque*. As with Sporck's Bethlehem, the interest was partly – but only partly – religious, since Bayreuth had for some time been a centre of Pietism, of the sort favoured in Fénelon's writings. Her father-in-law had had *Télémaque* translated into German.

It is therefore a French influence, the influence of a French writer, which is felt at Sanspareil, but the scenes created are for a wilderness which is far from the luxurious 'hermitage' erected for Louis XIV at Marly. The earliest engravings, in 1749, show the small central buildings with a *parterre de broderie* in front of them, but the other scenes are contrived in the rocks with a naturalness which is truly remarkable for the period. The idea of the garden was first mooted in 1744, and the work of contriving

the sequence of scenes from Fénelon's story began in the following year, and was completed in 1748. In the history of gardens, it is a most unusual development, comparable only with the activities in England of Henry Hoare at Stourhead, and William Shenstone at the Leasowes, at roughly the same time, each imagining that this landscape might 'resemble an epic poem.' Sanspareil must indeed have been 'incomparable' when it was first made. In 1749 Wilhelmine wrote to her brother: 'The situation of this place is unique. The buildings we have made are in exquisite taste. Nature herself was the architect.' Her words, and her cliff-garden, are extraordinary. In England they could easily have been understood, but in Germany they must have puzzled a great many people.

THE ROCOCO GARDEN

Sporck's Bethlehem was an isolated and exceptional phenomenon, and I venture to think that Wilhelmine von Bayreuth's *Felsengarten* at Sanspareil in the 1740s was still exceptional in Germany. Much more widespread in western Europe was the mood and style of the rococo, a term as liable to abuse as any other overall name for a characteristic 'movement' in the arts, such as 'baroque' or 'classical' or 'romantic', and nonetheless as valuable and as viable as these undoubtedly are. Dating approximately from the death of Louis XIV in 1715, the *seriousness* of baroque classicism gives way to a lighter and more frivolous mood, in which the relief and delight at the end of Louis' solemnity is expressed, not in a rejection of classical models (that was beginning quite separately in England, and is another story, closely linked with the birth of the landscape garden), but in a playful, light-hearted and more delicate treatment of the forms and themes of the past half-century.

This is delightfully evident in certain gardens in Germany, where by a most happy accident these fragilities have been preserved. Near Würzburg, at Weikersheim in Baden-Württemberg, a garden with a totally formal outline – a perfect rectangle, some 250 × 130 yards in size, with straight tree-lined walks round all four sides, and with four walks quartering the garden to meet at a central circular *rond-point* with a sculptured fountain in the middle – was laid out in 1709, and was to all intents and purposes completed with the construction of the double-orangery at the far end of the garden in 1723. Tediously symmetrical? Not in the slightest. This garden is endlessly intriguing and entertaining, being not only of proportions which are perfectly allied to the garden in front of the castle (and – unlike some much grander and more ambitious gardens – of proportions which do not overawe the visitor), but enlivened by fifty or more sculptures which say: 'We are here to give pleasure.' If we begin to read the list of these sculptures (by Johann Jakob Sommer and his three sons, begun in 1708 and finished in 1724), we might think that it was no more than a provincial echo of Versailles – the four winds, the four elements, the four seasons, many figures from classical mythology, centered round the fountain group in the middle of the garden, where Hercules wrestles with the Hydra. But sixteen of the fifty-odd sculptures are of servants and hangers-on and personalities connected with the court at Weikersheim, and all given the grotesque proportions of dwarves – the master of the hounds, the court fool, the shepherd, gardener's girl, good-for-nothing, cook, drummer and so forth. And when, leaving the printed list in the guide-book, we inspect the statues in the garden, we see that the oppressive solemnity and consequent boredom of the grand French manner has been exchanged for an alertness, a movement, and a humorous sense of reality which is wholly delightful. No doubt the visitors to Graf Carl Ludwig von Hohenlohe's garden were impressed, as they were impressed at Versailles. But they must have been entertained in a way which was immensely more enjoyable. At the centre, the wrestling Hercules is 'putting on a show'; at the four corners of the garden, the Winds swirl up like whirlwinds, or the horn of a unicorn or a *turritella* shell. They have the surging movement of Bernini's equestrian statue of Louis XIV – which he could not abide and wished to destroy – and the great gods on the balustrade of the orangery, Zeus, Hercules, Hermes and the rest, are *sitting* while we look on and observe their dangling legs.

The design of the orangery (by Johann Christian Lüttich) must be mentioned.

Built in 1719-23, it closes the far end of the rectangular garden – but not completely. It is in two equal halves, dividing to leave room for a statue (once an equestrian statue of Carl Ludwig, now exchanged for the somewhat sinister regal figure of 'Europe'), and dividing also to allow a most lovely and inviting prospect of the fertile and cultivated slopes of the Taubertal. Beyond the garden, the countryside – it is almost as if Addison's line in the *Spectator* of 1712 had penetrated to Germany: 'a Man might make a pretty Landskip of his own Possessions.' The glimpse, the *Blick* of the vine-clad slopes beyond the orangery is intentional, an essential part of the human scale of the garden. It is a further reminder of the continuing strength of the Italian tradition, with the villa garden set on a hillside slope, enjoying here and there the views of the surrounding countryside.

Covetousness, *convoitise*, is a disease in writers of history – 'I wish I had been Cesare Borgia' – and Weikersheim is my *faiblesse*. Near Athens there were the groves

119 At Rozendaal, near Arnhem, an intricate formal garden was added to the moated medieval castle in the seventeenth century. This was followed by the shell gallery, a semi-circle of superbly decorated shell-encrusted alcoves spouting and dripping with water. This photograph shows a detail of one recess. The entire gallery has recently been restored and is a fine example of rococo shell work

174

120 Pasteboard Gothic – in watercolour. The little-known artist Thomas Robins (1716-70) painted a fair number of English garden scenes, and delighted in showing the frail moments of garden chinoiserie and Gothic, which have now vanished from the landscape. Framed in twining tendrils, this scene (*c.* 1750) shows a lightweight Gothic chapel ringed with a ha-ha and overlooking a busy river, probably the Thames. We are still far from the solemn, gloomy scenes of Betz, Wörlitz, Wardour or Fonthill

of 'the divine Hecademus' where Plato had his Academy. For me, near Würzburg, there is Weikersheim. I know no other garden where I would freely and unhesitatingly scrawl on the door 'Est, est, est'.

Lighter still is the mood at Veitshöchheim in Bavaria, a few miles north of Würzburg. Here, all is given an intimacy which denies seriousness, since the hedges everywhere divide the garden into small regions, with sculptures which no longer strive to any kind of heroism, but smile or joke. The gardens, begun in the early 1700s, owe their present form to J. P. Mayer, who laid them out between 1763 and 1776, and who designed the Residenz garden at Würzburg, and the sculptures are the work of Ferdinand Tietz, in 1765-8. At Veitshöchheim there are no countryside views, and not many of the castle. All is private, and all is fun – the enticing view from one trellis-work summerhouse to another, suggesting a maze-like path, which you must follow in order to get there; or the carved dragon, creeping slyly down the steps to devour the flowers and fruit in a stony basket. The dragon is carved in lifelike detail, yet does not frighten us – on his back there are not scales, but a pattern of leaves and fruit.

In its very lightness, the rococo tended to be fragile, and in garden matters, fragility spells an early demise. In England, the gardens of a rococo kind have all perished entirely, their lattice-work frivolities decaying and giving way to the more urgent and sweeping changes of the landscape garden. Yet they existed – in particular the paintings of Thomas Robins (1716-70) depict them with a naive and moving grace. Robins's work is little known, and the gardens he painted with such care have gone, with their tender frameworks of tendrils and leaves, birds, butterflies and flowers. Already in the late 1740s and 1750s, when most of his paintings were made, gardens in England were changing to the landscape style: the formal, foursquare divisions stand beside areas with winding, serpentine paths, and the pillared temples (in wood and plaster) look out as often on flowery glades as on straight hedge-lined paths.

CHINOISERIE

Chinoiserie is at first a divergence, like rococo, from the heavy seriousness of baroque classicism, and in gardens this is true from its first appearance at Versailles, in the Trianon de Porcelaine, made in 1670-1, until well into the eighteenth century. The connection with China, Chinese architecture and Chinese gardens was never convincingly close – in 1665, Jan Nieuhof's *Gezantschap . . . an den grooten Tartarischen Cham* was published, describing the Dutch mission to the imperial court in Peking, and was soon published again in English, French and German, with its many pictures of Chinese life, buildings, flora and countryside – and it is no

exaggeration to suggest that all the pagodas and Chinese garden-buildings in Europe for the next century could have been designed from Nieuhof's illustrations. Of course, there were other books and sources, but for most of a century the additions which they brought to the West's knowledge of Chinese gardens were minimal, or else, like M. Ripa's accurate engravings of Chinese architecture, not widely known. Chinese *gardens* never really caught on in Europe – Nieuhof's picture of the preposterous 'Cliffs made by Art' (pl. 118) suggests why. He says that 'the like Artificial Rocks are to be seen in the Emperor's Court, where the great *Tartar Chan* often refreshes himself in the heat of the Summer', and the picture appealed enough to be twice republished in the eighteenth century. But few gardens in Europe contained imitations until the 1770s, unless we count the rock garden of Sanspareil near Bayreuth (and this was modelled not on a Chinese, but a French and classical theme).

Until the 1770s, chinoiserie in gardens is a matter purely of pagodas, steeply curved bridges, and lesser architectural decorative motifs, such as tip-tilted eaves, with or without bells, and reticulated lattice-work screens, applied to walls, fences, and endless varieties of furniture. It is decorative rather than structural. Countless pagodas were built all over Europe – even at Stowe. A small palace and attendant buildings, the Kina, was built between 1753 and 1769 at Drottningholm in Sweden; in Frederick the Great's garden of Sans-souci at Potsdam, there was a 'Chinese tea house' built in 1754-7, surmounted by a seated mandarin carrying a parasol (a miniature version of this 'tea house' was built by Tietz at Veitshöchheim); and at Wilhelmshöhe, near Kassel, there was an entire Chinese village, called Moulang, built in 1781. The Chinese pavilion at Stowe has gone, though others, even Moulang, survive entirely or in part. But if we want the full delight and intricacy of chinoiserie decoration, we must look at interiors, in palaces and mansions rather than in summerhouses; for example at the Eremitage near Bayreuth in Germany, at Claydon House, Buckinghamshire, in England, or at Capodimonte near Naples in Italy.

The idea of the Chinese garden has appealed to Europeans for a long while, ever since Sir William Temple wrote *Upon the Gardens of Epicurus* in 1685 (published in 1692), contrasting the European liking for symmetry and straight lines with the 'Chinese scorn' for 'this way of Planting'. In contrast, he writes,

their greatest Reach of Imagination is employed in contriving Figures, where the Beauty shall be great, and strike the Eye, but without any Order or Disposition of Parts . . . And though we have hardly any Notion of this Sort of Beauty, yet they have a particular Word to express it, . . . the *Sharawadgi*. [A mysterious word, as yet not convincingly explained, though enough has been written about it to fill this book.]

Addison echoes this briefly in the *Spectator* (25 June 1712), as do others down the century. Details of 'this Sort of Beauty' were not forthcoming until the Jesuit, J.-D. Attiret, sent back from Peking a long description of the beauties of the emperor's palaces and gardens, the Yuan Ming Yuan, which was published in French in 1747, in English in 1749, and again in 1752 as *A Particular Account of the Emperor of China's Gardens*. Attiret stresses their extent, their pleasing and irregular plan, the total absence of straight roads or walks, and the tendency for paths and even bridges to follow a winding or a zig-zag course.

But Chinese *gardens* were still not designed in Europe, only buildings. A nudge in the Chinese direction comes in Sir William Chambers' *Designs of Chinese Buildings* (1757), in which he outlines the 'three different species of scenes' – 'pleasing, horrid, and enchanted' – which are favoured in Chinese gardens, and touches briefly on 'artificial rocks', remarkably like those in Nieuhof's picture:

> In compositions of this kind the Chinese surpass all other nations . . . When they are large they make in them caves and grottos, with openings, through which you discover distant prospects. They cover them, in different places, with trees, shrubs, briars, and moss; placing on their tops little temples, or other buildings, to which you ascend by rugged and irregular steps cut into the rock.

Chambers was invited to adorn the gardens at Kew with exotic buildings, which he did, and these, including the pagoda, illustrate his *Plans . . . and Perspective Views of the Garden and Buildings at Kew* (1763). But he did not make a Chinese garden at Kew, or anything like it. In 1772, his *Dissertation on Oriental Gardening* extends the analysis of the 'three different species of scenes', by adding a great many alternatives to his earlier list of 'scenes of terror'. Chambers was by 1772 caught up in the wholly European admiration for the *sublime,* which was to prove both the climax and the downfall of the landscape garden.

Chambers was writing with architect's tongue in gardener's cheek: 'To add both to the horror and sublimity of these scenes' with concealed 'foundries, lime-kilns, and glass-works', whose flames and smoke give the appearance of 'volcanoes' in a mountainous scene. Echoes of Chambers' sublime scenes might be seen in the grottoes built in the second half of the eighteenth century, but these are more truly derived from the general impulse towards ever wilder natural scenes which is characteristic of the later landscape garden. By the time G. L. Le Rouge printed three *cahiers* of engravings of scenes from the Yuan Ming Yuan in the mid-1770s, in his *Détails des Nouveaux Jardins à la Mode,* it was virtually too late. His huge collection of engravings shows many a pagoda, tea house and Chinese bridge in European gardens, all built and complete, and none of them has a landscape which can honestly be compared with those in his real scenes of the palaces and gardens of Peking.

122   Stourhead – the temple of
Apollo, overlooking the lake,
roughly midway between the
stone bridge and the Pantheon

12

Leaping the Fence

Writing long after the event, Horace Walpole saw, exactly and correctly, that the *ha-ha* marks the dividing-line between the formal gardens of French and Dutch origin and the landscape garden born in England in the eighteenth century.

Other symptoms, other characteristics there are of course, and we shall discuss them – indeed there are many landscape gardens in England and elsewhere which do not boast a ha-ha at all. But the ha-ha has the status of a technological advance in the craft of gardening which is quite exceptional, and can only be compared for its impact with Budding's invention of the rotary mower, and Ward's invention of the Wardian case in the nineteenth century.

THE GENIUS OF THE PLACE

In various ways, people concerned with garden design in the early 1700s came to feel that the formality of French and Dutch gardens was too rigid, too pompous, and somehow 'unnatural'. In this they were backed and influenced by the philosophical attitude of Shaftesbury (Anthony Ashley Cooper, 3rd Earl of Shaftesbury, 1671–1713). In *The Moralists* (1709) the character of Theocles (who voices Shaftesbury's view) expresses deep, indeed passionate approval of 'Nature', the spirit of what is good, beautiful and true in the world. Though there are points of difference, his attitude is not far from pantheism, in which worship is a state of what Shaftesbury terms 'enthusiasm', a receptive and yet outgoing unity with the unspoiled manifestations of the natural world. In contrast with nature are the products of artifice, and Shaftesbury chooses as an example the formal garden. This opposition of 'natural' and 'formal', to the detriment of the latter, will be maintained throughout the century; it is at the heart of Rousseau's attitudes to nature and to society (one good, the other corrupt) and underlies Burke's admiration for the 'sublime' which later nature-lovers came to appreciate in ever wilder and more savage forms.

The following extract from *The Moralists* expresses the conversion to Theocles' view of the other character in the dialogue, Philocles.

> Your *Genius*, the *Genius* of the Place, and the GREAT GENIUS have at last prevail'd. I shall no longer resist the Passion growing in me for Things of a *natural* kind; where neither *Art*, nor the *Conceit* or *Caprice* of Man has spoiled their *genuine Order*, by breaking in upon that *primitive State*. Even the rude *Rocks*, the mossy *Caverns*, the irregular unwrought *Grotto's*, and broken *Falls* of Waters, with all the horrid Graces of the *Wilderness* itself, as representing NATURE more, will be the more engaging, and appear with a Magnificence beyond the formal Mockery of Princely Gardens.

This philosophical attitude was not matched immediately with a corresponding 'theory of gardening', but was rather evident in piecemeal, separated objections to particular aspects of formal gardening. Joseph Addison (1672–1719) in the *Spectator* (25 June 1712) objects to the fashion of topiary, producing 'a Mathematical Figure' from a tree's 'Luxuriancy and Diffusion of Boughs and Branches'; instead of 'an

Orchard in Flower' we have 'Cones, Globes and Pyramids', and 'we see the marks of the Scissars upon every Plant and Bush.' He speaks of the pleasure derived from his confused and irregular estate, 'a Confusion of Kitchin and Parterre, Orchard and Flower Garden', which has almost the air of 'a natural Wilderness' (6 September 1712), while in the earlier essay he suggests that an entire estate 'may be thrown into a kind of Garden' by thoughtful additions and plantations. In this way Addison is carrying the garden further out into the countryside, and converting the countryside into a wider and more spacious garden scene, a picture: by the help and improvement of 'some small Additions of Art . . . a Man might make a pretty Landskip of his own Possessions.' Addison's beginning here is a cautious one; he wishes to 'improve' the countryside. Later in the century the wish will be to bring the countryside into the garden, to 'improve' the garden by making it look like the countryside.

These points were taken up by Alexander Pope (1688–1744), first concerning topiary, in the *Guardian* (29 September 1713), and then in a more general way in his 'Epistle to Lord Burlington' (1731). In the *Guardian*, Pope contrasts the unadorned and happy simplicity of the gardens of Alcinous, in Homer's *Odyssey*, and of Virgil's old bee-keeper in the *Georgics* with 'the modern Practice of Gardening', in which we do our utmost to get as far away from nature as we can. Pope here confines his satire to topiary, inventing a 'Catalogue of Greens' which 'an eminent Town-Gardiner' wishes to advertise. Among other items are:

123   Gilbert White's ha-ha at Selborne, built in 1759-61. White's journal for 24 January 1761 reads: 'Long the mason finish't the dry wall of the Haha . . . it looks likely to stand a long while. The workmanship, exclusive of carting the stones, cost £1: 8s: 10d.' In the 1780s, this ha-ha was frequented by White's tortoise Timothy

A Pair of Giants, *stunted*, to be sold cheap.
A Queen *Elizabeth* in Phylyraea, a little inclining to the Green Sickness, but of full growth.
ANOTHER Queen *Elizabeth* in Myrtle, which was very forward, but Miscarried by being too near a Savine.
AN old Maid of Honour in Wormwood.

In his 'Epistle to Lord Burlington' Pope mocks the bad taste of the wealthy Timon, whose garden is unnatural in its regularity and its symmetry: 'Grove nods at Grove, each Alley has a Brother,/And half the Platform just reflects the other.' Nature within the garden is made monstrous by artificialities while the entire garden is cut off from the country round about: 'On ev'ry side you look, behold the Wall!'

Pope contrasts this sterile conception with the advice, endlessly repeated throughout the century, to seek and follow 'nature', the *genius loci* or 'spirit of the place', which '*Paints* as you plant, and as you work, *Designs.*'

Pope's words, like Addison's, must be read with caution. The fashionable garden practitioners of the 1710s and 1720s did not instantly plunge into a frenzy of mountainous, jungly or marshy excess. Their gardens – those of Pope at Twickenham, or of Philip Southcote at Wooburn in Surrey, for example – seem tame and restrained when set beside landscape gardens made in the 1770s. Pope's famous grotto, to him almost the abode of nature, and Southcote's *ferne ornée* (an 'ornamented farm', the literal interpretation of Addison's suggestion in the *Spectator*) were both relatively formal creations, and I am sure that neither Shaftesbury nor Addison nor Pope envisaged anything as wild, as 'natural', as Payne Knight's sublime landscape at Downton, or William Beckford's vast paradise at Fonthill.

THE HA-HA

But to the ha-ha. Addison wished to 'throw . . . a whole Estate into a kind of Garden', to 'make a pretty Landskip of his own Possessions', while Pope saw an obstacle to this in Timon's garden. 'On ev'ry side you look, behold the Wall!'

So long as gardens were enclosed – to obtain privacy, to keep out cattle, to mark a boundary between the garden and the surrounding land – an enclosure, a wall, a hedge, a fence was necessary. And so long as the garden was thus enclosed, its relationship with the surrounding land, with the landscape and with 'nature' was inevitably limited. Behind a wall, the garden was inward-looking, tied to the house, its aspect and its proportions, the perfect example being at the villa di Papa Giulio in Rome. The garden remained architecture on the flat.

The ha-ha solves this problem in one easy process: instead of a *raised* enclosing barrier, a *sunken* barrier, shaped like a ditch or a dry moat, was dug round those parts of the garden which were to be made into 'a pretty Landskip'. The ditch needed to be deep and wide enough to prevent cattle from crossing from the land outside to the garden inside, and to be as near unnoticeable and invisible as possible, to create the illusion that the garden and the surrounding countryside were one and undivided. Hence the name 'ha-ha'. Let Walpole explain. In the development of the landscape garden, he says, 'the capital stroke, the leading step to all that has followed, was (I believe the first thought was Bridgeman's) the destruction of walls for boundaries, and the invention of fossés [ditches] – an attempt then deemed so astonishing that the common people called them Ha! Ha's! to express their surprise at finding a sudden and unperceived check to their walk.'

Charles Bridgeman (d. 1738) may or may not have been the first in England to build a ha-ha. The term first appears in *La Théorie et la Pratique du Jardinage*, by A.J. Dézallier d'Argenville (1709): 'une claire-voie qu'on appelle autrement un *ah, ah*, avec un fossé sec au pied.' This is soon translated into English by John James, in *The Theory and Practice of Gardening* (1712): 'an Opening, which the *French* call a *Claire-voïe*, or an Ah, Ah, with a dry Ditch at the Foot of it . . .' He writes 'At present we frequently make Thorough-Views, call'd *Ah, Ah* . . . This Sort of Opening is, on some Occasions, to be preferred, for that it does not shut up the Prospect, as the Bars of a Grill do.' This implies that d'Argenville had seen such a device in France 'frequently'; but he is not specific, and the ha-ha remains rare in France. The learned seekers-after-ha-has have pointed out that d'Argenville is suggesting one when he recommends the use of a water-barrier at the end of an *allée*, to allow the view to continue outwards, but the essential quality of unobtrusiveness in the ha-ha is lacking: one might claim as well that Pliny's and Alberti's hillside prospects were the same thing, which is garbage. The nearest convincing antecedent for the ha-ha is, I think, the now derelict garden of Hillesdon House in Buckinghamshire, where in the 1660s garden beds and paths were built out to the edge of raised fortifications (dating from 1644), to give an unimpeded view across the countryside. Yet here there is no documentation to support the idea, and the garden may then have been, probably was, of unimpeachable formality, *contrasting* with the landscape, and not blending with it, and the edges of the raised fortifications may have been stressed, not hidden, with urns and hedges of box. This has been done, in innocence or indifference, at West Wycombe, at Syon Park, and at the Wakes at Selborne, where in the last two centuries the lines of the ha-has, or parts of them, have been made *more* conspicuous by the addition of urns, chains, geraniums and other inappropriate materials.

124 A view of West Wycombe, in Buckinghamshire, by W. Daniell (*c.* 1781), which artfully combines several features in this outstanding garden landscape – the house with its striking double colonnade, the distant church surmounted by the golden ball, the Dashwood mausoleum nearby. In the foreground is a ha-ha, showing a lady and children on one side, wild deer on the other

I mention Hillesdon deliberately, since the idea of fortifications is mildly allied to the ha-ha in its early years, at Blenheim, at Stowe, at Duncombe, where ha-ha walls and bastions with fossés or ditches were built, like those of a seventeenth- or eighteenth-century fortification, preventing entry but allowing an unimpeded outward view (compare the fortress walls of Furttenbach's ideal princely garden, pl. 94, though there no outward landscape-view was envisaged). It may be that Stowe had the first genuine ha-ha, since Bridgeman was working there from 1713. But Blenheim was earlier – in 1712 the peripatetic antiquary William Stukeley passed by Blenheim, and described a feature which is unmistakably a ha-ha, though he does not give it the name: 'The garden is . . . taken out of the park, and may still be said to be part of it, well contriv'd by sinking the outer-wall into a foss, to give one a view quite round and take off the odious appearance of confinement and limitation to the eye.'

The one Stukeley saw at Blenheim still stands, and the one at Stowe, and other good examples are at Rousham, at West Wycombe, at Bowood, at Levens Hall, and at Sezincote. Modern ha-has are still occasionally constructed – as at Villiers Park in Oxfordshire, and at Abbots Ripton, Huntingdon – and have come into their own in an unusual way in zoos, where they give visitors unimpeded yet safe views of fierce animals. The best of these is surely at Phoenix Park, in Dublin, with the alarmingly open prospect of the rhinoceros.

The ha-ha wall built by the naturalist Gilbert White in his garden at Selborne is still there, though disfigured with bedding plants along its edge. It marked the end of White's home garden, and the beginning of the wider prospect towards the wooded slopes of the Hanger. In the 1780s, thirty years after the ha-ha was built, it was visited by a remarkable character, White's tortoise Timothy. He acquired the tortoise in March 1780, when Timothy's owner Mrs Snook died at the age of 86. White first allowed the tortoise to hibernate, but as the spring advanced, so Timothy woke up, and ventured out and along the garden, devouring the young greens: 'his favourite food is lettuce, and dandelion, cucumber, and kidney-beans.' At last, on 27 May comes the news that Timothy 'when he arrives at the haha . . . distinguishes the fall of the ground, and retires with caution, or marches carefully along the edge.'

I have called this section 'leaping the fence', since in his famous passage about the ha-ha, Horace Walpole associates the greatest progress in creating the landscape garden with William Kent. With the ha-ha invented, Kent, says Walpole, 'leaped the fence, and saw that all nature was a garden.' Walpole's phrase is deeply perceptive. Before the ha-ha, fences, walls, hedges *prevented* the artist-gardener from seeing how his garden could become a part of nature; and it prevented him from seeing how all parts of nature, the rough and the smooth, could be considered fit elements of a garden. Between about 1710 and 1800, from d'Argenville's reference to the ha-ha and Addison's essays in the *Spectator*, until the making of William Beckford's Fonthill at the end of the century, the English landscape garden is born, and develops, tentatively, piecemeal, but always advancing, until at last an extreme of 'total landscape' is advocated which led beyond the resources in money and in land of garden owners, and beyond the reasonable capabilities of the garden itself.

BACK TO ARCADY

In this period of almost a century the art of gardening held a central place in European culture, as it had since the time of Louis XIV and the creation of Versailles. In the eighteenth century, there is hardly a poet, painter, politician or philosopher, hardly a lord or lady, landowner large or small in western Europe who does not participate in gardening or garden talk, garden writing or the visiting of gardens. Without excessive distortion we may say that this is because man in the eighteenth century achieved the great 'rediscovery of nature', and because this 'rediscovery' took place in large part via the garden. Opponents to the process there most certainly were, such as Voltaire or Dr Johnson, but their very opposition engaged them in consideration of gardens and garden theory. The thought of the century is linked to gardens with a strength unknown before or since.

The landscape garden, born and perfected in England, has two main stages in its development. The first is intimately connected with William Kent, the second with 'Capability' Brown. The first stage leads to the creation of 'ideal' landscapes, in which the nature portrayed was of an Arcadian or Elysian antiquity, and in which there was often a desire to recreate or echo in a three-dimensional form the views of the Roman countryside seen in the landscape paintings of Claude Lorrain (Claude Gelée, or Le Lorrain, 1600–82) and Gaspard Dughet (sometimes called Gaspard Poussin, 1615–75).

Though these artists and their many imitators painted numerous different landscapes, both real and imaginary, their most popular and characteristic rural scenes are of the area round Tivoli, fifteen miles or so to the east of Rome. Here, in a steeply hilly, almost precipitous landscape, the river Anio or Aniene plunges down in spectacular cascades towards the Campagna, the level plain which extends for miles towards Rome. The small and ancient town of Tivoli stands above the *cascatelle*, and perched on a jutting corner of the hillside is the ruined and beautiful temple of the Sibyl (sometimes called the temple of Vesta). These scenes, and this temple, are numerically the most frequent in the *oeuvres* of both Claude and Gaspard; for example, the temple of the Sibyl figures in over forty of Claude's surviving drawings and paintings, and I would think that views of Tivoli and of the temple form an even greater proportion of Gaspard's work than they do of Claude's. The works of a third painter, Salvator Rosa (1615–73), which tend to show wilder, stormier and more craggy aspects of the Italian landscape, are often associated with those of Claude and Gaspard, but attempts to emulate the spirit of Salvator's landscapes in gardens are rarer, and mostly confined to the second half of the century. Through a confusion of their names, Nicholas Poussin (1593–1665) is linked with Gaspard Poussin or Dughet (Gaspard was Nicholas' son-in-law, and took Poussin's name), but his paintings, though we may now consider them to be 'greater' than those of Gaspard, did not have anything like the same influence on landscape gardening, since their backgrounds are predominantly architectural, and not so much of the countryside.

An instructive reference to the three painters occurs in 1748, in James Thomson's *Castle of Indolence*, where a colourful, rural, natural and atmospheric scene is said to contain 'Whate'er Lorrain light-touched with softening hue, Or savage Rosa dashed, or learned Poussin drew.'

He then reinforces the Arcadian quality of this scene with music–'Aerial music in the warbling wind'–the music of the Aeolian harp. This instrument consisted of a series of strings stretched across a sounding-board, and suspended so that the wind caused the strings to vibrate. Though named after Aeolus, the Greek god of the winds, it did not exist in Greek times, being invented in the 1640s by Athanasius Kircher. It had considerable popularity in the eighteenth century as an instrument which produced 'natural' music, since the musician, the 'harpist', was the wind. Thomson's poem makes this clear–all you had to do was

> sidelong to the gently-waving wind
> To lay the well-tuned instrument reclined;
> From which, with airy flying fingers light,
> Beyond each mortal touch the most refined,
> The god of winds drew sounds of deep delight.

Thomson's reference is backed up in another poem, his 'Ode on Aeolus's Harp', also published in 1748, the year before his death. Until Thomson's time the Aeolian harp had not attracted much notice, but from the 1750s it was a frequent accessory in gardens of a would-be Claudian and sentimentally natural kind. The extraordinary cliff garden of Sanspareil, near Bayreuth, made in the late 1740s, has several features connected with the god of the winds – a cliff, a grotto, and a tower – and the 'tower of Aeolus' was equipped with the proper instrument.

The Aeolian harp was not always welcome. For many years the two eccentric 'ladies of Llangollen', Lady Eleanor Butler and Miss Sarah Ponsonby, had one, or maybe several, in their sentimental garden in north Wales. When they were visited

125   Claude Lorrain, like his contemporary Gaspard Poussin, was fascinated by the landscape at Tivoli and by the temple of the Sibyl in particular. This drawing by Claude (c. 1645) is one of many presentations of the temple, shown here in a river-side setting quite different from its original hilly site

in 1792 by the French lady novelist Mme de Genlis, whom they admired for her extreme sensibility, she was honoured by having the harp hung outside her bedroom window. It must have blown a gale, for the airy twangling kept Mme de Genlis awake all night, and she departed earlier than had been planned.

As late as 1809 one of Turner's most Claudian paintings – a view of Richmond on the Thames, but glowing with an Italian sunset light – brings these elements together again. The painting entitled 'Thomson's Aeolian Harp', has in the foreground an Arcadian scene, with peasants resting beside the fragments of a classical building. Shaded by an Italian-looking clump of trees is a stone inscribed 'Thomson'. On this, the poet's grave, stands a harp. A maiden adorns it with a garland, while others prepare to dance. Turner has united the great English poet of nature, the English landscape, Claude and Arcadia in a single painting.

WILLIAM KENT

William Kent (1685–1748) was first trained as a painter. His career as an architect and garden designer came later. From 1712 until 1719 he was in Italy studying painting, his time there paid for largely by wealthy patrons, Burrell Massingberd and Lord Burlington. We know from a letter written to him in 1713 that Massingberd instructed him to acquire copies 'after Poussin and Clodio Lorenzo', and we know that in later years he himself owned originals or copies of paintings by Claude. When he returned to England, his first published work, in 1720, was a frontispiece to the *Poems on Several Occasions* of John Gay, and this shows a view of the temple of the Sibyl; in 1734 the temple of Ancient Virtue in the Elysian Fields at Stowe was built from Kent's design, and modelled on the Sibyl's temple at Tivoli, and a year or two later he made a drawing of the Sibyl's temple in a steep hillside setting for a proposed remodelling of Grillet's formal cascade at Chatsworth. The temple of the Sibyl, introduced by Kent, was the most frequently imitated ancient building in the landscape garden. Twenty or more versions of it were built in the British Isles, and as many more on the Continent. Some, like Kent's temple of Ancient Virtue at Stowe, were built complete, and later, more daring versions like the temple of Philosophy at Ermenonville (*c.* 1775) were deliberately built in a ruined state, not for the sake of architectural and historical accuracy, but because the idea of the *ruined* building carried with it associations of greater antiquity, mingled with melancholy at the transience of human memorials. Much of this approval of old, rather than new, and of ruined rather than complete buildings comes from a wish to avoid the brash, authoritarian and worldly attitudes which – so the English thought – typified the formal gardens of France. The aesthetic of Versailles was perceived as an expression of Louis XIV's absolutism, the spanking new buildings, the geometrical gardens, the clipped hedges and the audacious fountains seeming to express a domineering attitude towards man and nature which the British now wished to challenge.

Joseph Warton's poem 'The Enthusiast', written in 1740, published 1744, has much of this feeling, shown in a contrast between 'Versailles' and the hilly landscapes of Tivoli (the river Anio) or England (the 'Gothic battlements'):

Rich in her weeping country's spoils, Versailles
May boast a thousand fountains, that can cast
The tortur'd waters to the distant Heav'ns;
Yet let me choose some pine-topt precipice
Abrupt and shaggy, whence a foamy stream,
Like Anio, tumbling roars; or some bleak heath,
Where straggling stands the mournful juniper,
Or yew-tree scath'd; while in clear prospect round,
From the grove's bosom spires emerge, and smoke
In bluish wreaths ascends, ripe harvests wave,
Low, lonely cottages, and ruin'd tops
Of Gothic battlements appear, and streams
Beneath the sun-beams twinkle.

126, 127 Kent's design for Venus' Vale, at Rousham (top), and a modern view across the pool, looking in the opposite direction to the top picture. Kent saw landscape with a painter's eye, designing his gardens as 'landscapes' modelled on the Italian views of Claude or Gaspard

The alternatives to the tyranny of Versailles were varied: not only were the gentler visions of Claude preferred, like the ruins of antique buildings, but the older, and often dilapidated gardens of Italy were found to have their charm. Not least among the attractions of these Italian gardens was their setting, on hillsides with country views round about, and further enriched with physical and atmospheric reminders of antiquity. Already in 1700 Timothy Nourse, in his *Campania Foelix*, had written of the use and pleasure of country life and of the qualities of a 'country house' in terms which recall Alberti and later Italian gardens (rather than the model of Versailles).

Kent's training led him to see gardens not only in terms of Claudian landscapes, but as compositions of a three-dimensional yet essentially painterly kind, where the visitor proceeds from one 'landscape picture' into another, and so onwards through the garden. Each 'picture' will have associations with nature and with the ideal aspects of the past through its architecture and sculpture, either within the immediate composition, with urns and statues, or with larger elements such as temples or the residence itself, or at a distance, like the 'Eyecatcher' at Rousham in Oxfordshire, where a crudely castellated tripartite archway was built in a field on the skyline a mile or more from the gardens to provide a distant and appropriate object to complete the view. Kent worked at Rousham in the late 1730s, on a site which had already been planned out in a semi-formal way by Charles Bridgeman. 'Nature' at Rousham appears to have been sedulously respected, for the sinuous curves of the river Cherwell which bounds the gardens to the east and south are echoed by the meandering paths, and by the S-shape of the serpentine stream which curls through the woods down to the lake in Venus' Vale. In his work at Rousham, Kent obliterated most of the formal elements which Bridgeman had used, leaving only the large rectangular lawn in front of the house, and the straight avenue from below Venus' Vale towards the statue of Apollo. The many 'pictures' the garden affords in its small compass have been created by Kent with a masterly use of the different levels of the ground, by dividing up the overall areas by means of jutting groups and spurs of trees, which separate and frame the views, and by arranging the direction of the paths so that one is given many varied glimpses of the scenes from different levels, angles and distances. Walpole felt that it was Kent's best work – it was 'Kentissime' – and he added in his *History of Modern Gardening* that 'the whole is as elegant and antique as if the Emperor Julian had selected the most pleasing solitude about Daphne to enjoy a philosophic retirement'–in other words, it could be compared with an ideal landscape of antiquity.

The same intention was present in the creation of Lord Burlington's garden at Chiswick, where again Bridgeman, followed by Kent, had worked in the late 1720s. At Chiswick, the imitation of antiquity was more open, more continuously in evidence, the imitation of nature less so. It was a 'mixed' antiquity related also to post-Renaissance Italy, with the models of recent architecture and recent garden design allied to models from ancient Rome. Burlington's villa was an adaptation of Palladio's villa Rotonda at Vicenza (1550–1), while round it the gardens were meant to echo certain qualities of Pliny's villa gardens. I say 'certain qualities', for the hillside prospects did not exist, and the elaborate topiary was eschewed, both features which the gardens of the Italian Renaissance had adopted. Instead, there was emphasis on the division between a fairly formal part, and a rustic or country part to the gardens. At one point, a semi-circular *exedra* was bordered with antique statues, and a *patte d'oie* with straight radiating walks between tall, clipped hedges led to classical architectural features. The hedges and the statues and also the buildings have an Italian feel, as if one had strayed into a damper, more grassy villa Medici. Elsewhere, in the 'rural' part, the lake has a mildly serpentine outline, with a rustic cascade by Kent similar to his three-arched cascade at the mouth of Venus' Vale at Rousham, or to his cascade by the lake at Claremont in Surrey. In 1728 Robert Castell, a protégé of Burlington's, published *The Villas of the Ancients Illustrated*, a translation of Pliny's letters referring to his villa gardens, with a commentary by Castell in which this contrast between the formal and the natural in the Roman gardens is stressed. Some parts reveal 'an Art that was visible in every Part of the Design', characteristic of 'the most regular Gardens', but others – Pliny's *imitatio ruris* – 'were possibly thrown into such an agreeable Disorder, as to have pleased the Eye from several Views, like so many beautiful Landskips.'

As at Chiswick and at Rousham, William Kent followed on the heels of Charles Bridgeman at Stowe, though here these two form part of a long succession of architects and garden designers. Kent was involved at Stowe from around 1730 until his death in 1748, and designed – or helped to design or re-design – several buildings and several regions in the gardens. The area most firmly connected with Kent is the valley of the Elysian Fields, which he developed as a separate feature to the east of the main north-south vista, which was still in a relatively formal state. This long and slightly winding valley is hidden from the main vista, and from the expanse of Hawkwell Field further to the east, by dense clumps of trees, which, growing high on either side, help to give a feeling of depth to the valley. At the top of the valley is a deeply recessed grotto, which was overhung with gloomy yews, and the stream issues from the base of the grotto to flow through the 'Elysian Fields'. Half-way down the valley, the water is held back to form a small woodland lake, and flows out through the Shell Bridge (before 1742), a characteristic tripartite Kentian design, with equally characteristic rough masonry. In the lower half of the valley the trees do not come so far down the slopes, leaving space on either side for a sweep of grass on each bank. On the eastern side is Kent's temple of British Worthies (*c.* 1735), a strange and unique building, being a curved section of wall with niches in which busts of notable Britons are displayed. This memorial faces across the stream, called here the river Styx, to a broad lawn leading up to the temple of Ancient Virtue, Kent's version of the temple of the Sibyl (*c.* 1734). The scene is firmly Claudian, with an obvious symbolism. On their death, the noblest Britons are to cross the river of the underworld and enjoy the Elysian Fields and their share of the temple of Ancient Virtue, which, perched on the edge of the valley like the temple at Tivoli, will remind the viewer of the Roman landscapes made familiar in the paintings of Claude and Gaspard.

In speaking of Stowe I have chosen to begin with Kent and the Elysian Fields, and this is indeed a memorable and beautiful section of the gardens. But Stowe is, like Versailles, which it emulated in the size and richness of its garden monuments, a vast and complex political and artistic creation; and, in contrast with Versailles, which was largely planned and executed between 1661 and 1688 (both the Trianons are separate and virtually independent ventures), the creation, modification and extension of Stowe lasted almost a century. Though many architectural garden features at Versailles have been changed, both during Louis XIV's reign and afterwards, the essential formal *plan* of the garden has not been touched since the 1660s. At Stowe the garden *buildings* have remained, more or less, while the plan of the gardens around them has been radically changed. The first house and gardens were already there, and impressive, when Celia Fiennes saw them in 1694, and major work on both continued until around 1776. This period begins when gardens were formal, and ends after half a century of reaction against such formality. The early plans of the gardens at Stowe show a rigidly geometrical vista in front of the house, beginning with symmetrical parterres to left and right, divided by a broad walk at right-angles to the house, lined with clipped, regularly spaced trees, punctuated with a fountain in the centre, and a formal lake, the Octagon, with a *gulio* or tall narrow pyramid spouting water in the centre.

The Octagon lake was flanked by identical small temples, the Lake temples, which still exist, though re-sited further apart. Other features, notably the Rotondo (by Vanbrugh, modified in 1760) were created to the west, with straight walks crossing and recrossing the main vista. The design so far is largely the work of Vanbrugh (who had planned the first form of the gardens at Blenheim and Castle Howard), and of Bridgeman, who may have been responsible for the miles of ha-ha which enclose most of the gardens. When Kent joined in, around 1730, a process of 'softening' the geometrical outlines of the gardens took place, and this was continued more thoroughly by Lancelot Brown ('Capability' Brown, 1716–83), whose career began at Stowe around 1740. Kent and then Brown removed all traces of the walk along the central axis to make an open expanse of lawn down to the Octagon, bordered with clumps of trees which swiftly came to resemble natural woodland. In

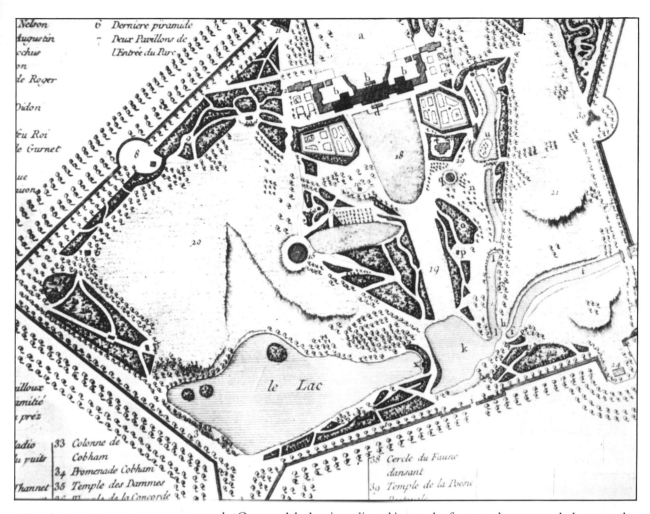

Within the plan image, the following labels are visible:

Nelson
Augustin
chus
on
de Roger

Didon

du Roi
le Gurnet

rue
tuons

6   *Derniere piramide*
7   *Deux Pavillons de*
    l'Entrée du Parc

le Lac

illour
amitié
t préz

adio   33 *Colonne de*
lu puits   *Cobham*
         34 *Promenade Cobham*
channel   35 *Temple des Dammes*
              de la Concorde

38 *Cercle du Faune*
    dansant
30 *Temple de la Poésie*

128   A plan of the gardens at Stowe in the 1770s. The earlier formal layout has been softened, so that the great avenue from the house towards the Octagon lake remains only in outline

1744 the Octagon lake lost its *gulio* and its regular form, and was extended eastwards, below the Elysian Fields, to be terminated with the view of the Palladian bridge. (Similar bridges were built, first at Wilton, in 1737, and then at Prior Park in Bath, *c.* 1755, with the same aim of adding an antique and classical character to the landscape.) At this point in the gardens another vista of a 'natural' kind was created, running northwards, beside and separate from the Elysian Fields. This vista is a spacious, undulating area of grass, the Hawkwell Field, bounded with an irregular belt of trees, with temples at either end (the Queen's temple to the north, the temple of Friendship to the south), and with glimpses of other features such as the Palladian bridge, or Cobham's pillar (1748), and of the palatial house itself in the distance. Midway, and at the highest spot in Hawkwell Field, so that it is visible from many points, stands the Gothic temple (by James Gibbs, *c.* 1741). This building, made of reddish ironstone, three-sided, battlemented, and uncompromisingly knobbly, irregular and 'un-classical', was first called the temple of Liberty, and represented Saxon or Gothic architecture, the natural and native British style, a memorial to British freedom, in contrast to the despotism endured in France. Over the doorway there used to be the inscription, from Corneille's play *Horace*, 'Je rends graces aux Dieux de n'être pas Romain', 'Thank God, I am not a Roman' – a line which summed up the tragic heroine's rejection of autocracy.

GARDEN GOTHIC

The temple at Stowe is not the earliest 'Gothic' garden object built in England: the first seems to have been at Shotover, in Oxfordshire, where the vista at the end of the long canal is closed by an arcaded building with three pointed arches, small

129, 130 Palladian bridges at Prior Park (left) and at Stowe (below left). The best sited of all the Palladian bridges in English gardens is the one at Prior Park in Bath. This is unaccompanied by other monuments in the landscape, and seen from the mansion at the top of the valley it appears to span an important river. In fact, as with so many landscape bridges in the eighteenth century, this is a deception. The bridge at Stowe was built around 1744, and differs from those at Wilton (1737) and Prior Park (*c.* 1755) in having a sloping approach instead of steps at each end. It serves a more practical purpose, carrying the peripheral coach road round the estate

pinnacled towers to each side, and a battlemented pediment in the centre. The date 1721 has been suggested, but I doubt if it is quite as early. 'Gothic' structures quickly became a characteristic ingredient of the landscape garden, for they were seen as representing the ancient, original architecture of the nation, and having therefore a 'natural' quality like that of the unspoiled countryside. If a landowner was fortunate enough to possess a genuine specimen of Gothic architecture, a castle, for example, or a chapel, so much the better. If not, a Gothic addition or extension could be arranged, and the conversion of existing buildings, both inside and out, to the Gothic style was to become a veritable mania, as was the building of separate edifices, such as that at Shotover and the Gothic temple at Stowe, in what was thought, or hoped, to be the 'Gothic' style. These 'follies' as they were quickly called were erected all over the British Isles and were soon rivalled on the Continent. They formed viewing points in or near landscape gardens, like Kent's crudely battlemented Eyecatcher near Rousham, or the pointed windows and battlements added by Kent to Cuttle Mill, another small building within the viewing area of the Rousham garden.

It was not long before the qualities of *ruined* Gothic buildings were valued as highly for the additional associations of gloom, of melancholy and of mystery as were buildings which had not yet begun to collapse. If one did not possess a ruin, then –

131 Horace Walpole not only wrote about gardens, and commented on his friends' – and enemies' – success or failure in designing them, but made his own, at Strawberry Hill, round the Gothic mansion which he fabricated from 1747 onwards. This engraving of the 'Chapel in the Garden' (1771) combines architectural with gardening enthusiasms – a sombre mass of pines overshadowing the solemn yet intriguing Gothic building, whose design is taken from a tomb in Salisbury cathedral

need I add, 'of course'? – even a ruin could be created. The first 'Gothic' ruin was built in 1747, at Hagley in Worcestershire, when Sanderson Miller, notable among the architects of the Gothic revival (he had already built a 'Gothic tower' at the entrance to his own property at Radway Grange in Warwickshire), put up a section of ruinated castle wall for Lord Lyttleton. Horace Walpole, the arbiter of Gothic taste (*he* began to convert his cottages at Strawberry Hill near Twickenham in 1747, a labour of love which was to continue for nearly half a century, with ever more battlements, fan-vaulting and the rest), said approvingly in September 1753 of the ruin at Hagley that 'it has the true rust of the Barons' wars.'

As early as 1709 Vanbrugh suggested, but without success, that the old fragments of Woodstock Manor should be kept in the new landscape at Blenheim, and at Studley Royal (begun in the 1720s) and at Duncombe (begun in 1713), two widely separate estates in Yorkshire, the gardens, which each began as landscapes of a purely Claudian kind, were eventually extended (and thus completed) by their different owners to embrace the medieval ruins of Fountains Abbey and of Rievaulx Abbey respectively. John Aislabie had apparently planned this from the start of his work at Studley, but the adjacent land with the ruins of Fountains was not acquired until 1768, while Thomas Duncombe's scheme was completed in 1758 by his grandson. The Claudian qualities of both gardens are strong: at Studley, the exquisitely curved and symmetrical moon-ponds (still formal, being designed in the early 1720s) stand between, and distance the viewer from the temple façade, which is backed by the encircling and rising natural woodland, so that the three-dimensional spectacle is, at first sight, really like a painting which one sees, and does not enter. At Duncombe, not one but two circular temples like the Sibyl's remind the visitor that the high terraces looking out over the plain are 'like' the hillside at Tivoli.

STOURHEAD

This ideal of the Claudian landscape was sought after by garden designers for half a century, until the 1760s. The grandest, most extensive and yet most severe was the immense Yorkshire landscape of Castle Howard, taken up by Vanbrugh in the same period as his work on Blenheim and Stowe. Vaster than either of these, Castle Howard has in parts a bleakness, an emptiness which is depressing. But the prospect of the temple of the Four Winds (by Vanbrugh, built after his death in 1726 by

132   Shotover, looking from the pavilion towards the house. This lake – the largest formal garden canal in Britain – was made soon after the house was built in the 1710s, and marks the high point of the influence of Versailles on British gardens. Yet as early as the mid-1720s, the view from the house was completed by the building of the pavilion, which is not 'classical' but 'Gothic' in style, with pointed arches, a rose window, and, *mirabile dictu*, with battlements along the top

133 Stourhead – one of the most complete and best preserved garden landscapes of the eighteenth century. As at Rousham, the Leasowes or Bowood, the visitor was intended to meander through and round the landscape, appreciating the varied 'prospects'. At Stourhead, the effects were consciously classical and Claudian, with buildings such as Flitcroft's version of the Pantheon, on the far side of the lake, to recall the glories of ancient Rome, set in natural scenes reminiscent of paintings by Claude or Gaspard

Hawksmoor), the Roman Bridge (c. 1744) and Hawksmoor's Mausoleum (begun in 1728, finished c. 1745) is the noblest of these ideal landscapes ever to be created. No single photograph can do justice to this three-dimensional scene, where the visitor, though moving slowly through the garden and among these buildings, remains a spectator and not a participant in a re-creation of an antique landscape.

On a smaller scale, and more fully successful, is the garden landscape at Stourhead in Wiltshire. An amateur creation, it was made for the most part by two members of the Hoare family, Henry Hoare (1705–85) and his grandson Richard Colt Hoare (1758–1838). Begun in 1735, the main features of the gardens were virtually complete by 1783, and they have been little changed since then, apart from the introduction of ornamental and exotic trees and shrubs, particularly rhododendrons, in the nineteenth century – a process which was in fact well under way in the lifetime of Richard Colt Hoare. The landscape is set at some distance from, and below the house, which does not form part of the scene, and it is a landscape which is at nearly every point self-contained, with wooded slopes around an irregular three-limbed lake. On the shores, or higher up the slopes are a variety of garden buildings, some classical and some Gothic. By and large, these buildings were each meant to be viewed in a distinct and separate scene, and usually from across the lake. The

134 One of Bampfylde's views of Stourhead (left), engraved by Vivares in 1777, showing a characteristically Claudian scene – a 'natural' landscape of rural and lakeside features, with tokens of the classical and Gothic past: the temple of Flora, the stone bridge, Bristol cross and the parish church. As at Prior Park, Blenheim, Stowe, Castle Howard or Kenwood, the bridge appears to cross a river of some consequence, yet its necessity is principally aesthetic

Claudian feeling is strong, and intentional. Among the paintings of Italian scenes owned by Henry Hoare is a Gaspard of Tivoli, and a copy of a famous Claude, the 'View of Delphi with a Procession' which has among its buildings an edifice based on, but slightly different from the Pantheon at Rome (cf. Claude's 'Coast view of Delos with Aeneas', now in the National Gallery). Henry Hoare had this building reproduced by Henry Flitcroft at Stourhead in the 1750s – not exactly Claude's, but a 'Pantheon' incorporating some of Claude's features (pl. 133). In several ways Stourhead goes beyond the painterly scenes of Kent's Rousham, though I would not say it betters them. Stourhead is a more costly Rousham: the numerous buildings are bigger, more elaborate, and in a fascinating way more literary, both in the detail and size of the classical reconstructions, and in the form of itinerary which was offered to the visitor. At Rousham, one might walk, I think, this way or that along the paths, and choose this or that turning, but at Stourhead, when the form of the gardens was established, the instructed visitor was meant to perambulate in a certain direction, following and receiving a succession of hints and statements provided by grotto, inscription, urn and temple which alluded to episodes in Virgil's *Aeneid*, book III. Not only was the garden an image of nature, but the sequence of its features alluded to a particular part of the fabled past. It is an idea which appeals, but it should not be taken to mean that Stourhead 'tells a story' of the naive sort which has been imposed on the Japanese garden at Kildare in Ireland. Henry Hoare seems to have hit on this idea at about the same time as William Shenstone, who suggests 'I have sometimes thought that there was room for it [the landscape garden] to resemble an epick or dramatic poem.' But neither Shenstone nor Hoare carried this out to the letter.

PAINSHILL

Charles Hamilton's garden at Painshill, near Cobham in Surrey, is another creation important in the history of the landscape garden. He acquired a lease of the land in 1738, and was gardening at Painshill for some thirty years, leaving the estate in late 1772 or 1773. The garden buildings he had erected – and in whose design he himself

XXXI The Elysian Fields, Stowe, looking across the river Styx, the river of the underworld, to the temple of Ancient Virtue. This temple, modelled on the ruined Sibyl's temple at Tivoli (pl. 2), was designed by William Kent and built c. 1735. Kent built it in a ruined form, and changed the pillars from Corinthian to Ionic. At Ermenonville, c. 1776, the temple (pl. 141) was at last built in a ruined state, but with simple Doric columns

XXXII   An early ha-ha, at Rousham in Oxfordshire, with the 'sunk fence' doing exactly what it is meant to do – keeping cattle out of the garden, while allowing people within the garden an unimpeded view out into the countryside. Rousham was first designed by Bridgeman, and altered and completed by Kent. Horace Walpole considered Bridgeman the first to have used the ha-ha in England, and saw Kent as the greatest landscape designer – he 'leaped the fence and saw that all nature was a garden'

took a hand – are as diverse as those at Stowe or Stourhead. Classical, and we may say 'Claudian', were the temple of Bacchus and the Roman arch, which was built in a ruined state, like Chambers' Roman arch at Kew. Gothic, and more mysterious, was the Abbey – built as a ruin – and the delightful and unruined Gothic temple or 'Gothic tent'. There was also a 'Turkish tent', now vanished, but like those at Drottningholm or at Haga park at Stockholm (though much smaller) or like the modern version at Groussay in France.

Later writers who described Painshill – Uvedale Price, for example – said that Hamilton had studied Italian painters in designing his garden, and that the spirit of Salvator Rosa was evoked with particular success. This spirit, unlike the glowing and peaceful evocation of Arcadian beauty in Claude, was one of wildness and gloom: 'savage' and 'impetuous' are adjectives which the century attached to Rosa's art. At Painshill this came no doubt from the 'Gothic' buildings, but more from the extensive plantings of conifers (said in 1781 to be the most varied collection in the world) and from the famous and 'primitive' grotto works which looked out over the lake. These were built (before 1765) by Joseph Lane, who had probably begun to learn about grottoes when working under William Privett, the mason who made the grotto at Stourhead. Lane's son Josiah Lane later designed and made other grottoes, particularly in Wiltshire, at Bowood, Wardour and Fonthill, while Hamilton himself was involved in designing the cascade at Bowood to which Lane's grotto was attached. There is therefore a chain in these grotto-building activities extending for sixty or more years, and linking the landscape gardens of Stourhead, Painshill, Bowood and Fonthill.

The grottoes at Painshill were remarkable for the wholesale use for the exterior of limestone tufa, called by contemporaries *pierre antidiluvienne*, or 'pre-diluvian stone', because of its pitted and supposedly water-worn appearance. Later in the century, the 'primitive' was to be much in demand in landscape gardens, and the Painshill arches and caves of tufa mark a notable advance towards this wished-for wildness.

*   *   *

The ingredients vary. The eighteenth century in Britain is a great age for amateurs in garden design, and much thought, money and time was spent by the brightest, and by the less bright, in making gardens and garden landscapes up and down the land. Some, like Aislabie at Studley Royal, or Hamilton at Painshill, began from scratch, and sometimes, as at Studley, at Rousham, or at Stourhead, the gardens have also resisted or avoided later changes in taste, surviving in a form not outrageously different from what was first intended. Some owners, and some gardens, show a mixture of tastes and influences: at Stowe, one fashion comes down on top of another, to make a sort of garden palimpsest; this is true also of Chatsworth, while at Melbourne, Bicton, Chiswick and Syon Park reasonably large sections of the original layout survive, with later additions tacked on more or less successfully to one side. This applies, of course, to many gardens in other countries – to Versailles, with the Petit Trianon and its Hameau, to Schwetzingen, with its 'English garden', to Wilhelmshöhe at Kassel, with its formal and its 'English' gardens, to Drottningholm with its Kina at Stockholm, and to Sturefors, also in Sweden, with its main seventeenth-century formal garden, its round temple like that at Tivoli high up at the end of the central axis, and its *jardin anglo-chinois* beyond and beside the formal area.

XXXIII   The grotto at Painshill was constructed in the 1760s by Joseph Lane for Charles Hamilton. In 1765 William Gilpin wrote: 'A sweet view catches the eye behind the grotto among the islands and along the water.' The brick archway is made to look wild and even gloomy by the addition of jagged, irregular blocks of tufa, simulating the natural outline of a cave. Joseph and Josiah Lane later made other grottoes, notably at Bowood (where Charles Hamilton had designed the cascade), at Wardour and at Fonthill

135   The 'Priory ruin' – one of
several Gothic structures erected
by William Shenstone at the
Leasowes

13

This Perfectly Arcadian Farm

WILLIAM SHENSTONE AND THE LEASOWES

William Shenstone was born in 1714, and died a bachelor in 1763. Going up to Oxford in 1732, he discovered and indulged a taste for literature, discussion and mild potation with like-minded friends which was to continue all his life. By 1735, when he was twenty-one, he had written and published a small volume of poetry; indefinitely postponed his academic studies, and inherited the small grazing farm, 'The Leasowes', where he lived for the rest of his life. The Leasowes was a farm of some 300 acres, on fertile, well-watered and moderately sloping ground near Halesowen, six miles south-west of Birmingham.

At Oxford in the 1730s, Shenstone imbibed the gardening ideas formulated by Addison and Pope, and put into practice by Pope, Southcote and Kent. His friend and biographer Richard Graves suggested that Shenstone experienced the 'new gardening' at first-hand at the Graves' estate at Mickleton, in Gloucestershire, and that the only major garden he could have imitated was Lord Lyttleton's, at Hagley, adjoining the Leasowes, since Shenstone had not travelled sufficiently to visit any others. Be this as it may, in the 1740s and 1750s Shenstone certainly travelled to London several times (though never to the Continent), and frequently left the Leasowes to visit gardens within a radius of thirty miles or so, Hagley, for example, Enville and Barrels. He conceived a deep affection for the Leasowes, regarding it not as a farm, but as land to be beautified, to be made into a *ferme ornée* (the term was invented by Philip Southcote). His income was small, £300 a year, imposing a modesty in his gardening efforts which made some later observers, such as Dr Johnson and Horace Walpole, smile at the frailty of his 'Gothic screens' (rather as other observers had smiled at Walpole's first flimsy battlements at Strawberry Hill, destroyed by the storms of a season). Yet he spent up to and beyond the limit, so that wags suggested that 'his groves were haunted by duns as well as by fawns and wood-nymphs'; and on his death, the Leasowes had to be sold.

The estate passed rapidly from hand to hand. His house was pulled down around 1775 and a new one built. The gardens were neglected, altered, neglected and altered. Today, a fair part of the estate survives as a golf-course, with the post-Shenstone building used as the club-house, but although the outlines of the Leasowes can still be traced the details have gone, and indeed barely survived beyond 1800. Already in 1773 Oliver Goldsmith had written, in the *Westminster Magazine* (1 January 1773), that 'in less than ten years, the [estate] has gone through the hands of as many proprietors . . . could the original possessor but revive, with what a sorrowful heart would he look upon his favourite spot again!'

Nonetheless, from about 1745 until a decade after Shenstone's death the Leasowes was at the heart of English landscape gardening. Shenstone corresponded with and advised other enthusiasts, while scores of visitors came to view the Leasowes, to describe its walks and to record the inscriptions which graced its seats and memorials – or to check them against the text of Robert Dodsley's 'Description of the Leasowes', with its accompanying numbered plan, published in 1764, a year after Shenstone's death. Probably more visitors thronged to admire the wonders of Stowe, but many would go there to admire the temples and monuments as examples of *architecture,* proud appendages of a mighty building. The visitors to the Leasowes went to see a *landscape garden*, and as such it was for a period immensely important—well-known, talked-about, admired, and influential. Among visitors to the Leasowes were Pitt, Lyttleton, Spence, Johnson, Dashwood, Goldsmith, John Wesley, Jefferson, Gilpin, Wordsworth, Loudon, and the French Marquis de Girardin.

Shenstone was a sensitive, sociable, intelligent, modest, much-liked and very likable man. He was also inclined to bouts of depression when left on his own, which happened with annual regularity, when wintry weather discouraged people from making sight-seeing journeys out to the country. The smallness of his income prevented his garden-building from having permanent features, prevented his travelling widely and prevented him from marrying, since the ladies whom he found congenial were generally of higher rank and wealthier than himself. Especially touching is his long correspondence with Lady Luxborough. Her husband had suspected her of infidelity, and rather than divorce her, he banished her to a country estate at Barrels, near Henley-in-Arden. Shenstone's acquaintance was obviously attractive to this rather lonely, but witty and well-read woman, and their correspondence, over years, reveals not merely a shared interest in gardens, literature and people, but a discreet yet powerful bond of friendship, which was strengthened by many visits made by one to the other.

In his sombre moments Shenstone regretted his necessarily quiet country life, but most often he was aware of the privilege of his rural retreat, and enjoyed it, like poet-gardeners in China: there is much to allow a passing comparison between Shenstone, a cultured, sensitive poet and gardener, and his contemporary Yuan Mei, the Chinese poet and garden lover. Rural retreat after a stormy passage in the world is a recurrent theme in both England and China (less so in France), and in England there are quite a few people who adopt gardening as a way of saying 'no' to the busy world. Apart from Lady Luxborough, banished from city society by her husband, and Shenstone, there are Aislabie, creating the gardens at Studley Royal after the collapse of the South Sea Bubble, and Beckford at Fonthill.

Shenstone's rural retreat has an engaging modesty. His garden features, his buildings and his memorials are not extensive or grand, and yet his genius achieved much in a small way. In his 'Unconnected Thoughts on Gardening' (printed in 1764, a year after his death), the first garden features he mentions are ruins, small ones, and he adds that 'an able gardener should avail himself of objects perhaps not very striking . . .' Of the cascade, with a fall of twenty feet, Dodsley wrote:

Other cascades may possibly have the advantage of a greater descent and a larger torrent; but a more wild and romantic appearance of water, and at the same time strictly natural, is what I never saw in any place whatever. This scene, though comparatively small, is yet aggrandised with so much art, that we forget the quantity of water which flows through this close and overshadowed valley: and are so much transported with the intricacy of scene, and the concealed height from whence it flows, that we, without reflection, add the idea of magnificence to that of beauty.

His view of the rural life – necessary, and at the best, admirable, yet not always what he wholly desired – comes out, I think, in the inscription from Virgil (*Georgics*, II) which he set beside a view of tranquil meadows and water:

Ruro mihi, et rigui placeant in vallibus amnes,
Flumina amem, silvasque inglorius

Let fields and streams gliding in the vallies be my delight:
may I court the rivers and the woods inglorious and obscure.

Shenstone divides gardening into three kinds: kitchen gardening, parterre gardening, and 'landskip, or picturesque gardening', and this third kind is the sort he admires. Landscape gardening is in turn seen as having three main aspects: the 'sublime', the 'beautiful' and the 'melancholy or pensive'. Just as Edmund Burke, in his *Enquiry into the Origin of our Ideas of the Sublime and the Beautiful* (1756)

136 A vignette from Shenstone's *Works* (1764), published by his friend Robert Dodsley, who also wrote the 'Description of the Leasowes'. Though this picture illustrates one of Shenstone's poems, the scene is so 'overshadowed with trees that grow upon the slopes of this narrow dingle' that it could in fact have been sketched at the Leasowes

summed up the developing concept of the sublime, so Shenstone summed up the eager incorporation of this concept into the aesthetics of gardening. For him, the sublime appears in scenes of rugged grandeur – the massive lines of a 'large mountain' or the sight of 'a large, branching, aged oak' – while the beautiful is less awesome, more regular, and generally smaller and gentler, a force which he rates less highly than the sublime, since it stirs our imagination less powerfully. It is 'the merely beautiful'. But for Shenstone both qualities are necessary to give the *variety* which completes a landscape, and he adds that the 'melancholy or pensive' scene (related often to the presence of a ruin) may be imagined as midway between the sublime and the beautiful.

Variety is essential if nature is to be respected. The plan of the Leasowes attached to Dodsley's 'Description' shows the variety and moderate irregularity of the *ferme ornée*, and indicates better than any other plan I know the genuine difference between the rational and geometrical gardens of the seventeenth, and the landscape gardens of the eighteenth century (pl. 137). Whereas the formal gardens of the past are condemned – Shenstone is so out of touch with the symmetry of Versailles that he writes 'It is not easy to account for the fondness of former times for straight-lined avenues to their houses' – the irregularity, the alternation of contrasting scenes and elements in the landscape are considered vital. He finds that one of the attractive qualities of a ruin is the irregularity of its surface, 'which is VARIETY', so providing a stimulus for the imagination. Ruins, and 'Gothic' structures generally, appealed to him strongly (Shenstone was active in the eighteenth-century rediscovery of the past, since it was he who suggested to Bishop Percy the collection of old English poetry which in 1765 appeared as the *Reliques of Ancient English Poetry*). 'Identity' of parts in a garden means loss of variety and cramping of the imagination – to pass along many miles of a straight vista 'must be as disagreeable a sentence, as to be condemned to labour at the gallies.' Instead, seek variety: of vegetation, for trees have an 'annual variety' in their blossom and foliage; of terrain, with alternation of steep, sloping and level ground (Dodsley says in praise of the Leasowes 'nor is there to be seen an acre of level ground through the large extent to which the eye is carried'), and of view. So far as the imaginative reward is concerned, tedium is the result if we walk along a straight path towards an object which is already in sight. 'The foot should never travel to [the object] by the same path, which the eye has travelled over before. Lose the object, and draw nigh obliquely.'

Again Shenstone sums up contemporary thought by seeing landscape gardening as an extension of painting. A landscape should have enough variety 'to form a picture upon canvas', and Shenstone adds 'I think the landskip painter is the gardener's best designer.' A successful garden landscape 'should contain variety enough to form a picture upon canvas.' As early as 1748, he wrote for 'a convex glass to see landscapes with', in other words, a 'Claude-glass', a viewing instrument with a convex oval mirror which gave a rounded, shaded-off appearance to the scenes one looked at, thought to be characteristic of a 'Claudian' landscape.

The paintings he would like landscape gardens to represent were indeed those of Claude or Rosa: varied 'natural' scenes, made more interesting with signs of man's nobler activities, such as a bridge, a farm, a ruin, an urn or a memorial. The scenes are to be 'natural', in that the slope of the ground, the placing and growth of the trees and the movement of streams should appear wholly spontaneous. These things are 'nature's province'. Should man's artifice be apparent here, then 'night, gothicism, confusion and absolute chaos are come again'; in other words, *leave nature alone*. But for Shenstone man is still essential in those scenes, and we are a long way yet from the jungle forest of Chateaubriand's *Atala* or the eerie unpeopled landscapes of Caspar David Friedrich. Shenstone's nature is still a relatively friendly realm in which man moves with assurance, albeit with gentle, respectful, or melancholy step. Within 'nature's province', the landscape gardener may add 'suitable appendages' to point up the characteristics of the scene ('for instance, the lover's walk may have assignation seats, with proper mottoes – urns to faithful lovers – trophies, garlands'), and the entire scene, like a Claudian landscape, may benefit immensely from historic associations. Shenstone asks rhetorically: 'What an advantage must some Italian seats derive from . . . being situate on ground mentioned in the classics?' Should one's garden be lucky enough 'to have been the scene of any event in history', then 'mottoes should allude to it, columns etc. record it.'

In his art the landscape gardener may go so far as to 'collect and epitomise the beauties of nature', making a poetic composition out of his garden's various scenes. In a sentence which we may apply in the crude sense of a 'story', and in the nobler sense of a 'sustained imaginative experience', he says of the landscape garden: 'I have sometimes thought that there was room for it to resemble an epick or dramatick poem', an idea which occurred also to Henry Hoare at Stourhead, and to the Margravine Wilhelmine of Bayreuth at Sanspareil near Bayreuth.

To turn to the Leasowes. His garden practice corresponds to his theory. If we look at the long 'Description of the Leasowes', we see exemplified the idea of an evolving and varied imaginative experience. Dodsley knew W. S. for many years, and their close friendship and correspondence, reinforced by Dodsley's visits to Halesowen and Shenstone's to London, dates from around 1750. Dodsley's 'Description' is an attempt 'to perpetuate those beauties, which time, or the different taste of some future possessor, may destroy'.

The visit to the Leasowes is in the form of a long, roughly circular walk, proceeding by gentle stages through and around the grounds. Not until the end of the walk does one enter the house: the landscape is enjoyed from point to point during the walk, and the views from the house itself are barely mentioned. The detailed plan shows this clearly. The stages of the walk, numbered 1 to 40, take you round in an anti-clockwise direction, through woods and lanes, past streams, cascades and lakes, into vallies and up hillsides, with constantly varied views, both of the objects within the grounds, such as the Priory ruin (9), the 'Gothic alcove' (19), the cascade (12), and the house itself, and of distant features, like the spire of Halesowen church or the top of Clent hill. On the way round, there are over forty seats or benches, 'intended', as Dodsley says, 'as hints to spectators'. These 'hints' are sometimes straightforwardly pictorial, indicating that *here* we should stand and stare. But more often than not, an imaginative and poetic 'hint' is added by means of inscriptions – dedications to friends, to noble visitors, or to a relative who died while still young, and verse in Latin or English expressing the 'spirit of the place'. At point 4 on the plan, there is 'a small root-house', where a tablet carried verses written by Shenstone, the song of the fairies who lived there:

Here in cool grot, and mossy cell,
We rural fays and faeries dwell;
Tho' rarely seen by mortal eye,
When the pale moon, ascending high,
Darts thro' yon lines her quivering beams,
We frisk it near these crystal streams.

The path and stream beside the root-house are 'overshadowed with trees that grow upon the slopes of this narrow dingle', and contrast with a previous scene of open lawn surrounding the house. Suddenly, therefore, the visitor finds himself in a 'cool, gloomy, solemn, and sequestered' place, which seems almost a 'subterranous kind of region'. The poem, Dodsley remarks, is a lovely description of 'the abode of fairies', and is also an apt 'hint to spectators' to show what their reactions should be: 'These sentiments appearing deep in this romantic valley, serve to keep alive such enthusiastic images while this sort of scene continues.'

Elsewhere, statues of Faunus or of Pan, or urns, or diverse 'Gothic' structures (the Priory ruin, the Gothic alcove, the Gothic seat, the Gothic screen) intensify the 'hints' which serve to 'collect and epitomise' the beauties of nature, and to direct the visitor through the 'poem' which came from, and was a walk round the Leasowes. In Shenstone's hands, the grazing farm had become, as Dodsley puts it, 'this perfectly Arcadian farm'. At the climax of the walk (32 on the plan), there is a view of distant, nearby and immediate scenes – hills and mountains 'at a prodigious distance', with woods, valley, and swelling slopes nearby. Here Shenstone set the simple inscription DIVINI GLORIA RURIS – 'The glory of the divine countryside'. Both Shenstone and his admirers were anxious to maintain how natural the scenes

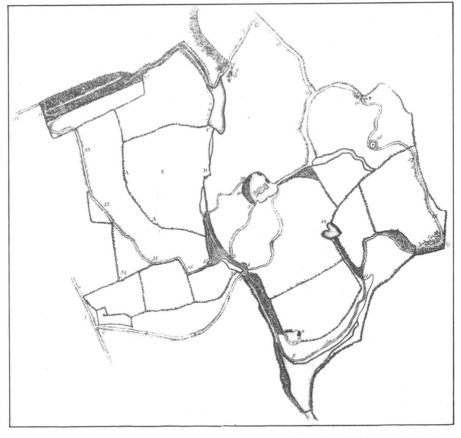

appeared, and yet wished to make clear that art, or artifice, the guiding and selecting touch of the artist, had perfected the means of seeing nature's materials. When William Pitt remarked that 'Nature had done everything for him', Shenstone mildly but firmly replied that he hoped he had 'done something for Nature too'.

Shenstone is hardly an innovator. Rather, he stands at a mid-point in landscape gardening, between the tentative adventures of Pope, Southcote and Kent, and the wild, dare-all extravagance of Monville at Retz, and Beckford at Fonthill. His garden and his writing sum up the developments of the first half of the eighteenth century. For his contemporaries, his work represented an achievement which was not only perfect of its kind, but embodied a modesty of attitude and of scale which many might endeavour to imitate, unlike the grandeurs of Castle Howard, or Stowe.

WEST WYCOMBE

Before Brown, and before the 'total landscape' of the late eighteenth century, two gardens must be mentioned, one in England, one in France. Both are the creations of their talented amateur owners; both are, more or less, influenced by Shenstone, since both owners visited the Leasowes, and both imbibed the century's enthusiasm for the Claudian and natural landscape.

In England and in France there are few rivals to the eighteenth-century gardens of West Wycombe in Buckinghamshire, and of Ermenonville, north of Paris. West Wycombe is the creation of a single patron, Sir Francis Dashwood (1708–81). He succeeded his father when he was only sixteen, and was throughout his life deeply involved both in the scandalous and the serious concerns of the century. Both sides are embodied in the park at West Wycombe. It is, more than any other in Britain, an integrated landscape, a park with distant rising slopes to the south and north which close the view, and within whose limits the owner-patron-designer has made a landscape, a painting, a poem (each term is appropriate) in which, to follow Addison's suggestion in 1712, a man has indeed made 'a pretty Landskip of his own

Possessions'. As Shenstone hinted, Dashwood found that there was 'room' for his garden to 'resemble an epick or dramatick poem'; but this poem is not simply Claudian, though now we might be forgiven if we thought so. Dashwood's landscape incorporates his mansion, the expanse of lawn and the ha-ha in front, the gardens and temples to the right, and behind, as a noble backcloth to the scene, the steep hill with the parish church of St Lawrence at the top, and to one side the Dashwood mausoleum. The church is crowned in turn with a golden ball, and overlooks both the whole Dashwood landscape and the mausoleum on the slope of the hill, an edifice which is egregious not only as an unroofed thin-walled flinty hexagon, but also in its half-in, half-out nature, being built partly within the consecrated area of the churchyard, and in part without. It is like Voltaire's pyramidal memorial in his chapel at Ferney, built half in the church and half out, a hedging of bets in characteristic eighteenth-century deist style.

Today it is hard to sort out the original and daring thought of West Wycombe. The integration of the church and the mausoleum into the landscape – both of them not at all what they might be in traditional opinion, being stripped as nearly as they could at the time of all Christian tokens, and left as memorials of a belief in deism – was more than the sentimental borrowing of a neighbouring 'Gothic' object, as it might have been with Shenstone or Charles Hamilton; it was evidence of the owner's personal belief and interests. The rebuilding and redecoration of the nave of the church – notable now for its most lovely ceiling, painted by Giovanni Borgnis, who also painted the frescoes in the open colonnade along the south front of the house – is comparable with Voltaire's chapel building at Ferney, with its inscription *Deo erexit Voltaire*. But Dashwood's taste led him to the darker side of religion as well as to the light. In later life he and Benjamin Franklin worked together to produce a shortened version of the Book of Common Prayer, a serious undertaking which the Episcopalian Church in the United States was later to make use of; but in his giddy youth and active middle age, he was engaged in ventures which were variously profane, sacrilegious and debauched. Accurate details of the society he founded in the 1740s, the 'Monks of Medmenham', commonly called the 'Hell-Fire Club', are hard to come by, but it is certain that at one stage of its history the society's meetings were held within the labyrinth of chalk caves excavated in the hill beneath the church of St Lawrence. The 'Hell-Fire Caves', as they are now called, hardly feel like a garden ornament, but through the aura of ice-cream, souvenirs and ticket-office which this century has wished on it, the flinty Gothic approach, shaded with sweeping yew trees, still has authority: here is a grotto, gloomy, mysterious and deep . . . The caves and their purpose were a part of Dashwood's landscape, just as much as the lake and gardens, which were 'laid out by a curious arrangement of streams, bushes and plantation to represent the female form' (*Victoria County History, Buckinghamshire*, III).

138   Both the open rotunda of the temple of Venus and the wooden bridge have now gone from the West Wycombe landscape, but the lake and islands, with Revett's temple of Music, still remain (see the titlepage). William Woollett's original engraving was the other way round, with the bridge to the right. This version, in Le Rouge's *Détails des Nouveaux Jardins à la Mode* is reversed

The gardens have been much changed since they were laid out for Sir Francis Dashwood in the 1740s. A gardener named Thomas Cook was called in in the 1760s, and at the turn of the century Humphry Repton was asked to advise. Though the many temples and ornaments have been thinned and simplified – the temple of Venus, an open rotunda on top of a conical mount, has gone, and the rockwork of the cascade at the foot of the lake has been reduced to a minimum – those that remain, for example Revett's temple of Music (c. 1780), on the island in the lake, the temple of Apollo or 'Cockpit arch' beside the south front of the house, or the flinty temple of the Four Winds beyond the trees to the south-east, are still eminently successful in holding together the nearer parts of this private and most lovely landscape.

ERMENONVILLE

The Marquis René-Louis de Girardin (1735–1808) did not begin to design his estate at Ermenonville until 1766, on the death of Stanislas Leczinski, the exiled king of Poland. Girardin had previously held the rank of captain in Stanislas' service, attending his miniature court at Lunéville, near Nancy in Lorraine. While at Lunéville he would have been many times through the formal gardens of the palace, and seen the tentative beginnings of the 'English' fashion to one side; and while serving Stanislas he was absent for long periods travelling abroad, in Italy, Germany and England. In England the new gardens captured his affections, especially the work of Shenstone at the Leasowes.

Between 1766 and 1776 Girardin created the landscape at Ermenonville. His father had a small formal garden near the château, but Girardin eliminated this, and transformed his estate into the most lovely landscape garden in France. The château lies in the centre of the estate, which is crossed by the river Launette running from south to north. To the south of the château is one garden landscape, with the lake and the Ile des Peupliers, the poplar-ringed island which now holds the tomb of Jean-Jacques Rousseau, and to the north is another, broader and more varied, with the hilly, heathy Désert, a large lake, and the extension of the Launette. Though the garden landscapes were all made in the period 1766-77, the northern areas diverge in different ways from the feeling of the southern part, and they are discussed later in this history. To the south the feeling is almost always Claudian, for here Girardin has made a landscape which Shenstone, had he had the means, would have loved to create. As at the Leasowes, the estate has a circular walk – necessarily round the lake – in which the scenes are given deeper meaning through monuments and inscriptions discovered along the way. There was a memorial to Shenstone, and the grotto of the Naiads, beside the cascade at the foot of the lake, bears verses in French not so different from Shenstone's on the fairies. Variety is achieved to perfection, since the irregular shape of the lake obliged the visitor to see the scenes and monuments in many changing perspectives – Shenstone's 'draw nigh obliquely' is beautifully obeyed.

Girardin did not just copy Shenstone; he had a wide and tolerant knowledge of the classics and of modern history and literature. For Rousseau he had deep veneration: he had met him briefly, corresponded with him, and followed his lonely fortunes with compassion. His garden landscape reveals these tastes: in Rousseauan style there was the shrine of Rêverie, and the Jeu d'Arc, the butts, a construction made to encourage rustic and virtuous pastimes among the tenants; and in a Claudian mood, there were the lovely Arcadian Fields to the south; while on a slope to the west, looking across the lake, was the temple of Philosophy, built in 1776. This temple, modelled on the Sibyl's temple at Tivoli, is deliberately built in a ruined state, unlike Kent's temple of Ancient Virtue at Stowe, to indicate the still fragmentary nature of the edifice of philosophy. Six columns are standing, each dedicated to a different thinker; Newton, Descartes, Voltaire, Penn, Montesquieu and Rousseau. The temple as a whole is dedicated to Montaigne; 'qui omnia dixit', 'who has said everything'. One pillar lying on the ground is inscribed 'quis hoc perficiet', 'who will complete this?' – a thought which is oddly tied to Montaigne's own reflections on the Sibyl's temple in Italy, which he saw in 1581. Montaigne's journal had been discovered in 1770 and published in 1774, when Girardin's creativity was most active. The temple of Philosophy at Ermenonville is therefore more important as a *symbol* in the landscape than a *building*. It is, like the 'hints' at the Leasowes, an indication of what you, the visitor, should think and feel at this point. At the temple, looking out over the lake, the sad inadequacy of human effort should strike you; yet, inspired by such beauty, what may not be achieved in time to come? As ruins go, this has the most cogent message of any in the eighteenth century, the most moving original, and a setting as good as any short of Tivoli itself.

Though he was helped by professional artists and designers, like J.-M. Morel, who wrote a *Théorie des Jardins* (1776), and the painter Hubert Robert, Girardin was his own designer. Ermenonville is his creation, and the thought behind the landscape is embodied in Girardin's treatise, *De la Composition des Paysages*, written in 1775, published in 1777. And all this was done *before* Rousseau came to live, and to die at Ermenonville.

Jean-Jacques Rousseau (1712–78) fell on evil days. He was invited by Girardin to live at Ermenonville, and spent his last six weeks – from 20 May until 2 July 1778 – as Girardin's guest. Girardin was a passionate devotee of Rousseau, and started

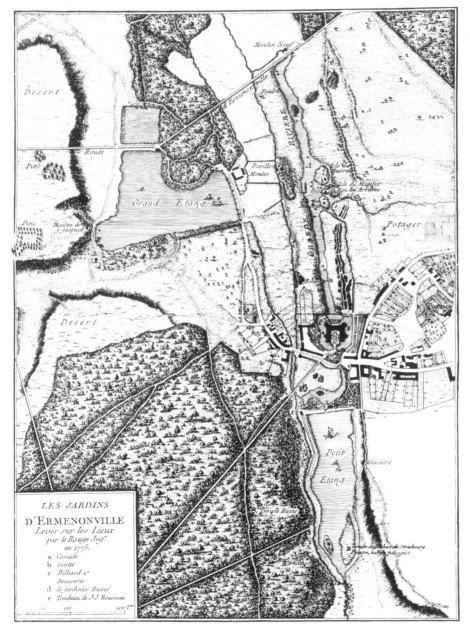

139 The gardens at Ermenonville. This plan was made in 1775, when most of the monuments were virtually complete, and was amended after Rousseau's brief residence, death and burial at Ermenonville in 1778. Rousseau's tomb is on the smaller island in the lower lake (the Ile des Peupliers), while the temple of Philosophy and the Dolmen are close to the western shore

206

140, 141 Two views of Ermenonville: Rousseau's tomb on the Ile des Peupliers (right), and the temple of Philosophy (below right). The Ile des Peupliers had already been planted with poplar trees when Rousseau died at Ermenonville in July 1778, and was an obvious choice for his tomb. Designed by Hubert Robert and carved by J.-P. Lesueur, the tomb shown here replaced a smaller one which was quickly erected in 1778. The temple of Philosophy overlooks the Petit Etang and the Ile des Peupliers. Modelled on the ruined temple of the Sibyl at Tivoli, it was built by the Marquis de Girardin in a deliberately ruined state to suggest the still incomplete nature of human systems of philosophy. The temple is dedicated to Montaigne, 'qui omnia dixit', 'who has said everything'. Girardin's temple is smaller than the temple of the Sibyl and simpler, with Doric instead of Corinthian columns

preparing a rustic residence for him in the northern part of the park. But Rousseau could not wait. He was buried on the Ile des Peupliers, and a first monument was set up, quickly replaced by a second, designed by Hubert Robert and carved by Le Sueur. This island monument is now the visual and emotional centre of the southern part of Ermenonville. The trees and the tomb both stand out in the landscape, and as you walk round the lake it is this island and this tomb which draw your attention. Since Rousseau's death other memorials have been added to the park, giving it an additional melancholy which was not at first planned; though Girardin seems to have accepted and later encouraged the elegiac mood which Rousseau's memory bestowed upon the scene.

142   Bowood – designed and
created in the 1760s by Lancelot
'Capability' Brown, and the best
surviving landscape by him

14

The Total Landscape

Soon after 1750 the ideal of the Claudian garden landscape began to lose some of its appeal; or at least to undergo changes which made later landscape gardens less clearly Claudian. Some (like Shugborough, for instance, or Kew) acquire such a miscellany, such a jumble of buildings and monuments, in such a diversity of styles so thoughtlessly juxtaposed that the landscapes in which they are built lack coherence. At Stowe this very real danger has been avoided thanks to the great extent of the grounds, and to the most careful and effective use of the modest contours of the land, and the planting of screens of trees. Other gardens acquire wild or primitive features which do not accord with the Claudian ideal, and which since they are largely connected with primitive architecture of a British or northern European kind – Gothic ruins, hermitages, wild grottoes, and primitive buildings like those of the Ancient Britons, especially Stonehenge – do not always coincide too well with the wilder yet still Italian landscapes of Salvator Rosa. A third development is that particularly associated with Lancelot or 'Capability' Brown, whose gardens, neither cluttered nor wild, have a natural quality and a simplicity which takes them beyond the Greek and Roman allusions which dominate the scenes of Rousham or Stourhead.

Similar developments take place on the Continent, some prompted by English examples, some arising because of other influences. The wildest excesses of the landscape garden are carried out on the Continent, and some of the most daring experiments. By 1800, in Britain, France and Germany, the pursuit of the 'natural' had led to extremes as absolute as those of the formal garden a century before, and much of the gardening of the nineteenth century was, in reaction, an exploration of past styles, collected from various countries and many ages.

CAPABILITY BROWN

The great gardener in this second half of the eighteenth century is Lancelot Brown (1716–83). After apprenticeship in the north of England, Brown moved to Walton in Oxfordshire, and then in 1740 to Stowe, where he seems to have worked at first in the kitchen gardens. At this time Kent was the director of the main gardens at Stowe and remained so, visiting Stowe at regular intervals, until his death in 1748. Brown was then in the position of head gardener, and remained at Stowe until 1751, when he left to set up in practice on his own as a landscape gardener. He was called 'Capability' Brown from his way of saying, when asked to give his opinion on a property, that the landscape or scene in question had 'capabilities' which he might be able to bring into proper prominence if allowed to undertake the task. His nickname is a good way of approaching his art, for the development of the latent capabilities of a site, the *natural potential* of a scene, is what his best work succeeds in doing. It is, I think, the inspired detection, analysis and encouragement of the *genius loci*, the 'spirit of the place', in which Brown excels, much as Pope had recommended this in 1731, in his 'Epistle to Lord Burlington'. Brown's 'nature' is much less concerned with the re-creation of painterly and allusive scenes than Pope's; and it is far more simple, more open, and on a larger scale, so that though Pope's advice in the 'Epistle' could read as a general rubric for Brown's creations, I doubt whether Pope would have found the long, clear sweeps of lawn and the smoothly evolving line of the lake at Bowood in Wiltshire (the best preserved of Brown's major landscapes) altogether what he had in mind. Pope would, I think, have found this, like many of Brown's scenes, too simple, too open, and desperately lacking in the hints and statements which ruins, memorials and statues had provided in his own garden at Twickenham. Brown for his part would have wondered in Pope's grotto below the garden at the injunction, 'Approach! Great Nature studiously behold!', when confronted with the jackdaw collection of crystals, shells, stalactites from Wookey Hole, minerals from Peru and Mexico, and pieces of looking glass in angular forms. Brown's 'nature' is much advanced on Pope's, purer and bleaker. His critics towards the end of the century said that he was too simple, that in striving to make a garden part of *nature*, he had often made it so effectively part of the countryside that in no way did it remain a *garden*. It is the very opposite of the criticism levelled at Le Nôtre, and in the same way as the rigidity and sterility of his – inferior – successors were blamed on Le Nôtre, so Brown has been blamed for the emptiness and excessive plainness of some landscape gardens made by his followers.

Bowood – to return to Brown – is neither empty nor plain, though it is simple. Brown first visited Bowood in 1757, but did not submit his plan for landscaping for some years. His work seems to have extended roughly from 1762 until 1768, and coincides with the designing of several architectural features by Robert Adam; principally the mausoleum (commissioned in 1761), and in 1768 an aqueduct bridge, which was never built. Brown himself was responsible for the small Doric temple (little more than a facade) which stands on a jutting hillock midway along one side of the lake. Of the mansion itself, only the extensive and sumptuous stable block remains, faced by the small Italian garden created in the nineteenth century by George Kennedy. This garden is well contained by the terraces, and does not cause any conflict with the lines of Brown's landscape. Apart from this block, the only notable building in the landscape is Brown's Doric temple (the mausoleum is some distance away behind the site of the mansion, and does not form part of the lake scenery), and one's viewing and visiting of the scene is free of other buildings. The Doric temple itself is unpretentious, and serves as a human touch in the landscape, and as a small focal point in a scene which constantly moves and evolves as one walks round the lake. By using only this one monument, Brown has not only simplified the 'landscape-painting' of Kent, but has also unified the landscape garden, since the entire scene is now a single, multi-dimensional composition, in which the contours of the land and the lake, and the relationship of trees and grassy lawn vary continuously as one walks onwards, experiencing not many different and separated 'pictorial compositions', but innumerable variations on a single theme. Above all Brown succeeds with the lake, which he made. Brown made many lakes, and all in the same way; by placing a dam at the foot of a valley and allowing the water from a river or stream to accumulate behind the dam. As it rose, the water spread out along the natural contours of the valley, producing a lake which was 'natural' in the irregularity of its outline. Usually Brown concealed the artificial dam by curving the shore of the lake so that its end was not apparent (making it seem as if the lake flowed on like a broad river), or by masking it with trees. At Bowood, massive beeches now grow along the line of the dam, and Brown's artifice is hidden until one reaches the shade of the trees.

Lakes of this kind are Brown's most notable addition to the British scene. They are his hallmark, as the geometrical and symmetrical fountain-jet is Le Nôtre's. Often, the 'lake' which he made was in fact composed of two or more lakes, separated by dams cunningly disguised and concealed so as to extend the grandeur of the expanse of water. The most famous of these effects is at Blenheim, where Vanbrugh's huge bridge and causeway stretched out high and long across a modest canalized stream (the Glyme) which was obviously not big enough to deserve such a bridge. Lakes to left and to right were joined by the narrow canal of the Glyme, but were both too far from the bridge to justify it. Brown solved this (between 1764 and 1774) by creating a 'natural' landscape with proportions to match the heroic qualities of Vanbrugh's bridge. The stream was dammed more effectively, raising the level of the water several feet, while wholesale excavation of earth also made it appear as if the bridge had now to strike across a great and ample river extending far round two sides of the palace. The ponderous height of the bridge was also diminished, or seemed to be, by the water coming higher up the arches, while it now lapped along the sides of the bridge, which had previously been dry and clear of the stream. 'Thames, will you ever forgive me!' Brown is supposed to have said when he dammed the Glyme and deprived the Thames of its waters.

In his work at Blenheim Brown not only created the lake but swept away practically all traces of the original formal gardens made by Vanbrugh, London and Wise, and Bridgeman. Only the walled vegetable garden remains from this earlier period, and a stretch of ha-ha – possibility the one observed by Stukeley in 1712 – far away beyond the south front of the palace. Between this ha-ha and the palace, where the south parterre used to be, is now an immense expanse of lawn, coming almost to the flight of steps. This destruction of the formal gardens immediately around the house, and their replacement by sweeping stretches of grass is another of Brown's characteristic practices, not always appreciated by his critics. At Nuneham Courtenay in Oxfordshire, where Brown had worked both on the landscape (beginning in 1779) and on the house itself from 1781 (he had become fashionable as an architect in collaboration with his son-in-law Henry Holland), the grass came right up to the front of the house, so that Fanny Burney, visiting Nuneham in 1786, complained that when she got out of her carriage to enter the house she stepped down into the wet grass. Nuneham, incidentally, is one of the landscapes where Brown did not need to create a lake, for he had the Thames, and his success lay in so controlling the vistas from the house and from the grounds that a single and therefore less interesting 'stare view' of the river was converted into many glimpses of the scene, endlessly varied as the visitor walked round the park. The procedure is therefore similar to that at Bowood.

The 'walk round the park' or 'the drive' in larger estates is coupled in Brown's gardens with his third characteristic device: the *belt* of trees, i.e. an encircling or partly-encircling strip of woodland which by exaggerating the contours, by concealing boundaries and unwelcome objects, and by revealing desirable ones, lends a feeling of greater variety and extent to the landscape. He destroyed many of the formal avenues of trees which had in other gardens emphasized and extended the geometrical rigidity of the parterres closer to the house; and in place of these avenues clumps and isolated groups of trees were left, allowing views further into the landscape, or ornamenting the summit or the slopes of the hillside. None of these features of the Brownian landscape – the lake, the sweep of grass, the undulating, encircling belt of trees – is absolutely new, but Brown's use and combination of them is distinctive and was acknowledged as such by his contemporaries and by other garden designers who imitated his work. The irregular lake was to appear all over the British Isles, the most remarkable being the enormous expanse of Virginia Water, created in the southern part of Windsor Park in the early 1750s and enlarged in 1768 by Thomas Sandby, who also designed the cascade where the surplus water flows over the dam. Virginia Water is the largest artificial landscape lake in Britain, and we may reasonably think of it with its irregular contours, its remote and shadowy inlets, its hanging woods and sweeping stretches of grass as the English answer to the great Canal, rigid, cross-shaped, geometrical, at Versailles. On a far smaller scale, but still imitating the Brownian style, is the early nineteenth-century park landscape at Spetchley in Worcestershire, where the irregular 'natural' lake is held in by a sluice, and where the lawn stretches open and uninterrupted from the lake right up to the house. The formal enclosures, herbaceous borders and remarkable tree-plantings to the east of the lake and lawn at Spetchley are mainly modern and do not clash with the park landscape, but rather complement it as they lie to one side.

Just as Brown obliterated older parts of the gardens he redesigned, so Brown's work has in turn been altered by his successors, who from the early 1800s brought back the terraces and formal divisions which Brown had banished from the area adjacent to the house. Again, the coloration of the Brownian landscape was often radically altered by the introduction of new and exotic trees. One of Brown's best landscapes is at Sheffield Park in Sussex, where his two original lakes have been planted round – mainly in this century by A.G. Soames – with trees and shrubs which give a brilliant and indeed un-English display of colourful flowers or foliage for most of the year. The contours of his two lakes remain but the colours round them have changed. It is interesting to compare the muted and limited tones of Bowood with the vivid and extensive spectrum of Sheffield Park. A similar – and I think successful – colour revolution has taken place at Syon Park by the Thames near Brentford. Working for the first Duke of Northumberland between 1767 and 1773, Brown designed a small but characteristically sinuous lake, running like a broad river down towards the Thames. At its inland end, there is a perfectly contrived bend, to conceal the conclusion of the lake. Since Brown's day, the surrounding landscape has been planted with rare and exotic trees – swamp cypress, a catalpa, and colourful maples, for example – and in the last twenty years the gardens have been adapted as a centre to exhibit garden plants and materials. Brown's lake and landscape survive, and provide a setting which has absorbed a difficult diversity of ingredients remarkably well. The beauty of the lake views in particular has been splendidly and imaginatively preserved.

THE SUBLIME GARDEN

Brown's critics, as I have said, complained that his gardens could not be told apart from the surrounding natural countryside. Yet after Brown the principal excess in the development of landscape gardens was in trying to make them more natural, not less so. The wish was coupled with the ideals of the sublime and the picturesque, both familiar terms in the eighteenth century, and both applied to landscape gardening theory and landscape gardens. In 1757 Edmund Burke had published his *Philosophical Enquiry into the Origin of our Ideas of the Sublime and the Beautiful*, and in 1782 William Gilpin had at last published his *Observations on the River Wye . . . Relative Chiefly to Picturesque Beauty made in . . . 1770*, the first of a series of books describing and depicting the 'picturesque' qualities of British scenery.

In his treatise Burke had codified the division of beauty into two kinds: the beautiful, for things which were smooth, regular, delicate and harmonious, and the sublime, for things which also moved us to aesthetic approval, but were rough, gloomy, violent and gigantic. This second group tended to include the manifestations of untamed and uncivilized nature which had only been appreciated since the writings of Shaftesbury, such as the wilder parts of the countryside, mountains, volcanoes, storms and cataracts, and scenes of a lovely, savage and primitive kind. Gilpin for his part, while accepting Burke's division, felt that a further refinement was needed to sort out the qualities necessary to make a landscape suitable for a painting. In Gilpin's work the picturesque qualities of landscape are descended from the hilly countryside views of Claudian painting, but are translated into British landscape, generally of a wild, rugged and gloomy kind, and most often with the buildings, if they appear, of a ruined and Gothic character.

It is not hard to see that these interests do not fit within a garden. If the garden is to be 'natural', and if to be 'natural' means to be wild, rugged, solitary, gloomy, precipitous, riven with chasms and livid with the gleam of cataracts, then the garden is in difficulties, especially if it is small. If the owner was lucky enough to have a large estate, on terrain which was already divided with steep hills and deep vallies, then something might be done. If he was rich.

RUINS, BONES, HERMITS AND GROTTOES

A further – and several-horned – complication arose with the proliferation and extension of the Gothic. At an early stage, it was possible to incorporate into one's garden a Gothic tower, the fragment of a ruined arch, or a stretch of battlements along one side of the house without too much stir. But the taste for what was more and more 'natural' was applied to the Gothic. One's Gothic should be ever more ancient and original, more rude, more ruined, more wild, more primitive. And if the primitive is desired, then Gothic itself is too sophisticated, and the original forms of architecture which led to Gothic must be sought out. Already William Kent had been criticized for excess in this search for the natural: 'he imitated nature even in

XXXIV   Rousseau's tomb (near right, top) on the Ile des Peupliers at Ermenonville. In 1794, Rousseau's body was removed to the Pantheon in Paris, but the tomb remains, forming the emotional centre of the gardens

XXXV   A sublime detail at Fonthill – 'a rude erection in imitation of a Cromlech' (near right, bottom). This was one of several rocky creations designed by Josiah Lane for William Beckford in the 1790s. Now swathed in ivy, the jagged slabs of tufa look much more genuine than most eighteenth-century imitations of prehistoric monuments. Beyond the Cromlech, Fonthill lake can be glimpsed – an artificial lake made by Beckford's father twenty years earlier

XXXVI   Vanbrugh's bridge and Brown's lake at Blenheim (far right). Before Capability Brown dammed the little river Glyme, the majestic bridge spanned a small, almost puny canal only a few feet wide. When the lake had filled, Brown is supposed to have exclaimed, 'Thames, will you ever forgive me!' – for depriving the major river of the Glyme's modest trickle

XXXVII   The cascade at Virginia Water (bottom) is the most impressive of the outlets designed for the many artificial lakes which were so central a feature of the landscape garden. All these lakes – like those at Blenheim, Bowood, Stourhead, Ermenonville and Fonthill – are formed by means of a dam, holding the water within the irregular contours of a natural valley. The lake at Virginia Water was formed in the 1750s, and is the largest of its kind – about 120 acres in size

watercolour of the richly sombre scene at Fonthill. Bitham Lake, resembling 'the crater of an ancient volcano', gleams in the foreground, while the misty yet glowing towers of Fonthill Abbey are just visible on the horizon. Beckford wrote of this scene: 'from out of these forests rose the Castle of Atlas with all its windows sparkling like diamonds! Nothing I've ever seen in my life can equal this unique vision in grandeur of form or magic of colour'

143   This plate (below) from Humphrey Repton's *Observations on the Theory and Practice of Landscape Gardening* (1803) shows one of the last – and certainly the most curious – of the many buildings inspired by the temple of the Sibyl at Tivoli. While Girardin's temple of Philosophy at Ermenonville retained an essentially truthful form of the original, Repton's is grotesquely 'primitive', like the root- and bone-houses for hermits so popular at the end of the eighteenth century. Yet his visitors are genteel, and most of his gardens have little to do with the sublime

her blemishes, and planted dead trees and mole-hills, in opposition to parterres and quincunxes' (*The World*, 8 February 1753). Even the classical buildings in landscape gardens acquired a primitive cousin, with the new fashion for Greek Doric, beginning in the 1750s with the rediscovery of the temple at Paestum in Sicily, and the depictions of it by Piranesi (1778) and Cozens (1782). As early as 1758 the first temples with the simpler kind of column (lacking the base of the Tuscan Doric) were built in the gardens of Hagley and Shugborough, and this style was to be pursued to its supposed logical origins with bark-covered tree-trunks for pillars, supporting a pediment and roof of branches and thatch. Such a garden temple, the Temple Rustique, was sketched at Ermenonville in 1788 (it was probably erected some years before). To my mind the ultimate in this return to the origins of classical architecture in gardens appears in Humphry Repton's *Observations on the Theory and Practice of Landscape Gardening* (1803), where a rustic model of the temple of the Sibyl is recommended, with trunks for pillars and a conical thatched roof.

These were not the only primitive materials. Walls were made of roots, to form 'root-houses', and floors of bones (the knuckle-bones of sheep were popular) with 'rustic stonework' of the most knobbly and irregular kind. Few early roothouses survive – an example from the 1820s can be seen at Spetchley in Worcestershire – but bone-floors are fairly common. In Ireland, an entire building was faced with bones, at Lord Orrery's park at Caledon, county Tyrone. Work began in 1747, and though all other monuments in the garden have gone, impressive stretches of the wall are still standing. Britain's first temple was not forgotten, and several gardens in the British Isles had miniature imitations of Stonehenge: in 1770 Arthur Young saw a 'Druid's temple, built in a just style of bark, etc.' at Halswell in Somerset; the irascible Dr Thicknesse built one around 1770 near Abergavenny in south Wales, while at Park Place, Remenham, on the Thames, a prehistoric stone circle was set up in 1787, having been brought piecemeal from its original site in the island of Jersey. Horace Walpole called it 'little master Stonehenge'.

Hermitages and grottoes flourished, the primitive abodes of solitary, contemplative and simple people. A few early eighteenth-century grottoes have already been mentioned, but later landscape gardens could hardly be considered complete if they did not have something of the kind, or a hermitage, or both. Already in 1735 Kent had designed the Hermitage at Richmond for Queen Caroline, together with Merlin's Cave, a building whose symmetrical plan was tricked out with buttresses, a Gothic archway and a roof of thatch. Merlin's Cave had an appropriately unsophisticated tenant and custodian, the thresher poet Stephen Duck. At Stowe, there was the thatched hermitage of St Augustine, and at Stourhead there was the Gothic nunnery, remote in the woods; at Hagley, another hermitage was built of boulders, roots and moss. All this, remember, in a staunchly Protestant country, where this flirting with a 'medieval' aspect of the Old Faith was yet another departure from what was modern, and social, and civilized.

By the mid century, books with designs for these places were fairly common. The best-known British ones are W. and J. Halfpenny's *New Designs for Chinese Temples, Triumphal Arches, Garden Seats, Palings, etc.* (1705–2), Paul Decker's *Gothic Architecture* (1759), and W. Wrighte's *Grotesque Architecture . . . Plans . . . for Huts . . . Hermitages . . . Cascades, etc.* (1767). Inhabitants were often required, and the sad dismissal of Sporck's real hermits for heresy around 1720 is matched by the comic loss of hermits from gardens in England. Several landowners hired, or tried to hire, a 'hermit' to live in their 'hermitage', including Charles Hamilton at Painshill. These characters were supposed to live an austere, unkempt and hairy life and thus lend verisimilitude to the hermitage whenever the owner showed guests round his estate, but the combined and stipulated austerities – no speech, no company, no comforts, no ladies, no liquor – generally proved too much, and the hermits, detected with drink or a dairymaid, were sacked.

Grottoes, like hermitages, became more primitive. The later work of the Lanes, father and son, is less adorned with shells and crystals and is rougher, closer to the spirit of a mountain cave. At Bowood in 1785 Josiah Lane built a grotto-tunnel to go across and through the cascade at the foot of Brown's lake. (The cascade itself had been designed – another contribution by an amateur – by Charles Hamilton,

supposedly after a painting by Gaspard.) At Wardour Castle, also in Wiltshire, Josiah Lane built one of the prickliest of all grottoes in 1792, a superb example of primitive rockwork, facing through dark conifers the medieval ruins of Wardour Castle. The grotto at Wardour, masterly though it is, strains our credulity. Such crags, such rocky clefts . . . in rural Wiltshire?

THE TERRIBLE GARDEN

One of the breaking points in the evolution towards total 'naturalness' is apparent in the analysis of Chinese garden-theory in the work of Sir William Chambers (1723–96). Chinoiserie, as I have said, had been a small but noticeable ingredient in rococo gardens for some time, providing a playful lightening of the heavy seriousness of baroque architecture. With Chambers' *Designs of Chinese Buildings, Furniture, Dresses etc.* (1757) and his *Dissertation on Oriental Gardening* (1772), he not only gave a fillip to the architectural taste for chinoiserie (several of his oriental fantasies were actually built at Kew, and his tall pagoda survives, though shorn of much of its 'Chinese' decoration), but stated in the most absolute terms that Chinese gardens were 'natural' in a way that English gardens, as yet, were not. In the *Dissertation* of 1772, he goes beyond the fairly gentle statements of Temple and Attiret that the Chinese aim to have gardens which are varied and irregular, and divides the Chinese gardens into three kinds, 'the pleasing, the terrible, and the surprising'. In this, Chambers is drawing less on his own knowledge of the Chinese (once in the service of the Swedish East India Company, he went twice to China, in 1744 and 1748, and spent some months in Canton) than on Burke's theory of the

144   In the wooded and mountainous region west of Bayreuth, the grotto-garden of Sanspareil was created in the 1740s by Wilhelmine, Margravine of Bayreuth and sister of Frederick of Prussia, who made his own garden of Sans-souci at Potsdam. The tortuous cliffs and caves have as their theme the adventures of Telemachus, son of Odysseus, as related in Fénelon's *Télémaque* (1699). This scene, the cliff beside Calypso's grotto, was noted for the daring escape of Telemachus and his tutor. The tiny plaque attached to one of the trees shows them leaping from the cliff

Sublime and the Beautiful. The 'beautiful' is less interesting for Chambers than the 'terrible' and the 'surprising', just as the 'sublime' appealed more to the eighteenth century than the 'beautiful'. Chambers describes the Chinese 'scenes of terror' in terms which could illustrate Burke's *Enquiry* of 1757:

> The buildings are in ruins; or half consumed by fire, or swept away by the fury of the waters: nothing remaining entire but a few miserable huts dispersed in the mountains, which serve at once to indicate the existence and wretchedness of the inhabitants. Bats, owls, vultures, and every kind of bird of prey flutter in the groves; wolves, tigers and jackals howl in the forests; half-famished animals wander upon the plains; gibbets, crosses, wheels, and the whole apparatus of torture are seen from the roads.

Should this not be enough in one's garden background, effects are provided from 'foundries, lime-kilns, and glass-works' to simulate the noise, flames and smoke of erupting volcanoes. If 'terror' palls, then 'surprise' can provide variety: the visitor may glimpse

> . . . dark passages cut in the rocks . . . colossal figures of dragons, infernal fiends, and other horrid forms . . . from time to time he is surprised with repeated shocks of electrical impulse, with showers of artificial rain, or sudden violent gusts of wind, and instantaneous explosions of fire . . .

'Indeed terror' writes Burke, 'is in all cases whatsoever, either more openly or latently, the ruling principle of the sublime.' This is Chambers' true source, more than a smattering of Chinese buildings and a reading of Nieuhoff, Temple, du Halde and Attiret. Neither in Britain nor on the Continent did chinoiserie extend beyond the architecture of gardens. A true and complete Chinese garden, of the kind described in chapter 3, has not yet been made in the West.

Too much into too little. No 'garden' could contain every one of Chambers' ingredients, and most could hardly manage this sort of thing at all. It is the eclecticism of these poorer landscape gardens which is their downfall. With less variety, less straining after *all* the possibilities of the extreme, they would have been better. In England, satirists had seen this early on: in the same periodical, *The World,* which had made fun of Kent's tree-stumps, the folly of Squire Mushroom, taking pains 'to torture his acre and half into irregularities' is exposed (no. xv, 1753):

> At your first entrance, the eye is saluted with a yellow serpentine river, stagnating through a beautiful valley, which extends near twenty yards in length. Over the river is thrown a bridge, *partly in the Chinese manner,* and a little ship with sails spread and streamers flying floats in the midst of it . . . you enter into a grove perplexed with errors and crooked walks, where having trod the same ground over and over again, through a labyrinth of horn-beam hedges, you are led into an old hermitage built with roots of trees, which the squire is pleased to call St Austin's cave . . .

On the Continent, it was worse – even more ridiculous, and striving more earnestly towards the sublime. English travellers saw the comic side, just as they mocked the formal gardens which managed to survive. Horace Walpole, in 1771, writes (to John Chute, 5 August) of a Monsieur Boutin, who has

> three or four very high hills, almost as high as, and exactly in the shape of tansy pudding. You squeeze between these and a river, that is conducted at obtuse angles in a stone channel, and supplied by a pump; and when walnuts come in, I suppose it will be navigable . . . This new *Anglomanie* will literally be *mad English.*

A few years later William Beckford, visiting Schwetzingen in 1780, is angry to be asked to admire 'a sun-burnt, contemptible hillock, commanding the view of a serpentine ditch, and decorated with the title of Jardin Anglais.'

THE SUBLIME GARDEN IN GERMANY AND FRANCE

But neither Walpole nor Beckford visited any of the truly remarkable *jardins anglo-chinois* which were made in Germany and in France, and which reach out to the sublime with deep enthusiasm. The baroque plan of Wilhelmshöhe near Kassel was extended to either side by du Ry and Jussow in the 1780s and 1790s with a miscellany of exotic pleasures, including a Chinese village, a ruined aqueduct of Roman inspiration, the 'Jussow temple' (yet another version of the Sibyl's temple from Tivoli), and several medieval and Gothic features, such as the Teufelsbrücke (the Devil's Bridge) and the ambitious Löwenburg (the Lion Fortress), built by Jussow between 1793 and 1798 as a residence in the Gothic style and as a fit building to house a huge collection of antique furniture, tapestries, weapons, stained glass and the like.

At Hohenheim, near Stuttgart, Herzog Karl Eugen von Württemburg (1737–93) set to work in 1774 to make an entire park look as if it was constructed over the ruins of an antique city. Here and there, fragments of wall, tower or archway protruded from the greenery, and 'later' constructions were added, to give the appearance of subsequent settlements, by peasants perhaps, or fallen descendants of the Romans, now living among the rubbish, the débris of a lost civilization. The intended effect was certainly sublime – like a series of three-dimensional scenes from Piranesi's view of Roman ruins, which owe much of their effect to the contrast between the colossal scale of the antique buildings, and the diminutive figures of the shepherds and beggars who animate the ruins. Such was the intention, but the sixty-odd features, all on a fairly small scale, and dotted around the park, were of such an indiscriminate mixture – medieval castles, Chinese pagodas and rococo dairies – that the grandeur, melancholy and strangeness of the sublime degenerated into the bizarre and almost the grotesque. The site remains, but retains only a few of these features, though many of the remarkable trees planted there still flourish, the nucleus of the 'exotic garden' of Hohenheim university.

At Wörlitz, near Dessau in East Germany, one of the most serious attempts to achieve the sublime was made. Here there is an English landscape on an ambitious scale, created between 1764 and 1800 by Fürst Leopold Friedrich Franz von Anhalt (1740–1817). The prince had twice visited England in the early 1760s, and had been to Italy in 1765. Like so many others, his garden has a Sibyl's temple, but on a wooded hilly site which responds fully to the requirements of a Gaspard landscape. The landscaping at Wörlitz is imaginative, and through size and boldness it escapes from the quaintness of Hohenheim. Wörlitz is the only garden which really possessed Chambers' ultimate in sublimity – supposedly a Chinese device – the volcano. The mountain, Der Stein, or the Vulkankrater, was equipped to produce black, smoky fires which simulated volcanic activity. We may think it ridiculous, but it is identical in spirit with the monstrous effects achieved and enjoyed in the modern cinema.

Goethe was deeply influenced by the gardens at Wörlitz: using them in part as a model for the gardening schemes which form part of the background to his novel *Die Wahlverwandtschaften*, mocking them in Act IV of his dramatic poem, the *Triumph der Empfindsamkeit* (1787), and himself going on to advise on the design and ornamentation of the court gardens at Weimar.

French gardens contained similar advances towards the sublime. Most came in the years just before the Revolution in 1789, though at Ermenonville the landscape was begun in the late 1760s. I have already discussed the Claudian and elegiac landscape to the south of the château at Ermenonville. Other features conceived at roughly the same time are aesthetically outside the peaceful elegiac scheme. The medieval occurs in the landscape north of the château, with the round and battlemented tower of Gabrielle d'Estrées, seen in contemporary engravings decked with pennants, and with visitors slipping past in rowing boats and skiffs like so many minstrels or courtiers with their ladies. Further steps into the past are taken in the woods beside the southern lake, with the narrow Gothic bridge, and higher up the slope, with the ultimate in prehistoric monuments, the Dolmen. The huge stones which form the Dolmen were brought here (unlike, say, the stone masses at Bomarzo or Sanspareil, which were natural outcrops), and the largest was too big to

145 The Maison du Philosophe overlooks the Grand Etang, the large lake in the north-western part of the Ermenonville landscape (see pl. 139). After Rousseau's brief stay at Ermenonville, it was renamed the Cabane de Jean-Jacques. But Rousseau never lived in the rock-and-thatch abode: though his tomb bore the words 'L'homme de la nature et de la vérité', 'the man of nature and of truth', such a 'return to nature' was more than he could contemplate

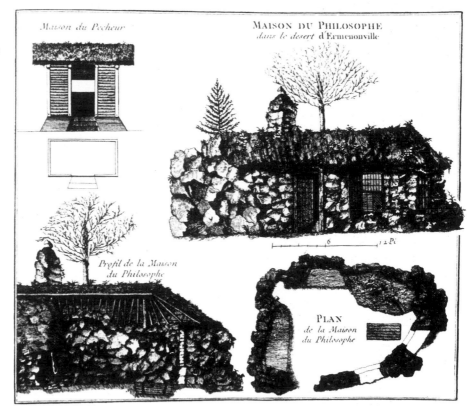

be transported in one piece. It was therefore split up, and reassembled and cemented together on the site, as the sharp and cynical Walpole noted, writing on 7 December 1782 to William Mason (the designer of the somewhat Rousseauan Flora's Garden at Nuneham Courtenay):

> Take a mountain, break it into pieces with a hammer, number the fragments and observe their antecedent positions: place them in their original order, cover the junctures with mould: plant ivy and grass and weeds, which will hide the fractures, and so you may have a cart-load of Snowdon or Penmenmaur in the middle of your bowling-green, and no soul will suspect that it did not grow there.

Flaubert will remember the Dolmen as well, with Bouvard and Pécuchet's 'potato', mentioned later. Dolmen, tower, Gothic bridge, all go beyond the meditative spirit of the southern lake. But sublimer still is the wild, heathy area to the north-west called the Désert, where the hilly landscape overlooks an irregular lake, and where the rocks jutting from the slopes and the uncultivated land round about promote feelings of crude and untainted seclusion.

The attempt to achieve a total landscape, either in terms of the multiplicity of ingredients, or in the absolute sublimity of the features, was repeated in France several times. Around 1774, the painter and architect Carmontelle began work for the Duc de Chartres on the park at Monceau, on the outskirts of Paris. By 1779 much of the work was complete, and is depicted in Carmontelle's gorgeous work, *Le Jardin de Monceau*. The area of the park was restricted, but Carmontelle aimed, as he explains in his 'Prospectus'; 'to bring together all ages and all parts of the world in a single garden'. The phrase is taken from Rousseau's *La Nouvelle Héloïse*, where it was a criticism of the number and variety of the monuments at Stowe. At Monceau, the attempt was deliberate, with many scenes and styles adequately separated – or so it was hoped – by plantings of trees. Carmontelle envisages a two-hour promenade round the garden, with carefully arranged viewpoints (rather like Kent's Rousham half a century earlier), to create the maximum number of illusions, the maximum of variety, surprise and novelty. Unlike Kent, whose compositions were careful modulations of a principal theme, Carmontelle crowded his site with Roman, Egyptian, Chinese, medieval, prehistoric and Levantine follies, and with a fantastic enclosed 'winter garden', with strange artificial trees beside exotic real ones, and arrangements for illumination by night. The illusions were light-hearted but elaborate: around a *tente tartare* (very like the 'Turkish tents' at Painshill in England, or at Drottningholm or Haga in Sweden), the vegetation was chosen for its 'oriental' qualities, and the engraving of the tent in Carmontelle's book shows in the foreground two characters in 'eastern' dress, one of whom holds the bridle of a caparisoned camel, no doubt hired or kept like the hermits in British hermitages.

Now in Belgium, but then in the French-governed part of Flanders, were the gardens of Beloeil belonging to the Prince de Ligne. In the early eighteenth century, his father had set up a formal garden *à la Le Nôtre*, and he himself added to this scheme from 1775 onwards. His plans, either achieved or intended, are described in the editions of his *Coup d'oeil sur Beloeil* (1781, 1786 and 1795), and his views of other picturesque gardens are given in the second half of the book. This work is a characteristic summary of the desperate search on the Continent for variety, stimulation, and the bizarre – all expedients to achieve the *sublime* with the *garden* – as characteristic as are the quiet phrases of Whately's *Observations* in describing the tempered discipline of the Brownian garden in England.

The conceptions in the *Coup d'oeil sur Beloeil* were indeed sublime, the intention exciting, but the execution was debatable. The Prince de Ligne has no principle except that of interest and variety, and this must be pushed to the uttermost. A single mood or theme – as at Rousham, or Bowood, or at Versailles – is not enough. Instead, he will have a kind of tower in an 'archi-Ostrogothic' style, to be a temple of Mars, and each feature or building seems to have a variable or double purpose which is certainly ambiguous and intriguing, and to me perplexing. He will have an 'Indian temple', where he may eat cream; a 'Chinese temple', which will serve as a dove-cote, while 'a mosque will surround the ice-house which was built some time ago.' He also wants a hermitage, to commemorate the memory of a hermit 'whom I saw die at the age of a hundred and twenty-three', and inside the ruined building, all is ornate and elegant, with a *salle de glaces*. On the lake and the connecting streams float the vessels of 'a sizable fleet', and 'since it would be too predictable to have an *island* in the lake, I have thought of constructing a thirty-gun frigate. Visitors will not be able to understand how it got there. It will appear to be at anchor, and will in fact be built down to the bed of the lake.' There is no end to the varieties of Beloeil – a Russian bath, a Turkish tent, the garden of Helen – and there is no centre.

These diversities are matched by more single-minded excesses. In France at Betz (Oise), the Princesse de Monaco superintended the construction of one immense, and several subsidiary Gothic ruins on her estate, beginning around 1780. A 'ruined castle' is the central feature, and as at Hohenheim, other ruined or partly-ruined fragments are scattered over the wooded slopes of the small river Grivette to appear as if they are the melancholy, sublimely moving remains of a vanished medieval city. At the Folie Saint James near Neuilly, Bélanger worked from 1778 to create its most notable monument, the temple façade built beneath the – equally fabricated – gigantic cliff or cavern. The total effect is wholly in the domain of the sublime, with the pure outline of the temple gleaming but menaced by the monstrous, overhanging 'natural' shape of the cliff.

In 1774 the large estate at Retz, in the neighbourhood of Marly, was acquired by de Monville, and over the next eleven years he built at Retz (the grounds were called the Désert de Retz) some sixteen garden buildings in a landscape to which they were wholly related, and in which no other distracting element – such as the city of Paris, at Monceau, or a central residence, a house, mansion or palace – were allowed to intervene. Space was unlimited, and the features do not clash, nor does one need much screening from another. De Monville, a wealthy man, sought and achieved the sublime, but in his *maison chinoise*, in which he was able to live from 1776 onwards, he also created a major piece of chinoiserie, supported by lesser features in the same style. Other 'oriental' items included a *tente tartare*, like that at Painshill. The grotto, with larger-than-life-sized fauns carrying flaming torches to light visitors through the gloomy archway, could come from the pages of Chambers ('dark passages cut in

146 A wilder moment in the Désert de Retz, de Monville's large estate near Marly, where the *maison chinoise,* the grotto and the ruined column were built between 1774 and 1785. The grotto was one of the features of the landscape garden where the qualities of the *sublime* could most easily be sought, achieved and appreciated – dark, wild, primitive, natural and frightening

the rocks . . . colossal figures of dragons . . .'), while the masterpiece, the *ruined column,* built in 1780–1, is a conception which any garden-builder on the grand scale must envy and admire. The column is about fifteen yards across, and its scale and proportions imply that if it were complete it would be between 300 and 400 feet tall. As it is, built as a ruin, the height above the ground is over sixty feet. The sloping ground, like the accumulated detritus of time, half covers the base, and the top is jagged, as if shattered in a storm of titanic proportions back at the beginning of the world. Set in the gigantic fluting of the column are windows, marking the puny habitations of modern men, who live among the fragments of a greater past. The architect, Barbier, contrived within the column a cellar and four floors above the ground. The upper rooms are illuminated through irregular apertures in the wall, disguised by the gaps and fissures which run downwards from the fractured top.

There is a drawing by Henry Fuseli, executed in 1778–9 and now in the Kunsthaus at Zurich, which shows the artist sitting, pensively, beside the enormous fragment of a statue – all that remains is a foot and a hand – which towers up beside the human, dwarfing him. The idea has just that aspect of the sublime which the ruin-landscapes of Hohenheim, Betz and Retz endeavour to convey in different three-dimensional ways; unsolvable mystery, a certain terror, and a tingling melancholy at the irrevocable nature of passing time.'

FONTHILL

Two more gardeners and two more gardens, one real and one fictional, must complete the eighteenth-century progress towards the total garden. In practice, the Englishman William Beckford (1760–1844) went furthest towards achieving a garden landscape which was wholly natural while remaining a garden; and in theory, the Frenchman Rousseau expressed the disturbing doubts which must lie in the mind of those trying to reconcile 'nature' with the 'garden'.

Beckford, inheriting a vast fortune at an early age and finding his social and political ambitions thwarted, turned to the solitary embellishment of his enormous estate at Fonthill in Wiltshire. In 1793, he decided to surround the estate with miles of wall, twelve feet high, 'not quite so long or so high as that of China', and within a few years this boundary wall had been extended to a total of fifteen miles or more. Inside, at the centre of his estate, Beckford had created and designed (with the help mainly of the architect Wyatt) his Gothic folly of Fonthill Abbey, begun in 1793 and more or less completed in 1813. This building, with the tallest spire in England, its overall area far larger than most cathedrals, and built entirely from scratch, was the greatest of all landscape follies, in England or elsewhere, in the audacity and extravagance of its conception and building, in its physical size, in its end – the tower collapsed not once but twice, and most of the Abbey had been destroyed within half a century of its being built – and in its isolation. Beckford wished for no near neighbours and surrounded his 'Castle of Atlas', as he called the Abbey, with a densely wooded landscape (he planted on a heroic scale, in 1796 'above a million of Trees'), interspersed with glades and pasture, avenues and paths, and many garden features – a flower garden, a 'Norwegian hut', a 'thornery', a herb garden, a rosarium and other delights. The Beckford estate extended even outside the miles of wall, and he had on either side landscape lakes (artificial, as they nearly all were) which Brown would have approved, one made by his father, once Lord Mayor of London, and one by himself. There were separate complexes of caves and grottoes on either side of the larger lake, constructed in the 1790s by the Josiah Lane who had worked at Painshill for Hamilton (who was related to Beckford by marriage). Near to those parts of the grottoes called the Hermit's Cave and the Hermit's Cell is a convincingly prehistoric construction, a 'rude erection in imitation of a Cromlech', now and I imagine then wreathed in ivy, and, apart from the Hermit's Cave, distant from any human habitation.

Nearer to the Abbey is Bitham Lake, dammed up by Beckford and surrounded on three sides by steep rising slopes mostly covered in dark conifers, but brightened on one side with the exotic colours of the American Plantation. Back in 1782 Beckford took the artist W. A. Cozens with him to Italy. Cozens painted several views of Lake Nemi, the waterfilled bowl of an extinct volcano in the Alban hills, with the palace of Castelgandolfo high up on the rim of the crater. Beckford had this image – both Claudian and sublime – in his mind when creating Fonthill, and his Abbey could just have been perceived over the top of the slope, like Castelgandolfo above Lake Nemi. Chambers recommended an imitation volcano, of a crudely eruptive kind, and this is what was aimed for at Wörlitz; but Beckford's 'fine pellucid lake . . . having the appearance of the crater of an extinct volcano' avoids this vulgarity.

It lasted only for a moment. Beckford overspent, sold up the Abbey, moved to Bath in 1822, and gardened again, but never on such a scale. What he had undertaken (in his time he was the richest private citizen in England, and maybe in the world) was beyond the scope of ordinary rich men and, more important, beyond the scope of the garden itself. Beckford's Fonthill is a turning point in garden history. It marks the absolute limit of the English landscape garden, and from this point a return to less absolute and less deeply philosophical garden convictions occurs. From now on, gardens such as Beckford's are acknowledged to be possible only in fantasy, and in fiction. In 1798 Coleridge wrote *Kubla Khan*, describing the 'stately pleasure-dome' of Kubilai or 'Kubla Khan' in Xanadu, written about by Marco Polo and describing as much the ground of Kubla Khan's palace as the palace itself. Beckford and Coleridge had both read Marco Polo, and both had also read accounts of the recent British embassy, led by Macartney, to Peking in 1794, in which, *en passant*, the size, princely splendour and paradisial qualities of the Yuan Ming Yuan are extolled.

> So twice five miles of fertile ground
> With walls and towers were girdled round

Coleridge thought first of Kubilai and his pleasure palaces, but his imagination was urged on by the recent news of Peking and its paradisial garden, and urged on too, I think, by news of Beckford's wall and fertile paradise within.

> And there were gardens bright with sinuous rills,
> Where blossom'd many an incense-bearing tree;
> And here were forests ancient as the hills,
> Enfolding sunny spots of greenery.

147   Bitham Lake, at Fonthill. This lake, artificial, as at Bowood or Virginia Water, was created by William Beckford, with the Italian Lake Nemi (the site of an extinct volcano) as his model. There, the palace of Castelgandolfo was set high on the rim of the water-filled crater, while at Fonthill the towers of Beckford's own creation, Fonthill Abbey, could just be perceived over the trees

223

But Coleridge's paradise is in the mind. His 'sunny dome', his 'caves of ice' take leave of the Abbey and the grottoes of Fonthill, and exist in the realm of the imagination. Once, in the mid-nineteenth century, Beckford reappeared in fictional form – but only in fiction. In 1884, Edgar Allan Poe wrote a story, *The Domain of Arnheim*, in which the hero, Ellison, inherits 'inconceivable wealth' and becomes the richest man in the world. Ellison debates what to do with his money, and decides that 'the richest, the truest, and most natural' province of art is 'the creation of the landscape-garden'. Previously, this aim could not be achieved since no-one, neither kings nor private citizens, had the means, and perfection had only been suggested 'on the canvas of Claude', and in reality, and to a *modest* degree, at Beckford's Fonthill! Poe's description of his hero's achievement is a fantasy, extravagant and disappointing. By this time, the formality of Victorian gardening was in full and oppressive flower, and he could respond only with immensities and superlatives of cliffs, forests and cascades. By no stretch of the imagination can the 'Domain of Arnheim' be called a 'landscape garden': it is a lake-and-jungle countryside, and a fiction.

JEAN-JACQUES ROUSSEAU

Though Rousseau's name has occurred in connection with Ermenonville, I have refrained from mentioning his views on gardening until now as, although his fascinating section on 'Julie's garden', the 'Elysée', was published in 1761, in *La Nouvelle Héloïse*, its full significance was not accepted by his contemporaries. Commonly and rightly, Rousseau is associated with the rejection of society (as being corrupt) and the embracing of a free and 'natural' way of life away from the harmful constraints of civilization. Within this general context, his description of 'Julie's garden', the *verger* or 'orchard' near her country residence at Clarens, is seen as advocating a 'natural' style of gardening: he attacks the formal gardens of the French, the accumulation of garden buildings at Stowe, and the pettiness of floral mania among the Dutch, in favour of a garden which appears to grow spontaneously and without straight lines, and in which visitors of a vulgar or unsympathetic kind are not allowed. The 'Elysée' is concealed by thick trees and bushes, and its existence is unsuspected by the passer-by. Rousseau's partisans and contemporaries hailed this as a sensitive variation on the English 'natural' garden, and many a monument, bust or inscription was erected in leafy, flowery, private parts of the garden to commemorate and imitate the 'Elysée' and 'l'homme de la nature et de la vérité', 'the man of nature and of truth' (the inscription on his tomb at Ermenonville).

These memorials range from the Prince de Ligne's black memorial and 'flower bed outlining a grave' to the sensitively arranged Ancien Verger prepared by Girardin (and visited by Rousseau himself) at Ermenonville – now vanished, alas! – and to the intimate and attractive Flora's Garden designed by the garden-poet William Mason at Nuneham Courtenay in the 1770s. The landscape of Wörlitz, troubled by its Vulkankrater, was also appeased by an island dedicated to Jean-Jacques, ringed with a circle of poplars, and there is another at Sturefors in Sweden. But each and every one of these is, in its memorial nature, with tablets, urns, temples of Flora and the like (even with a thatched cottage in the 'orchard' at Ermenonville) a contradiction of what Rousseau wanted. When Rousseau's hero, in *La Nouvelle Héloïse*, first enters the 'Elysée' he exclaims 'O Tinian! O Juan Fernandez! Julie, the end of the world is at your door.' His words refer to the *uninhabited* yet fertile islands in the south and central Pacific where Commodore Anson with his exhausted sailors had been able to recuperate on their voyage round the world in the 1740s. The idea of the 'Elysée' being like a fertile desert island is repeated several times in Rousseau's analysis, and in contexts which show the qualities Rousseau thought belonged to such places. They are, literally, uninhabited – *no* people go into such gardens – and literally uncultivated, untended, without design or human intervention. Such places have 'virtue' in direct relation to the 'naturalness' of the scene and its freedom from human contamination.

Rousseau's contemporaries could expatiate over the equation 'nature = virtue', and at Nuneham Courtenay, at Ermenonville, and at Canon (Calvados) in France

148   One of Turner's views of Fonthill Abbey, which he sketched and painted in 1799. This sombre engraving (published in *The Anniversary*, 1829) shows the isolation and sublime wildness of Fonthill, which William Beckford had begun to enclose with a wall some fifteen miles in length in 1793. Fonthill Abbey was begun in the same year, and was the ultimate Gothic folly of the eighteenth century. Round the Abbey were the densely wooded but immensely varied landscapes of the Fonthill estate

various competitions and rewards were instituted by the owners to encourage their peasants to persevere in rural and therefore 'virtuous' pursuits. Joseph Heeley writes of the morally uplifting effect of a scene at Hagley in Worcestershire where the – to him – superlative naturalness of the scene is enough 'to disarm a villain' (*Letters on the Beauties of Hagley, Enville and the Leasowes*, 1777). But Rousseau looked beyond this. To him, logically, both gardens and people were a blemish in nature, and only an un-gardenlike garden without people could begin to resemble nature. The process could not be considered complete until the uninhabited site had lost all resemblance to a garden. After *La Nouvelle Héloïse* in 1761, Rousseau has little to say about gardens as he left them to explore more natural surroundings to herborize and to indulge in *rêverie*. His final comment on gardens comes in a letter to the Duchess of Portland written on 12 February 1767, where he says decisively:

> The plants that grow in our woods and on our hills are still as they were when they left the Creator's hands, and it is there that I look to study nature – for I must admit to you that I no longer feel the same delight in botanizing in a garden. I find that nature, in a garden, is not the same: she has more brilliance, but she does not move me as much. Men say, they make nature more beautiful – but I believe they disfigure her.

149   The Italian garden at
Bowood, designed by Kennedy in
the 1860s

15

Gardens in the Nineteenth Century

FROM PICTURESQUE TO GARDENESQUE

A good moment to begin with nineteenth-century gardens is in 1806, when Wordsworth, writing on 23 December to Lady Beaumont, recommends for her 'winter garden' a reconstruction of the 'herber' or trellis work arbour described in the old English poem 'The Flower and the Leaf'. The advice is wholly characteristic of the century – tidy, imaginative, historically-based, attractive, and with a comfortable and human scale. The entire garden of which this bower is to be a part will be enclosed, secluded, 'shut up within [a] double and tall fence of evergreen shrubs and trees', to hide the 'cold, decayed, and desolate . . . face of Nature' outside. Another region will have a border of flowers, 'edged with boxwood', and another – *mirabile dictu* – a fountain. He remarks, with caution, 'Shall I venture to say here, by the bye, thât I am old-fashioned enough to like in certain places even *jets d'eau*?'

Lady Beaumont lived at Coleorton in Leicestershire, but Wordsworth lived in the Lake District, in surroundings which had not long before prompted William Gilpin to his most enthusiastic perceptions of the sublime. In Gilpin's time, what wildness might have been prescribed for a 'winter garden'! Yet Wordsworth's gardening always has modest proportions, and his poetry, especially the *Prelude*, begun in 1797, shows why. Like Chateaubriand in *Atala* in 1801; like the painter Caspar David Friedrich a few years later in the 'Monastery at Eldena' (1810) or the 'Wreck of the Hope' (1822); or like Goethe as early as 1774 in the *Sorrows of Werther,* in the hero's terrible letter of 18 August, Wordsworth had explored the grandeur, the sublimity of nature with a seriousness which most nature-lovers of the eighteenth century had not attempted. It is a commonplace to talk of Rousseau as a lover of nature, and as common to add that the 'nature' he loved was gentle, his scenes rural, his weather mild. Rousseau did not like jungles, mountains or storms; and when those a generation younger than Rousseau came to explore the extremes of natural violence and wildness, few found them welcoming. Interesting, fascinating, worthy of a lifetime's scientific study, yes; but not made to the measure of man. Even those like Wordsworth, whose study and whose knowledge of nature is of the deepest, are occasionally appalled, or filled with fear at what they discover. Nature is too great, and man not equal but inadequate; not a welcome guest, but a stranger.

Around 1800, therefore, gardens generally turn away from the wildest forms of nature; or seek to make these savage prospects less forbidding. On the grand scale, the garden practice of Humphry Repton (1752–1818, his career as a garden designer did not begin until 1788) shows this exactly. In many ways the successor to Capability Brown, his numerous landscape gardens were at first difficult to distinguish from Brown's; but as his confidence grew and the predelictions of his patrons developed, his gardens again and again revealed a softening of Brownian principles. Repton's further prospects, his middle distances even, resemble those of a Brownian scene. But the areas round the house are – I dare the word – *prettified*. While Brown brought the sweeping lawn up to the front door, Repton would interpose a drive, a terrace, a balustrade – and beds of flowers – and, a further emphatic dash is allowable here – he reintroduced the *fountain*, that emblem of artificiality, of the unnatural which the eighteenth century had struggled to destroy. In 1800 he designed a greenhouse for Harewood in Yorkshire with a fountain inside, and in 1811, his design for a rosarium at Ashridge includes a fountain at the centre. Already in 1803, in his *Theory and Practice of Landscape Gardening,* he had written: 'Flower gardens on a small scale may, with propriety, be formal and artificial'; and this small beginning was to allow an entire century of the same, not always on a small scale. Yet his own formalities were restrained. His most famous legacy, more famous than any of his gardens (his work remains, partially or substantially, at Welbeck in Nottinghamshire, Cobham in Kent, Uppark in Sussex and Sheringham Hall in Norfolk) is the couple of hundred surviving 'Red Books', the red-morocco-bound manuscript volumes in which his suggestions for particular garden and landscape designs were contained, and in which he demonstrated his ideas by the ingenious and simple use of 'before and after' pictures. The 'before' state of the landscape is changed to his proposed 'after' state by lifting a flap of paper superimposed on the page. Beneath the flap of paper, which Repton called a 'slide', a more picturesque, a *prettified* garden or landscape is found, often involving substantial modifications to the owner's house as well. For our purposes, the before-and-after views of the small area in front of Repton's own cottage in Essex are the most memorable – from a rather bleak village green, disturbed by the passing coach and the importunate beggar, Repton contrives a flowery, private, somewhat cosy scene.

In these scenes – always presented, as far as I know, in watercolour – Repton was not impartial. He made the original scene more severe, and the new one more welcoming, and generally his clients accepted his proposals. At this moment in garden history, the frontiers are shrinking, ambitions are fewer. The sublime and the 'picturesque', cherished for half a century, are exchanged for the 'gardenesque', those qualities which are 'calculated for displaying the art of the gardener'. This phrase is from John Claudius Loudon (1783–1843), who appears in the first half of the nineteenth century as the great popularizer. It is a descent which Kent, Brown or Beckford in England, which Watelet, Girardin or Carmontelle in France, and Hirschfeld, Pigage or Sckell in Germany would have abhorred, but which in the early years of the nineteenth century was neither wrong nor silly. It was within the reach of ordinary men, as are the recommendations of William Sawrey Gilpin (1762–1845), the nephew of the Rev. William Gilpin. His uncle had preached the picturesque, and though William Sawrey Gilpin begins from the same ground, his *Practical Hints for Landscape Gardening* (1832) are firmly in agreement with Repton. With propriety, the *formal* and *artificial* may be admitted, and the *small* and *floral* are just as welcome.

Poets and painters a short while after Wordsworth turn to these qualities with interest and approval. Sir Walter Scott, in his essay 'On Ornamental Plantations and Landscape Gardening' in the *Quarterly Review* of 1828 draws an absolute distinction between the 'park, chase, or riding' and the garden, 'with its ornaments': the one is open, natural, and expansive, and the other within a 'certain limited portion of the domain'. The garden is 'necessarily surrounded by walls', containing 'green-houses and conservatories . . . susceptible of much ornament, all of which . . . must be the production of art . . . in its most obvious phasis.' He sums up with the resounding phrase, 'Nothing is more completely the child of art than a garden.'

Varying this theme, John Keats admires the riches of nature rather than nature's wildness, and the features of the actual world in which he takes delight are small, modest and controllable. The London garden in which the 'Ode to a Nightingale' was conceived in 1819, and the natural abundance of the 'Ode to Autumn', in the same year, are both paralleled in the natural world of Samuel Palmer's sketches and paintings from his Shoreham period (*c.* 1824–30). Palmer's painting 'In a Shoreham Garden' (*c.* 1828) is the visual equivalent, for richness and abundance, of the 'Ode to Autumn'; it is the time for flowers, not fruit, but the clotted heaviness of the blossom, weighing every plant and tree, and seeming even to burst in the sky above, are wholly in the spirit of Keats's poem. The scale of the garden is right also, both for Keats's nocturnal, scented and music-laden scene, and for the smaller gardens which will appeal to a part of the nineteenth-century sensibility.

Already in the previous century there had been a theme of 'rustic simplicity', which formed one of the ingredients of the picturesque landscape, but this was usually a part of a larger scheme, to alternate with other exoticisms or approaches to

150, 151 Before and after: two views of Repton's cottage garden in Essex from his *Fragments on the Theory and Practice of Landscape Gardening* (1816). In the first, the 'garden' is no more than a strip of lawn, two trees and a lattice fence, made embarrassing by the one-eyed and one-legged veteran, noisy by the passing coach, and vulgar by the sight of the butcher's shop. Lifting the flap or 'slide', the improved view is revealed: the garden has been pushed outwards, hiding the coach and – apparently – burying the beggar in a flowerbed. Climbing roses on a trellis frame neatly obscure the dangling sides of meat

the sublime. Towards the end of the eighteenth century, the Swiss cottage became a tiny part of this recipe, carrying with it post-Rousseauan clichés of mountainous seclusion, ever-flowing cataracts, and the innocence of pastoral manners. In the nineteenth century, this ideal gradually came together with the general interest in the small and simple gardens which had existed in the countryside for generations, barely affected by the changing fashions of the great formal or landscape gardening movements, and by the 1880s the English cottage garden was to have a sizable and serious influence on the gardening ideas of William Robinson and Gertrude Jekyll. Meanwhile in the 1830s the growth of a more educated and ambitious middle class in England encouraged garden fashions of a modest kind. The flood of gardening manuals and gardening periodicals which is unleashed in England in the first half of the nineteenth century has, it is true, strong links with the botanical innovations which were taking place, and which will be discussed later in this chapter; but it is just as much connected with the rise of the urban and educated middle classes. Loudon's writings on gardening cover every aspect of the activity, and certainly do not omit the grander side. But his *Encyclopedia of Gardening* (first issued in 1822), his *Gardener's Magazine* (founded in 1826), and his *Arboretum et Fruticetum*

Britannicum (1838) were to cover topics and aspects of gardening which people of modest means would also follow, while some of his writings were specifically addressed to the middle classes; for instance his *Suburban Gardener and Villa Companion* (1838). His wife, Jane Loudon, née Webb (1807–58), worked with him on later projects, and on his death in 1843 carried on with gardening journalism, her most influential book being the *Ladies' Companion to the Flower Garden* (first published in 1841, and many times reissued).

BUDDING'S LAWN-MOWER

In the 1830s two of the vital technological steps in the history of gardening occurred: the invention of the lawn-mower, and the invention of the 'Wardian case'. The Wardian case will be described when flowers are discussed later in this chapter, but this is the proper place to discuss the mower, since its use was to make the closely-cut lawn, previously cropped by sheep or mown laboriously with a scythe, into a garden feature which could easily be the property of a modest householder, without sheep or even a team of gardeners to do the work.

Edwin Beard Budding (*c.* 1796–1846) signed 'articles of agreement' with an engineer, John Ferrabee, on 18 May 1830, covering the finances required to make a machine for 'cropping or shearing the vegetable surface of lawns, grass plots or pleasure grounds', and the patent for his 'machine for mowing lawns' is dated 31 August 1830. Soon after, Budding and Ferrabee entrusted the manufacture of the lawn-mower to the firm of Ransome's of Ipswich, who quickly issued advertisements illustrating and describing the machine. The first clear indication of the success of the venture is the page devoted to 'Budding's grass shearing machine . . . employed at the Zoological Gardens', in the *Mechanics Magazine* of 25 August 1832. The text beneath the engraving explains:

> The person places it so as to bear his whole weight on the cast-iron drum A and the wood roller B; he then takes hold of the handles, as represented in the figure, and . . . pushes the machine steadily forward along the greensward, in the direction of the arrow . . .

'Steadily forward along the greensward': the three pictures of the mower and its operator show the progress of Budding's invention both physically and socially. The first and earliest shows a bare-headed and wild-faced rustic, clearly struggling with the machine. The two later pictures show controlled and tranquil operators, both dressed far more elegantly. It is fascinating to see that the original picture of the machine has been used, but a deliberate *embourgeoisement* of the operator's stance and clothing has taken place.

In 1840 Mrs Jane Loudon's *Instructions in Gardening for Ladies* gives advice on the 'frequent mowing' of the lawn, and adds 'this is an operation which a lady cannot very well perform for herself: unless indeed, she have strength enough to use one of

152, 153, 154   Three advertisements for Budding's lawn mower illustrate the machine's rapid social progress, as the operators change from a rustic (top left) to an elegant and composed gentleman (above), who might be the proprietor himself, beautifying his suburban villa

XXXIX   Alton Towers (right) – the pagoda designed by Robert Abraham. The pinnacle spouts water, completely un-Chinese in spirit, but entirely in accord with the eclectic nature of these gardens, created between 1814 and 1827

230

Budding's mowing machines.' A year later, Mrs Loudon's *Ladies' Companion to the Flower Garden* cautiously welcomes

> A substitute for mowing with the scythe [which] has lately been introduced in the form of a mowing-machine . . . It is particularly adapted for amateurs, affording an excellent exercise to the arms and every part of the body; but it is proper to observe that many gardeners are prejudiced against it.

By the 1870s, in Beeton's *Dictionary of Gardening*, lawn-mowers have triumphed: 'Their use is too well known to need description . . . These useful machines are fast supplanting the scythe both on large and small lawns.' Just as the invention of the ha-ha made the landscape garden possible, so Budding's invention of the mower encouraged both the spread of middle-class gardening, and the return to formality, since a neat and tidy lawn was now within everyone's grasp.

THE EIGHTEENTH-CENTURY TRADITION

It would be quite wrong to imply that the landscape garden expired when Wordsworth suggested a medieval garden design to Lady Beaumont. The eighteenth-century struggle for the sublime, for the natural, for immensity carries on, and eventually merges with some of the grander schemes of the nineteenth century. At Sturefors in Sweden a version of the Ile des Peupliers was made in around 1820, a small island thick with poplars, set in a meadow like the Prairie Arcadienne at Ermenonville, and with a black memorial at its centre. (Herr Bielke told me that this beautiful yet melancholy small island was designed as a wedding present by an earlier Bielke to welcome his new bride – a strange *cadeau de noces*!) At Chatsworth as late as 1845 there was a section of the gardens called 'Tinian' to commemorate the desert island which both the English sailor Anson and Rousseau's hero St Preux had found so valuable and inspiring. The Claudian or Graeco-Roman landscape is continued after the Revolution in an eccentric way in Languedoc, where the château de Castille near Uzès was itself ornamented, and the surrounding grounds well-nigh smothered in countless forms of classical columns, either singly, or in sweeping colonnades imitating Bernini's at St Peter's, or as a part of classical monuments or buildings; versions of the Pantheon, a composite tower, or circular temples. These objects were put up between about 1812 and 1820 by the Comte Louis de Castille. Though they were all smaller than the antique originals, they were sizable. There was even a small imitation of the nearby Roman aqueduct, the Pont du Gard.

No less eccentric, but far grander, was the suggestion of the French architect Gabriel Thouin in 1820 (in his *Plans Raisonnés de Toutes les Espèces de Jardins*) that an enormous tract of land to the south and west of Versailles – at least three times the area of the vast park established by Louis XIV – should be constructed as a *jardin anglais* of the largest, most varied and most extravagant kind. It was, literally, to be a countryside, contrasting with Le Nôtre's ruler-straight *allées* and Canal, and with a lake and waterway system connected to the old Pièce des Suisses and the great cross-shaped Canal so that one might sail through this paradise for miles and miles. Besides the gardens of Versailles and the Trianon, Thouin's garden will include gardens which are sylvan, pastoral, rustic, Chinese-romantic and French-romantic. In the 'sylvan garden' there will be a Colossus of Rhodes, standing at the head of one of the huge lakes and at the end of Le Nôtre's Canal, facing the château of Versailles. Thouin will have this monster 'serve as a viewpoint for the château, and also for navigation.' And in the 'French-romantic' garden, beyond the Pièce des Suisses, there will be the Temple of Peace, under which (Thouin does not explain why) he proposes 'a factory for producing the barrels of rifles, etc.'

Thouin's map is fascinating, but remains a fantasy, like Edgar Allan Poe's Domain of Arnheim. Most impressive and beautiful of the early nineteenth-century landscape gardens still in the tradition of the eighteenth century is that made in Germany round the medieval castle of Dyck, near Düsseldorf. Here the Scotsman Thomas Blaikie, who had worked with Bélanger at Bagatelle just before the

Revolution, was called in by Fürst Joseph zu Salm-Reifferscheidt-Dyck to design an 'English garden' in which the prince's collection of rare and beautiful trees and shrubs might be displayed. In 1834, many years after Blaikie's visit to Schloss Dyck, the prince produced his small but solid *Hortus Dyckensis*, the catalogue of his tree and plant collection. Among these treasures the succulents (with a unique collection of mesembryanthemum) were under glass, and these were soon lost, but the hardy trees remain in Blaikie's uncluttered parkland, and form one of the best of the large arboreta to be created in the nineteenth century in all Europe. Often, they are merely bulky and lugubrious collections of unassorted tree-trunks, but at Dyck they are essential ingredients of a composed landscape. Blaikie was not only a garden designer but an experienced botanist and plant collector, and I suspect that much of his success at Dyck came from an understanding of the nature and requirements – and appearance when mature – of the remarkable trees for which the grounds were designed.

EXOTIC PLANTS AND WARDIAN CASES

I have deliberately mentioned Schloss Dyck as the last of the great eighteenth-century landscape gardens, since it combines this with a tree-collection firmly in the nineteenth-century tradition of using new plants, introductions from other countries, and new cultivars developed by horticulturists eager to experiment and improve on older forms. The nineteenth century is the century *par excellence* for the discovery and the exchange of plants from different parts of the world, and for the introduction of these plants into other people's gardens. Of course flowers were grown in the eighteenth century: we know that Philip Southcote had a planting scheme for flowers in parts of his *ferme ornée* in the 1730s. At the same time there were amateurs with botanical collections, the most famous in Britain being the eighth Lord Petre (1713–42), who corresponded with the naturalists and plant-collectors Collinson and Bartram to increase his plant treasures. He planted lavishly and with discrimination at Old Thorndon Hall in Essex. At his death it was reckoned that his nurseries contained over 200,000 plants, many of them exotic. Collectors with equal enthusiasm existed throughout Europe; like J. C. Volkamer, whose *Nürnbergische Hesperides* (1708–14) has already been mentioned for its pictures of German gardens. This great book, however, was intended primarily to display Volkamer's collection of fruit-trees – lemons, oranges, pomegranates and the like – and for the author the garden illustrations were definitely of secondary importance. The botanic gardens in different European countries increased their collections as the century progressed, and botanists corresponded with each other and with their agents to discuss, extend and classify their collections. The Chelsea Physic Garden (founded in 1673) had its period of greatest influence under the direction of Philip Miller (1691–1771), who was Keeper from 1722 until 1771, and his *Gardeners' Dictionary*, first issued in 1724 and enlarged and many times reissued in his lifetime, is not so much a work of gardening as of botanic importance. While Miller's influence on eighteenth-century gardening was – to be brutal – minimal, his influence on the introduction, study, understanding and classification of *plants* in Britain is immense. In 1768 the eighth edition of the *Gardeners' Dictionary* went over to the Linnaean system of classification, a matter for hot dispute in the eighteenth century. Carl von Linne, or Linnaeus (1707–78), the greatest botanist of the age, corresponded with Miller from Uppsala in Sweden, where his botanic garden still survives; and while he corresponded with botanists like Collinson, Miller or Buffon in centres of learning, his colleagues, disciples and agents – like Hasselquist, Förskal or Sonnini – explored the known world to bring back specimens, flowers, seeds and plants, to fill out the world's ever-growing *catalogus plantarum*.

For all this enthusiasm, the new plants did not escape into the eighteenth-century landscape garden. Even the royal example at Kew, where the Botanic Garden was founded in 1759, with Queen Caroline and Lord Bute as patrons, did not much affect the plants grown in the 'natural' or would-be 'sublime' garden. From the lengthy descriptions in Whately or Repton, or the more succinct ones of Walpole,

155, 156   Two ornate 'fern cases', the most popular adaptations of the Wardian case. If you imagine either case stripped of its decorations, the essential Wardian case – a sealed box, with wooden ribs and glazed on the sides and top – is revealed. From Shirley Hibberd's *Rustic Adornments for Homes of Taste* (1856)

157 The conservatory at Bicton (c. 1820) is one of the most handsome, as well as the earliest, of the big nineteenth-century greenhouses. Though the 'stove' – a heated room for protecting plants against the winter frost – was used in the sixteenth century, the idea that tender plants needed not only warmth but adequate light was not generally appreciated until the 1800s. The early orangeries were often more like heated cellars than greenhouses. The Bicton conservatory is still backed on to a wall, but it is high enough to allow palms and other tempting exotica to be grown indoors

George Mason, Uvedale Price or Payne Knight, one might conclude that virtually all up-to-date landscape gardens made between 1750 and 1790, or even 1800, had only a sprinkling of native flowers growing, modest and inconspicuous, in the sombre shadow of the trees; while the trees themselves were just as quiet in their colouring, being praised for their tones of green, grey, silver and brown. Brown, we should remember, was a colour more admired then than it is today. Trees which 'embrowned' the prospect were doing their job well. Similar conclusions may be drawn from the pictures of the time: the exotic plants which are illustrated are almost always part of a 'collection', grown under glass, and not allowed out into the landscape.

At the turn of the century, new plants were reaching Europe – usually Britain first, though not always – in greater and greater numbers. Private collections, like that at Dyck, increased. By the 1830s Loudon could boast that he had around 2,000 kinds of plants in his own small London garden. In 1804 the Horticultural Society was founded (to become the Royal Horticultural Society in 1861), and increased its influence by commissioning travellers, merchants and explorers to obtain rare plants from abroad; and in 1815 the end of the Napoleonic wars allowed new freedom of travel in Europe and beyond which had been restricted for nearly twenty years.

Three other factors were immensely effective in promoting the nineteenth-century fascination with new, exotic plants: the development of the greenhouse, the birth and popularity of horticultural periodicals, and the invention of the Wardian case.

The greenhouse, conservatory or hot-house has a long and complicated history dating back to the sixteenth century, when such an enclosed and warmed space might be called a 'stove' since it contained a heating apparatus of some kind. Orangeries of course are a part of the process; rooms where half-hardy shrubs could be wheeled in to spend the winter months. But the – to us – essential idea of a greenhouse, that it should be a *glasshouse*, a building allowing as much light as

possible to enter, did not really gain much favour until the late eighteenth-century, when the improvement in metal-frame construction and in glass-making techniques allowed much more daring and elaborate structures. The best early greenhouse in Britain is that at Bicton in Devon (c. 1820), built as a semi-circle against a south-facing wall, and other striking examples were at Syon House near Brentford (c. 1820), at Kew (begun in 1844 by Decimus Burton and R. Turner), at Chatsworth (the Great Stove, 1836-40, designed by Joseph Paxton), and the culminating giant structure of the Crystal Palace (1851, and also by Paxton). Of these, the greenhouses at Bicton, Syon House and Kew remain. Similar buildings with wooden or iron frameworks were erected on a smaller scale all over Europe in the nineteenth century. They encouraged the wholesale growth of tender plants: often the larger conservatories, like that at Kew, were called 'palm houses', since they would be built tall enough to contain specimens of palms growing to their full height (or nearly so).

Gardens and botanical periodicals – like Loudon's already mentioned, and the *Journal* of the Horticultural Society – proliferated to satisfy the curiosity of the public; and nurserymen who had in the past principally been concerned with the supply of trees and shrubs for landscape gardens extended their potential for the supply of rare plants, and themselves commissioned plant hunters abroad, like Robert Fortune, to find and to send back coveted discoveries. Of these firms, Loddiges and Veitch were foremost in the first half of the century: Conrad Loddiges and Sons even produced their own periodical, the *Botanical Cabinet* (1817–33); while the Veitches developed into James Veitch and Sons in Chelsea, and Robert Veitch and Son in Exeter.

The Wardian case is, with the ha-ha and the lawn-mower, one of the great inventions in garden history. Its invention virtually coincides with Budding's invention of the mower, and is chronicled in accurate and succinct detail by the

158   The conservatory of Syon House, c. 1820, is one of the best in Britain, comparable with the later marvels at Kew (still standing) and Chatsworth, and with the Crystal Palace. The erection of such giant structures depended upon cast iron and plate glass, whose manufacture was immensely improved in the nineteenth century. In this photograph, the iron pillars holding up the glass and iron roof can be seen, while the height of the building may be appreciated from the size of the tropical plants grown inside

inventor, Dr Nathaniel Bagshaw Ward, in his book *On the Growth of Plants in Closely Glazed Cases* (1842).

Ward was a doctor and in his spare time an ardent grower of ferns – a characteristic nineteenth-century plant enthusiasm. He was also interested in moths and butterflies and used to observe their metamorphoses. He built a rockery, but found that his ferns would not grow in the dirty, smoky London air. And then came the discovery (like that of penicillin, the result of accurate reflection following a chance occurrence). He writes, after the failure of his rockery: 'I was led to reflect a little more deeply upon the subject, in consequence of a simple incident which occurred in the summer of 1829.' The 'simple incident' was this:

> I had buried the chrysalis of a Sphinx [the Hawk Moth] in some moist mould contained in a wide-mouthed glass bottle, covered with a lid. In watching the bottle from day to day, I observed that the moisture which during the heat of the day arose from the mould, became condensed on the surface of the glass, and returned whence it came; thus keeping the mould always in the same degree of humidity. About a week prior to the final change of the insect, a seedling fern and a grass made their appearance on the surface of the mould.

Ward was puzzled. How could a fern, which would not grow when he tried to cultivate it, come up of its own accord? He thought, and concluded that in the bottle, *the atmosphere was free from soot*, and there was *light, heat, moisture* and moderate circulation of air. So he applied 'the test of experiment' (that most English of activities):

> I placed the bottle outside the window of my study – a room facing north, and to my great delight the plants continued to grow well ... They required no attention, the same circulation of water continuing, and here they remained for nearly four years, the *Poa annua* once flowering, and the fern producing three or four fronds annually.

The experiment was a success, and Ward considered how his discovery could be applied. To him, it led to a better fernery – and he built his *Tintern-Abbey House,*

> from its containing in the centre a small model, built in pumice and Bath stone, of the west window of Tintern Abbey. The sides were built up with rustic-work to the height of about five feet, and a perforated pipe runs round the top of the house, by means of which I can rain upon the plants at pleasure ... It contains at present about fifty specimens of ferns, and [other] flowering plants.

In the second edition of Ward's book (1852), the 'Tintern-Abbey Case' was worth a frontispiece, and the mid-Victorian era seized upon the invention with rapture. It provided indoor gardens, successful in miniature, which smaller bourgeois households required, just as they welcomed the lawn-mower invented by Budding. Among the many advocates of the 'fern case' – as Ward's invention was known in his day – Shirley Hibberd is the most remembered, and his illustrations of fern cases in, for example, *Rustic Adornments for Homes of Taste* (1856) and *The Fern Garden* (1869) are informative and horrifying for their indication of Victorian taste. Hibberd's 'fern case' is the basic Wardian case with ferns inside, albeit with a Gothic pedestal; while 'Rosher's-fern-case' goes most of the way to the pagoda at Kew, sealed in a glassy dome, and sprouting ferns at every storey.

But Ward saw two other uses for his invention, one philanthropic, the other botanical. With a touching naivety, he thought it would help in 'improving the condition of the poor', who might grow flowers, ferns and ivies for pleasure, and 'all the vacant spaces may be employed in raising small salads, radishes, etc.', which will 'in the course of a twelvemonth pay for [the] case out of its proceeds.' How many families quickly paid for their Wardian cases in this way has never been calculated; but Ward's other idea was far more practical. Within months of the conclusion of his original experiment, he had decided on a further 'test of experiment'. Until Ward's time, plants, seedlings and young trees shipped from foreign parts – China, South America, India, the Cape – mostly died before reaching England, because the changes in temperature and the variations in humidity were so extreme, as the ships carrying the young plants crossed and recrossed the Equator, and passed from cold to torrid, and torrid to cold regions. Fresh water was always scarce, and cabin-boys paid to water the plants were known to have used sea-water to avoid 'wasting' the ships' precious supplies.

Ward therefore prepared two cases of the typical 'Wardian' pattern; a sturdy rectangular box with sides and sloping top of glass, sealed with putty at the joints to make it airtight. 'In the beginning of June 1833, I filled two cases with ferns, grasses, etc., and sent them to Sydney [in Australia].' The contents arrived fit and flourishing. An acknowledgement from the ship's captain Charles Mallard, dated 23 November 1833, says happily that 'all the plants have grown a great deal, particularly the grasses which have been attempting to push the top of the box off'; and the cases were refilled at Sydney in February 1834. On their way back to England, the temperature varied between 20° and 120° Fahrenheit, and at the coldest moments 'the decks were covered a foot deep with snow.' Yet the cases were on the deck of the ship throughout the voyage, and were not once watered. The ship reached London docks on 24 November 1834, and when Ward came to examine the cases, he had a professional nurseryman with him. Ward writes: 'I shall not readily forget the delight of Mr George Loddiges, who accompanied me on board, at the beautiful appearance of the fronds of *Gleichenia Microphylla*, a plant never before introduced alive into this country.' It is fascinating to think that this very first 'round trip' of the Wardian case should have brought back a new plant alive to England, and that a representative of one of the great nursery firms should have been there to see, and to take the hint. Loddiges were to adopt the Wardian case at once to promote the importation of new species. Loddiges stated firmly in 1842, after the Wardian case had been used for a decade, 'Whereas we used to lose 19 out of 20 cases during the voyage 19 out of 20 is now the average that survive.'

While the Victorian use of the fern case has dwindled to the sale of broad-bellied bottles for miniature gardens, the use of the Wardian case for shipping young plants overseas has deeply affected the speedy dissemination of new plants from all over the world.

The history of gardens is not the history of plants, but this is a proper moment to indicate some of the more important newcomers to arrive in Britain (though the date of introduction may precede even by decades the successful general propagation). I have already referred to some of the plants and trees introduced before 1700. The sketchy list opposite continues the story:

It is offensively narrow to pretend that this movement was solely towards the British Isles. The dissemination was world-wide, though there is no room here to record it. As examples, it is illuminating to learn that the Cedar of Lebanon reached America in 1683 (in England by 1659), the Tree of Heaven, the ginkgo and the Lombardy poplar all in 1784, while the geranium or pelargonium did not arrive until 1810. The monkey puzzle and the wistaria both reached the United States in the same years that they reached England, 1795 and 1816 respectively. The expedition of Captain Bligh to the South Seas in 1787–9 may have ended in mutiny, but its aim was to take the plants of the breadfruit from Tahiti to the West Indies, and *en route* to plant useful seeds and roots from Europe in Tasmania. Tasmania received plantings of onions, cabbages, potatoes, apple trees, and the like, but the thousand-odd roots of the breadfruit acquired in Tahiti were soon after thrown into the sea by the mutineers. And the prickly pear, indigenous to Central America, the bougainvillea from Brazil, and the eucalyptus from Australia now grow extensively and freely on the northern coasts of the Mediterranean.

Year introduced	Vernacular name	Botanical name	Source
1701	Ivy-leaved geranium	*Pelargonium peltatum*	South Africa
1710	Pelargonium	*P. zonale*	South Africa
1707	Red-hot poker	*Kniphofia*	South Africa
1730	Iceland poppy	*Papaver nudicaule*	Siberia
c. 1730	Magnolia	*M. grandiflora*	North America
before 1732	Ice plant	*Mesembryanthemum*	South Africa
1736	Witch hazel	*Hamamelis virginiana*	North America
1751	Tree of Heaven	*Ailanthus altissima*	China
1754	Maidenhair tree	*Ginkgo biloba*	Japan
1758	Lombardy poplar	*Populus italica*	Italy
1789	Tree paeony	*P. moutan*	China
1789	Hydrangea	*H. macrophylla* (from which h. hybrids are descended)	China
1792	Lupin	*L. arboreus*	California
and 1826	Lupin	*L. polyphyllus*	British Columbia
	('Russell lupins' are a cross between these two, achieved in the early twentieth century)		
1792	Eschscholzia		California
and again in the 1820s			Oregon
c. 1793	Chrysanthemum	*C. sinensis x indicum*	China
1795	Monkey puzzle tree	*Araucaria araucana*	Chile
1804	Tiger lily	*Lilium tigrinum*	China
1805	Kerria	*K. japonica*	Japan
1816	Wistaria	*W. chinensis*	China
1827	Mahonia	*M. aquifolia*	North America
1844	Japanese anemone	*A. japonica*	China, via Japan
1844	Forsythia	*F. viridissima*	China
c. 1850	Forsythia	*F. suspensa*	Japan, via Holland
1844	Winter jasmine	*J. nudiflorum*	China
1849	Berberis	*B. darwinii*	Patagonia
1879	Cotoneaster	*C. horizontalis*	China
c. 1890	Russian vine	*Polygonum baldschuanicum*	Russia (Bokhara)
1896	Buddleia	*B. davidii*	China

(but *B. globosa* from Chile, 1774)

ECLECTIC GARDENS

For several decades the nineteenth century had no distinctive garden style, but remained unsettled, eclectic and searching, as it did in architectural form, in furniture and in clothing.

If any style went out of fashion, it was that of the simple landscape garden: in Britain and on the Continent I can think of few attempts after Repton's death in 1818, while in the United States, the development of New York's Central Park in something resembling this style, by F. L. Olmsted, is a rare survival. Other styles were taken up with haphazard enthusiasm: the 'Indian' at Sezincote in Gloucestershire (around 1805) and at the Larmer Tree Gardens in Wiltshire, by General Pitt-Rivers in the 1880s; or the 'Swiss' at the Swiss Cottage at Old Warden in Bedfordshire, where in the 1820s four acres were converted into a series of flower-decked and intimate glades with humpy bridges (in cast iron), floral arcades (supported on huge iron hoops), sentimental memorials, a thatched roof encircling the trunk of a beech tree, and at the centre of the gardens, a wooden cottage with thatched roof, and split, bark-covered log decoration like that in the root house at Spetchley.

'Chinese' was popular – at Dropmore in Buckinghamshire there is still a handsome metal-and-tile Chinese aviary, built around 1800, and at Alton Towers in Staffordshire there is the lovely pagoda built by Robert Abraham in 1827, more delicate and far better sited than that of Chambers at Kew. At Alton Towers there is also a Chinese lookout tower, but this today has lost its chinoiserie.

The masterpiece among Chinese gardens – and I think the only western example to come anywhere near realizing the atmosphere of the originals – is at Biddulph Grange in Staffordshire, where in the 1850s the owner James Bateman and his friend, the artist, Edward Cooke, designed a region for the gardens known as 'China', properly and solidly isolated from the rest of the estate by immense elevations of rocks and soil and trees. Entry to 'China' is obscure and difficult, and it is invisible from outside. Through a rocky tunnel, longer and darker than most garden tunnels, you arrive inside a Chinese pavilion, and look out from its crimson-painted balcony across a small, still lake, surrounded by bamboos, antique massy stones, and exotic trees. Across the lake, a lacquered bridge, reflections, and beyond, high up as if in a mountain range, a weather-worn tower in the Great Wall . . . Walking from the temple, your path leads you to one side, and round the lake – in miniature, it is not impossibly remote from T'ang I-fen's painting of 1826. I could not say as much of any other 'Chinese' garden in the west.

In the late nineteenth century, the fashion for japonaiserie led to interest in Japanese gardens and gardening styles – the books by Josiah Conder, *Landscape Gardening in Japan* (1893) and *The Floral Art of Japan* (1899), are the most serious attempts to understand them – but no physical imitation of a Japanese garden in the west succeeded until well into the present century. The Japanese garden at Kildare in Ireland, begun genuinely enough in 1906 by a Japanese Tassa Eida, and the section called Japanese at Newstead Abbey in Nottinghamshire are typical in their exploitation of stepping-stones and stone lanterns to excuse lavish, attractive but un-Japanese plantings of rare and colourful plants.

The Victorian seach for excitement in gardens went as far as the volcano at Wörlitz – to monsters. After the Great Exhibition of 1851 had closed, Paxton's Crystal Palace was dismantled and moved from Hyde Park to a permanent site at Sydenham in south London (where it remained until it was destroyed by fire in 1936). At Sydenham, Paxton not only designed striking Italianate terraces which still remain, but arranged the landscape for a collection of concrete dinosaurs, most of which still leer or rear from their island sanctuaries, painted to the life and appropriately labelled. In 1854, a group of Fellows of the Royal Society dined within one of them, an iguanodon. But whereas Chambers' scenes of terror and the volcano at Wörlitz were meant to arouse a certain *frisson*, the monsters at Sydenham were educative. This mid-Victorian parallel to Darwin's *Origin of the Species* is a reminder of the didactic, rather than sentimental purpose of these gardens. In visiting the Great Exhibition of 1851, and to a lesser and more discreet extent in visiting the eclectic British gardens of the 1850s, one was to admire, to be impressed, and to learn, briefly, that of all the animals of creation *man* had worked his way to the top, and that among the countries of the world, Britain had done a similar prize winning sprint.

The eclectic impulse was strong – maybe to show that all kinds of garden could be built, maybe as an indication that a dominant style had not yet been found. Alton Towers boasted beside the pagoda and the Chinese watch-tower, numerous Grecian, Roman, Gothic and Indian buildings, an alpine garden, a topiary garden, and a version of Stonehenge; while Biddulph Grange, whose 'China' is outstanding, has still a plethora of other areas within its twenty acres – the remains of an arboretum, a few traces of a 'stumpery' (a Victorian creation, a region of picturesque roots of trees, deriving from the hermitages and roothouses of the previous age), an Egyptian scene with sphinxes and pyramidal topiary, an Italian terrace, a lake garden, and at the intersection of several of these, a tunnel-cum-building which begins on one side as an Egyptian tomb, hesitates as a chapel, and comes out on the other side as a Swiss-looking Cheshire cottage! To compare with this feature is the fern house within the grounds of the Swiss Cottage at Old Warden. Here a small cruciform building has Gothic ends to each of the four arms, like a nave with north and south transepts. When you go in, the intersection of the four arms is in rough heaving shapes of tufa, to simulate a grotto, while up and down the 'nave' ferns, or the places for ferns, are illuminated through the curved glass roof – a greenhouse on top. The end wall of the building, in the 'chancel', is pierced by a rose window of stained glass, and its tinted churchy light shines on a marble tablet with an inscription of scriptural and botanical solemnity. This is indeed *multum in parvo*, while the many garden aspects within the Crystal Palace rejoiced in ample space.

On the Continent, two great gardens mark the middle and the late nineteenth century: Muskau in East Germany, and Weldam in Holland. Weldam is discussed near the end of this chapter, but it is more appropriate to mention Muskau now.

Fürst H. L. H. von Pückler-Muskau was a properly devoted gardener – he called himself 'der Parkomane', or the park maniac – and wrote a book on the subject, *Andeutungen über Landschaftersgärtnerei* (1834). He spent his adult life pursuing his landscape and garden ideals to the utmost, i.e. to the point of bankruptcy. He took over his father's estates at Muskau on the river Neisse, and Branitz near Cottbus in 1811. Between 1815 and 1845, he worked on the principal estate, at Muskau, and then, rather like William Beckford at Fonthill a few years earlier, he was forced by his own extravagant schemes to sell up, and retire to the lesser estate at Branitz. There, like Beckford at Bath, he gardened again until his death in 1871.

The park at Muskau was large, with hills and woods to allow varied scenes; for example an observatory, a mining-scene, a vineyard, a race-course, a mansion-scene and a fortress-scene. Most interesting and idiosyncratic was the 'pleasure-ground' (he used the English words) near the mansion. Here, the scene had features of a characteristic 'landscape' nature, but there were also in the vicinity of the mansion scattered flowerbeds of the most formal and artificial kind: he himself wrote 'I always give a firm and definite form to individual flowerbeds, and prefer to enclose them in a framework of iron, wood, earthenware or trellis.' Some were edged with box, others defined by urns, or by pebble designs. Though they were loosely placed in the landscape, the beds were themselves representational, in ways which had been rejected by the main garden designers for over a century: a fan, a letter 'H' set in a star pattern, a cornucopia, a dice, a gigantic flower made up from several beds joined together to look like petals, and a design to imitate a bunch of peacock feathers.

When he moved to Branitz, the terrain was less favourable, flat, marshy and bleak. Pückler-Muskau designed a smaller area of flowerbeds round his castle, and one remarkable monument – a pyramid made of earth, sixty feet high. He was buried in it in 1871.

Readers will now have seen how these geographical and historical juxtapositions needed care, taste, skill and money if they were to avoid being ridiculous. Just as the excesses of formal gardens were mocked by Pope and Walpole, and as the natural and picturesque were mocked by Colman and Garrick in the *Clandestine Marriage* (1766), or by Thomas Love Peacock in *Headlong Hall* (1816), so nineteenth-century eclecticism was pilloried by Gustave Flaubert. In his novel *Bouvard et Pécuchet*, begun in 1874 and published posthumously in 1881, he tells how in the 1840s two middle-aged clerks come into a fortune, and spend it, disastrously, on one ill-conceived enthusiasm after another. In the two sections describing their gardening adventures, Flaubert shows the middle-class failure to cope with any elevated or sensitive ideas, such as the eighteenth-century concepts of the sublime or of the melancholy, and the equally lamentable inability to bring together disparate and grandiose ideas in a small place.

Having just failed in a scheme to grow fruit, his comic heroes wonder what next to do. Fortunately, in their library, they come across Boitard's work entitled *The Garden Architect*.

Gardens are divided by the author into an infinity of styles. There is, first of all, the melancholy and romantic style, which is distinguished by everlasting-flowers, ruins, tombs, and 'a votive tablet to the Virgin, marking the spot where a nobleman fell under the blade of an assassin.' The sublime and awesome style is composed with hanging rocks, shattered trees, and burnt-out huts. The exotic style is achieved by planting Peruvian lilies 'to bring back memories to a settler abroad, or to a traveller'. The solemn style should offer a temple of philosophy, as at Ermenonville. The majestic style is characterized by obelisks and triumphal arches; the mysterious style by moss and grottoes, and the thoughtful style by a lake. There is even the fantastic style, which was seen at its best in a garden in

Württemburg – there, you would discover in turn a wild boar, a hermit, several sepulchres and a boat which would glide away from the bank of its own accord, to carry you to a boudoir where you would be drenched by fountain-jets when you reclined on the sofa . . .

Bouvard and Pecuchet then got to work on their own garden:

> The hedgerow was opened here and there to lead into the coppice, which was filled with serpentine paths to make a labyrinth. They had hoped to make an archway in the wall of the fruit garden, through which the perspective would be revealed. As the coping-stones wouldn't stay in place, this had resulted in an enormous breach, with ruins on the ground. They had sacrificed the asparagus in order to build an Etruscan tomb – that is to say, a quadrilatral in black plaster, six feet tall, and looking like a dog-kennel. Four spruce trees at the corners stood guard over this monument. They intended to top it with an urn, and to embellish it with an inscription.
>
> In the other part of the vegetable garden, a sort of Rialto spanned an ornamental pond, having a shell-work of mussels, encrusted with barnacles. The ground just drank up the water – but no matter! A layer of puddled clay would form at the bottom, and then the water would hold. The garden shed had been transformed into a rustic cottage, by the use of panes of tinted glass. At the top of the little vineyard, six squared-up tree trunks supported a sort of bonnet in tinplate, with upturned corners, and this represented a Chinese pagoda.
>
> They had gone down to the banks of the river Orne to pick out blocks of granite; they had broken them up, numbered them, and brought them back in a cart, and had then stuck the fragments together with cement, heaping them up one on top of another, and so in the middle of the lawn a rock reared up, looking like a gigantic potato.

The 'fantastic style' is obviously from Hohenheim, while the 'gigantic potato' is an echo of the Dolmen, at Ermenonville. Had Flaubert seen some text of Walpole's letter to Mason? It is most unlikely, yet the waspish style of the two attacks on such monuments is strangely similar.

CARPET BEDDING AND TOPIARY

In their search for a style, and helped – or impelled – by the technical and botanical changes I have described, nineteenth-century gardens found two forms of expression which are characteristic, memorable and widely spread in Britain, the Continent and the United States. One, the practice of massed bedding of flowers is more or less new in the history of gardening (Le Nôtre's floral bedding at Trianon is the most notable exception); the other, the adaptation of a neo-Italianate style in garden design, comes from the formal gardens of Italy, with a side-glance at Versailles. And these two forms of expression, characteristically Victorian, are most often used in conjunction, the bedding illuminating the grass, gravel and statuary of the Italian-style gardens.

Massed or *carpet* bedding became possible with the introduction of greenhouses in which immense numbers of tender annuals could be raised ready for wholesale use, to be taken up after flowering and discarded while another filling for the bed, likewise raised up in quantity, was put in. Many nineteenth-century gardening books give plans and plant-lists for such beds, and Loudon's are typical. He gives both details of actual bedding in particular gardens, and suggestions of his own; while Nathan Cole's *Royal Parks and Gardens of London* (1877) indicates the planting which Cole himself arranged at Kensington gardens and saw with approval elsewhere in London, or suggested for private gardeners to copy.

This practice of massed bedding was inevitably tied to a more formal gardening style, with orderly 'separation of kinds'; lawns, beds, taller plants behind – or, in island bedding, in the centre – and then massed shrubs and trees. Many mid-century gardens retain an undulating line, their paths meander and the outline of the beds

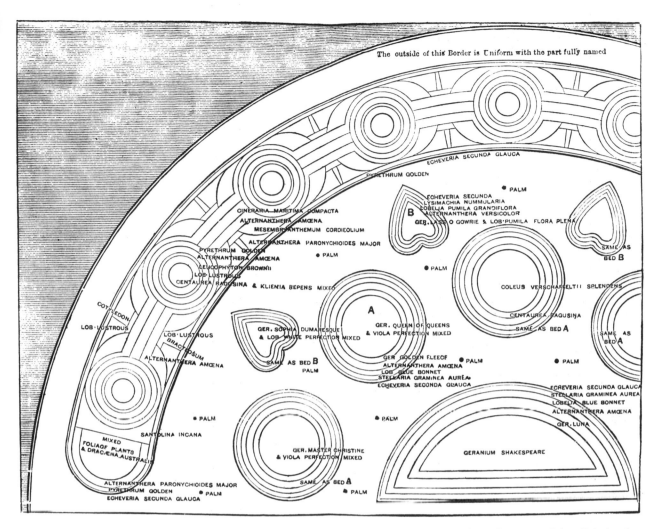

The outside of this Border is Uniform with the part fully named

ECHEVERIA SECUNDA GLAUCA

PYRETHRUM GOLDEN

CINERARIA MARITIMA COMPACTA
ALTERNANTHERA AMŒNA
MESEMBRYANTHEMUM CORDIEOLIUM

ALTERNANTHERA PARONYCHIOIDES MAJOR

PYRETHRUM GOLDEN
ALTERNANTHERA AMŒNA
LEUCOPHYTON BROWNII
LOB· LUSTROUS
CENTAUREA RAGUSINA & KLIENIA REPENS MIXED

ECHEVERIA SECUNDA
LYSIMACHIA NUMMULARIA
LOBELIA PUMILA GRANDIFLORA
ALTERNANTHERA VERSICOLOR
GER. LASSO GOWRIE & LOB·PUMILA FLORA PLENA

• PALM

B

SAME AS
BED B

• PALM

COTYLEDON

LOB· LUSTROUS

LOB· LUSTROUS

BRACTOSUM
ALTERNANTHERA AMŒNA

A

GER. SOPHIA DUMARESQUE
& LOB· WHITE PERFECTION MIXED

SAME AS BED B
PALM

GER. QUEEN OF QUEENS
& VIOLA PERFECTION MIXED

GER GOLDEN FLEECE
ALTERNANTHERA AMŒNA
LOB· BLUE BONNET
STELLARIA GRAMINEA AUREA
ECHEVERIA SECUNDA GLAUCA

• PALM

COLEUS VERSCHAFFELTII SPLENDENS

CENTAUREA RAGUSINA
SAME AS BED A

SAME AS
BED A

• PALM

ECHEVERIA SECUNDA GLAUCA
STELLARIA GRAMINEA AUREA
LOBELIA BLUE BONNET
ALTERNANTHERA AMŒNA

GER. LUNA

• PALM

SANTOLINA INCANA

MIXED
FOLIAGE PLANTS
& DRACŒNA AUSTRALIS

GER. MASTER CHRISTINE
& VIOLA PERFECTION MIXED

• PALM

GERANIUM SHAKESPEARE

ALTERNANTHERA PARONYCHIOIDES MAJOR
PYRETHRUM GOLDEN   • PALM
ECHEVERIA SECUNDA GLAUCA

SAME AS BED A

• PALM

159   From Nathan Cole's *Royal Parks and Gardens of London* (1877). Cole was in charge of the planting at Kensington Gardens, this section of his bedding plan is typical for the geometrical regularity of the design, for the massed treatment of the flowers and for the brightness – we might think it was garish – of their contrasting colours. The use of several of these – *echeveria secunda glauca, alternanthera, kleinia repens,* coleus and various geraniums and pelargoniums – is still accepted practice in modern municipal bedding

may be fluid – ovals, crescents, kidney shapes – but the control implicit in the closely-mown lawn and the rigid block planting of brilliant annual flowers is a world away from the undulating landscapes of Capability Brown.

Many bedding schemes were openly formal, with symmetrical balancing of parts, and with a reproduction of parterres which, in black and white, are not always so different from those of the seventeenth and eighteenth centuries. In colour, they are instantly separated, since plants – begonias, salvias, geraniums – provide the main colour contrast rather than occasional gravels, sand or crushed shells. One of the most overwhelmingly elaborate schemes is in Scotland at Drummond Castle in Perthshire, where an area of thirteen acres below the castle courtyard was laid out formally in the 1840s. Being at a much lower level than the castle, this enormous space can qualify as a parterre, since it is wholly visible from above. But once within its framework of paths and avenues, its unity is less clear. It is impressive, an immense spectacle, but when compared with other rectangular gardens with not dissimilar situations such as Weikersheim the plan appears inadequate and dull.

Round this dazzling and orderly display of flowers, the nineteenth century's most characteristic garden style is neo-Italianate, a framework of clipped hedges, balustrades, statues, straight gravel walks, and regular pools with fountains. With the flowers, and with the massive scale employed for many of the gardens, this led to a rigidity of plan which had been unknown since the early eighteenth century, and to gardens of a brightness which Italy had never seen; though Italy was not to escape the fashion. The villa Garzoni today maintains bedding of a lurid crudity which comes straight from nineteenth-century England.

The reintroduction of formality round the house, begun by Repton, was followed

by an extension of formality further into the garden, and many old gardens which had lost their parterres in the days of the landscape garden acquired new ones, or at least new formal features, in early Victorian times. At Chatsworth, for example, the great parterre had gone long before Joseph Paxton designed the new formal garden to the east, completing it with the towering Emperor fountain (1844). At Trentham in Staffordshire a big Brownian landscape was made to seem merely a background – of lake and island – beyond the enormous terraces laid out by Sir Charles Barry (1795–1860) who redesigned the house. In the garden, Barry was helped by W. A. Nesfield (1793–1864). Barry (who designed the Houses of Parliament) worked on his own with Nesfield on several gardens, while Nesfield reintroduced a formal area at Castle Howard, focusing on the huge fountain sculptures brought from the Great Exhibition of 1851, and designed the formal gardens and layout radiating from Burton's Palm House at Kew. Barry's garden work survives in England at Trentham, at Cliveden in Buckinghamshire, and at Shrubland Park in Suffolk. This last is his most grandiose design, and echoes and tries to outdo the villa d'Este with terraces, balustrades and stairways. In the far north of Scotland, Barry is thought also to have designed the three parterres, one of them circular, at Dunrobin Castle. Few large gardens of this type now survive as they were in their heyday: often the 'bones' of the garden may still be there, as at Trentham, with great geometrical areas framed in straight paths, and with ironwork pergolas stretching on either side. But the intensely concentrated bedding which gave them colour and some kind of an excuse has nearly always been abandoned in favour of diluted and less costly schemes, leaving the areas of beds thinly covered with rose-stumps, or reduced to grass, and with an uneasy, empty feeling, as in an abandoned car park. An admirable,

160   Another illustration from *Royal Parks and Gardens of London.* Victoria Park still retains outstanding areas of carpet bedding, set in scenes of lake, lawn and single trees. The circular bed to the left rises up in characteristic 'wedding cake' fashion, with low, neat plants on the outside and large, showy plants (these might be cannas) in the centre. Practically all the plants used in such massed displays would be annuals, and would be raised in their tens of thousands in the giant greenhouses which were also a feature of nineteenth-century gardening

detailed, clear and accurate record of these gardens at their peak is in Inigo Triggs's large work, *Formal Gardens in England and Scotland* (1902), where large plans and photographs show how lavishly the gardens were maintained, and show that when their bedding was complete the overall effect of the designs was both grand and reassuringly solid.

The worthwhile survivors are generally the smaller ones, frequently when they form a subordinate part of a larger whole – as at Bowood in Wiltshire, where George Kennedy designed the terraces in front of the house and a partly sunken formal area beside the stable block. These additions perfectly achieve the slight separation of house and landscape in the Reptonian manner, and serve rather to increase the amplitude and dignity of Brown's greatest landscape.

With the neo-Italianate garden came not merely clipped hedges as borders and framework for formal areas of bedding, but clipped bushes and trees of great size – as at Biddulph, where the 'Egyptian' area is triumphantly backed and flanked by towering clipped yews, to resemble the monumental entrance to a tomb and, *mirabile dictu*, topiary. Often the topiary of Victorian times has vanished with the bedding it outlined, or has become irregular, swollen or patchy, but its use was widespread, and good topiary gardens made at the end of the century can be seen still at Ascot in Buckinghamshire and at Haseley Court in Oxfordshire. On the Continent there is a striking topiary garden of this period at Twickel in Holland. Quite the most remarkable topiary garden of the time was made in the United States, at Green Animals in Rhode Island, by Thomas Brayton. He acquired the land in 1872, and lived until 1939. Over half a century he developed a menagerie of box and privet animals and birds which stand, green and larger than life, round smaller beds of box, and among rosebeds or topiary of abstract or architectural forms. A camel, giraffe, terrier, bear, swan, ostrich, hippopotamus, a horse and its rider, a goat and a peacock – the list goes on. Parts of the seven acres of garden are – though inhabited by such wild creatures – formally designed, others less so, and it is fair to compare the oddity of Green Animals with that of the vanished villa Quaracchi in Florence, with its topiary marvels, or even in a light-hearted way with the strange garden of Bomarzo, with stone monsters and sculpture which are today both enigmatic and inconsequential.

To my mind the best preserved of the great nineteenth-century formal gardens and one of the best in quality is in Holland, at Weldam. Here an old moated castle stands in the middle of the garden site, which forms a hollow square round the castle. On the outside, as so often in Holland, the level terrain is bounded by straight drainage canals.

The designer, Edouard André, worked at the close of the century, and made his garden as a series of 'compartments' round the castle. As the site is flat, the overall view of each part of the garden is possible only from viewpoints in the castle itself – indeed some features, like the gigantic topiary scrollwork to the rear of the castle, or the chest-high topiary letters to one side, cannot be appreciated by the visitor who is actually in the midst of the hedges. To the front, the parterres are somewhat lower than the paths around them, and a wider view is possible, but in the main the garden at Weldam is intentionally divided into sections by the massive hedges, and yet given a sense of unity by the body of the castle in the background and by the firm lines and right-angles of the hedges.

Weldam returns to the Dutch seventeenth century as much as to a more general European formal style. This is so both from the divisions I have mentioned and from certain features, notably the pleached hornbeam tunnel and the maze. The tunnel is the grandest of its kind, tall and long as a cathedral nave, and doing that rare thing in garden design, providing an axis which is covered from one end to the other. The tunnels in Dutch garden engravings often look improbably extended, but Weldam proves that they are possible. This tunnel runs along one whole section of ornamental topiary – box and yew – and leads to the maze, which is so extensive and so tall that even when the explorer reaches the top of the wooden platform at the centre, the foreground view is mainly of the perplexing hedges of the maze.

Weldam is almost entirely in the nineteenth-century formal manner, and modern simplifications have not reduced the bedding to bleakness, nor has the unity of

162   After a century of
disapproval, topiary returned to
the Victorian garden. This view of
the topiary garden at Twickel
(above), in the Netherlands
(*c.* 1900), shows the calculated and
striking association of stepped
hedges – trimmed to resemble
peacocks – with geometrical
borders of box and a central
ornament elaborately carved in
stone

161   A view of the Egyptian
Court at Biddulph Grange (left),
one of the most successful of the
eclectic gardens of the nineteenth
century. Having passed through
this tomb-like entrance, the
visitor goes on into a 'Cheshire
cottage', while the gardens and
buildings of 'China' occupy an
entire and secret area to one side

manner been affected by introducing other elements in distracting styles. Another
nineteenth- and twentieth-century Dutch garden, at Twickel, has a fine landscape
garden, with good trees and shrubs around a beautifully contoured lake (somewhat
reminiscent of Schloss Dyck), and a first-rate enclosed topiary garden beside an
orangery. While these areas, which form the main part of the estate, are in
themselves excellent representatives of the early and late nineteenth century, the
recent and irregular flower garden which links them is neither mature, nor as yet
successful. A third notable garden of this mixed kind was laid out in 1900 at
Oostermeer, near Ouderkerke aan de Amstel. Here, the designer, Leonard A.
Springer, has used both formal elements derived from French tradition, and the
freer movement of the English landscape style.

HERBACEOUS BORDERS

Towards the end of the century, there were moves to reform the more florid excesses
of the Italian style, or to annihilate it. The most important reformer was Sir Reginald
Blomfield (1856–1942), whose *Formal Garden in England* (1892) urged a return to
the simpler architectural formalities of Renaissance and seventeenth-century
gardens, while in the early 1900s Sir George Sitwell was to make his garden at
Renishaw the best and most persuasive demonstration of this opinion. But while
Blomfield wanted *better* formal gardens, others had for some time been uneasy, and
at last wholly opposed to formality. By the 1830s, the idea of the *herbaceous border*
was forming. This is often ascribed to Loudon, but others hit on the idea
independently. The herbaceous border (though it is most often contained in an
exactly rectangular area with a straight wall giving strict vertical backing) is the

247

beginning of floral informality. It contains perennial plants (though there may be a small admixture of annuals), associated in colour, and graded in height and form to make a variegated but harmonious whole. It admits as its principles the importance of the *plant* – its colour, foliage, and shape – and the display of flowers for as long as possible.

In 1806, in his letter to Lady Beaumont, Wordsworth describes a border 'edged with boxwood', 'to receive the earliest and latest flowers', with snowdrops backed by crocus in front, and in the middle 'hepatica, jonquils, hyacinths, polyanthuses, auriculas, mezereon, and other spring flowers and shrubs that blossom early; and, for the autumn, Michaelmas-daisy, winter-cherry, china-asters, Michaelmas and Christmas rose . . .' By 1829, William Cobbett, in *The English Gardener*, distinguishes between flowers in *beds* ('a mass of one sort of flower') and in *borders*, 'where an infinite variety of them are mingled together, but arranged so that they may blend with one another in colour as well as in stature.'

The earliest surviving example is at Arley Hall in Cheshire, where a lovely double border based on a dated plan from 1846 has been maintained with good sense and fidelity. From around 1900, the herbaceous border was to become more subtle, under the influence of Gertrude Jekyll, with the making of 'tonal' gardens in which flowers and foliage of a single dominant colour were to be grown.

The revolution comes later: with William Robinson (1839–1935), a man of words, imagination and bad temper. In his late twenties he went to Paris as a horticultural correspondent for *The Times*, and quickly expressed his views on French gardens in two books, *Gleanings from French Gardens* (1869) and *Parks, Promenades and Gardens of Paris* (1869). These views are deeply at odds with the gardens of Barry, Nesfield, and their kind. He appreciates, admires, understands the botanical collections (though not the conservatories which contained them), and the plants – their structure, their form, the use each may have in combination with others or on its own – but he *loathes* (italics are weak to express Robinson's detestation) the straightjackets in which they are confined. His comments on Versailles in *Parks, Promenades . . .* are quite enough:

This being one of the most celebrated gardens in the world, it behoves us to examine it somewhat in detail – were we, however, to treat of it in proportion to its real merits as a garden, a very small amount of space would suffice.

Nothing in Versailles much pleases him. The best he can do is, as I would have predicted, at Hubert Robert's romantic Bains d'Apollon. This, since it has a grotto, and hanging trees, and water flowing downwards as it wills, he calls: 'The most striking and satisfactory in the gardens at Versailles.' Elsewhere, the visitor is faced (or, if Robinson himself, exacerbated) by the 'indescribable emptiness and ugliness of the scene'.

Robinson found words to formulate his solution. In 1870, he produced *Alpine Flowers for English Gardens*, which is virtually the beginning of the irregular alpine or rock garden in Britain, a pseudo-mountain setting for the often tiny plants discovered in Switzerland, Scandinavia and the Pyrenees, and imported to Britain to be grown in or on that most lamentable of all pretences to the natural, the rockery. While most are an embarrassment to the visitor who observes not only the plants but the artificiality in which they are planted, a small number succeed, as at Hergestcroft in Herefordshire (*c.* 1900), where a small pool and rock garden achieves colour, form, and a happy accommodation between the size and shape of the plants, and the rocks among which they grow. Even this is not strictly an alpine garden, and I insist that I have not yet seen one where the plants would not have been better displayed back in their natural habitat.

In the same year Robinson published *The Wild Garden*, and in 1883 *The English Garden*, many times reissued. These books both had a more general and more healthy influence. For Robinson, the garden was a place in which rare and interesting plants should be grown, with attention, respect and even veneration for their form, foliage and colour. These qualities should govern the 'design' of the garden, if such a word may be allowed.

XLI   The prehistoric monsters at Sydenham (right) still lash their concrete tails – a relic of the Great Exhibition, and of the fascination with the earliest inhabitants of the earth which surrounded Darwin's *Origin of the Species*, published in 1859. These monsters, frozen like the figures on Keats's Grecian urn, are safe on the islands in the lake, and resist the passage of time rather better than the Renaissance monsters of Bomarzo, now the prey of meddling tourists. Beside this scaly creature a monkey puzzle (*araucaria araucana*) dispenses a prickly, exotic shade

XLII   This heroic arbour (far right) in the garden at Weldam, in the Netherlands, is a modern reminder of the magnificence of Renaissance carpenter's work. While all contemporary examples have disappeared – the wooden framework needs frequent attention and renewal – pictures survive which show that the height and length of this creation at Weldam is not excessive

XLIII   In London, the carpet bedding at Victoria Park is still faithful to the principles which governed the fashion in the nineteenth century. Geometrical patterns, raised up in the manner of padded embroidery, are executed with massed plantings of annual plants. Frequently the same plants are used – for example echeveria, sempervivum, coleus, cineraria, lobelia and many varieties of pelargonium

XLIV The sunken garden at Hergest Croft in Herefordshire, laid out at the turn of the century, and developed continuously as a semi-wild setting for the display of remarkable plants. This section, with plants and shrubs admirably juxtaposed among rocks round a small woodland pool, is one of the most successful and convincing examples in Britain of the rock garden

Robinson's words were wilder than his garden (his own, at Gravetye Manor in Sussex, which he bought in 1884 and developed for many years, has several surprising architectural sections) and led to much necessary but foolish rejection of control in favour of colour, and of form in favour of foliage. One of Robinson's more extraordinary commissions was to re-work Barry's Italianate garden at Shrubland, where the terrace, balustrades and formal stonework are now writhen over by shrubs and climbing plants.

Miss Gertrude Jekyll (1843–1932) met Robinson in the 1880s, and accepted many of his views on the need to understand and interpret plants in relation to their surroundings. But she was a more thoroughly educated person than Robinson, and had an understanding of the total needs of a garden which was greater than his. No doubt Robinson set things off: Gertrude Jekyll made sure they went in the right direction. She appreciated 'wildness' – and this is clear from her *Wood and Garden* (1899) – but she saw also the control which a wild garden needed, and which she appreciated in English cottage gardens, the rural and village gardens. In these for a long while (as in Palmer's passionate and idealized painting 'In a Shoreham Garden') flowers and trees had been assembled without formality, and yet with a feeling for the necessity of simplicity and a respect for the space and setting available. William Robinson was determined to place 'plants of other countries . . . in places where they will flourish'; but Gertrude Jekyll wanted a more solid basis for such introductions. In her collaboration with the architect Lutyens, she brought together Robinson's desire for the plants themselves to be respected, and the more important need for them to be given a controlled and human setting. The scale and planting of the cottage garden are curiously close to Jekyll's best work, and to her own invention – I do not think any other gardener can claim it – of the 'tonal' or colour border, the herbaceous border in which the colours are so controlled that they are all tonally related in shades of silver, or white (the dullest) or yellow or blue. This invention no doubt springs from her insight into the potential qualities of the flower and foliage of the cottage garden. She travelled when younger, and she may indeed have seen the peasant gardens in the Tirol and Switzerland which have lived on for centuries as an extraordinary and attractive miniature of the formal gardens of the baroque. There, box hedges and straight paths outline patches of tulips or vegetables; and all within the compass of a few square yards. The Swiss *Bauerngärten* are a fraction more formal than are those of Gloucestershire or Surrey, but they have a similar message. Order is combined with colour; there is a pleasurable confusion of leaves and flowers in which the individual leaves of ivy or lavender have as great a value as the plants that bear them; and almost as great as the narrow paths and paving stones, the gates and waist-high walls which divide the garden from the farm.

XLV The survival of the Renaissance garden is nowhere more striking than in Switzerland, where for centuries farmers' gardens have transmitted the formal edging of box – in this garden, at Kappel (Solothurn), at least a hundred years old – and the delight in floral and vegetable variety from the earlier traditions of Italy and southern Germany

163   The long, curved
laburnum walk at Bodnant – when
in flower, the most brilliantly
coloured 'arbour' in Britain

16

The Modern Garden

NINETEENTH-CENTURY SURVIVALS

'If you analyse a group of important English gardens constructed at any time between 1900 and 1930 you will see that they are based on designs borrowed from every period of European garden design.' Russell Page, the outstanding garden designer of the middle years of this century, made this observation in 1962 (*The Education of a Gardener*). It could be extended to the present day and, indeed, to the rest of the world without altogether shaming the truth.

Eclectic gardens like Biddulph or Alton Towers continue to be made, and with enough money, a complaisant and competent gardener, a tolerable space to garden with and enough imagination, there is no reason why they should not be made almost anywhere. Without attempting caves of ice or desert pleasure domes, the sequence of gardens at Compton Acres in Dorset, and those at Dumbarton Oaks, near Washington, do approximately what Biddulph did in the 1860s, but with a richer planting of recent introductions and cultivars. Individual imitations of styles also continue, with varying success. Among many 'Japanese' gardens which serve as an excuse for cherries, wistaria, kerria and dwaft azaleas (and often have the unfortunate hallmark of stone lanterns and bronze cranes), there are two recent creations of deep sensitivity and un-European restraint: one is in England, in Michael Pitt-River's estate at Tollard Royal in Wiltshire, and one made within the decade in the austere and arrogant confines of Hitler's pre-war Nordpark at Düsseldorf.

Quite the most surprising of the eclectic gardens made this century is in the United States – the Duke Gardens at Somerville, New Jersey. Begun before the war, these gardens are entirely under glass in a series of eleven large greenhouses each containing the necessary elements (layout, appropriate plants, bushes and trees, garden buildings, furniture and objects, pool, streams, paths, rocks and sand) for gardens in different styles. In the American mode are a Colonial and a Desert garden. The East is represented by Indo-Persian, Chinese and Japanese, and old Europe by Italian and French gardens. Tropical and sub-tropical gardens present an exotic contrast to the typically Edwardian garden, while the English garden contains the styles of several centuries with its knot garden and herbaceous border, Victorian bedding, topiary and a lawn. The word 'sumptuousness' was used by the Elizabethans to describe the quality they strove for in their richest garden effects. The Duke Gardens have just this. Faultlessly and lavishly maintained, they have the sumptousness which the eclectic garden must achieve to convince the visitor that all is there. In their way, Miss Doris Duke's greenhouses are an American Crystal Palace, superbly equipped, rich in plants and always imaginative in design.

Eclectic gardens, then, are common, but not the only gardens to be made. There are exceptions, though admittedly they are rare. And the derivative qualities of most gardens are not necessarily a bad thing, any more than the resemblance of a child to its parents.

Nineteenth-century gardening moved vigorously intact into the twentieth century. In the public domain, the enthusiasm for massed formal bedding continues to this day, with 'wedding cakes' and tiered fountains still plentiful along the promenades of seaside resorts. Such displays are also, almost inevitably, to be found

in many town or city parks both in Britain and Europe – London's Victoria Park has a particularly impressive expanse of massed bedding.

The villa Garzoni, at Collodi, still has its garish armorial bedding at the foot of the terraces; by the lake in Geneva, there is the floral clock; in France, at Bourg-en-Bresse, and not all that far from Geneva, there is a floral clog and across the square a floral cock (part of the town's heraldry). These last three I remember neatly bristling with sempervivums; while in Austria at Mirabell in Salzburg dwarf, pale pink begonias mimic the earlier parterre, and at Lunéville near Nancy the green of Stanislas' *compartiments de gazon* is now set off with salvias along the edge. (Salvias, incidentally, are extensively used in municipal gardening in Peking.) In England as I write, in Reading, polyanthus rule, at the Forbury gardens, on the roundabouts, and in parts of Caversham Court. Even the fairly genuine pattern of the knot garden at New Place in Stratford-on-Avon is bedded out, the spaces between the box strapwork stuffed and bulging with auriculas and dwarf hyacinths. Colourful, but not what Shakespeare saw. Tourists are rarely garden or plant historians, and the great majority are happy with anachronism, so long as it is gay.

THE MODERN RENAISSANCE GARDEN

Surviving more generally is the nineteenth-century version of the Italian Renaissance garden. Inigo Triggs's *Formal Gardens in England and Scotland*, already noted as an accurate record of Victorian gardens, also serves as a pointer for the continuing Italian tradition, seen at its purest and best in England at Renishaw in Derbyshire. Here Sir George Sitwell planned, laid out, considered, changed and rearranged the formal terraced garden to the south of Renishaw Hall over several decades, beginning in the late 1890s. His views on gardening are superbly expressed in his *Essay on the Making of Gardens* (1909) and as superbly recorded in the volumes of his son Sir Osbert Sitwell's autobiography. *On the Making of Gardens* is the best book in English on the nature of gardens since the days of Shenstone and

164   A fine detail in the gardens of Dumbarton Oaks, Washington. The gentle effect of the stairs has been achieved by planting grass over the broad treads. Any feeling of artificiality is dispelled by the generous width of the stairs, and their undemanding, leisurely ascent

Walpole. Though it deals mainly with the gardens of the Italian Renaissance, its considered asides on other gardens and styles give it a wider scope and authority; and the garden at Renishaw shows today the understanding of its creator. The central garden is geometrical, dropping away from the house in terraced lawns, and crossed by walks at right angles to the main axis. To counter the horizontal expanses of lawn, tall yew hedges mark the divisions of the garden. Their strong vertical effect is reinforced along the central axis by two massive pairs of statues, by the soaring central fountain jet, and by the woodland which rises up sombrely on each side of the formal garden. Since Sir George Sitwell's time, the bedding has been simplified – he objected vehemently to brightly coloured flowers, and Miss Jekyll is said to have made suggestions for tonal borders, two of which remain in the central lawn – and the hedges have grown. In *Left Hand, Right Hand!*, the first volume of his autobiography, Sir Osbert describes the gardens of Renishaw, and how he 'grew up, year by year, with its yew hedges'. And he adds: 'I never remember a time between the ages of three and seventeen when we were not the same height, though now they overtop me.'

Today the hedges are eight feet tall and their clipped and steeply sloping sides and level tops provide a grand control for the garden, leading the eye to statues or water, back to the battlemented house, or vistas beyond the ha-ha wall and across the open countryside. These hedges are reminiscent of those other yews, even taller and

165   The terraces at Dartington Hall. Round an ancient manor house, gardens entirely of this century have been designed, principally the creation of Percy Cane. These terraces, sharply cut like the grassy amphitheatre at Claremont, designed by Bridgeman in the eighteenth century, rise in six stages to a final viewing platform, on which a sculpture of a reclining woman by Henry Moore looks out over the Devon countryside

equally Italian in feeling, at Sandemar in Sweden; and while direct allusions at Renishaw to Italian gardens are many, one is reminded of the villa Garzoni, looking down past cross-walks formed in massy hedges, towards the thin, tall jets in circular pools. There are echoes too of the villa Lante, with its *bosco* to the left, and its terraces dropping downwards to the formal water garden, while allowing wider views outwards over the plain.

The Italian garden was the inspiration for a small garden made in this century, the work of Sir Clough Williams-Ellis around his home at Plas Bron Danw in North Wales. The house is set in the mountains, and their grandeur is glimpsed along the axes of the garden. Indeed the main hedge-lined axis appropriates the sharp peak of the 'Welsh Matterhorn', Cynicht, in the best Japanese manner of 'borrowed scenery', and at one point even jokes with it, where the jet of a small fountain seems to be rising from the tip of the mountain three miles to the north. Much use is made at Plas Bron Danw of dark granite, the local stone, which merges finely with the heavy green hedges and topiary. Contrast is achieved with statuary in lighter-coloured stone, and with the occasional introduction of light blue as a background for statues in dark or lichen-darkened materials. The openness of some parts of the garden, with sloping lawn and scattered orchard trees, prevents an over-artificial separation of the garden from the surrounding countryside. These trees are often tilted and shaped by the prevailing wind, and the formality of the tall and relatively narrow hedges is reassuring, leading to enclosed and intimate areas of flowers and to shadowy recesses gleaming with carved stone or the glint of water.

In Italy itself one triumphant example of the Renaissance-inspired garden has

166 William Robinson would have approved of this moss and water scene as a modern 'wild garden' of the most admirable kind, and just such abundant moss grows beneath the beech trees in the Savill garden in Windsor Great Park, created in the 1930s. Yet this garden, the Kokedera or moss garden of the Saiho-ji temple, Kyoto, was designed six centuries ago. It remains a continuing demonstration of the appeal of such 'natural' scenes

167 An overall view of the gardens of Vizcaya, in Florida. Created in the first decades of this century, these gardens combine the exuberance of semi-tropical vegetation with the equally exuberant yet disciplined qualities of the Italian Renaissance garden – lavishly carved stonework, abundant fountains and intricate detail in grottoes and the arabesque scrollwork of parterres

been created at the Papal country residence of Castelgandolfo, where the derelict gardens were wholly renovated from 1929 to 1933. Not all the gardening at Castelgandolfo is a success. There is no adequate centre, such as a mansion, a lake or a watercourse would normally provide, and in some parts the sight of wide metalled roads and lamp posts with climbing roses recalls a rather opulent cemetery. But one splendid feature, the largest, designed by Dr Emilio Bonomelli, is now after forty years in a state of perfect maturity. It is a parterre some 200 yards long, patterned in box in a strictly regular manner, and meant, as are all proper parterres, to be seen best from a commanding viewpoint. Here the parterre is overlooked at the eastern end by the Belvedere terrace, and along the northern side by a high balustraded wall. From the Belvedere the eye looks down on the two sides of the parterre to scan the walls, the globes and dividing-lines of box, the gravelled paths around, and the rectangular pond which gives breadth and substance to the first area of the parterre. Halfway along, there is a change of height, and the second section takes the eye farther away towards a wall of closely planted cypresses, whose deep, almost blackish green silhouettes a white statue at the end of the long central axis. 'Half way along', that is, from the viewpoint of the Belvedere. In fact, the proportions of the two sections of the parterre are so arranged as to make them look the same – the farther section actually being longer, a trifle thinner and with a more robust pattern than the nearer part. This audacious composition is faultlessly executed, with entire mastery over the proportions and the materials. The parterre runs east-west along the side of a hill, so that its horizontal balance is countered by the tall balustraded terrace, backed by a dense stand of holm oaks, to the north, and by the line of a low

257

terrace on the south side, marked and given lively colour by terracotta pots. Towards the farther end it is lifted upwards by thick cypresses, through which the plain – as in all good Italian gardens! – can be seen. This combination of a plan extending regularly in one direction, with a terrain which slopes across the direction of the plan, is reminiscent of the villa d'Este, where the side axes slope steeply across the regular downhill direction of the main central axis. At Castelgandolfo another magnificent and wholly traditional achievement is in the scene looking downhill and across the plain, from the same Belvedere terrace.

In the United States, the eclectic nature of many early twentieth-century gardens ensures – as it does in Britain – the existence of echoes and imitations of Italy. There is Filoli, for example, in California, designed in 1915, and maintained by only two proprietors until 1975, with an equally fortunate stability in the slow succession of head gardeners. This is a garden on the most lavish scale (the whole estate is over 700 acres in extent) and it has many sub-divisions, in a variety of styles; 'Japanese', 'Dutch', 'wild', 'kitchen', and so on. One area, the sizable 'walled garden', has six sections within its enclosure. But the framework of the garden is firm, and predominantly inspired by the geometrical control of the Italian Renaissance garden, with borders and hedges of box and myrtle, and avenues of stone pines or Irish yew. All is of the grandest and most spacious, and though individual areas have both intimacy and elegance, others have an Elizabethan 'sumptuousness' in the number and quality of flowering shrubs.

Because of its very size, Filoli is difficult to comprehend as an entity. A smaller and superlatively successful Italian garden is at Vizcaya, close to Miami in Florida. Though originally larger, it is now an estate of about thirty acres, of which the garden covers ten, and surrounding woodland the remainder. The buildings and gardens were designed and built between 1912 and 1916, and have as their inspiration the villas and gardens of Italy, modified, with genius, to suit the hotter, moister climate of Florida and to incorporate the indigenous and exotic plants now available. Architecturally it is a stone and water garden. The mansion resembles an Italian palace, with balustrades, stairs, stone-lined pools, urns, obelisks and sculpture. Facing the mansion, along the main axis, is a smaller pavilion, like an Italian casino. Water is abundant, for the garden was formed from a mangrove swamp on the coast. An inlet from the sea comes round behind the small casino on the south, and the east front of the mansion leads down to the sea itself. From the casino, elevated to look down on pools, lawn and parterre in the main axis, a double flight of steps descends beside a step-cascade. The steps are enclosed between rising walls, like the approach to the private casino, the villa Farnese, at Caprarola, and within the depths of these walls on either side are the elaborate arched entrances to a grotto. The curling scrollwork of the parterres, more French than Italian, is executed not in box but in jasmine (*J. simplicifolium*).

It is all immensely appealing – the Italians of the Renaissance would not have been

168   The stone boat at Vizcaya (left), which can be seen in the top right hand corner of pl. 167, is a fantasy midway between Bernini's Roman 'Barcaccia' and Isola Bella in Lake Maggiore

uneasy – and the exuberance of the fountains and sculpture is matched with the shapes and colours of mangroves, tulip trees, and varieties of palm. But the greatest achievement of Vizcaya is by the east front of the mansion, where the shore has been converted into a sea-wall. It curves round on either side like a shallow horseshoe and between the extremities of the 'horseshoe' a stone boat has been built, with plants growing vigorously at either end. This extravagant and beautiful creation is exactly in scale with the dimensions of the mansion and the gardens. Though only a fraction the size of Isola Bella, this stone boat is immediately seen to be a descendant, a cutter or a longboat belonging to that great galleon. It would be fascinating, and indeed amusing, to hear the opinions of Sir George Sitwell on Vizcaya (for he too had intended to build a stone boat in the lake below the formal gardens at Renishaw); and the opinions of James Deering, the owner of Vizcaya, and of Paul Chalfin and the others responsible for the design of the gardens, on the wholly un-tropical Italian garden of Renishaw. Here and there they might agree to differ; but they would all agree on the power and excitement of the Italian inspiration.

WILLIAM ROBINSON AND GERTRUDE JEKYLL

The other major influence coming from the nineteenth century is that of William Robinson and Gertrude Jekyll. Miss Jekyll (1843–1932) may even be considered as much of this century as of the last, like her friend and colleague Sir Edwin Lutyens (1869–1944).

One of the best Robinsonian gardens I have seen is in Holland, created in the past twenty years by Miss C. M. Cremers at Wassenaar. It is far smaller than, say, Robinson's own woodland garden at Gravetye Manor in Sussex, being essentially a woodland dell contrived round a small lake to the rear of the house. But it has a lightness of touch, a delicacy of colour and form and a naturalness which Robinson would acknowledge, with a fine integration of plant shapes into the overall design. Sometimes these 'wild' gardens are built on an old framework as at Pusey House, in Oxfordshire, where a Brownian landscape with lake and lawn and excellent ha-ha has been superbly planted over since 1935. The paved garden terrace was designed by Geoffrey Jellicoe, and in the garden as a whole there are now many discrete and separate areas, arboretum, water plants, heathers, roses, and one of the best curving herbaceous borders in England.

At Nuneham Courtenay there is not only the intimate eighteenth-century Flora's Garden hidden within the landscape, but a Robinsonian dell concealed just as effectively in a narrow, turning valley in the north-western area, between the church-temple and the Thames.

At Abbots Ripton, in Huntingdonshire, the late eighteenth-century garden has virtually disappeared apart from the pair of magnificent yew hedges which face the house across the lawn, and which divide at the central axis to show mixed bedding as exciting as that at Pusey. To one side a long silvery border, backed by a brick wall and faced by a line of *Cedrus arizonica glauca* has a tonal perfection which Gertrude Jekyll would have envied. The gardens at Abbots Ripton were designed by the late Humphrey Waterfield – there is a memorial to him near the eighteenth-century bridge – and are the best surviving example of his work.

At Sezincote, in Gloucestershire, there is a valley garden designed by Graham Thomas. It runs down the estate to one side of the house, with its stream descending in a sinuous, extended line from shell-surrounded grotto to narrow channel, cascade and bridge and snake-fountain, to a long and open stretch of grass, and to the calm pools at the foot. This valley garden is only 'Indian' in an occasional way, with a tiny temple, the bridge and the bull motif, and the three spitting snakes of the fountain. Elsewhere, it is simply a specimen of the Robinsonian wild garden at its best, using 'foreign' rather than indigenous plants and trees, from bamboos and gingko at the upper end to gunnera and – covering an entire island in the lowest pool – a prostrate juniper.

The cadence of this narrow and exotic glen is perfectly controlled, yet it is fragile and perishable. Graham Thomas also designed the admirable formal garden on the other side of the house, in an 'eastern' and geometrical style. We might reflect that,

169   A clematis-covered
archway at Hidcote in
Gloucestershire, where the
gardens were designed by
Lawrence Johnston in the early
years of the century, leads the eye
to the garden beyond. The chief
delight of these gardens lies in
their diversity and in the wealth of
lesser gardens and surprises

given a decade's neglect, the formal garden would survive, and could be restored, while the valley garden might, alas, go under. This has certainly been the fate of so many 'wild gardens' when the enthusiasm or the owner has gone.

The partnership of Lutyens and Jekyll extended to France, where at Bois des Moutiers, near Dieppe, Lutyens designed the house in 1898, and Gertrude Jekyll helped advise the owner, Guillaume Mallet, on the design of the gardens. Within the precincts of the house there are formal areas, with paving and tonal bedding (a white garden is especially good), while farther away, beyond a grassy terrace, is a 'wild' and woodland garden which is remarkable for its trees and shrubs, well planted to allow vistas towards the sea or back to the house.

Also in France, and unconsciously a part of the same movement led by William Robinson and Gertrude Jekyll, in which the plants themselves are the centre of interest, since their shapes, colours and characteristics are valued above the architectural qualities of the garden, is the garden of Claude Monet (1840–1926), the greatest of the Impressionists. In 1883 Monet moved to Giverny, on the Seine, midway between Paris and Rouen. With occasional intervals he lived there, painting scenes in and around the garden, for over forty years. Parts of his garden were arranged with a geometrical plan, but his paintings – the many versions of the 'Japanese bridge' over one part of the pool, or the symphonic series of *nympheas,* the water lilies, now exhibited in the Orangerie, in the garden of the Tuileries beyond the Louvre – describe views in the garden which are 'wild' in the Robinsonian sense. In the paintings of the *nympheas,* no garden borders appear, no artificial form or constraint; only the flowers, their leaves, the water, and the changing reflections of sky, clouds, flowers and leaves.

In the Jekyll-Lutyens tradition are the tiny but fine enclosed garden at West Wycombe, and the famous, much visited and lovely gardens of Hidcote, in Gloucestershire. Hidcote was begun and completed while Robinson, Jekyll and Lutyens were alive and flourishing. It was the work of a talented amateur, the American Lawrence Johnston, who began work on the site in 1905. Attached to a Cotswold manor house, the garden has a T-shaped framework, the main view from the house running along the top of the T, and a secondary axis coming down at right angles from the middle of the T. This framework is outlined with hedges of beech, holly, and at one point of hornbeam, sufficiently tall to control the garden, and to allow an immense variety of subdivisions in the areas between the two main axes.

In the tradition of Hidcote comes Sissinghurst in Kent, begun in 1930, the work of Sir Harold Nicolson and his wife Vita Sackville-West; and the garden of the lodge house at Badminton, designed by Russell Page. Each of these gardens, like Hidcote, has a multiplicity of divisions within the main plan; as Russell Page says of the garden at Badminton, 'a very decisive framework – all rectangles linked by narrow openings, forcing one to go and see what it is that lies beyond.' This characteristic use of a small, enclosed area for a tonal or single colour range, or for a single group of plants with only secondary backing from others, is the most permanent legacy of the Jekyll style, and is more likely to have lasting influence than the variety so often lacking form or firmness of the 'plantsman's garden'. Miss Jekyll's profound understanding of the qualities of plants is jokingly acknowledged in Ian Hamilton Finlay's re-use of the line from Gertrude Stein – 'A rose is a rose is a rose Gertrude Jekyll' – painted round a watering can.

PLANT GARDENS

Though most visitors to Bagatelle in Paris or Keukenhof in Holland will go there to see plants, in both cases they will enjoy them more because the settings are well planned. Bagatelle, in the decade before the Revolution, was planned and laid out for the Comte d'Artois by Bélanger and the Scotsman Thomas Blaikie, who also designed the garden landscape at Dyck in Germany. The fragments of the *jardin anglais* are no longer picturesque, having suffered after 1789, but in 1905 the house and gardens were bought by the city of Paris and were almost at once designated as a centre for horticultural and floral display – a French Kew. The area and existing features were then redeveloped with this in mind, and Bagatelle is now celebrated for

its rose garden, close to the pretty eighteenth-century orangery, for its specialist collections of narcissi and tulips, and for the magnificent trees and shrubs which are scattered through the erstwhile *jardin anglais*.

Keukenhof in Holland is more recent, more single-minded, more colourful. Canals frame the essentially level site, as they did the great gardens of seventeenth- and eighteenth-century Holland, and the design and development of the gardens are remarkably successful both in varying the landscape and in absorbing the tens of thousands of visitors who may come to the gardens on a single day in the spring and early summer. For Keukenhof is a display centre for plants: tulips, of course, but many other bulbs, such as hyacinths, narcissi, crocus, fritillaries, and other plants such as ericas and dwarf azaleas are also displayed. The flatness of the terrain is brilliantly disguised by banks of earth thrown up to vary the level and to split up the area, while stands of trees backing these banks, fountains and abstract sculpture provide more distracting verticals. The irregularly contoured lake serves to disperse the visitors and provides curved, sweeping and separate areas for the eighty or more permanent exhibitors to display their plants. It is probable that the pressure of commercial competition will ensure that Keukenhof remains a coherent, handsome and forcefully confident garden.

170   The main grass walk at Hidcote (above), framed between tall hedges. At the far end is one of the two summerhouses which mark the cross-axis of the gardens. This formal vista conceals the smaller and widely varied sections to left and right; indeed, by the steps in the foreground, a steeply-banked stream crosses the path, forming an unexpected, irregular and 'wild' area

171, 172   Sissinghurst – two views (above and right) illustrating the variety achieved within this remarkable modern garden. As at Hidcote and at Cranborne, the planning of the gardens at Sissinghurst Castle in Kent involves the skilful subdivision of the whole into a wide diversity of garden areas. These allow intimacy, as in the brick-paved arbour, where roses climb freely over the trunks of larger trees, many of them old orchard apples; wider prospects, along the lime walk, and, above all, the creation of a garden in which one part or several will be beautiful at every time of the year

Plant gardens can change rapidly if they have only a moderate or lightweight framework. In his *Education of a Gardener*, Russell Page described the 'astonishing achievement of Sir Eric Savill' in creating the Savill gardens in Windsor Great Park, which he considers 'the best existing example of current English gardening'. Elsewhere he writes less enthusiastically of the Royal Horticultural Society's garden at Wisley, in Surrey, which he finds 'a series of charming incidents beautifully gardened but incoherent and unrelated to the site'. That was in 1962: today the positions of these gardens are reversed. Wisley, after another sixteen years' solid and thoughtful development, hangs together well, while the Savill gardens, begun in 1932, have somehow lost their coherence. Plants on their own, whether giants or dwarfs, however rare or grand or beautiful, do not make a garden. In my own herb garden the sixty or so kinds fascinate me with the beauty of their leaves and the oddity of their uses, but they do not *ipso facto* constitute a garden, any more than would a single *Metasequoia glyptostroboides* or a collection of bromeliads. Kew, Bagatelle, Wisley, Keukenhof and the Savill gardens make this clear.

173   Bagatelle, on the outskirts of Paris. Once celebrated for its 'jardin anglais', designed by Bélanger and Blaikie just before the Revolution, Bagatelle now has several areas in formal styles, like this nineteenth-century *allée* with box hedging in geometrical curves, backing displays of tulips, and a line of light metal archways shrouded in wistaria – a plant not introduced to Europe until 1816. Bagatelle is now also a centre for floral exhibitions

RECONSTRUCTED GARDENS

Two groups or categories of gardens have not seriously been attempted until relatively recent times: those that have been restored and reconstructed in a historically accurate manner, and sculpture-gardens.

The first group can be found in many countries, and their degree of authenticity, and hence success, depends usually on the documentation available to the restorers

174   The main lake within the gardens of Keukenhof in the Netherlands. Primarily designed for the display of tulips and daffodils by scores of different growers, these gardens are a brilliant example of landscape design, achieving variety, concealment and surprise in a terrain which is essentially as level as that which dictated the rectilinear gardens of the seventeenth century

or on the state of dilapidation of the original garden.

One of the earliest and most famous reconstructions is in France, at Villandry in Touraine, where Dr Joachim Carvallo recreated a complex sixteenth-century scheme in the area round the château. Dr Carvallo bought the property in 1906, when all trace of the original garden had gone, and no records of it survived. The gardens of Villandry are therefore a reconstruction based on the numerous designs of du Cerceau, published in the 1570s, to show what sort of gardens such a château might have had. One may question several of the interpretations: the general use of box for edging, the *art nouveau* curves of the patterning in the flower gardens, and the occasional anachronism in the choice of flowers and vegetables. But these are minor criticisms beside the overall achievement, which has been an inspiration to subsequent restorers.

Elsewhere in Europe, damage caused during World War II has led to wholesale or partial reconstruction of gardens, at the Zwinger in Dresden, for example, at Ludwigsburg near Stuttgart, in the garden of the Residenz at Würzburg, and to a lesser extent at the villa Lante at Viterbo.

In Britain, the restorations have usually been on a smaller scale – the best, most successful and authentic being at Edzell in Scotland, where the tiny square enclosure beside the castle keep had a garden in 1604, but where all trace of the garden had gone for decades when the Government took it over in 1932. As at Villandry, a totally new but historical reconstruction has been attempted, a knot garden of a generally rectilinear design with modest scrollwork appropriate for the early 1600s. The only anachronism (minute, sensitive and entirely acceptable!) is the spotting of

269

red from *Tropaeolum speciosum* which twines through the central drum of yew. Tropaeolums – nasturtiums or 'Indian flowers' – only reached Europe in the 1570s, and *T. speciosum* was introduced to Britain from Chile in 1847!

Also in Scotland, not far from Edzell, is the restored garden of Pitmedden House. The garden made in the 1670s had gone, but the extensive box-edged beds were redesigned in 1955 with patterns considered appropriate to the original. The patterns themselves and the box edgings are convincing. The detail of the scrollwork of box and lavender, combined with contrasting gravel, is the best in Britain. But the flowers used inside the larger beds are both anachronistic and, particularly the throbbing orange of the tagetes, difficult to admire. Pitmedden is administered by the National Trust for Scotland, and the National Trust has played an important role in garden conservation and restoration throughout Britain.

By far the most enterprising, extensive and fascinating restoration work has taken place in the United States, at Williamsburg, the colonial capital of Virginia. Here garden after garden has been remade in the colonial style of the early 1700s. Plans, journals, plant lists, contemporary garden books, and physical excavations have been used to achieve results which are staggering in their thoroughness, both in detail and general effect. In 1930-1 major excavations took place in the region of the Governor's Palace, and in 1964 and 1968 excavations were made in the garden

175 Looking north over the *jardin d'ornement* towards the château at Villandry (above). Dr Joachim Carvallo's garden is imaginatively based on French Renaissance designs, but there is a sense of overall unity and control far stronger than in the original French gardens of the period

LIII A genial climate and a perfect site have helped in the creation of the garden at Ninfa, in Italy, a 'wild garden' in William Robinson's sense, where plants of all kinds, homely and exotic, may grow freely in natural situations

176 The great lime avenue at Villandry (right) runs from east to west, and provides a firm axis for the gardens, on which both the *jardin d'ornement* and the equally formal *potager* are based

LIV From the terraces below the castle at Powis (top left), the view is partly closed by the parallel bank and the sizable stand of trees; but it opens briefly to allow a glimpse of the countryside beyond the urn in the centre of this picture. Though only a small part of the scene, the urn serves as an 'eye-catcher' from this part of the gardens, rather like Brown's modest temple beside the lake at Bowood (pl. 141)

LV A garden in Brasilia (left) designed by Burle Marx – indoors, and yet out of doors. Where a medieval cloister garden was closed in with walls, but open to the sky, this garden is enclosed completely, with a surrounding colonnade and with beams crossing over the top; yet the light enters freely from the open sides and the roof. The distant view and the open sky are both parts of the composition. The attitude goes back to the Italian Renaissance – but the architecture and the plants are firmly in the New World

region of John Custis's house. The findings from these and other researches have been described in an illuminating small book by A. N. Hume, *Archaeology and the Colonial Gardener* (1974). In this, flowerpots, tools, seeds, twigs and leaf-cuttings from plants in a disused well, postholes in the ground marking the line of the fence, ashes and gravel marking the paths, bell-glasses for forcing, watering pots and cans, and stone and cast-iron rollers are discussed. With such enquiries afoot, the restored gardens of Williamsburg could be more 'authentic' than the eighteenth-century gardens of Europe, continuously maintained and as continuously changed, little by little, with the passing of time.

SCULPTURE

Sculpture has appeared in gardens from early times, often with a religious purpose. It was an important feature in the gardens of the Romans, and Renaissance gardens proudly displayed the Roman sculptures which had been rediscovered. Lord Burlington's villa at Chiswick displayed statues in the *exedra* which he had acquired from Hadrian's villa near Tivoli, while baroque and rococo gardens generally had

statues, grave or gay, to reinforce the classical allusions of the architecture. But in the twentieth century a handful of gardens exist in which the display of sculpture, or of sculptural or architectural objects, is the principal concern. In the Netherlands, there is the garden of Kröller-Müller at Hoge Veluwe, while in Britain the two most notable sculpture gardens display the work of Henry Moore and Ian Hamilton Finlay. Henry Moore has placed various of his sculptures in the grounds of his home in Hertfordshire, and Ian Hamilton Finlay has done the same with his works, sited in the wilder and more picturesque garden of Stonypath, south-west of Edinburgh. Finlay's garden is far more integrated, since his creations are a conscious and repeated expression of a poetry which makes itself felt through several media and several craftsmen: *idea,* from Finlay (derived, it may be, from one or more earlier sources), carried into a solid, usually sculptured *form* by another craftsman, *sited* in some chosen and adapted garden spot, and individually received and *appreciated* in its (more or less constant) intellectual and (constantly changing) visual and physical forms by each new visitor. Such is the case with 'The Great Piece of Turf', an echo and image of Dürer's watercolour, 'Das grosse Rasenstück', where Finlay has set a stone inscribed with Dürer's characteristic monogram among a boggy group of rushes, reeds and grasses; or – most cogent in this history of gardens – the 'Elegiac Inscription', a stone inscribed (by John Andrew) '*See* POUSSIN *Hear* LORRAIN', and placed before a tiny landscape which, with wind, weather and time of day, invites the *participant* in this scene to seek the sense and spirit of Finlay's words.

Gardens of this kind are liable to criticism, and collapse like the plantsman's paradise if they are not rigorously maintained, and if their original design lacks coherence. An intriguing and tragic instance of this is in France, in the park at Groussay, where Emilio Terry designed several of the garden buildings for the late Charles de Bestegui. These buildings have a surrealistic oddness reminiscent not only of the architectural fantasies of Ledoux, but of the sculptural monsters at Bomarzo in their unconnected or weirdly juxtaposed woodland situation. Such is now the case at Groussay, where the grounds appear neglected and shaggily overgrown, and where a brick and stone pyramid with a waterfall gushing from its side confronts a Palladian bridge; where a tiny pavilion stands naked and alone on a grassy mound; and where an iron 'Turkish tent' (copied from the one at Drottningholm, or maybe from pictures of the one which was at Retz), wholly lined inside with blue and white tiles from Delft, stands facing an obelisk in a murky pond, which has Ali-Baba-sized Chinese jars at the corners.

178 The permanent exhibition in the gardens of the Kröller-Müller Museum at Otterloo in the Netherlands is one of the most striking of modern sculpture gardens. Here, the level and tranquil planes of water and grass contrast with the 'Floating Sculpture' by Martha Pau, the 'Song of Vowels' by Jacob Lipchiz and 'The Shepherd of the Clouds' by Jean Arp

TWENTIETH-CENTURY GARDENS

I want now to concentrate on modern gardens which are both thoroughly of this century, and thoroughly good. In a slightly artificial way, they can be divided roughly into two groups – those which begin with an older framework and those which begin more nearly from scratch – though they are all descended from the great and common mixture of wild and formal which this book has described.

Begun in 1875, the gardens at Bodnant in North Wales have been developed over most of a century by the first Lord Aberconway and his son, and by the talented gardeners of the Puddle family. For many visitors, the rhododendrons and azaleas (some hybrids actually developed at Bodnant) are the strongest attraction. There is a covered laburnum walk, and a secluded rock and water garden. But to me the triumph of Bodnant is its sequence of five great open terraces descending in front of the house towards the prospect of the river Conway and the mountains of Snowdonia beyond. This is 'borrowed scenery' indeed, and the scale and dignity of the terraces, designed by the second Lord Aberconway, responds to the grandeur of the scenery. Each terrace is different, in height, in outline, and in its horticultural and architectural components. Each is deep enough to mask in part what lies below, so that the descent is a series of lavish surprises. At the top, one is conscious of the house, with paving-stones extending its domain. Beyond, one sees a semi-circular pool, and lawn; beyond and below that, another pool, shaded by gigantic cedars. At the sides, intricate pergolas descend, twined round by wistaria, and then come together to make a rounded front and covered promenade for a lower terrace. Stretching the entire width of the terrace is the long rectangular canal, with the Pin Mill at one end, and a theatre of tall clipped yew at the other, through which one reaches the specialist gardens of flowers and shrubs.

Both Bodnant and Powis Casle (also in Wales, near Welshpool) are maintained by the National Trust; and though some may find Bodnant more to their taste, for me Powis is today the most beautiful garden in Britain. Its setting, like Bodnant's, is spacious and hilly; it has a good selection of flowering shrubs, and it may be

considered a 'terrace garden'. But there the resemblance stops. Powis is nowhere near as immense as Bodnant, and its framework is both older, more marked, and more enclosed. Below the old castle, a red sandstone mass high on the skyline, a steep terraced garden was built in the late seventeenth century, with brick walls, carved stone balustrades, urns and statuary, some in lead and of high quality (a group of shepherds and shepherdesses, some playing instruments, some dancing). Set within one of the terraces is an orangery.

Of the original bedding and planting at Powis, nothing but yews – such yews! – remains. The yews, on the highest terrace, must have begun like those at Hampton Court, as modest cones or globes, but now they tower over the wall, swelling and flowing like dark green castles. Below them, the narrow south-facing terraces extend the whole width of the garden, and have been planted to perfection with climbers, roses and magnolias, and with shrubs and bedding plants. This terrace area descends to a broad lawn, bounded by hedges at each end, and faced by a narrow, sheltering ridge which runs parallel with the terraces. The lawn is thus enclosed on three sides by the terraces and the encircling arm of the ridge. Up on the ridge there is a woodland area, planted with fine trees and rhododendrons. The planting is interrupted opposite the centre of the trees to allow a cutting, marked by an urn, and a view through to the distant countryside. At the open end of the valley the gardens

continue with tall zigzags of box going down to an area still being developed, with formally trained apple trees in lines, a vine pergola, and a mountain far off to complete the view.

Powis, though it has no flowing water, and only one woodland pool, is in feeling much like the villa d'Este at Tivoli. Its success comes from the similar pleasure one feels in walking the terraces, coming from one delight down to another, while enjoying the continual attraction, the appeal, of the other parts of the garden – the lawn in the valley, the eye-catching urn up on the ridge, the hedges and pergola and rows of apple-tree cones in the kitchen garden beyond the lawn. Walking the ridge to the other side of the valley, one has an ever-changing view of the terraces, now revealed, now hidden by the bushes and coloured leaves of acers, and the undulating domes of yew which lip smoothly over the topmost terrace next to the castle walls. How might one feel if the villa d'Este were planted in this way?

Almost as successful, in my estimation, is Cranborne in Dorset. Here, round an Elizabethan mansion far more beautiful than Powis, the garden is split up into hedges and distinct sections, some of great age. A mount is supposed to have been designed by John Tradescant in the seventeenth century, and the kitchen garden is easily as old. But the continuous care of the gardens dates only from the mid-nineteenth century, and their present beauty has been achieved in the last two decades. Not every part of Cranborne has an equal appeal. The bedding round the mount, for example, seems confused, and the stream and water garden is still too new. But the lines of fruit trees facing the great loggia are exactly harmonious in tone and scale. The knot garden, walled on three sides and with low box pillars on the fourth, is the best in the world. The long arching lime avenue, like that at St Paul's Walden Bury, is a yearly excitement as the leaves and twigs burst out and shade the walk; and the sprinkling of small flowers – crocus and fritillary, cowslip and anemone around the beech tree (a girth like Falstaff's) – would wring approval from the crusty William Robinson.

Other modern gardens have such moments, and it would be churlish to deny them a word. Crathes Castle near Banchory in Scotland has, like Cranborne, a modern, firmly divided garden round a towering ancient house. I like the formal pool and hedge garden best, while others remember the separate 'colour' gardens, echoes of the Jekyll theme. In the south of England, at Barnsley House in Gloucestershire, a Cotswold manor house has two and a half acres of varied garden scenes, created since the 1950s by Mr and Mrs Verey. Beside Bodnant, this is a miniature; but with understanding two acres can seem a world, and hold like Cranborne or Crathes separate and successful gardens. Barnsley has outstanding borders, a laburnum walk which vies with Bodnant, and the recent addition of a knot garden.

These gardens all have a framework, a plan, and most often a firming, reassuring support from the house. Gardens are just not plants, not architecture either, but inextricably both. This is true even of the newest gardens, though they come straight from the woods, and are still earthy behind the ears. Let us finish with a handful of modern gardens which are wholly new – or more or less so, for history abhors an absolute – and made in the last thirty or forty years.

To Italy, for the most beautiful of all modern gardens, to Ninfa, fifty miles south of Rome, begun by the Duchess of Sermoneta and her son Prince Caetani in 1922. Imagine an immense amphitheatre of mountainous cliffs, miles across and a thousand feet tall. Imagine a plain, watered by the clearest of rivers, the *Nympheus* of Roman times, and in the plain, fertile soil and a climate which says 'Grow!'. Imagine a castle keep, and the ruins of a medieval town, gate-towers and walls and doorways, the lines of buried streets and buildings. Make here a garden, using the exotic and shapely, colourful and varied plants the world has released in the last two centuries: giant bamboos from the east, acers from Canada, gunneras from Brazil, climbing roses and tall palm-like acanthus from Italy itself. Frame them against straight yet crumbling antique walls; contrast them with the minute shapes and rainbow colours of countless eschscholtzias grown in the walls themselves, with creepers and mosses and ferns along the shaded aqueducts; mirror them in the water of the river; outline them against the sky and mountains far away. It is a modern form of Poe's Domain of Arnheim, or of the garden set in Roman ruins at Hohenheim; but unlike these, it is real, it succeeds.

A smaller, but similar garden, made in the last ten years by Mr and Mrs Twyman, is at Kazaphani on the north coast of Cyprus. The Kyrenia mountains are on one side, on the other the sea. The house gives a human scale to this prospect, and at the same time takes brilliance from climbing bougainvillea, now naturalized in Cyprus and elsewhere in the Mediterranean, though only introduced to Europe from South America in the 1820s. Horizontal form is given by paths and irrigation channels, vertical strength by palm, olive and bead trees (*Melia azederach*), and by the mountains beyond.

South American plants, with their striking and often almost architectural shapes, play an important part in the gardens of Roberto Burle Marx. In particular, this amazingly versatile Brazilian architect, sculptor, painter, stage designer and above all landscape gardener is fascinated by Heliconia, relatives of the banana family, and in the course of several expeditions into the interior he has brought back no fewer than ten previously unknown species. If the Italians of the Renaissance brought their gardens into the house by decorating the walls with flowers, leaves and birds, Burle Marx reverses the process by bringing the architectural forms of modern Brazil into the garden, where beds of ground cover plants – deep pink, ochre, red or silver – in firm, swirling arabesques or bold squares echo and complement the shape of the buildings. More than any other gardens described here, those of Burle Marx are wholly of the twentieth century, owing more to cubist art than to any preceding style of landscape gardening, and wholly American.

Owing more to past traditions, in this case the old Spanish gardens, are the small gardens of America, and especially of southern California. It has been impossible to give more than an occasional glance at small gardens, whether those of Swiss farmers or the Victorian middle classes, but these must be mentioned. They are often a combination of room and garden, where facilities for cooking and entertaining play as large a part as the plants. The delights of Pliny's villa gardens or the Sultaniye

181 At Ninfa, in Italy, the mountains come halfway round, while the fertile plain (reclaimed from level marshland) stretches far in the other direction – contrast on a magnificent scale. The vertical plumes of cypresses and the occasional straight lines of partly-hidden streets provide internal order in this, the most beautiful of all 'wild' gardens. The garden covers the site of a long-abandoned medieval town, of which little remains beyond two towers and a few walls

kiosk were for the privileged few; now, in a more democratic world, the joys of garden entertaining are brought within reach of the majority. Social change is also reflected in the choice of plants: in the days of cheap labour, the Victorian middle-class gardener could afford luxuriant and time-consuming flowerbeds; the modern American gardener, in contrast, has turned to minimum care plants, such as palms, which will look attractive all the year round, and in particular to drought-resistant plants from South America or Australia which can be left to fend for themselves when the family is on holiday.

But to return to the old world, and to large gardens – in Holland, the modern part of the garden behind the old castle of Wildenborch is outstanding. Apart from formal areas, with a lovely curved and covered arbour round copies of Bernini's *Apollo and Daphne* – divided, as they are at the villa Garzoni, I suppose to make the pursuit more poignant – there is a landscape garden which contrives a brilliant synthesis of Brownian lawn and lake with the simplest of rose pergolas beside the water, more Jekyll than Repton. There is a small 'secret lake' approached through a summer house and surrounded by beech hedges; and aligned on a different side of the house from the main lawn, a long vista framed by sections of beech hedge, allowing both the full prospect and the temptation of separate enclosures to visit as one walks along. This harks to Hidcote in England or to Veitshöchheim near Würzburg, or to the vast axial *allées* of Versailles, where the parallel lines of trees are crossed by other avenues, and the crossings are marked, and made interesting, by the fountains of the Seasons.

This sounds ponderous, but Wildenborch is notable for the lightness, the delicacy with which this strength is used. This is true, and just as vital, in two gardens designed by Russell Page, one English and one American: the smaller area round Coombe Priory, in Dorset, and the woodland lake at Kiluna farm on Long Island. At Coombe, Page's treatment resembles that of the garden at Ninfa, but in a less exuberant climate. The limestone house looks out to a long and steeply rising site, narrowing and hemmed in by trees at the top. Near to the house is a sunken lawn, with a raised terrace divided by steps in the centre. The steps lead upwards to the higher part of the garden, and to further lawn. Most modern gardens would capitulate to the slope, and treat it merely as rockery, which would be 'natural', possibly beautiful in its detail, but shapeless overall. At Coombe, however, the rectangular quality of the sunken garden has been made stronger by planting a pair of clipped box drums on the raised corners of the steps, and by broadening the beds, both on the level of the sunken lawn and on the upper slope of the terrace. Apart from the yews, the planting is not symmetrical or formal, but the underlying effect is to extend the formal control of the house farther into the garden, and so to gain coherence in a quiet and effective way.

At Kiluna, owned by Mr and Mrs William S. Paley, the relatively formal and traditional gardens have been extended and made exceptionally beautiful by the creation of a woodland lake to the rear of the house. In a hollow in the woodland a fair-sized lake was made, and surrounded by a band of lawn, then by low plants and bushes, and finally by the taller trees of the wood. From the house, the lake is hidden by a rising bank, and by growths of rhododendron, juniper and taller trees. This may sound little more than 'a lake in a wood', but Mr Page has done much more. The lake is perfectly oval, with a clearly marked outline, and the long axis of the oval is aligned with the two main entrances to the glade surrounding the lake. The lawn forms a concentric oval around the lake, and the levels and thickness of the adjacent plants and bushes form a further controlled and rising outer oval framework. This is, therefore, an exercise of the most difficult kind, the achievement of a symmetry which is felt, but concealed; which controls, but is not obvious.

At Kiluna the lake itself is symmetrical, but the apparently free-growing azaleas and dogwood, and the varied and abundant ground cover distract one's thought, as do the irregular reflections of trees and blossom in the water. In a lesser way, the steps leading down from the house-approach to the lake achieve the same effect: they are regular, broad and symmetrical, but their authority is disguised by the width of the treads, and, as at Dumbarton Oaks, by the grass which covers them.

This success at Kiluna is like that at Courances in France, where the symmetry of the great formal *bassin* is softened by the rounded and tumbling exuberance of the chestnuts which stand near its banks. The symmetry is essential, yet we hardly notice. 'Ars celare artem', we were told at school: 'the task of art is to conceal art.' Yet if there were no art to conceal then our gardens would not be gardens, but a jumble and a wilderness, and as Shenstone put it: 'night, gothicism, confusion and absolute chaos' would come again.

*   *   *

This history goes back three thousand years, and it will continue for a while yet. Old motifs will be used again, and forgotten or neglected plants or plans will be rediscovered; new styles, new attitudes, new interests and necessities will increase the stock of garden themes. In England, at Abbots Ripton, a grotto in the Italian style has just been designed, and a lake which did not exist when I began this book is to be adorned with a version of the Sibyl's temple from Tivoli – the most beautiful of all garden buildings. At the university of Düsseldorf, in Germany, a botanic garden is being built which incorporates modern and Renaissance ideas, to respond to requirements which are both new, yet as ancient as science itself.

Tradition and innovation, an old story endlessly renewed. Gardens are one of the best stories – the sort we read again and again.

BIBLIOGRAPHY

This brief list only mentions works published or republished since the 1870s. The books are grouped in the following categories: General; Plants; Classical Gardens; Medieval Gardens; Australia; Britain; China; France; Germany; Ireland; Italy; Japan; Persian and Islamic Gardens; Switzerland; and United States.

GENERAL

CLIFFORD, Derek *A History of Garden Design* 1966

GOTHEIN, Marie-Luise *Die Geschichte der Gartenkunst* 1914, tr. 1928 as *A History of Garden Art* (the first solid general history, still good on the sixteenth and seventeenth centuries)

ROHDE, Eleanour Sinclair *The Story of the Garden* 1932 (contains a 32pp bibliography of works on gardening up to the 1830s)

TRIGGS, H. Inigo *Garden Craft in Europe* 1913

The periodicals *Country Life* (1897-) and *Garden History* (1972-) contain many valuable items on aspects of garden history – gardens, gardeners, plant introductions and the like.

PLANTS

COATS, Alice M. *Flowers and their Histories* 1956
  Garden Shrubs and their Histories 1963 (Miss Coats is the *doyenne* of plant historians; her knowledge is deep and extensive and her style felicitous – a rare conjunction)

HARVEY, John H. *Early Gardening Catalogues* 1972
  Early Nurserymen 1974

HUI LIN LI *The Garden Flowers of China* 1959

KEIMER, Ludwig *Die Gartenpflanzen im alten Ägypten* 1924, 1967

LEMMON, Kenneth *The Golden Age of Plant Hunters* 1959

OLDENBURGER-EBBERS, C.S. and HENIGER, J. *Ornamental Plants in 16th and 17th Century Gardens* 1975

CLASSICAL GARDENS

AELIAN *Of the Characteristics of Animals* tr. A.F. Scholfield 1959

ATHENAEUS *The Deipnosophists* tr. C. B. Gulick 1927-41

CATO and VARRO *On Agriculture* tr. W.D. Hooper and H.B. Ash 1954

COLUMELLA *On Agriculture* tr. H.B. Ash 1941-55

Diodorus of Sicily tr. C.H. Oldfather 1933-

GRIMAL, Pierre *Les Jardins Romains* 1943, 1969

HERO OF ALEXANDRIA *Pneumatica* tr. Bennett Woodcroft (1851) 1971

HERODOTUS *The Histories* tr. A.D. Godley 1950-61

HOMER *The Homeric Hymns* tr. H.G. Evelyn-White 1936
  The Odyssey tr. E.V. Rieu 1959

JULIAN *Works* tr. W.C. Wright 1913-23

LONGUS *Daphnis and Chloe* tr. Moses Hadas 1953

OVID *Fasti* tr. J.G. Frazer 1921

PLINY THE ELDER *Natural History* tr. H. Rackham and W.H.S. Jones 1949-

PLINY THE YOUNGER *Letters* tr. Betty Radice 1969

SIDONIUS *Poems and Letters* tr. W.B. Anderson 1936, 1965

TANZER, Helen *The Villas of Pliny the Younger* 1924

THACKER, Christopher 'The Temple of the Sibyl' *Park und Garten in 18 Jahrhundert* 1978

THEOKRITUS *Idylls* tr. Barris Mills 1963

THEOPHRASTUS *Enquiry into Plants* tr. Sir Arthur Hort 1948-9

XENOPHON *Memorabilia and Oeconomicus* tr. E.C. Marchant 1923

MEDIEVAL GARDENS

BOCCACCIO, G. *The Decameron* tr. G.H. McWilliam 1973
CRISP, Sir Frank *Medieval Gardens* 1924
The Goodman of Paris (Le Menagier de Paris) tr. Eileen Power 1928
PEARSALL, D. A. and SALTER, E. *Landscapes and Seasons of the Medieval World* 1973
The Romaunt of the Rose and Le Roman de la Rose: a Parallel Text Edition ed. R. Sutherland 1967
STRABO, Walafrid *Hortulus* tr. R.S. Lambert 1924, also tr. Raef Payne 1966
WILKINS, Eithne *The Rose-Garden Game* 1969

AUSTRALIA

BLIGH, Beatrice *Cherish the Earth: the Story of Gardening in Australia* 1973

BRITAIN

ALLEN, B. Sprague *Tides in English Taste, 1619-1800* 1937, 1958
AMHERST, Alicia M.T. *A History of Gardening in England* 1895 (still excellent up to 1600)
BECK, Thomasina *Embroidered Gardens* 1978
BLAIKIE, Thomas, ed. Francis Birrell *Diary of a Scottish Gardener* 1931
BLOMFIELD, Sir Reginald *The Formal Garden in England* 1892
CHASE, Isabel W. *Horace Walpole: Gardenist* 1943 (contains an edition of Walpole's *History of the Modern Taste in Gardening*)
COLE, Nathan *The Royal Parks and Gardens of London* 1877
DESMOND, R.G.C. 'Victorian Horticulture: a Guide to the Literature' *Garden History* Vol 2 (Summer 1977)
The Diary of John Evelyn ed. William Bray (1818) 1945
The Garden Book of Sir Thomas Hanmer ed. Eleanour Sinclair Rhode 1935
HADFIELD, Miles *Gardening in Britain* 1960
A History of British Gardening 1969 (a solid reference work for most periods)
HELLYER, Arthur G.L. *The Shell Guide to Gardens* 1977
HENRY, Blanche *British Botanical and Horticultural Literature before 1800* 3 vols, 1975
HONOUR, Hugh *Chinoiserie: the Vision of Cathay* 1961
HUNT, John Dixon *The Figure in the Landscape: Poetry, Painting and Gardening during the Eighteenth Century* 1976
HUNT, John Dixon and WILLIS, Peter *The Genius of the Place: the English Landscape Garden 1620-1840* 1965 (a rich and indispensable anthology of basic texts)
HUNT, Peter ed. *The Shell Gardens Book* 1964 (an essential companion volume to the *Shell Guide*)
HUSSEY, Christopher *English Gardens and Landscapes 1700-1750* 1967 (a balanced, erudite and beautifully illustrated study)
JEKYLL, Gertrude *Wood and Garden* 1899
JOHNS, William Earle *The Passing Show* 1937 (typical of the period – preoccupied with plants and neglecting design)
JONES, Barbara *Follies and Grottoes* 1953, enlarged 1974
LOUDON, Jane *The Ladies' Companion to the Flower Garden* (1841) 1879
LOUDON, John Claudius *An Encyclopaedia of Gardening* (1822) 1871
MALINS, Edward *English Landscaping and Literature, 1660-1840* 1965
MANWARING, Elizabeth *Italian Landscape in Eighteenth-Century England* 1925, 1965
PAGE, Russell *The Education of a Gardener* 1962, 1971 (a modest yet impressive survey of the author's experience and achievement)
ROBINSON, William *The English Flower Garden* 1883
The Wild Garden 1870
RØSTVIG, Maren Sophie *The Happy Man* 1962-71 (an essential study of the theme of rural retirement in Britain)
SCOTT-JAMES, Anne and LANCASTER, Osbert *The Pleasure Garden* 1977
SELLAR, W.C. and YEATMAN, R.J. *Garden Rubbish* 1936 (a joyous satire on contemporary garden folly)
SITWELL, Sir George *Essay on the Making of Gardens* 1909, 1951 (experience, authority and poetry – unequalled in this century)
STROUD, Dorothy *Capability Brown* 1950, enlarged 1975
Humphrey Repton 1962
THACKER, Christopher 'England's Kubla Khan' *William Beckford Exhibition 1976* 1976
Masters of the Grotto: Joseph and Josiah Lane 1976
TRIGGS, H. Inigo *Formal Gardens in England and Scotland* 1902 (superb and detailed plans and photographs)
WHITE, Gilbert *Gardeners Kalendar* 1975 (facsimile ed.)
WOODBRIDGE, Kenneth *Landscape and Antiquity . . . Stourhead 1718 to 1838* 1970

CHINA

AYSCOUGH, Florence 'The Chinese Idea of a Garden' *A Chinese Mirror* 1925

BEURDELEY, C. and M. *Giuseppe Castiglione: a Jesuit Painter at the Court of the Chinese Emperors* tr. M. Bullock 1972

BOYNTON, Grace M. 'Notes on the Origin of Chinese Private Gardens' *The China Journal* July 1935

CAO XUEQUIN *The Story of the Stone* tr. David Hawkes 1973

CHANG, H.C. *Chinese Literature* 1973

CHUIN TUNG 'Chinese Gardens' *T'ien Hsia Monthly* October 1936

DANBY, Hope *The Garden of Perfect Brightness* 1950

INN, Henry and SHAO CHANG LEE *Chinese Houses and Gardens* 1940, 1950

KOTEWALL, R. and SMITH, N.L., tr. *The Penguin Book of Chinese Verse* 1970

MAI-MAI SZE *The Tao of Painting* 1957 (with a translation of the *Chieh Tzu Yuan Hua Chuan*, cf. Petrucci)

MALONE, C.B. *History of the Peking Summer Palaces of the Ch'ing Dynasty* 1934

PETRUCCI, R. ed. and tr. *Kiai-Tseu-Yuan Houa Tchouan, Les Enseignements de la Peinture* 1918 (cf. MAI-MAI SZE)

POLO, Marco *The Travels* tr. R. Latham 1958

SIRÉN, Osvald *The Gardens of China* 1949 (the first and still the best survey of this immense subject)

WEN CHENG-MING *An Old Chinese Garden* ed. and tr. Kate Kerby 1922

WALEY, Arthur *One Hundred and Seventy Chinese Poems* 1969
    Yuan Mei: Eighteenth-Century Chinese Poet 1956

FRANCE

CHARLES, Le Prince de Ligne *Coup d'Oeil sur Beloeil* ed. E. de Ganay (1781) 1922

DE GANAY, E. *Les Jardins de France* 1949 (detailed if crowded survey)

DE NOLHAC, Pierre *Versailles et la Cour de France* 1925-30

DU CERCEAU, Jacques Androuet *Les Plus Excellents Bastiments de France* (1576-9) 1972

GWYNN, Stephen *Claude Monet and His Garden* 1934, 1936

JOSEPHSON, Ragnar *L'Architecte de Charles XII, Nicodème Tessin, à la Cour de Louis XIV* 1930

LOUIS XIV 'La Manière de Montrer les Jardins de Versailles' tr. Christopher Thacker *Garden History* vol I, 1, September 1972 (a translation of successive texts of Louis XIV's instructions to subordinates taking visitors round the gardens)

MARIE, Alfred *Jardins Français Classiques des XVIIIe et XVIIIe Siècles* 1949
    Jardins Français Créés à la Renaissance 1955

MARIE, J. and Alfred *Marly* 1947

THACKER, Christopher 'Voltaire and Rousseau: Eighteenth-Century Gardeners' *Studies on Voltaire* XC 1972

VERLET, Pierre *Versailles* 1961

GERMANY

BACHMANN 'Anfänge des Landschaftsgartens in Deutschland' *Zeitschrift für Kunstwissenschaft* vol. V 1951

HENNEBO, D. and HOFFMANN, A. *Geschichte der Deutschen Gartenkunst* 1962-5 (invaluable study, ending *c.* 1870)

RICHARDI, Hans-Günter *Die Schönsten Gärten und Parks* 1975

    See also the exemplary guides to great houses and their gardens open to the public issued by regional authorities, e.g. *Eremitage*, 1975, and *Schönbusch*, 1963, both by Erich Bachmann; *Nyphenburg*, 1975, by Gerhard Hojer and Elmar D. Schmid; *Schloss Benrath*, 1975, by Irene Markowitz, and *Schloss Weikersheim*, 1976, by Klaus Merten.

IRELAND

MALINS, Edward and THE KNIGHT OF GLIN *Lost Demesnes, Irish Landscape Gardening 1660-1845* 1976 (a detailed and moving record of many vanished gardens)

ITALY

ALBERTI, Leone Battista *Ten Books on Architecture* tr. J. Leoni (1724) 1965 (a translation of *De Re Aedificatoria*, 1485)

CANTONI, Angelo *La Villa de Bagnaia (Villa Lante)* 1962

COFFIN, David R., ed. *The Italian Garden* 1972 (articles by Eugenio Battisti, Elisabeth MacDougall, Georgina Masson and Lionello Puppi)
    The Villa d'Este at Tivoli 1960

COLONNA, Francesco *Hypnerotomachia Poliphili* (1499) tr. 'R.D.' (1592) 1946

DE MONTAIGNE, Michel *Journal de Voyage en Italie* ed. C. Dédéyan 1946

D'ONOFRIO, Cesare *La Villa Aldobrandini di Frascati* 1963

FRANK, C.L. *The Villas of Frascati* 1966
MASSON, Georgina *Italian Gardens* 1961, 1966
MATTHEWS, W.H. *Mazes and Labyrinths* 1922, 1970
MORTON, H.V. (*The Waters of Rome* 1966) *The Fountains of Rome* 1970
SHEPHERD, J.C. and JELLICOE, G.A. *Italian Gardens of the Renaissance* 1925, 1966

JAPAN
BOWNAS, G. and THWAITE, A., tr. *The Penguin Book of Japanese Verse* 1972
CONDER, Joseph *The Floral Art of Japan* 1899
    Landscape Gardening in Japan 1893, 1964
HARADA, Jiro *The Gardens of Japan* 1928
ITO, Teijo *The Japanese Garden* 1972 (superb photographs, clear and helpful plans)
KUCK, Lorraine *The World of the Japanese Garden* 1968 (a full, balanced and well-illustrated
    history)
LADY MURASAKI *The Tale of Genji* tr. Arthur Waley 1935
LADY SARASHINA *As I Crossed a Bridge of Dreams* tr. Ivan Morris 1975
TAKAKUWA, G. and OKAMOTO, T. *Invitation to Japanese Gardens* 1960 (good black and white
    photographs of Kyoto gardens, with a lucid text)
YOSHIDA, T. *Gardens of Japan* 1957

PERSIAN AND ISLAMIC GARDENS
BEVERIDGE, Annette Susannah, tr. *The Babur-nama in English* 1922
ELDAM, Sedad H, *Turk Bahçeleri* 1976
GOTHEIN, Marie-Luise *Indische Gärten* 1926
The Koran tr. N.J. Dawood 1964
MACDOUGALL, Elisabeth B. and ETTINGHAUSEN, Richard, eds *The Islamic Garden* 1976
    (perceptive articles by Annemarie Schimmel, William L. Hanaway, Ralph Pinder-
    Wilson, James Dickie and Susan Jellicoe)
PARPAGLIOLO, Maria Teresa Shepherd *Kabul: The Bagh-I Babur* 1972
PECHÈRE, René *Iran: Etude de Jardins Historiques* 1973
VILLIERS-STUART, C.M. *Gardens of the Great Mughals* 1913
    Spanish Gardens 1929
WILBER, Donald N. *Persian Gardens and Garden Pavilions* 1962

SWITZERLAND
HAUSER, Albert *Bauerngärten der Schweiz* 1976

UNITED STATES
HUME, Audrey Noel *Archaeology and the Colonial Gardener* 1974
LEIGHTON, Ann *American Gardens in the Eighteenth Century* 1976
    Early English Gardens in New England 1970
MCGOURTY, F., ed. *Handbook on American Gardens – a Traveler's Guide* 1970
MANKS, Dorothy S., ed. *America's Garden Heritage: Explorers, Plantsmen and Gardens of
    Yesterday* 1968

ACKNOWLEDGMENTS

The author would like to thank the following for their kind permission to reprint extracts from their books:
pp. 11, 14, 16 – reprinted by permission of Penguin Books Ltd from Homer *The Odyssey* (pp. 89–90, 359–60,
115), translated by E. V. Rieu, Penguin Classics, 1946; pp. 14–15 – reprinted by permission of Doubleday &
Company, Inc. from *Three Greek Romances* (pp. 78–79), translated by Moses Hadas, 1953; pp. 21, 22–3 –
reprinted by permission of Penguin Books Ltd from *The Letters of the Younger Pliny* (pp. 77, 143), translated
by Betty Radice, Penguin Classics, 1969; pp. 48, 49 – reprinted by permission of Penguin Books Ltd from
Marco Polo *The Travels* (pp. 225–7, 108–9, 127), translated by Ronald Latham, Penguin Classics, 1958; p. 50
– Cao Xuequin *The Story of the Stone*, vol. 1 'The Golden Days' (pp. 324–5, 327, 344, 365), translated by
David Hawkes, Penguin Classics, 1973; p. 51 – reprinted by permission of George Allen & Unwin (Publishers)
Ltd from *Yuan Mei* (p. 48), by Arthur Waley, 1956; p. 56 – 'The Flower Market' by Po Chu-i, reprinted by
permission of Constable & Company Ltd (United Kingdom) and Alfred A. Knopf, Inc. (United States) from
One Hundred and Seventy Chinese Poems, translated by Arthur Waley; p. 56 – poem by Ou-Yang Hsiu
reprinted by permission of Penguin Books Ltd from *The Penguin Book of Chinese Verse*, translated by Robert
Kotewall and Norman L. Smith, Penguin Poets, 1962; p. 57 – reprinted by permission of Edinburgh University
Press from *Chinese Literature* (p. 394) by H. C. Chang (extract from *The Story of the Stone* by Cao Xuequin);
pp. 63–4 – reprinted by permission of George Allen & Unwin (Publishers) Ltd (United Kingdom) and
Houghton Mifflin Company (United States) from *The Tale of Genji* translated by Arthur Waley; pp. 64, 65 –
reprinted by permission of Anthony Sheil Associates Ltd from Lady Sarashina *As I Crossed a Bridge of Dreams*
(pp. 84, 75–6, 67–8) translated by Ivan Morris, Penguin, 1975; pp. 92, 93 – reprinted by permission of
Penguin Books Ltd from Giovanni Boccaccio *The Decameron* (pp. 516–17, 232, 233) translated by G. H.
McWilliam, Penguin Classics, 1972.

INDEX

PICTURE CREDITS